Buck Perley

The Great Ride of China

*One couple's two-wheeled adventure
around the Middle Kingdom*

www.thegreatrideofchina.com

An imprint of:
Great Ride Press

www.greatridepress.com

*For my parents, who always supported me no matter how crazy the idea,
and Amy and the many more great rides I look forward to sharing with you in our life together.*

How To Make The Most Of This Book

The story is in chronological order so if you'd just like to read it as is then feel free to jump right in! Below, however, are some tips to get a bit more out of your experience.

For photos, the middle of the book has black and white images. If you would like more photos and in color, the book is broken into sections roughly by region of the country represented in the story. At the end of each section is a page with a QR code (a square with a black and white checkered-like pattern). If you scan that QR code with your phone it will take you to a dedicated website with photos from that section. If you have the latest version of iOS on an Apple device, all you have to do is open your camera app, point it at the code, and wait for the prompt to open your browser. On both Apple and Android devices, the mobile Chrome browser has a built-in QR Code scanner.

For those readers interested in keeping track of the Chinese vocabulary used in the story, the first appendix at the end of the book has the Chinese characters, Pinyin (Romanization), and translations.

The second appendix has a list of references, organized by chapter, that were used for the facts and figures seen in the book.

That should just about cover it. I hope you enjoy the story!

- Buck Perley

The Great Ride of China

Introduction

I started riding motorcycles in China a few months after I accepted my first job out of college, at the Beijing office of an American company doing supply-chain management in China. I had been hooked on bikes ever since starting to ride during my sophomore year of college a few years earlier. With a couple cross-country U.S. trips already under my belt, there was no question that I would need a motorcycle once I moved. So in the sub-freezing temperatures of a Beijing night in January 2011, I gathered up as many extra layers as I could, went out to the outer rings of Beijing, and picked up a second-hand 250cc Golden City motorcycle from the seller I had found online.

After two years on Chinese roads, in the fall of 2012, I finally applied for my driver's license. On the urging of a friend, another foreigner who rode in Beijing, I made my way on the Golden City to Beijing's equivalent of the DMV, "The Beijing Municipal Public Security Bureau Public Security Traffic Management Bureau of Vehicle Management" (sic). Their headquarters, the only place in a city of over 20 million where you could apply for a license, was in the far southeast of Beijing, a 30–40 minute drive from the city center. As soon as I arrived, I was turned away and told I needed to first get a health checkup at one of the officially approved hospitals (none of which were within even a five-mile radius). After coming back the following week, with a signed form that recorded my height as eyeballed by a nurse who, in addition, affirmed that I was indeed not blind, I paid a fee of $8, filled out the remaining paperwork, and was given a large book to study from for the written test. The book contained over 900 sample questions. Of these, I was told that 100 would appear, verbatim, on the test. Memorize the 900 questions and

1

I'd have no problem getting the minimum 90% needed to pass the exam.

For some of the questions, my years of experience on Chinese and American roads worked in my favor. For example, I was relatively confident I knew what to do when another driver asked me for directions.

A. Ignore it
B. Answer with patience
C. Find an excuse to reject
D. Answer for a pay

Answer: B, Answer with patience

I also found myself well equipped to answer the more technical based questions.

True or false: Depressing the accelerator pedal reduces the rotation speed of the engine and releasing the pedal increases the rotation speed of the engine.

Answer: False

For others though, I felt somewhat less confident. For example, had I still remembered the first aid training that I'd done back in high school, I might have been better prepared to deal with this problem:

When there is a bleeding in an upper limb or shank without bone fracture or joint damage, the bleeding can be stopped by _____.

A. Tourniquet
B. Compression dressing
C. Cushioned limb folding
D. Pressure bondage

Answer: C, Cushioned limb folding

For still others, it seemed that neither past experience, technical expertise, nor further cultural immersion would be able to help me. When faced with a counter-intuitive question/answer pair, my last resort would have to be rote memorization.

> After a vehicle falls into water, the wrong method for the driver to rescue himself is to _____.
>
> A. Close the window to prevent water from flowing into the vehicle
> B. Immediately use hand to open the door
> C. Let the water to fill up the driver's cab so that the water pressure both inside and outside is equal
> D. Use a large plastic bag to cover the head and tight the neck closely
>
> *Answer: A, Close the window to prevent water from flowing into the vehicle*

Though I have never personally had to deal with a car being submerged into water, I was glad to have learned that using "a large plastic bag to cover the head and tight the neck closely" is among the best ways to survive such an ordeal.

It took me two tries before I passed. Because I was converting a foreign license to a Chinese one, I luckily did not have to take the practical test. It was only later that I discovered that taking the test at all is more of a formality. As it turns out, you can pay an agent to go through the whole process for you, a common practice for many licensed Chinese drivers. Pay a little extra, and they can take the practical for you as well.

***

Amy and I first met in the summer of 2010. I had just graduated from the University of Toronto with a Bachelor's Degree of Arts and

Sciences, majoring in economics and Chinese language and society. At the time, I was interning at the sourcing company that would later offer me full-time employment. Amy was practicing architecture in Oxford, where she'd been for the past few years, and was in Beijing visiting family. She is half-Chinese and half-British. Both her mom and her aunt, sisters who had grown up in Beijing during the Cultural Revolution, had married foreigners when they were in their early 20s. It was an act that was as unusual as it was frowned upon at the time.

Amy's parents separated when she was six years old. Her mom, Wang Ying, was young, Chinese and barely able to speak English at the time. Amy ended up staying with her father, Tim Mathieson, in Switzerland where they had moved as a family. When Amy was 14, her dad moved the family once again, followed not long after by another divorce. This time they moved back to the U.K. where she finished high school and eventually studied architecture at Oxford Brookes University.

Meanwhile, Ying's sister Delianne stayed married to her foreign suitor. Her husband, a young Belgian with dual Australian citizenship named Michael DeClercq, and Amy's dad were some of the first foreigners to come to China at the start of the country's efforts to normalize relations with the West in the late 1970s. Michael studied Chinese at a local university in Beijing and soon found himself involved in the country's fledgling manufacturing industry. A young, enterprising foreigner who spoke Chinese as well as English, French, and Italian fluently, he took advantage of his unique position and found opportunities in the increasing number of foreigners looking to purchase cheap goods from Chinese producers. As the sector grew, so did the demand for Michael's services. Soon, to deal with the growth in his business, Michael founded China Performance Group with his wife, Amy's aunt. The company eventually grew to have dozens of employees in offices in the U.S., China, and Europe. It was Mr. DeClercq who in 2010 offered me my first job in China, helping to manage the company's digital marketing operations from their Beijing office.

When Amy came to visit, the building industry in the U.K. was still struggling to recover from the 2008 Financial Crisis. Work hours at the small architecture firm where she was employed were getting cut regularly. All over the country, people seemed to be disinterested and pessimistic. The summer we met, Amy described to me the lethargic atmosphere of the U.K., particularly in contrast to the energy of Beijing. She told me how before on past family reunions, she never particularly enjoyed her visits to the country. Her impressions were of a dirty, crowded, and disorganized place, not somewhere that she particularly looked forward to spending time in.

Her reaction this time around was different though. Now rather than repulsed, she was finding herself drawn to the energy, dynamism, and frenetic pace of Chinese life. Locals and expats alike were optimistic and ambitious. Rather than complaining about their circumstances, even the less fortunate seemed upbeat, looking forward to the opportunities ahead. The contrast to the monotony and cynicism of England at the time was invigorating, the ambition and pace inspiring. Within a couple months of her visit, Amy had moved out of her house in Oxford, broke up with her boyfriend, sold her car, quit her job, and moved to China.

Amy and I didn't start dating until a few months later, during the Chinese New Year of 2011. We found ourselves to be complementary opposites. Amy had proper, British sensibilities. She was subdued in her mannerisms and erred on the side of politeness. I rode motorcycles, had a couple of tattoos, and, like any good New Yorker, probably spoke what was on my mind more often than advisable. The contrasts worked well though, and Amy provided a pragmatic antidote to my sometimes outlandish notions. We had things in common too: we were both huge Lord of the Rings geeks, fans of Joss Whedon, and intoxicated by the energy of China.

The Golden City motorcycle I had bought in 2011 was small. 250cc is not a big engine, and being Chinese-made meant frequent quality issues. Amy and I nicknamed the bike *Mafan*, a Chinese word that most closely translates to "Trouble", because of all the maintenance and part replacements we had to do on it. But despite battery problems, a couple leaky gas tanks, and pretty bad suspension, it managed to take us both for some good rides. It was on *Mafan* that we discovered a passion for exploring the paths less traveled in China – a tolerance, if not enjoyment, of the chaos of its roads, and a drive to constantly see more.

There is a quote by Robert Pirzig in *Zen and the Art of Motorcycle Maintenance* that perfectly encapsulates what I feel it's like to travel by motorcycle and why it is an experience unlike almost any other:

> *In a car you're always in a compartment, and because you're used to it you don't realize that through that car window everything you see is just more TV. You're a passive observer and it is all moving by you boringly in a frame.*

> *On a cycle the frame is gone. You're completely in contact with it all. You're in the scene, not just watching it anymore, and the sense of presence is overwhelming.*

We had both moved to China to experience its unprecedented economic growth and its unparalleled history and culture first hand. We came to absorb its energy and Amy and I both found ourselves with a growing fondness for the country's past, present, and future. Amy had even started a blog with this in mind, *Project: China Building Restoration*, an opportunity to combine her interest in cultural preservation and vernacular architecture with a new interest in exploring her Chinese roots. In my opinion, there was no better way to be a part of it all than on a motorcycle.

We started off with small, weekend trips around Beijing. There were some scenic loops in the mountains near the Great Wall to the north that we enjoyed taking *Mafan* out on. Another trip was to an old Ming Dynasty-era village west of the city. There, less than 100 miles from one of the world's biggest metropolises, we found traditional homes, single-story buildings still heated by *kangs* (raised brick platforms, hollowed out underneath to burn wood, rice stalks, and other flammables) serving as both beds and dining areas.

With two riders, *Mafan* had trouble on hills, but there was storage space on the sides and back, and on flat roads we could cruise comfortably at around 50–60mph. She wasn't fast enough to try and sneak onto the expressways but, as long as we avoided the potholes, *Mafan* was still perfectly adequate for the National Highways.

Our trips became more ambitious as Amy and I grew more comfortable on the bike, increasing in distance and time. We started to explore farther afield during our work holidays. For our first multiday trip, Amy and I went 200 miles out to the coast, visiting the resort town of Beidaihe and the eastern terminus of The Great Wall, "The First Pass Under Heaven", where the wall enters the sea. Later, with an extended holiday from work, the two of us ventured down to the old German concession city and one of the top 10 busiest ports in China, Qingdao, a trip that took us over 1,200 miles along China's industrialized east coast.

Forbidden from entering the highways in China, motorcycles are relegated to the national, provincial, and county roads. In contrast to the well-maintained, well-marked, and well-regulated expressways, driving on these smaller roads presents one with a stark and present reminder that China is still a developing nation. There is a pervasive lawlessness to the driving habits of people on the *guo dao* (National Highway) network. It is an exhilarating and terrifying world where every truck, car, villager, stray dog, and scooter is out for him, her, or itself. Road signs and pavement markings are treated as mere suggestions rather than legal mandates. Potholes form easily and deeply as a result of years of pounding from overweight trucks with teeth shattering consequences when hit unawares. These poorly maintained roads have been neglected for so long that soot and dust have become a constant feature of the countryside. They are left to crumble for as long as possible, until they're finally dug up shoulder to shoulder for miles with an eye towards repairs but no consideration given to reroutes.

Our excursions on these wild, industrial roads turned out to be fascinating and unique opportunities to experience a more authentic, if less polished, version of China. Less than a day out of Beijing we would find ourselves meeting locals who had never seen a foreigner in person before. We drove through the outskirts of newly built cities, like the Special Economic Zone of Weifang in Shandong province, where we were the only vehicle driving along perfectly paved 8-lane roadways. Some places we would stay overnight didn't have accommodations that could legally accept foreigners. In one of these, I convinced an old woman who ran the hotel to input my ethnicity as "Han Chinese" in her computer system so that it would register me as a guest. In another town, when wandering the streets after dinner, Amy and I accidentally stumbled into an underground gambling house disguised as a children's arcade. The game tables, covered in flashing lights and cartoon animals, looked like they could have been plucked out of a Chuck E. Cheese's. The machines were not spitting out redeemable prize tickets though. Instead we found chain smoking Chinese men, shirts rolled up above their protruding stomachs, crowding around the tables, competing to have their voices heard as they placed bets and cheered for which flashing light they thought would get around the table first.

Over two years of motorcycling around China during our holidays, Amy and I had already visited dozens of cities along the east coast. It wasn't just the tourist sites either. We visited the beer factory in Qingdao, the Great Wall in Shanhaiguan, the Bund in Shanghai, and Sun Yat-sen's Mausoleum in Nanjing. But we had also been to cities rarely visited and sometimes not even heard of by foreigners, places with names like "Smoke Platform" (Yantai), "Level Degree" (Pingdu), "City of Zou" (Zoucheng), "Without Metal" (Wuxi), and "Port Connect-the-Clouds" (Lianyungang). In most cases the memories of these faceless Chinese cities, many larger than the largest in the U.S., and the roads that took us there, were more impactful than those listed in "Top 10" lists on Tripadvisor. The way was often brutal, causing me on two occasions to fall ill with fever from exhaustion. In two years I had been in three accidents, one while Amy was a passenger, more than in the five years and tens of thousands of miles I'd ridden in North America. We were consistently refused access to highways even when the alternatives were closed, and food poisoning was a constant risk.

Despite the difficulties and drawbacks, I was addicted. I found myself constantly escalating, trying to find new and longer trips. Meanwhile, Amy, who had never even been on a motorcycle before we'd met, continued to indulge me as the escalations continued and I kept pushing to see more.

Part I - Beijing to Inner Mongolia

千里之行，始于足下
- 老子
"A journey of a thousand miles begins beneath one's feet."
- Lao-tzu (604-531 BC)

Chapter 1 – A Record, a Charity, and a Motorcycle

Two roads diverged in a yellow wood
And sorry I could not travel both
And be one traveler, long I stood
And looked down one as far as I could
To where it bent in the undergrowth;

Then took the other, as just as fair,
And having perhaps the better claim
Because it was grassy and wanted wear,
Though as for that the passing there
Had worn them really about the same,

And both that morning equally lay
In leaves no step had trodden black.
Oh, I kept the first for another day!
Yet knowing how way leads on to way
I doubted if I should ever come back.

I shall be telling this with a sigh
Somewhere ages and ages hence:
Two roads diverged in a wood, and I,
I took the one less traveled by,
And that has made all the difference.

-Robert Frost, "The Road Not Taken"

Life, I think, really is just a series of decisions – the sum of choices we make and those we don't. Every day from the moment we wake up to that moment when we drift back into unconsciousness, we are making decisions that have the power to alter our lives. Often the opportunities to diverge go unnoticed. The clearest path is the one laid out directly in front of us, a continuation of the trail already held.

So when you arrive at the place where two roads diverge, how do you recognize that divergence? How do you choose which path to follow?

In June 2012, I decided to leave my job as Marketing Manager at China Performance Group. It wasn't a straightforward decision. I liked the people I worked with and was getting promoted in the company. I didn't have a more lucrative job lined up either. I didn't have a job lined up at all.

After two years living in Beijing I had found myself frustrated with a sense of stagnancy. I had moved to China not just because of the job, but also because of the opportunity to live in an exciting and foreign place. Life in Beijing, however, had become comfortable and easy. Living expenses were cheap and modern amenities were readily accessible. Most expats could afford a house cleaner, Amy and I ate out regularly, and Beijing was growing into a world-class cosmopolitan city with a wide range of international food and entertainment. None of these were what I had left New York, nor Amy London/Oxford, for. There was a pervasive expat bubble and it felt impossible to extricate ourselves from it.

Amy was finding similar frustration in her job as architectural consultant at a Chinese property development company. The one project she had been brought in to advise on back in 2010 was struggling to even break ground still two years on. Nobody in the company ever seemed to have any work to do, and it made her wonder what anyone had been hired for in the first place. It was almost as if the whole company existed as a conduit for favors to friends and associates of its president. *Guanxi*, or "relationship" is China's system of influence-based social currency that is often described as underpinning much of China's economy, and it seemed to be the primary currency at Amy's company. The novelty and intrigue of working for a Chinese company had been fading, and Amy was starting to have some of the same misgivings about whether we were making the most of our time in China given our reasons for having moved there.

My original plan wasn't anything ambitious. The idea was to go on something of a road trip: a month from Beijing to the scenic province of Yunnan in the Southwest. I argued that it would be a good excuse for Amy to quit her job and an opportunity for us both to reset and think about what we wanted to do next. Along the way we would have the chance to see more of China and expose ourselves to the diversity of culture and geography that the country had to offer. I argued that it could also be a chance to discover interesting material for Amy's blog too. Traveling by motorcycle would allow us to visit the harder-to-reach and more obscure examples of traditional architecture and discover how, if at all, they were being preserved.

While we had some misgivings about giving up our apartment and putting our careers on hold, it wasn't a hard sell given Amy's frustration at work and so we started to devise a rough plan. With start and end points set, we mapped out the destinations we wanted to visit along the way. The ancient city of Pingyao and the Hanging Temple in Shanxi, the "Avatar Mountains" in Zhangjiajie and Phoenix City in Hunan, Jiuzhaigou National Park and the giant Leshan Buddha in Sichuan, and of course the scattering of centuries-old traditional villages of the two dozen ethnic minority communities living in Yunnan all made it onto our list.

While our developing itinerary looked ambitious, it still felt like we were limiting ourselves. Our route was constrained to the land between Beijing and the Southwest. What about the former Russian-settled city of Harbin in the Northeast? Or the cave dwellings in the Loess Plateau of the North? Even harder to reach but still more enticing were places like the Great Wall fortress of Jiayuguan in the Gobi Desert, the ancient Turkish-influenced city of Kashgar in the far

West, and of course the seat of Tibetan Buddhism in Lhasa, high up on the Tibetan plateau.

As the list of "what ifs" grew, I became increasingly enthralled by the idea of visiting them all in one trip. If we were taking this time off anyway, and our goal was to immerse ourselves more deeply in China, why hold back? There was so much to see and this was the time we were setting aside for ourselves to see it. It wasn't difficult for me to justify this idea to myself and I soon convinced Amy that we should try a more extensive trip. I suggested that we stretch out our timeframe, broaden our aspirations, and put together a more ambitious itinerary, no longer limiting ourselves to what lay between Beijing and Yunnan.

For inspiration I bought a wall-sized map of China and mounted it on a board in our living room. I started with pins in all the places we had already decided we wanted to visit, and as more occurred to us, more pins continued to radiate out from Beijing, regardless of where they were in the country.

China of course is not just a large, homogenous country covered in bicycles, coal mines, and factories as it is often depicted. In fact, thanks in large part to its millennia of history, it is also incredibly diverse. There are 56 different ethnicities in China, many of whom speak their own languages, have their own writing systems, and practice their own religions. There have been eight different cities spread throughout the country that have at one time served as the capital of a Chinese dynasty or government. The food, culture, and architecture can vary tremendously from region to region and even province to province. This was going to be Amy's and my once in a lifetime trip, our chance to expose ourselves to as much of China as we could. With so much diversity spread around so many different places, why limit ourselves only to the ones we knew of by reputation? I wanted to actively seek out where roads diverged, where we would have the opportunity to encounter the unexpected. So why not ride our motorcycle through all 33 provinces in the country?

***

At this point all we had was an ambitious idea for a motorcycle trip around China. Unfortunately, money would be tight, especially if we wanted to go to Tibet, for which we would need a lot of paperwork and a guide to escort us through the province. Also, the motorcycle I had at the time, a used, 12-year-old 750cc Honda Shadow, was ill-suited for the conditions we would be facing on the road. Potholed *guo daos*, snowstorms on the Tibetan Plateau, and landslide-inflicted roads in the mountains of Sichuan would all likely be unkind to the low down, relaxed riding position of the Japanese cruiser. If we were going to make this work, some form of sponsorship would go a long way.

In the process of planning out a potential route and researching how to prepare, I stumbled upon a unique opportunity that would help get us there. The route I had sketched out, starting from Beijing and traveling counterclockwise around the country, would add up to approximately 14,000 miles covered in four months. In the past couple years there had been a relevant Guinness World Record established, first set by two Canadian brothers who had also motorcycled around China. Their record, just over 10,000 miles, was officially titled the "longest continuous motorcycle journey around a single country." That record had since been broken by an Indian named Moshin Haq who rode 11,400 miles around his home country, 2,600 miles shorter than our planned route. This added dimension to our trip, the branding of a Guinness World Record, would serve perfectly as our "unique selling proposition" if we were going to bring in some outside support.

The theme of our trip was China; the inspirations were it's past, present, and future. We were guests in the country though, and thus felt an obligation to give something back to our hosts. A record-breaking motorcycle trip would be a fantastic vehicle to raise money and awareness for a local cause. In addition, we figured that if we had the support of an established, Chinese organization such as a non-profit, it would also help when pitching to sponsors later.

Amy and I knew people in Beijing who worked in the non-profit sector. This gave us some insight into the industry and a partial understanding of how it operated. Our conversations with friends soon led us to "Free Lunch for Children". Founded by a former reporter turned philanthropist Deng Fei only a couple years before, the program provided free school lunches to children in rural China. They embodied many of the qualities we were looking for: education/children-focused, well established, and with an emphasis on the transparency of their finances. The scope of their operations, in 20 provinces and over 180 schools across the country, also aligned perfectly with that of our trip.

As discussions progressed, the people we met with seemed excited that we had been drawn to their organization. When we'd finalized the details of a partnership, "Free Lunch" even started to help us look for sponsors and media. Amy and I however began to grow concerned that this form of fundraising, a high-profile challenge used as advertisement, was an entirely new concept in China. Independent non-profits themselves were only a recent development in the country. The industry was still in the process of establishing local strategies for the problems they were trying to solve. This incongruity between our Western perspective and that of our Chinese counterparts became clear as we were posed with, at times, irrational concerns. Frantic and blunt questions like "what does a motorcycle have to do with children in China?" or "how will you get *us* money?" did not instill much confidence. In the end however, they proved to be

17

a well-known, fully Chinese non-profit in line with a cause Amy and I both supported. We were also running out of time.

By the time we had solidified a partnership with Free Lunch for Children, it was already April. The geography of China spans almost every type of terrain and climate on the planet including the subtropics, deserts, grass plains and high-altitude glaciers. In order to avoid adverse weather conditions, we had to time our itinerary carefully. The biggest concerns for us were typhoon season in the South, winter in the Northeast, and snows in Tibet. The first two constrained the direction we had to travel in and the last meant we could enter the Himalayas no later than September before the risk of road closures and avalanches would become too high. So if we wanted to make this work, we would have to start in July or risk not finishing at all.

My goal was to continue with the theme of China when looking for sponsors, especially for the motorcycle. The obvious reason for this was that it would be great to break the record with a Chinese bike. The practical argument was that in the event that anything went wrong on the road, it would be much easier to get parts than with a foreign brand. Unfortunately, Chinese companies did not quite have the infrastructure set up for these types of marketing campaigns. We found that, in contrast to their Western counterparts like Red Bull or GoPro, a lot of Chinese companies didn't seem to have marketing departments at all, to say nothing of sponsorship strategies. China was home to some of the largest motorcycle manufacturers in the world. Brands most may not have heard of, companies like Jincheng, Shineray, and Zongshen, had the largest sales volumes in the industry but also all seemed to have barely functioning websites. Emails too usually went unanswered and when I could get in contact with people, the conversation rarely moved past the sales questions the rep had been pre-trained to deal with.

Our luck broke though when Amy's stepdad Li Qiang, her mom's partner of 20 years, came to us with an idea. He had previously worked in the government, and a friend from his time there was the former Vice Chair of the China Association of Automobile Manufacturers. Because of the way that the industry in China had developed over the past two decades, the car and motorcycle manufacturers still had a lot of overlap. Similar to Japan where companies like Honda (piston rings) and Suzuki (looms) started off making things other than what they are known for today, many domestic motorcycle companies did not start off making motorcycles. These Chinese OEM companies eventually diversified from engines and engine components for foreign brands to become some of China's first motorcycle manufacturers. Li Qiang told us that he had talked to his friend about our trip and found out that, though retired, he still had some connections in the industry.

We met "Uncle Du" at a classic Chinese restaurant just a couple blocks from Tiananmen Square. Amy's mom instructed us to use the moniker *Bai Bai* (pronounced "bye bye") when referring to him, an informal but respectful title that translates to "uncle" and is indicative of someone that is not a blood relative and is older than your father. Du (pronounced "doo") was a short, dark skinned Chinese man. He wore an ill-fitting, brown toupee that looked like it was meant more for a Western than Chinese head, and spoke in a gravelly voice and with such an overt expectation of deference that it bordered on insecurity. Both host and guest of honor, he sat at the head of the round table in our private room of the restaurant facing the door, hunched and grimacing as he led the conversation.

Du and Li Qiang spent most of the dinner catching up, while Amy and I stayed almost entirely silent. I was anxious about getting an opportunity to talk about our trip, but I also knew that this was how business dinners were done in China. 90% of the time you talk about anything but business. By the end of the meal, if good *guanxi* has been established, then the last 10% is strictly an opportunity to hammer out the details. Often, though luckily not in this particular case, the experience is lubricated with the Chinese fortified sorghum wine, a drink known simply as *baijiu* ("white wine") that gets as strong as 65% ABV (for comparison, Vodka is usually around 40%).

Uncle Du had the condescending habit of punctuating his statements with the question *"ming bai ma?"* or "Do you understand?" Rather than a genuine concern for comprehension, this served primarily as a rhetorical device, to remind the listener that they were being given valuable insights and should be sure to take note. It was a turn of phrase I had encountered before in Chinese authority figures eager to justify their position.

"The motorcycle industry has been growing extremely fast in China over the past 10 years," he confidently explained to us. "It's the biggest in the world now. *Ming bai ma?*"

"A lot of the people I know used to produce engine parts. Now there's such an increase in demand and their technology is good enough so they're producing their own motorcycles. *Ming bai ma?*"

"In China, motorcycles aren't allowed on the expressway. You have to take the national highways. *Ming bai ma?*"

Eventually he began to ask more direct questions (ones where answers were actually expected), allowing us to describe our plans in more detail. I told him we intended to ride through 33 of China's provinces – careful not to say "all" since we weren't going to Taiwan. We would be leaving in the summer and the goal was to break a Guinness World Record. He asked what kind of motorcycle we would need and I described roughly the type and engine size we were looking for: at least 400ccs that could carry two people and handle tough terrain. At that, Uncle Du grunted his affirmation and without any further deliberation, he pulled out his phone. Within five minutes, the president of CFMoto, a motorcycle and ATV company based out of Hangzhou, Zhejiang, had verbally agreed with Uncle Du to give us a brand new 650cc motorcycle. Their 650TR model was the biggest Chinese-made bike available on the market. Only one other company I knew of, Jialing, was making anything comparable.

I had come across the TR during my research for the trip and managed separately to get in touch with someone at the company. Things ultimately fell through however because the TR didn't look like it would be suitable for the road conditions we would be facing. CFMoto got good reviews for reliability and 650cc was powerful enough to carry two people plus equipment. From that perspective it seemed perfect. Unfortunately, however, they only made road bikes, which meant models that were built exclusively for nicely paved, flat asphalt (i.e. expressways, the type of road Du had just reminded us we were forbidden from riding on). I reservedly voiced some of these concerns to Du, asking whether they had a bike that could handle the types of roads we were expecting. He quickly called back and communicated what I had asked.

"They need an adventure bike," he told the president of CFMoto, President Lai. He grunted to the phone and then, directed at me, asked, "Do you mean for off-road?"

"No, no. Not like a dirt bike," I replied. The classifications for the different types of motorcycle were a little less clear in Chinese so I tried my best to communicate what we needed. "Just something that can go on more difficult roads but is also good on highways."

Du again repeated back what I had said, and then confidently turned back to me and proclaimed, "Yes of course. Their bike is perfectly suitable."

So, less than two months to departure and it looked like we had a bike. While Uncle Du couldn't arrange actual sponsorship, he did explain to his friend about the record and helped to set up a meeting in a couple weeks for us to go down to the factory in Hangzhou, a city of about 8 million near Shanghai. There, we would have the opportunity to pitch upper management in person.

Amy's mom and Li Qiang also had meetings planned in Hangzhou and so in mid-June, the four of us left via overnight train from Beijing. I normally find the repetitive rocking and rumbling of the trains soothing and don't have a problem falling asleep on the stiff cots of the sleeper cars. But lying in the top bunk of the four-person compartment for the 12-hour ride, head propped up by the large beanbag sack that served as the pillow, all I could think about was the presentation I was about to give the following morning. What if my pitch didn't convince them? Would just a bike be enough? Could we afford the entry permit and guide we would need to enter Tibet on our own? What was our plan B? Was there another version of the 650TR that could go off-road that I had missed in my research?

We made it to Hangzhou at around 5am the next day. Amy also hadn't gotten much sleep. After a long, drowsy car ride out to the factory, a sterile complex of aircraft hangar-like buildings, we were dropped off at the four-story office building on the premises and shown up to a reception room where we waited for President Lai. The room was large, with a projector screen on the far wall and plush, oversized armchairs that seemed plucked from a 1950s American sitting room, arranged in a semicircle opened towards the screen. We took our seats around the room before being served tea by a quiet CFMoto employee. I blew on the hot water as I sunk into the deep cushions, anxious for the air-conditioning to fill the room before the 100-degree temperatures of June caused me to sweat through my formal, button-down shirt.

A soft-spoken man of average build, Lai had a weak handshake that felt as if the movement was unfamiliar and uncomfortable to him. He smiled kindly, was extremely courteous, and seemed genuinely pleased to meet us. He was accompanied by his immediate subordinate, the equally soft-spoken Manager Zhu, who was shorter but with a broader and more confident smile. Zhu came in dressed in one of the white, CFMoto branded jumpsuits that we had seen the factory workers wearing on the way in. It appeared Zhu was more of the hands-on manager at the company.

Since Li Qiang was the original source of the *guanxi* connecting us, he led the introductions and briefly spoke to President Lai and Manager Zhu about the adventure we planned to take their motorcycle on. Lai expressed his support almost immediately and showed clear interest in the challenge we would be embarking on. For sponsorship, we would be given the opportunity to present our proposal in more detail to Manager Zhu and their sales and marketing team. First though, he took us on a tour of their factory. He told us about the history of the company and proudly listed off their sales statistics, sharing that CFMoto was the second largest producer of ATVs in the world behind Can-Am. He also confirmed that they made the largest domestically manufactured motorcycles. The tour ended at a showroom where we were given a brief rundown of the different bikes and ATVs that they offered. Among the machines on display was a brand new, white 650TR.

With all the assurances I'd been given about the bike's suitability, I'd naively hoped that maybe there was another model of the 650TR more targeted to the adventure-touring market. To my disappointment (though I didn't show it at the time), the bike we would have for the trip was the same I had seen during my research.

A beautiful bike, the TR had a sleek, aerodynamic plastic fairing with a windshield, directionals, and headlight built into the front. It had hard side cases for storage, a space for a rear luggage case, and even small compartments built into the dash. Later, they invited me to ride a test model down the empty strips that ran between the factory buildings. It had a comfortable riding position with a slight forward lean and foot controls just behind where my knees bent. This was better than the leaned back, feet forward position I was used to on cruisers, but still closer to a racing bike than the upright position of an adventure motorcycle, which allows the rider to take bumps more easily. With smooth, steady pickup, the 650TR had a nice amount of torque that threw me back when I gave it some gas on the wide open runway-like strip of road. It felt great on turns too, leaning effortlessly when I tipped it over to slalom around the road markings.

My overall impression was that it was a solid bike. It felt well made with a lot of thought put into the engineering. Company management clearly took pride in the brand and their confidence in the bike's durability seemed justifiable. If motorcycles were allowed on the expressways and our goal was simply to ride 14,000 miles as quickly as possible, the bike would have been more than adequate. These were not, however, the conditions we were expecting. I was a little too tall for the bike and it barely had enough room for two people. The short frame, low ground clearance, small wheel diameter, and shallow tire tread were all concerns given what I knew Chinese roads could be like. In fact, months later, near the halfway point of our trip, a couple of the more subordinate members of the CFMoto team confided in me how their biggest concern during our pitch hadn't been whether *we* could handle the trip but whether their bike could.

Departure was only a month away now. The investment in *guanxi* had been deposited. Like it or not, we were wedded to this bike.

Amy's Mom, Li Qiang, and President Lai all had other meetings to get to so Amy and I were on our own for the sponsorship pitch after lunch. I was more familiar with the Chinese version of the presentation than Amy, so I took the lead. It took a couple slides before I overcame the knot in my stomach, but after my 20-minute presentation, where I covered everything from major stops, fundraising goals, and budget breakdown, the audience of six all seemed receptive to the project.

When we moved on to specific questions about our proposal, the only thing I was tripped up by was when they asked where we would be in mid-October. Apparently their decision seemed to hinge on whether we could make it to Chongqing, a provincial-level municipality in Southwest China, for the opening day of the annual CIMA motorcycle exhibition (the largest consumer motorcycle show in the world). The trip had so many variables between now and October that I hesitated to make any promises, but with us on the verge of getting the company's full support, I figured we'd find a way to make it work (and if we couldn't, with the Gobi Desert and the Himalayas between now and then, I'm sure we'd have a good excuse). So I reluctantly nodded my affirmation and the conversation moved to the details of a contract.

It had been a wild two days. We started with a sleepless overnight train from Beijing and ended with us negotiating a contract for full financial support and a brand new motorcycle. In between, there was a tour of a world-class motorcycle production facility, a stunt-riding performance, a one-hour crash course on the mechanics of the CF-650TR, and a couple celebratory meals with the management of CFMoto. With the start date only a month away, we now had a cause, a sponsor, and a motorcycle. All there was left to do was actually get ready for the trip.

The next few weeks were non-stop. We had barely gotten back from Hangzhou when Amy and I had to start moving out of our apartment. The lease was up at the end of June, which meant we had to pack up and move to a temporary lodging, an old place Amy's mom had out in the suburbs, for our last couple weeks.

After the move, including an afternoon running a yard sale in front of our apartment complex, selling off our extra things to curious Chinese "aunties," the three big projects left were to organize our gear, schedule our guide for Tibet, and put together a press conference to formally announce our trip. This last one was something that we had proposed to both Free Lunch for Children and CFMoto as something we would be happy to participate in as a way to help promote their brands. Unfortunately though, while both were interested, neither seemed willing to take any responsibility for it. Instead, Amy and I ended up fielding calls from both companies trying to get us to take care of things that we lacked the experience, resources, and, most importantly, time to organize in any way.

While Amy and I tried to abdicate from the project, instead focusing on more important tasks like arranging mail drops and figuring out how to fit four months of gear onto a single motorcycle, the ugly side of *guanxi* reared its head. When Uncle Du heard we weren't setting up a press conference for his friend's company, he called up Amy's mom to voice his displeasure. In this world, it's get a favor, give a favor. *Ming bai ma?*

Once Amy and I were successfully strong-armed into handling certain aspects of the event, our partners pitched in more themselves. Free Lunch for Children had a small army of volunteers come to help us prepare at the venue we had reserved and CFMoto provided gift bags for the guests, while Manager Zhu, the company's VP (also named Manager Zhu) and their Marketing Manager Chen Guanping took the train up from Hangzhou for the event. Uncle Du also made an appearance.

At the event, Amy and I introduced the trip and fielded some questions while each of the guests spoke a few words about the partnerships. There was an unveiling of our bike, a sleek black version of the 650TR that we'd picked up a couple days earlier, and an unfurling of a Free Lunch for Children flag with one of the charity's board members. That evening we had a party to celebrate with the volunteers and some of our friends at a rooftop cocktail bar in the city.

The following day back out in the suburbs and two days before departure, the house was a mess. Tools, equipment, spare parts, camping gear, multi-vitamins, everything that we needed to either take with us or mail ahead was strewn across every bit of open space. It took a concerted effort, with Amy and I each in charge of organizing different categories of the equipment, for us to steadily chip away.

When economizing space for such a long trip, everything you take needs to have a clear purpose and each arrangement a deliberate strategy. The right saddlebag would be for spare parts and the left for camera equipment; this bag was for camping gear; first aid supplies went in this ziplock bag while spare socks, underwear, and town clothes went in that one; tools could fit in with the parts, but the electronics chargers were sent to the back. Extra layers and warmer sleeping bags went into a box that was going to get shipped ahead to Lhasa in a couple weeks. We'd figure out how to latch that on to the bike when we we met with our Tibet guide in Kashgar.

The past six months had been an adventure in and of itself. We had gone from an idea for a one-month-long road trip to what we hoped would be a world record setting motorcycle ride through China. All of the planning and negotiating, the purchasing of gear and mapping out of routes, the research and preparation, it was all distilled down to a few piles of... stuff, stuff that represented the shelter, sustenance, entertainment, kitchen, and transportation that would support Amy and I for the next four months.

Sometime around midnight the night before departure, we were doing our final checks and addressing the boxes for the mail drops when I received an email. The message was from a friend of ours back home, Dan Zinn, also a motorcycle enthusiast who had been watching our preparations and the Guinness World Record closely. The subject line read, "So much for that". I opened up the email and my heart dropped to my stomach. His brief note simply said: "Well, there goes that. I just saw this... You guys leave yet?" The screenshot was from Guinness' website. There were some lines of text pictured in the preview. I opened up the attachment and read: "The longest journey by motorcycle in a single country is 28,049.66km (17,429.22 miles) and was achieved by Vishnu Mehta and Santanu Chakrabortty (both India)." The record had been broken, extended by over 6,000 miles, 3,500 more than our own target, and we hadn't even left Beijing yet.

Chapter 2 – The Road Angels of Manchuria

Amy and I had spent so much time focusing on everything except actually riding that I had forgotten how liberating it felt. The urban sprawl of Beijing dwindled away and we glided northward at 80mph. The expansive G45 expressway stretched wide on either side as it cut through the Yanshan mountains that border Beijing to the north. The wind blew over the aerodynamic fairing of the bike at incredible speeds and rushed through the open vents in my riding gear. Pounding heat from the mid-summer sun was effortlessly whipped away, taking with it all the meetings, contracts, conferences, *guanxi*, and world records that had attempted to squeeze the meaning out of our trip over the past six months. Now it was just me, Amy, the motorcycle and the tiny area of pavement that we occupied at any given time. In front of us, the whole expanse of China lay ready for us to explore.

The tall, sparsely forested Yanshan mountain range runs a few hundred miles from Shanhai Pass on China's east coast, over Beijing to the north, and eventually meeting the northern tip of the Taihang mountains to the city's west. These geological barriers once held the strategic significance of splitting the North China Plains to the south from the Mongolian Steppe in the north. Today their function is to place Beijing in a topological bowl that traps emissions, prolonging the adverse effects of air pollution until a strong southerly wind can blow the captured billows of smog off to sea.

Beijing is not just a city but also one of the four municipal provincial-level administrative regions in China (Tianjin, Shanghai, and Chongqing being the other three). Covering an area of over 6,300 square miles (Los Angeles by comparison is 500 square miles) and a population estimated at over 20 million people, it's not hard to see why. This made Beijing our first of 33 provinces. It is surrounded on three sides by the horseshoe-shaped Hebei province and in the south/ southeast touches with the neighboring municipality Tianjin, which we would not be visiting until months later, in winter, as our 33rd and final province.

One of the only major world capitals not established near a body of water, the city's location was instead chosen for its favorable feng shui properties (*fengshui* ironically translates to "wind water"), most notably the mountains which frame the northern section of the city. Modern Beijing is organized into six concentric "ring roads". Each road is an expressway with the Forbidden City at its center (the first ring is the only exception – it was once a 11-mile-long tramline in the center of the city but now has no official demarcation). The 6th Ring is of course the longest, with a maximum radius of 12 miles and a circumference of 140.

All of that was being put behind us now. The canal of asphalt and cement hurtled forward, moving effortlessly through mountains that for centuries immense human blood and capital had been spent to either reinforce or conquer. We continued into Hebei, province number two, and into the area of the Steppe formally known as Manchuria but today known to Chinese simply as *Dongbei* (literally "Northeast").

Our goal for day one on the road was a modest 150 miles to the city of Chengde. Chengde was built by the Qing, the last Chinese dynasty before the Republic was established in the early 20th century. Emperor Kangxi, the fourth Qing emperor, ruled over China for 62 years from 1661 to 1723. He built Chengde as a hunting retreat, a summer getaway from the heat and administrative pressures of the capital. It was subsequently developed between 1702 and 1792 and became known as the "Chengde Mountain Resort" (避暑山庄 *bi shu shan zhuang* which translates to "Escape the Heat Mountain Villa"). Manchurian by descent, the Qing were originally from the more open grass plain regions of the north and no doubt found the opportunity to get away from the city to hunt and exercise a particularly relaxing escape.

In modern-day Hebei there isn't much hunting going on anymore. Today, the wide open parks, eight lakes, 11 outlying lamasery temples, and dozens of ornate buildings and halls dispersed throughout the 2.2-square-mile area have become a popular tourist destination for Beijingers and Chinese from around the country. A different kind of invader, modern Chinese arrive in SUVs rather than on horseback. Armed with smartphones, tablets, and guides, the tourists descend on the greenery of the park seeking another form of respite from urban life than their Manchu predecessors.

We hadn't made it to the retreat yet though, and within just a hundred miles of our departure the fuel gauge on the bike had gone from full to nearly empty. I didn't mention the problem to Amy, but slowed dramatically to decrease air resistance and preserve fuel. I silently panicked. The whole time I had images flashing in my head – Amy and I in our full padded riding gear, helmets in hand, pushing the bike on the shoulder for miles under the hot midday sun. Only a couple hours out and we were already having problems with the bike.

We made it to the next service station without incident. I opened up the tank and was surprised to find it almost full. Fortunately, it appeared the problem was in the metering system. A leak or inefficient use of fuel would have been a much worse thing to deal with. The next day, as Amy and I took time off to tour the lakes, gardens, and temples of the hunting grounds, I called Fang Shujian, the jovial engineer from CFMoto in charge of helping us with any mechanical problems, to explain what happened.

"*Mei wen ti, mei wen ti!* No problem, no problem!" he told me after I described the issue.

"What do you mean '*mei wen ti*'?" I asked. "Of course there's a problem. The meter doesn't work. I have to guess how much fuel we have left."

"No, no. It's working. That's by design! It's supposed to look like it's empty before it's actually empty," he explained, matter-of-factly.

"But you said the bike could go over two hundred miles and it was empty by one hundred. I don't need to know THAT far in advance."

"*Mei wen ti, mei wen ti!* " he repeated. "Your odometer is working right?"

"Yes," I replied, cautiously.

"Well then, all you have to do is look at the distance you've traveled when you're filling up gas, add two hundred to that, and then you'll know when you run out!"

The modern Chinese approach to problem solving tends towards restorative rather than preventative measures. This was a lesson we would learn many more times on our trip. Whether you're dealing in automotive care, construction, or business negotiations, as a westerner you might try and bring up a concern with some argument about how it could cause problems further in the future. No matter how well thought out your reasoning may seem to you though, issues are apparently best dealt with when they come up. Speculation about tomorrow serves only to unnecessarily increase costs today. Simply put, "*Mei wen ti!*" "No problem!"

***

I was slightly ashamed at taking a day off in Chengde after only one half-day on the road, but Amy and I needed the rest. We were less than two hundred miles from Beijing, but our journey had formally started and it felt okay for the two of us to just take a moment for ourselves after so much build up, a time for us to reset and get into trip mode.

When we had fully recovered from all of the pre-trip stress, and gotten our first full night's sleep in months, we left the summer retreat and made our way through *Dongbei* into province number three, Liaoning. The province greeted us with miles of torn up National Highway roads, the *guo daos* that would be our guide for much of our time around China. A familiar battle took shape between smoothly laid asphalt, the potholes in various stages of bloom, and spurts of construction attempting to bring order. Dirt piles and poorly conceived detours littered the road until eventually the construction consumed it all. It seemed to go on in perpetuity with no pavement in either direction for miles. We drove through towns and construction sites, getting covered in dust as trucks and cars barreled their way through with no pavement or road markings left to constrain their paths.

Something Amy and I would muse over together throughout our journey was whether there was some universally distributed script for how to greet traveling foreigners. Whatever it was, almost every conversation we had, independent of age, gender, ethnicity, geographic location, or social status, started out with the exact same four questions in identical order: 1) What's your nationality? 2) What brand is your bike? 3) How much does it cost? and 4) What gas mileage does it get? The really inquisitive would sometimes add a bonus – "Are you married?"

At gas stations we sometimes had to repeat our answers several times per stop, once for the attendants and once or twice more for other patrons. Most people were more surprised by the fact that Amy and I weren't Russian (probably because of our proximity to the border) than by the idea that we were trying to motorcycle around China. Others wouldn't believe us when we told them that our bike was made domestically. They would tell us it was too big or the quality too high before labeling it another brand. Most insisted BMW, but there was one person who made the outlandish claim it was a Harley-

Davidson. Later, when Amy and I started to get tired of repeating the same conversation at every gas station, restaurant, and hotel around the country we joked about getting cards printed. Instead of business and contact information, we would provide the details that seemed most pertinent to our Chinese introductions: American and British, CFMoto (Made in China!), ¥40k, 1 tank 17 liters/300km, (flip the card over) boyfriend and girlfriend. We even mused about putting these on larger poster boards that Amy could hold up as passengers (and sometimes drivers) of passing cars stared at us through their windows in wide-eyed amusement. Amy could then flip through the cards one by one in order to participate in their internal monologue.

Broadly speaking, the experiences and interactions with people we met along the way were almost universally positive. On one of our first days in Liaoning we stopped for lunch in a small town that was, for the most part, inconsequential aside from the commerce it seemed to facilitate for passing freight traffic. After the formalities (American and British, CFMoto, ¥40k, 1 tank 17 liters/300km), we were greeted very warmly by the family that ran the small noodle house along the dusty side road we had stopped at. I felt like we were in an American Western, tired after a long day on the 'ol dusty trail, taking a break at a saloon in some frontier town. The family could tell we were hot in our motorcycle gear, the beige polyester material already starting to brown from the dust in the air, and offered us refrigerated bottled water to help cool us down. After we finished our meal and took some photos with the proprietors (another common practice among people we met throughout our trip), Amy and I made to pay the $3.50 for the meal and cold drinks we'd just enjoyed. The family, all four of whom lived in the upstairs of their restaurant, adamantly refused to accept our money. Amy and I, who had come on a motorcycle that cost more than they probably made in a year and had the luxury to quit our jobs to travel for four months, clearly had the means to pay. For this *Dongbei* family though, it was a matter of pride. They were our hosts

34

and they were proud to play the role of welcoming their foreign guests to the Northeast.

We called these people "Road Angels"[1], and we met more of them at another lunch break the following day. The parking lot we pulled into and the buildings behind looked like a vacant strip mall in American suburbia. Most of the lot seemed to be made up of shops selling wholesale tea, but on the far end we found a convenience store where we hoped to find some food. With high ceilings and half the shelves empty, the space was much too large for the amount of inventory they had. The other half wasn't stocked with anything of much nutritional value. All we could find were Chinese imitation Hostess-style cakes, over-sweetened iced tea and *fang bian mian* or "convenient noodles" (a staple meal for most of our trip). We were happy though just for the opportunity to sit down and relax after the two-hour pounding Amy's and my backsides had just endured on the Liaoning *guo dao*.

As we sat at a squat little table in the back of the shop eating our "convenient noodles", a couple of men walked in through the rear entrance. After picking something up at the store they walked back past us again on their way out, this time making eye contact and smiling. After asking us where we were from, they skipped the remainder of the script – to my surprise – and politely asked us if we would like some tea after we finished. Amy was skeptical of the encounter, and, after they had left, cautioned that it would be more prudent to get back on the road. It was getting late and she was nervous about making our destination before it got dark. She also had

---

[1] "Road Angel" was a term that originated from my time long distance hiking in the U.S. Hikers use the term "Trail Angel" to refer to someone you meet in your travels that shows you, usually unsolicited, acts of kindness. Whether it's a bottle of soda, a meal, a ride into town, or even a stay at their house and the opportunity to take a shower and do laundry, trail and road angels, via gestures big and small, can add tremendous meaning to a traveler's journey. In my experience these have been some of the most impactful encounters I've had while traveling, erecting a backbone of support that provides an adventure with its deeper significance.

a nagging suspicion that we had been targeted for some kind of scam (not an unjustified concern[2]). I, however, didn't want our schedule to get in the way of experience. I argued we could stop early or drive for a bit in the dark if we needed. As for getting ripped off, I figured that if we knew to be aware of the signs, we should be ok. I wanted to avoid the path of least resistance when possible and not let cynicism and tunnel vision shortchange us of any unplanned opportunities we might encounter along the way.

Behind the store was a whole second row of shops just like in the front towards the parking lot, with more tea shops as well as what seemed to be fake antique stores. A walkway ran between the rows of cookie-cutter, industrial buildings wide enough for vehicles to drive through, likely for deliveries. We were intercepted in the rear alleyway by one of the guys that had found us with our noodles before leading us to their "tea house" just a couple of doors down. The shop itself was modest, mainly just storage for their product which we soon found out was tea imported from the southern province of Fujian.

Our hosts were a family of three men, a young girl and a child of about eight, none of whom looked like they were over 30. They were all originally from Fujian and had migrated north to sell tea in *Dongbei*. Due to it's moist climate and year-round warm weather, Fujian province is where some of the country's most popular teas come from including Oolong, white, black, flower, and, of course, green tea. Fujian is probably best known for it's variety of Oolong tea named "Iron Bodhisattva" or *tie guan yin*. Oolong leaves are a cross

---

[2] Tea ceremonies are a popular form of scam in tourist areas around China. The foreign target will be lured in by a youngish-looking Chinese person who usually claims to be a student that would like to practice their English with you. They invite you to a nearby tea house where an elaborate show of serving the tea is performed. You will then be charged high prices, sometimes in the hundreds or even thousands of yuan, not just for the tea but also service charges for the ceremony itself. The "student" will usually offer to split the bill with you. This is just an empty gesture though meant to lure you into a false sense of security about paying since they are in the employ of the tea house anyway.

between a green and a black tea leaf, prepared using a process of partial fermentation. The flavor of *tie guan yin* is much stronger than what we're used to in our teas in the West. The lower quality varieties can be quite bitter, but you'll know a good one when you find it – the bitterness is cut before it passes fully over your tongue and the flavor becomes much smoother with an almost sweet aftertaste. *Tie guan yin* is also well known for its health benefits which include lowering high blood pressure, strengthening your heart, aiding digestion, and even improving eyesight and skin elasticity.

This was the tea we were being served as we visited the young Fujianese family's wholesale teahouse. As with the family in the restaurant the previous day, we were made to feel extremely welcome. The family conveyed immense pride in the opportunity to share their culture with us, childlike in their enthusiasm.

A traditional tea set was used to prepare and serve the tea. The set came on a wooden serving tray with a slatted top layer in order to allow any excess water used to rinse the cups to fall through to the bottom. First, the Oolong leaves were steeped in a small tea cup for 10–20 seconds after which the water was poured into a small, glass teapot. This weak tea water was used to rinse out the small saucer-like cups the tea is drunk from. After rinsing out the saucers and emptying the water into the grated surface, the tea leaves were steeped once again, this time for just under a minute before being poured out for drinking.

This entire delicate and precise process was carried out for us by the most unlikely of characters. A larger Chinese man whose stomach was nearly popping through his too-tight black t-shirt, he looked like he had seen some fighting in his day. Arms covered in lightly colored scarring, even his face carried some evidence of past violence. Through a warm smile and thick, gruff Mandarin accent, the man explained the whole tea making process to us as he carefully handled the tiny saucers and fragile glass containers with club-like hands.

After nearly 45 minutes of chatting and tea drinking, Amy and I explained that it was time to be on our way again. Just as we started to get up and go, the scarred man and one of his friends jumped up, exclaiming for us to wait. They ran to the back of the shop and rummaged around in a long freezer box laid along half of the length of the opposite wall. The man with the scars stuck his head up and, smiling, pulled out a box of about two dozen small, vacuum sealed packages of tea. Not wanting to impose any more, we tried to refuse by saying we didn't have much room on our bike. They insisted, however, and it became clear that it would be more rude to refuse than to accept. And so with that, we were equipped with a couple months' supply of some of the best Iron Bodhisattva tea I'd ever had.

***

After a few days, Amy and I started to settle into life on the road. Day by day we were finding comfort in our routines. The paradox of travel is how while your surroundings are constantly changing, and at times may even seem to conspire against you, the routines are constant. This regularity can offer a comforting bulwark against the unpredictable. Our daily activities were structured around the rising and setting of the sun. The trajectory we moved in was dictated by the realities of the road and the imperatives of food and shelter. Every possession we owned had its own nook in the sanctuary of our bike, prioritized by when we might need it during the day. Each night it all got unpacked because everything had a purpose. Each morning it got packed back up in the exact same way so it could be found again later. This was our new 9-to-5. While we would continuously adjust over the following months, Amy and I each taking responsibility for certain tasks, the relative consistency of this life would give us the framework to deal with the challenges we would face ahead.

After a couple days in Liaoning our trail eventually curved southward. Rains hit us as we made our way across the Liaodong Peninsula towards the Yellow Sea and the North Korean border. There was asphalt again now though and the roads were beautiful. The lush Qianshan mountains which form a gateway to the peninsula rose up from the flatness of the *Dongbei* steppe. The mountain roads were a welcome respite from the choking yellow of road work. They were a joy to ride – even in the rain.

Dandong lies in the armpit of the Korean Peninsula, right on the border between China and North Korea, at the mouth of the Yalu River. This 491-mile-long stretch of water forms most of the geographical border between the two countries. It flows from over 8,000 feet above sea level from its source at Changbai Mountain to the northeast and empties out into the Korea Bay and Yellow Sea to the southwest of Dandong. The Sino-Korean Friendship Bridge crosses this river and allows rail and vehicle traffic to cross into Sinuiju, North Korea on the opposite side. In 2013, trade between China and North Korea was an estimated USD $6.54 billion. 60–70% of this trade was facilitated through the city of Dandong.

Unfortunately, because of my American passport and the short notice, Amy and I would not be able to enter North Korea. We did however plan a visit to the Friendship Bridge the morning after our arrival at the city. There are two bridges at the site, the Friendship Bridge itself and an older one that was built at the beginning of the 20th century, just 66 yards away. The Friendship Bridge was built later on by the Japanese when they occupied Korea and Manchuria during World War II. Both had been bombed repeatedly for two years and again later by the Americans during the Korean War, when they were destroyed several times to stop the flow of Communist soldiers coming in to aid the North. Only the newer one had been repaired. The older one, which is today known as the "Broken Bridge", only allows you to walk part way out into the water, offering pedestrians a viewing platform of the relatively desolate North Korean city on the other side.

As we arrived at the bridge, Amy and I spotted a group of motorcycles parked near the tourist center. I immediately recognized fellow comrades of the road in the line-up of dust covered machines. Flags sporting the Motorfans logo, one of China's largest online motorcycle forums, flew from the back of each of their bikes. Spare luggage was wrapped in plastic bags and strapped tightly to the frames, webbing and bungee cords haphazardly holding them on like giant hands.

A bohemian-looking Chinese man with the greying facial hair of a martial arts master walked over to us as we surveyed the bikes. The man was dressed casually in a Motorfans polo shirt, reinforced rain pants, and wool socks beneath his sandals. We got to chatting and found out that they were indeed also traveling by motorcycle across China. The group, all members of the online forum, had been on the road for a month now. Coming from Guizhou province in the Southwest, they had come up through Inner Mongolia, making it all the way up to the Russian border. They were now heading back home.

The man had a thick southern accent which made it difficult to make out the details of what he was saying, but I was comforted by the familiarity of the conversation itself. Rather than questions of our nationality and the cost of our bike, we exchanged stories of the road. Discussing route suggestions and conditions felt like I was in a conversation with a biker back home despite the different language. It made me glad to think how this shared passion for motorcycles could so easily traverse the culture barrier. We were not foreigners to each other, but fellow adventurers.

A route I was eager to learn about in particular was the one our new friend had taken through Inner Mongolia. The idea of taking our bike across the vast expanses of the Steppe had been appealing to me ever since I started thinking about this trip. Our original itinerary however limited our time in the Northeast. After hitting our easternmost point at Harbin, the plan was to cut across the southern part of the province, which was the more industrialized area close to Beijing. The way the Motorfans group had gone though took them hundreds of miles farther north, ending deep in the grasslands at a border town with Russia called Manzhouli.

I knew Amy and I were going to have to find a way to extend our trip. Since leaving Beijing, I had chosen not to focus on the new Guinness World Record that had been set. I still hadn't even informed our partners at CFMoto or Free Lunch for Children about the development. This detour to the Russian border could add 1,000 miles and almost as much as a week (depending on the road conditions) to our route. The description of hundreds of miles through windswept grasslands enthralled me. Romantic images of horse-mounted hordes traversing a Mongol Steppe nearly unchanged after a thousand years passed through my mind. Unimpeded by train tickets or time frames, the flexibility to make our own trip was the whole reason we were traveling by motorcycle. My mind was convinced and Amy seemed happy to indulge. After we reached Harbin a few days later, rather than make our way back west we would turn north and into the wilderness of Inner Mongolia's steppe.

Chapter 3 – The Russian Capital and Mongolian Plains

We wouldn't be able to step foot on North Korean land, but Amy and I did manage to find a cheap, Chinese-run operation that would boat us across the Yalu River into D.P.R.K. waters. We zipped around on the small 8-seater motorboat among straw-hut military barracks and old WWII military installations built by the Japanese during their occupation in the early 20th century.

We shared the boat with a guide/driver and three other Chinese tourists. After entering the foreign territory, our companions revealed a carton of cigarettes. These were apparently to be used as offerings to any North Korean locals we happened to see. Before long we passed a fisherman on his boat and later a stoic, expressionless 16-year-old armed with a machine gun, both of whom were recipients of our carcinogenic oblations. For the boy soldier the offering was apparently more of a bribe. A pack alone, we were told, was the equivalent to a month's wage in the country and our tour was completely unofficial. We threw individual packs to him across the water from the safety of our boat and he remained without movement or expression throughout. Once satisfied with the offering, he waved us on with his weapon, his stone-cold gaze following us as we buzzed away.

It was a surreal, dehumanizing experience, like tossing food pellets to an animal at a petting zoo. I wasn't quite sure who I felt more embarrassed for, the people getting paid in tobacco or us for treating the experience as some novel form of entertainment.

From Dandong we started moving north again. The roads near the border along the Yalu River were phenomenal, some of the best I've ever ridden on (irrespective of it being in China). Bright, yellow daisies lined the roads for over a hundred miles and perfectly paved mountain "twisties" were a much better send-off from the province than the construction pit that had been our welcome.

Jilin went by quickly and uneventfully. The sunny flowers abruptly ended at the provincial border and we spent most of our time on wide, only occasionally pockmarked roadway. We stopped in Tonghua, a dark, industrial town in the mountains near the border with Liaoning, and Changchun, the sprawling urban capital of the province[3].

On our way from Jilin into Heilongjiang, province number five, we accidentally skirted an entrance barrier onto an expressway. While the smaller *guo dao* roads also have toll booths, two-wheeled traffic is exempt from having to pay[4]. So when our GPS led us towards one of these, it didn't occur to me that we couldn't pass. I read a sign over one lane that read *"zhuan yong che dao"* or "Specialized Vehicle Path", assumed the "special" categorization applied to motorcycles, and went through the space to the right of the barrier. With music playing in my headphones as I accelerated away, I didn't even notice the highway attendant that jumped out of his booth, yelling and waving after us in a futile attempt to chase us down. I remained blissfully unawares of this overeager traffic cop until Amy recounted the event to me at our next stop.

Generally speaking, one of the goals for our trip was to try and avoid the expressways as much as possible. Although motorcycles weren't technically allowed on them, you could still usually sneak on via spaces between the fulcrumed bar and the adjacent booth. Even if we could get on though, the highways were physically set apart,

---

3   The name of the capital, Changchun, means "Long Spring", ironic considering the winters there can last up to six months and have average lows of -4.6°F (-20.3°C)

4   This is considered a sort of subsidy to poor farmers and factory workers who use small scooters and motorcycles as their primary means of transportation. Special lanes exist at the national road toll booths without any form of barriers (sometimes there will be something limiting vehicle width) through which motorcycles can pass without paying a toll.

almost anachronistically, from the rest of the country. They were like sanitized versions of China, wiped of both the country's deficiencies and endearing characteristics. The easy driving on bland, monotonous roads distilled of any culture or character thus deprived us of the "real China" that we had initially set out to discover.

Because roads are so poorly signed and the *guo dao* in Jilin had been relatively wide and flat, it took me a while before I realized we were on an expressway at all. When I did though I was shocked by how relaxed I'd become. My muscles had been in a kind of sustained contraction since we left Beijing, maintaining a high level of preparedness for whatever the countryside might throw at me. Unwittingly, my stress levels had altered. No busses blaring cruise ship-like horns to announce their imminent passing within my lane. No over-packed trucks with axles rattling over potholes, projectiles periodically flung over the top of their towed containers. And I certainly didn't miss the stray animals, pedestrians, and scooters running unannounced across the road after peering in the wrong direction.

While this allowed me to zone out, trance-like, (and surely Amy was finding a similar level of Zen), the presence of a motorcycle on the highway caused many Chinese we encountered varying levels of shock, surprise, and bafflement. Other drivers seemed amused and would often have their passengers take photos, or, if they were solo, keep one hand on the wheel and do it themselves. Convincing gas station attendants to give us fuel proved especially challenging. Normally, motorcycles have to fill up away from the pump, pouring gas via a giant aluminum watering can. This is due to the fear that the exposed engine might cause a spark that could ignite the gas and travel up the pump, killing us all in a giant fiery explosion. Highways aren't equipped for motorcycles though so they didn't have the watering can. "*Tai wei xian!*" the attendants exclaimed when I tried to say how much gas we wanted, "Too dangerous!" This was a conversation we would have on almost daily basis.[5]

The most entertaining exchanges however were at the provincial border and the highway off-ramp where the tolls had barriers too broad for me to circumvent. Both times Amy and I preemptively decided on the "dumb foreigner" routine: pretend not to speak any Chinese and they would find us too much trouble to deal with and let us through. We sometimes felt guilty for doing this – it felt unfair that we could receive preferential treatment because we were foreigners, but it was a reliable strategy nonetheless.

At both stops on our way to Harbin the attendants seemed overwhelmed and had to call over a superior. The first time, the cop and his supervisor were pretty stern with us. They tried to explain how we weren't allowed on, including painful attempts at gesturing with their hands while still using Chinese words to communicate their meaning. Amy and I would just smile and nod in unison or shrug at what seemed appropriate times. Eventually, exasperated after ineffectually trying to explain the rules to us, we were finally waved through with a frown and a sigh.

At the second checkpoint the supervising officer seemed to find the situation so ludicrous that he started giggling uncontrollably, rubbing the top of his head several times in a sign of confused futility upon seeing two foreigners on a motorcycle.

"Jilin?" the man said with a laugh, pointing down the road behind us.

---

[5]   Amy and I would have to spend several minutes of careful reasoning and well-thought-out logic each time we wanted to fill up in an effort to convince them that our motorcycle would not cause an explosion. "Look, our engine is covered," I'd explain pointing at the faring, "so it can't catch fire." Or "This is a bigger bike, not like the farmer motorcycles, so the quality is better." If I was feeling particularly combative though I would just explain how no other country in the world made motorcycles fill up in this way and none of them had had any explosions either so just let us buy some gas and we would be on our way.

As if excited by a point of common comprehension, Amy and I began to nod enthusiastically and agreed, "Yes, yes! Jilin!"

Now that we had established some sort of conversation, I offered to continue it. "Harbin!" I exclaimed, pointing forward this time, still grinning widely, indicating the place we planned to go after Jilin. At that, the two officers looked at each other, let out a sigh, and with a giggle flagged us forward.

***

A crossroads of European and East Asian cultures in the heart of Manchuria, Harbin has had a fascinating and tumultuous history throughout the 20th century. It has passed through a succession of Manchurian (Qing), Russian, Japanese, and Chinese control. This has made it one of China's most culturally diverse cities.

Human settlement in the area dates as far back as 2200 BC and was occasionally used by Chinese dynasties, most notably the Jin around 1100 AD, to establish northern power bases. Harbin's true significance however came with the construction of the Trans-Siberian Railway at the end of the 19th century, in particular the 895-mile-long East Chinese Railway spur-line which runs from Chita in Siberia, southeast through Harbin, and ends at the Russian seaport of Vladivostok. The city of Harbin in its current incarnation was founded in 1898 when an agreement between the Russians and the Qing was made for construction of the railway. The Russians later used the city as a base for military operations during the Russo-Japanese War from 1904 to 1905.

After the Japanese won, many Russians remained and Harbin began to grow into a truly international, cosmopolitan city. By 1913, only 11.3% of the population was native born. 53 different nationalities were represented and a total of 45 languages spoken. By 1917, the population had grown to over 100,000, with the local census reporting over 40,000 being of ethnic Russian descent. After the establishing of the PRC however and as China continued to develop, Harbin lost much of its heterogeneity. Today, the city remains the largest in Heilongjiang province with a population of over 10.5 million. Han Chinese make up 93% of that number however, with much of the Russian population having emigrated away. Harbin is also Heilongjiang's largest economic hub, with local GDP in 2013 reaching ¥501 billion (USD $80 billion), with ¥55.43 billion (USD $8 billion) coming from tourism. Harbin is today probably best known for the annual International Ice & Snow Festival held during the city's frigid winters. The festival most notably features full-scale buildings made entirely out of ice, including a working hotel.

Ever since we decided to ride up through the Northeast, Amy and I had planned on visiting Harbin. Amy in particular was eager to tour the city's old Russian quarters with its traditional European style architecture, workshops, and marketplaces.[6] The site we were most interested in visiting was the 175-foot-tall, Russian Orthodox Saint Sophia Cathedral that stands in the center of Daoli district in downtown Harbin. The red brick, Neo-byzantine building, with it's green tipped onion dome and surrounding steeples, sits at the end of a historic Russian neighborhood. Its exterior has been beautifully preserved, standing proudly on its own in the center of a wide open square, an area that was swarming with tourists and couples taking wedding photos in front of the church when we were there.[7] It was

---

[6] This of course was all against the backdrop of a modern Chinese city consisting of giant billboards advertising generic electronics brands, Chinese and Western fast food chains, and the wafting scents and grating sounds of local Chinese hawkers.

[7] While fireworks and red envelopes are still a big part of Chinese matrimony, aspects of Western (and particularly American) romance have been imported where convenient. The stereotypes of Hollywood romantic comedies have been transferred to Chinese studios for example with dozens of new, boilerplate "rom-coms" coming out every year. In addition, thousands of yuan can be spent on full day photoshoots for soon-to-be-wed couples in long white wedding dresses and rented tuxedos. Despite there being no religious (and certainly no Christian) context for the Chinese wedding, if feasible, these sessions will be done with the

originally built as a symbol of Russian national pride after losing the Russo-Japanese war in 1907, but in 1997 was converted to serve as the Municipal Architecture and Art Museum with displays of Harbin's colorfully diverse architectural past. This consisted of pictures reaching back a century to the construction of the East Chinese Railway, the original city plans, and the Cathedral itself.

One other thing I wanted to visit while we were in Harbin was the remnants of a small Jewish community that had been established there. One little known fact about Harbin is that it was once home to the largest Jewish community in the Far East when, at the beginning of the 20th century, many immigrated to Harbin looking for opportunities associated with the railway construction and to escape persecution and civil wars back home. Throughout its history, as many as 20,000 Jewish people are said to have spent their lives there. Although little of the original community still remains, there are many Jewish schools, homes, and synagogues still standing in the city.

Harbin was Amy and I's first big milestone of The Great Ride of China. It was the farthest either of us had been from Beijing by motorcycle, the farthest point east we would travel on the trip, and also the first of only a couple mail drops we had pre-arranged. At our hotel, which we reserved before leaving Beijing, we picked up our package that included camping gear and a waterproof 21-gallon bag we could strap to the back of the bike for additional storage space. On the outskirts of town was also one of the region's only CFMoto shops. We took the opportunity to make sure everything was running properly after the bike's first thousand miles including getting a third

---

backdrop of a European style church. In addition to our witnessing this ritual being performed at the Russian built St. Sophia Cathedral in Harbin, on a previous trip along the east coast Amy and I also saw trains of brides and grooms emptying from vans in Qingdao lining up to take photos in front of the German cathedral that had been built there in the early 20th century.

party to confirm that our gas gauge was indeed malfunctioning and arrange to have a new one sent to us further on[8].

Harbin was the first time in a week of riding from Chengde that we took a day off, but unfortunately there wasn't much opportunity for rest. Aside from putting on our tourists' hats and dropping off the bike for repairs, there were chores to do. Carrying only a couple sets of clothing with us (one for riding, one for towns, and a couple spare pairs of underwear and socks), laundry was a major concern. There were also emails and blog posts to catch up on. Most of all though we needed to plan our new route north.

We knew now that we would have to add at least 3,000 miles to our original itinerary in order to get the Guinness World Record, but we also had to be conscious of two deadlines: the September cutoff for entering Tibet and the CIMA exhibition in Chongqing on October 17th. If the detour to Manzhouli took too long we could miss one or both of these. In addition, since the reroute lead us to a very remote area of the country, if we ran into any problems it could cause some serious delays.

I took the morning to look over maps and the calendar, planning an approximate route that would keep us on schedule. Out of Harbin we would follow the Motorfans biker's suggestion, heading northwest and through the city of Qiqihaer, across the sparsely populated plains of the Hulunbeier region of Inner Mongolia, and arriving at Manzhouli approximately three days and 650 miles later. After that we would head southeast, hugging the border with Mongolia for a couple of days before hooking south back into the industrial heart of China towards Shaanxi province and the Terracotta Warriors in Xi'an.

---

8   After the mechanic at the shop determined that the meter wasn't working correctly, Fang Shujian explained to us that the electronics couldn't be replaced but that he would send a full new dashboard to Xi'an for us, a couple weeks away. Still not wanting to lose any face with regards to whether or not the meter had been operating according to design, he explained that he would send us the dashboard made for the domestic market rather than the one we had which was meant for export, his explanation for the discrepancies.

It was raining the entire morning that we prepared to set out from the city. The dark and gloomy grey outside was an ominous backdrop as we packed up the bike at the CFMoto shop with our new gear.

A clerk, concerned about our safety, asked whether we still planned to leave if it was raining. I told her it didn't look like it would stop anytime soon. She shrugged and walked away, muttering half to herself and half at us, "*Tai wei xian.*" Too dangerous.

We made our way slowly out of the city. The rain was coming down hard so I took my time. I didn't rush to catch any yellow lights and avoided having to stop too abruptly. Just before the city limits, we came to an on-ramp for a bridge leading out of Harbin. Just as it looked like we'd soon finally have space to get some miles behind us, the bike, without warning and with no shoulder to pull off onto, sputtered and died.

I had no idea what was wrong and the traffic was coming up full speed behind us, merging to get onto the bridge. I tried one more time to start the bike but it just died out again. By my final attempt to start up, I could smell very strong whiffs of gasoline coming up from the bike and knew that we had to get down off the ramp as soon as possible.

I yelled to Amy over the rumbling of traffic and rain to jump off and help wave away the oncoming vehicles coming around the half-blind curve. I managed to do a three-point turn and rolled the bike in neutral down the ramp against traffic. At the base, under the overpass of the bridge, I noticed an impromptu police checkpoint, just a couple of parked cop cars and a few officers standing around pulling vehicles over at random. It looked safe, flat, and most of all dry, so I rolled the bike up next to them and hopped off to assess the damage.

Every time I tried to turn the bike on, gas would pour out from underneath and a safety automatically shut the engine off again. Still only a couple miles away, I gave the shop a call to see if the mechanic could come help. We were waiting there under the overpass for about 45 minutes before he showed up.

The three officers on duty at the checkpoint were incredibly interested by the two Chinese-speaking foreigners that had ridden a leaky motorcycle all the way from Beijing. They were nice, even buying us a couple bottles of water as we made small talk by the side of the road (American and British, CFMoto, ¥40k, 1 tank 17 liters/ 300km, plus the new one for rainy days: "It's ok, in the rain we just drive more slowly").

Finally the mechanic arrived and we showed him what was going on. He took off the seat and checked the gas line. Apparently he had failed to re-attach it properly after checking the gas gauge and in the ten minutes since we left it had shaken loose.[9] With everything tightened back up, the bike started without any problems. We waved goodbye to our policeman hosts and drove to a nearby gas station to refill our depleted tank.

After crossing the bridge out of town, we finally found our way onto the northbound National Highway. By early afternoon we had put Harbin behind us but the rain persisted at a steady drizzle. Between the smooth pavement and our neon yellow waterproofs, it was manageable. We had the road mostly to ourselves too, though we did pass some stretches of construction, patches of gravel and other evidence of a road not yet completed. These areas soon grew more frequent and since the road tires on the 650TR aren't built for gripping loose surfaces, I slowed down to avoid slipping.

---

[9]   Similar to Fang Shujian who tried to excuse himself of responsibility by insisting that the apparent problem with the gas gauge was by design, the Harbin mechanic told us that the screw was worn down which is why it had loosened. I had him show me exactly where it was in case I had to tighten it again later on. When I told Fang that we might have to change it at our next stop, he dutifully informed me that the mechanic had been lying. The screw was fine. He was just embarrassed about messing up and did not want to admit it. Fang turned out to be right of course and we never had to touch that screw again.

The lightly forested areas bordering the highway soon turned into small villages. They were the kind of commercial waypoints we were used to passing through on the *guo dao*, but the rain was adding even more stress to the usual chaos.

Not too long after however, the gravel turned to mud.

Construction on Chinese roads, excluding the expressways, is a patchwork affair. Nothing is planned with any sort of purpose. There are no detours and no signs. No thought is put into how digging up miles and miles of road might disrupt the flow of normal life. The construction was so dramatic in areas that some villages had deep trenches through the main street of the town, muddy declines as much as 10–20 feet deep which we had to inch our way down. There was certainly no consideration given to what might come of the loosely packed earth in the event that it rained.

As I got more used to techniques needed to keep us vertical and moving forward, I actually found myself starting to enjoy the experience. Never having done any off-roading before, the challenge of mapping out routes through the mud and other obstructions was fun, and I started to feel confident in my new found abilities.

The situation was much more stressful for Amy. Sitting in the back, she had absolutely no control over the efforts to keep upright. Totally helpless, she panicked every time she felt the tires slip a little in the deepening mud, tightening her grip around my waist or slapping me repeatedly on my back to get me to slow down.

We did what we could to help our chances. Amy even dismounted for each particularly steep incline or decline. After at least ten miles of endless mud though and the rain giving no sign of letting up, the situation was starting to feel hopeless.

Just after passing through another village, the mud road dipped down and detoured around a small construction pit. I pointed the nose of the bike left, into the curve of the main track, but, seized by the swing of momentum, the back wheel had other ideas. Unable to grab onto anything but slick mud, I started to lose control.

Like an out of body experience, I felt myself following each second of our fall as it happened. There was the moment of relief when I pulled in the clutch and the bike started to straighten out again, as well as almost immediately after when we started to fishtail. Easing back into gear, the wheel reengaged with a vengeance, whipping from side to side with nothing in the slush underneath us to grab onto. The back of the bike took one more swerve to the right and this time there was nothing I could do to bring it back. The wheels popped up and with one last screech from our futilely revving engine, we were in the mud.

As soon as we hit the ground I turned to check on Amy.

Amy had been in a minor accident a couple of years prior where a car had pinned her legs between its bumper and that of a parked car she was standing behind. There had been sensitivity in her knee since then and I was worried about aggravating any past damage. Amy confirmed that she was alright, after which I dug myself out from under the frame and lifted it up enough so she could drag herself out too. While still awkwardly pinning her to the ground, the left-side panniers of the bike had ended up taking the brunt of the fall and luckily kept most of the weight off of Amy's legs.

We were completely drenched through now from the rain. The fall had ripped holes in our rain gear and we were covered head-to-toe in the clay we had slid through (though it did have the benefit at least of cushioning our fall). After establishing that we were both physically okay I started to do a quick survey of any damage to the bike. Aside from the left mirror, which had snapped free from its plastic latch but was easily pushed back into place, and a few other mainly aesthetic odds and ends, everything seemed to have made it through alright.

The adrenaline-induced tunnel vision I was experiencing started to wear off now and I quickly surveyed where we had landed. On the right side of the road were a couple one-story, dark, shuttered buildings. Behind us was the small construction pit that I had been on my way around. To the left were open fields. Next, I noticed, sitting on a stool in the doorway of a shop closest to where we fell, a chapeaued dwarf staring at us from his perch. Unmoving with his arms crossed and hat casting a shadow over his eyes, he seemed nonplussed by what had just transpired in front of him.

A sheet of rain covered the area and the bike still lay in the mud. Fully packed it was too heavy for me to lift up on my own, especially in the slippery mud, so Amy and I unpacked everything we could and I propped the bike back up again. As we went through the slow process of our recovery, several locals had passed by, lazily making their way down the muddy trail. Some walked by wordlessly while others attempted to converse. Not in the mood for 20 Questions, the indignation in my voice seemed to discourage most from inquiring much past our nationality. One man however did stop on his way down the road. Finding the spectacle too engrossing to pass up, he decided to linger and took up a spot just a few feet down the road to rubberneck a little while longer.

I finally managed to get the bike upright again and wanted to see if we could try and rinse everything off a bit before strapping the bag back on. I turned towards the dwarf and asked if there was any water available we could use to wipe down the bike. He didn't respond, and just continued staring expressionlessly at me. Fortunately, our rubbernecker was more forthcoming. Sidling over through the mud-caked road, he quickly helped communicate our request to the dwarf who, with a grunt and a nod, was finally moved to action. He hopped off his stool and cautiously withdrew into the shadows inside before reappearing with a wash basin full of water.

As Amy and I went about the work of rinsing ourselves and the bike of some of the mud, I noticed that the building the dwarf was sitting in front of had a sign hung up indicating it served food. A rural restaurant. My stomach suddenly and vocally reminded me of how long it had been since breakfast. Throughout all the commotion of the day – our leaking gas tank, chatting with policemen under a bridge, and our first fall of the trip – I realized that it had been a long time since our early breakfast at the hotel in Harbin. After re-attaching the bags to the bike and finally having a moment to relax, I turned and asked the dwarf about food. While still unable to deign himself to speak with us, he did respond by shaking his head vigorously from side to side. Luckily the other man was able to give us some more information.

"None of the restaurants on this road are open now," he said.

"What do you mean?" I asked, turning towards him now. "Isn't this the main national road? How is everything closed?"

"Yes, but the national road is closed now for construction. Since no traffic is coming through, everything is closed. The road ends in a few kilometers that way," he explained, pointing in the direction we had been heading in.

The fact that the road we were on was actually officially closed came as a bit of a shock to me. It's true that the road itself was in a state of complete disrepair, but that was something that we had come to expect on the National Highways. This didn't necessarily mean the road was closed. We hadn't passed any signs prohibiting thru-traffic or gone around any barriers. How could you just close down a main traffic artery without any sort of official detour? Everyone seemed completely complacent to the fact that almost all commerce in the area was now shut down as a result of a poorly planned road construction.

"So there's no way to move on on the national road? It's completely blocked?" I asked. "We're trying to go north towards Inner Mongolia. Is there any other way?" Both men (the dwarf still vacantly spectating, unwilling to participate) just shrugged.[10]

The two men finally conferred with each other and agreed that if we turned back the way we came, in about a mile we would get to an intersection in the center of the nearest village. There we would be able to ask someone for more specific directions on how to navigate around the road closings and continue north.

Amy was not thrilled about going back through all the mud, but we clearly had little choice. It was an uneasy five minutes back but we made it without another incident. At the first intersection we arrived at we spoke with another local, this one in an old pickup truck. Sighing in relief, we noted that the eastwardly road he pointed us down was paved.

We spent the next couple of hours navigating our way along extremely remote county roads, through wet, sleepy hamlets, and across half a dozen creaky plank bridges over swollen streams. Some of the roads we took were not even marked on our GPS. I was happy for the solitude though, feeling refreshed after days on highways and in the city. Soon we made it back to a major roadway, a four-lane provincial highway that was headed in the general northward direction we were aiming for.

That evening we arrived at a very strange but bustling city by the name of An Da (安达 or "The Arrival of Peace"). An Da itself was nowhere near as large as Harbin but it was still very busy and seemed to have plenty of hotels to choose from. What was weird about it

---

[10]   Inability to provide clear directions was a common problem we encountered in China. In contrast, back in the U.S. if you stop in a small town, most locals will know every road, from the interstate to the gravel foresting roads, within 100 miles of their area. I've stopped at a gas station before and had a ten minute conversation just about which roads were good and which to avoid. In China though, most people don't do much driving and what driving they do is restricted to the areas in which they work and live (usually not mutually exclusive). Life is still very much centered in the area where you were born. This means that most people rarely if ever venture outside of their hometown and when they do it's generally by bus or train. This makes getting directions in China, even to the next town over, a challenge.

though was the near-obsessive fascination with cows. I had never seen a place like it. We drove into the city via the south end of the main provincial road and were immediately greeted by life-sized statues of cows gazing contemplatively over our shoulders and out towards the countryside. As we continued on we saw cows displayed everywhere, on top of lamp posts, in murals on garbage cans, welded on manhole covers, even cow themed mosaics built directly into the sidewalks. Most of the street names also seemed to involve cows, with the character for cow, 牛 *niu* appearing at least once at every intersection. After having so much thrown at us that day, it was a relief when we caught a break finding a place to stay. It only took one rejection by a hotel that refused to register foreigners as guests[11] before finding what appeared to be luxury accommodations just off the the main road and beside a construction site. Entering the lobby with its vaulted ceilings, a large chandelier, and well dressed, smiling attendants Amy and I, dejected in our ripped and mud covered gear, walked up to the front desk and handed over our passports to check-in.

**

It took another day and a half to get to the border between Heilongjiang and Inner Mongolia. Rain persisted as a sporadic if somewhat more diminished threat, while road quality remained a

---

[11]   This is a common problem for foreigners traveling in China. Though much more lax compared to the early days of Deng Xiaoping's "Reform and Opening Up" when foreigners could not even leave designated areas in major cities let alone travel the countryside, the government still likes to keep track of anyone traveling. Even Chinese have to provide their personal identification card when checking in to a hotel so that guests can be registered with the local PSB (Public Safety Bureau). For foreigners, the paperwork is more detailed and the regulations more stringent. In some towns we couldn't find a single place that would register us. Others might only have one option, usually with a deceptively high-end sounding name that included some combination of the words "International" and "Business". Amy and I were almost invariably unimpressed by such establishments as "The New Century International Business Hotel" or "The Flourishing Mansion International Business Hotel", as we usually found them to be suffering from varying degrees of disrepair and neglect.

constant challenge. There were long stretches of road either dug up but never repaired and other areas pitted with frequent and deep potholes. Constantly bracing against the imminent bottoming out of our suspension and working to keep the bike, along with Amy and all of our luggage, upright over these areas proved to be an exhausting affair. Awkward and unfamiliar areas of my back, shoulders, and arms soon began to sting with the lactic burn of overworked muscles.

We arrived at the sign welcoming us to Inner Mongolia with a baking midday sun (finally) beginning to bore down on us. In a large grass clearing off the left side of the road was a collection of yurts, the cylindrical, tent-like structures that traditionally served as the homes for the nomadic Mongol people. Set up at the entrance to this little tourist park were a few middle-aged, dark skinned, ethnic Mongolian women selling fruit and nuts to passing travelers. In front of us, ominously laid down across the full breadth of the road, was a giant mound of dirt, defiantly standing 10 feet high blocking the advance of traffic. Beyond was a three-lane dirt track running down from the low plateau we were perched on and off into the hills in the horizon. It looked like the highway into Inner Mongolia had ended.

At a loss, Amy and I dismounted, deciding first to check out the migratorial Mongolian dwellings and have some snacks before figuring out where we would go next. We snapped some photos and then approached the Mongolian women to inquire about a way forward. They were very excited to learn that we could speak Chinese, giggling after each brief exchange, but graciously explained to us that we could drive around the dirt mound and up the path, hitting pavement again after about 15 miles.

After conversing for a few minutes Amy and I headed back to our bike to start getting ready to head off. Just as we were finishing up the complex ritual of packing up the bike and putting on our gear, the chattiest of the women ran over, grinning ear to ear. Hands cupped in front of her, she approached as if in supplication. As she got closer, I noticed a large sampling of the kumquat-like fruits she had been selling clutched in her hands. Arriving at the bike she jovially shoved the offering towards us and insisted above all protestations that we accept her gift. Another selfless show of hospitality from a local whose means were far below our own.

After managing to find a nook in the bike where we could cram the newest addition to our travel apparatus, Amy and I evaluated our options. I was skeptical about the implied ease with which we could proceed. If the road was open but under construction, why block the way with a wall of dirt? Several days earlier we had encountered a closed road with no official closing and here we were faced with a very obvious obstruction to thru-traffic but this road was open? There were no signs anywhere other than the one marking the border, and, as expected, now that we were this far north there were also no alternate roads on the map going forward.

As Amy and I stood, beginning to sweat in full riding gear and helmets, deliberating over our options, a couple cars came around the side of the barrier from the direction we were targeting. The exteriors of the vehicles looked a little worse for wear, but, we reasoned, they must have come from somewhere. So, with a hesitant shrug, Amy and I mounted the bike, waved goodbye to our entrepreneurial friends, and set off on our way, following the car tracks around the dirt pile.

It was slow going navigating through the gravel, sand, and diversions around drying asphalt. Twice, the road ended at a deep moat cut through the breadth of the road and we had to find alternate routes around on dirt side-paths through the adjacent woods. It was an exhausting exercise that ultimately took us an hour to complete. We were navigating an off-road track but relying on machinery designed exclusively for the forgiving conditions of level tarmac. The wheels slipped often and after our fall outside of Harbin Amy was much more anxious on the back. The hot sun made the work of keeping upright and steady even more draining. I gradually stripped layers off as we went along, strapping them haphazardly to the bike, but thinking this was still better than the alternative. Had we had rain and mud instead we may not have been able to proceed at all.

As a biker, there are few greater feelings than than that of unloading the throttle of a large capacity engine after struggling through miles of frustratingly slow and treacherous trail. When we finally hit the tarmac again, successfully making it through the gauntlet, I dropped down on the accelerator and jumped the bike forward, throwing Amy's and my combined weight backwards into our rear case. It was the biker's equivalent to a whoop of joy (I may have whooped a little in my helmet as well). To further punctuate the moment, after about ten minutes, the road lifted and rose up a small hill greeting us with a spectacular view.

We came out of a lightly forested valley and at the apex joined with another two-lane highway. As if laid out on a tablecloth, the tableau of the Mongolian steppe opened out in front of us. Looking out over the windshield of the bike, I marveled at the endless green expanse and the snaking black of our road as it was swallowed up on its way towards Siberia before it all dissolved into the crisp blue of the snow globe-like roof above us.

A storm hit just as we were passing through a small town on the borderlands of the Steppe. Rain in this area of China appeared to come in spurts all at once, in contrast to the gradual and sustained rainfall we'd encountered elsewhere. What started off as a dark blur in the distance soon transformed into a distinct wall of rain advancing with tremendous speed before eventually hitting us full force. I wanted to try and ride through it but the sides of the road were starting to flood. Dips and potholes in the pavement soon turned into hidden road hazards, a condition made more dangerous by the declining visibility that the splashing on my visor was causing. We waited out the rest of the storm under a gas station awning with a host of local cab drivers, many of whom were taking the opportunity to nap, evidenced by the pairs of legs sticking out from their passenger seats.

The rain stopped as suddenly as it began. The floating fortress of precipitation continued its trudging assault across the plains and the sun broke through, illuminating the aftermath.

Rain can be a fickle travel companion. It can be dangerous and sometimes life threatening. It can ruin your food, clothing, gear, and, most importantly, your mood. There are few discomforts in the world that can compare with the squelching of your last pair of clean socks after water has seeped into your boots.

What the storm did for the countryside though was magnificent. After the deep cleansing of the downpour, the Mongolian Steppe came alive. Rivers had formed from nothing, filling the gullies that ran on either side of the roadway. Power lines and trees stuck up above the muddy currents, giving evidence of the land that had been there only a few hours before. There were signs of more distant scars from seasonal flooding further out as recently deposited runoff glittered in the sunshine. Farm animals had come out of hiding too. Sheep and cows could be made out now on the lush greenery that surrounded us, lazily scanning the surrounding hillocks, unperturbed by fence or shepherd.[12]

The towns in the area were small, nothing more than watering holes for passing migrant workers and loading docks for farmers and factories to send away goods on trains. The hostel we stayed at for our first night in Inner Mongolia, which sat next to one of these train stations, didn't even have a computer system to register guests. The question of our nationality moot, the man who ran the building took

---

[12]   In some areas, the running water found its way onto the road as flooding overtook the barriers. Two times in particular the deluge had been so heavy that there was a current running over the road, inhibiting our progress. The foaming white of mini-rapids made crossing hazardous as it obscured the depth of the water as well as any obstacles that may have been hiding underneath.

down our personal information with a pen and paper and showed us to the white, cell-like room where we would be spending the night.

After changing out of our rain-soaked clothing, Amy and I wandered together down the main (and only) road in town to find a local restaurant for dinner. It didn't take long. We shared the main seating area with a group of fifteen high-spirited locals seated around a Chinese banquet-style table. The rosy-cheeked revelers took turns cheers-ing and making loud, barely comprehensible proclamations to the group. Clearly this was a celebration.

Two foreigners in a backwater town deep in *Dongbei*, it wasn't long before we began to draw the attention of some of them. They yelled introductions at us from across the room and Amy and I happily reciprocated.

"*Huan ying dao Nei Meng Gu!*" someone would yell, standing erect, chest out like a soldier on parade at their spot at the table. "Welcome to Inner Mongolia!"

"*Huan ying dao Zhong Guo!*" Welcome to China! another would proclaim.

"*Yi lu ping an!*" Safe travels!

Every declaration was punctuated with a raised glass and a *Gan bei*, Bottoms up! (literally "Dry glass") and to each one Amy and I would raise our glasses of 50-cent beer, downing our drinks in response.

We soon discovered that the group was a gathering of two families. They had come from around the province and neighboring Heilongjiang to celebrate the wedding of two of their progeny. Notably, the newlyweds lived and worked in Harbin and had been unable to celebrate or have a proper ceremony themselves. So their families, without bride or groom, had taken it upon themselves to congregate in this small town in order to celebrate the union.[13]

---

[13]   The story of this newlywed couple in Harbin caused me to think back on our visit to the St.

For the next hour Amy and I became informally adopted into this newly expanded family. Several members came over to our table to toast us individually. A particular shiver of excitement however went through the table when we brought out the camera. We wanted to capture some of the experience and caught one of the members of the group singing *a capella*. At this, everyone seemed to want to make their contribution to the record and by the end of the night we had filmed nearly half of the group in boisterous song.

As we were now deep in rural China, many, if not all, of the guests were farmers. This meant that life, much as with our schedule of the road, was dictated by the rising and setting of the sun. So, as if on cue, just after the sun had set at around 9 o'clock, the festivities wrapped up. In proper Chinese fashion, almost none of the plates in the center of their table were finished (a sign of politeness in China to show that no one is leaving the table still hungry[14]). About four of the middle-aged women however, the family matriarchs it would seem, made sure that nothing from the feast went to waste. While all the men had already stumbled their way to the gravel road outside, the four women retrieved a large stack of takeaway containers and plastic bags from the back of the restaurant and, sobered by the task at hand, calmly and efficiently packed away every last leftover.

Sophia Cathedral only a few days before. I noted the irony of the staged nuptials of the half-dozen couples we witnessed that day in front of the famous church in the open square. Dressed in western-style wedding attire, obsequious grooms tediously obeyed the orders of their white-clad brides and diminutive (but apparently visionary) photographers skittered about trying to set the scene just so. Meanwhile, hundreds of miles away, there were families such as these gathering together in what may appear as an unrefined but still unfiltered gaiety, an honest show of true celebration.

[14]   With a growing middle and upper class now with the means to over-order, China is beginning to experience serious problems with food waste. A 2012 study by the Beijing-based China Agricultural University's College of Food Science and Nutritional Engineering found that USD $32 billion worth of food is thrown away in China each year. Researchers in the Environmental Science and Technology publication also estimate that 19% of China's grain, 20–30% of fruits and vegetables and 3–15% of meat are wasted each year.

Our reroute to the North from Harbin had already been incredibly challenging. We had had our first fall and our first major mechanical malfunction. The poorly maintained infrastructure of this remote part of the country was making me question whether we had made the right decision. Would this take longer than the time we had allowed for? Would we still be able to make our other deadlines? How much of this rough road could our highway bike take? How many more days of rain did we still have to look forward to? Would the even more remote road back south be even more poorly paved?

Amy and I left the restaurant and began to make our way back to the railway tracks. I thought about what a special occasion we had just been lucky enough to be a part of, a unique experience in our combined six years in the country. The glow of a full moon lit our way, helping to compensate for the lack of street lights. I took in a deep breath. The air was fresh – the kind of crisp, clean freshness that can only come with the passing of a heavy downpour. I took hold of Amy's hand and thought of the days we had ahead riding through the plains, and smiled. There was nowhere else I'd rather be, no one else I'd rather be with, and no question we had made the right decision.

Chapter 4 – The Rains of the Steppe

It dawned on me that we had reached the periphery of the Han Chinese sphere of influence when the language of the road signs started changing.[15] As we went farther north, the terrain flattened out entirely. The small hills melted away and spread out into a distant, infinite expanse of green. Signs of life were sparse and the sun was unrelenting even at the high speeds that we were now able to hit on the open road. Our first glimpse of Mongolian writing was on a street sign at a National Highway tollbooth welcoming us to the Steppe. The inscriptions felt ancient and contrasted with the bright reflective green of the modern highway sign. The script was constructed out of vertical lines that connected a series of swoops and dashes which emanated outward. The way it was structured gave it the look of a long sword with serrated edge. Gliding against the peaceful backdrop of the windswept plains, it felt like a subtly martial reminder of the Mongols' imperial past.

Due to its proximity to Russia, Manzhouli serves as a bridge between China and neighboring Siberia, on whose border it sits. This has contributed to its becoming the busiest land port in the country. In 2012, USD $1.63 billion in exports went through the city, primarily in light industrial goods and textiles, while $4.17 billion worth of goods were imported from Russia, mostly natural resources. Manzhouli accounts for nearly 50% of all of Inner Mongolia's total foreign trade. Like Harbin, Manzhouli was also heavily influenced by

---

[15] This was something that would happen multiple times throughout our trip. In contrast to some countries where you may have one or two secondary languages (e.g. Spanish in the U.S., French in Canada, or French/Flemish in Belgium) we passed through many regions around China where completely new scripts were suddenly introduced alongside Mandarin, often wildly different from one another with little shared history or etymology.

the agreement between Russia and the Qing in the early 20th century to build the East Chinese Railway, the spur-line that cuts through China to the Sea of Japan. It was the first stop into China on the route, which gave it its modern-day name, which means "Into Manchuria". Rail remains a large part of the local industry and it is one of the four busiest rail ports of entry into China.

The Russian influence doesn't just show up in the statistics. Manzhouli is a crossroads of two very different cultures and acts as a conduit, in sometimes surreal ways, for their exchange. While it has become a popular tourist destination in recent years for domestic Chinese tourists, the primary source of traffic originates from the Russian side. In 2009, 3.6 million tourists visited the city, bringing in ¥3.5 billion in total tourism-related revenue. For the Russian tourists the allure is to hop the border and buy cheap consumer goods from their Chinese counterparts on the other side. In response, the enterprising residents of Manzhouli have built up businesses to accommodate their eager new customers. We found a multitude of Chinese-run Russian restaurants, clubs and cafes dotting the city. Signs were written in Cyrillic. Many locals had even learned the language in order to communicate with their patrons.

The local government and property developers were not shy about who their target market was either. Upon arriving at the city we were immediately immersed in an onslaught of tacky, over-the-top imitation Russian-style architecture. Approaching downtown was like entering an amusement park of follies and faux baroque-style buildings. All of Manzhouli seemed to have been set up in an effort to attract Russian tourists and shoppers. The contrast with Harbin was striking. Having at one time been home to a thriving Russian community, Harbin's evolution was organic and its cultural diversity authentic. Manzhouli on the other hand was an overt attempt at commercializing its proximity to a foreign population. It was a fake Russian city built and occupied by Chinese to attract Russian tourists (and shoppers). Almost everything in the town had been erected in the past 20 years. In fact, the only original buildings were the old train station and a few old log cabins. These former fur-trading posts, once a lonely outcrop of civilization in a sea of grass, have today become overwhelmed by a forest of towering edifices and mock palaces.

Before finding a place to spend the night, we made our way across the city towards the international border which lay in the plains on the other side. On our way, we admired the facade of blue, tin-roofed neoclassical follies made of imitation marble that lined the streets of Manzhouli. At one intersection, creepy bronze statues of babies – nude, and with muted smiles across their cherubic faces – pranced around the corner of a lamppost.

We exited on the north end of town and followed signs out to the border, but even in the outskirts the sights kept coming. We passed government buildings made from dark, reddish brick built to look like walled Russian Kremlins, domed roofs needling the sky. Farther along we passed an actual theme park made up entirely of giant Russian nesting dolls. The largest of these could be clearly seen from the road: a creepy, brightly colored Russian idol peering out nearly a hundred feet above our heads.

We finally arrived at the border and to signs welcoming us to the "Mutual International Trade and Tourist Plaza". This included several large parking lots, a toll booth welcoming us to Russia, and a viewing platform where you could look across the border (I was unable to confirm on whose side the grass was greener). The area itself was packed with tourists.

We approached the main plaza's parking lot and noticed a large group of motorcycles in a row by the entrance. I drove up and saw that the group was made up of at least a dozen Harley-Davidson bikes. The owners, who could be seen lounging around the lot or leaning on the bikes, all appeared to be Chinese and were dressed up, as if in costume, in their motorcycle leathers.

The bikers, who we soon learned were part of a club that had ridden from Hebei, looked as if they had emptied a couple Harley dealerships. Everyone was covered in some assortment of leather, American and Chinese flags, eagles, and of course plenty of skulls and flames. My dad is part of a couple of HOG (Harley Owners Group) chapters back home and if I blurred my vision a little bit, I maybe could have been looking at a group of my dad and his friends. Uncrinkle your nose though and rather than a greying collection of plumbers, dentists, and construction workers you realize these bikers are all Han Chinese, about 10–20 years younger, and rather than tattoo sleeves some literally were wearing sleeves with tattoos printed on them.

However quaint this group of Harley enthusiasts may have seemed initially, I found the scene quite remarkable, a snapshot of a society at or over the cusp of monumental change. Many of these bikers, a collection whose net worth likely measured in the millions of USD, had either had family members or had themselves been exiled to work on communes during the Cultural Revolution only a couple generations before. As present day China moved into the future with unprecedented speed and enthusiasm, its culture maybe wasn't keeping pace as many Chinese were becoming enamored with the romantic (small 'r') ideals of a foreign one.

From the abstract to the more practical, Harley-Davidson, and large displacement motorcycles more generally, have had a difficult time taking root in the country. China's luxury market, the category a Harley would fall into, has been growing faster than almost any other sector in the economy. Research in 2011 by McKinsey & Co. indicated that by 2015 China's market would account for 20% of global luxury good sales. Harley-Davidson has an obvious interest in carving itself out a piece of this pie. Unfortunately though, since opening their first dealership in China in 2006, sales have been uninspiring. By 2011 they had 11 dealerships in the country but the following year only managed to sell 268 motorcycles, barely half of what Harley sold in its home city of Milwaukee, Wisconsin alone.[16]

Despite all this, Harley's *brand* has appeal. This is particularly true of the *nouveau riche* who are attracted to the American-style "rebel" image the company actively cultivates. A big part of these initiatives has been to help establish local biker groups (HOG chapters) and official rallies around the country. The year-long 110th anniversary celebration of the company in 2012 saw a few such events, including a high-profile intercontinental rally in August where a group in China rode across the Tibetan Plateau while a simultaneous trip was coordinated in the U.S. from Seattle to Sturgis, South Dakota, which is home to one of the world's largest motorcycle gatherings.[17] In May 2013, Harley also hosted a rally in Zhejiang province near Shanghai where over 1,000 riders from all over the country were invited to gather and meet other enthusiasts. All this points toward Harley-Davidson playing the long game in China as it focuses on spreading brand awareness and laying the groundwork for future growth. The group at the tourist plaza and their enthusiasm for everything Harley seemed to indicate these efforts were having some impact.

After introducing ourselves to the bikers, we hung around for a little while. We traded stories about our trips, admired each others' bikes, and snapped photos to commemorate the meeting. One

---

[16]   There are two likely reasons for the slow adoption. The first is the high price tag. A Harley-Davidson motorcycle can be upwards of $30,000 in the U.S. In China, taxes and import tariffs can inflate this number by as much as 50% and in some cities just getting a license plate can cost $10,000 alone. The other reason is regulations. With almost every major city and all highways having rules that ban or restrict motorcycle use, it's hard to justify so much money on something you're not allowed to drive anywhere.

[17]   Sturgis is home to one of the world's largest annual motorcycle gatherings. Tucked away in the Black Hills of South Dakota, only an hour's drive from Mount Rushmore National Park, the town of 6,500 can get as many as a half a million riders over the course of the week for the event. The festivities feature unveilings of new bike models from companies like Harley-Davidson and Indian Motorcycle, custom build competitions, group rides around the area, and even beauty pageants.

conversation in particular stuck in my mind. The man, taller than me, was wearing a black bandana, an open leather vest, and a Harley-branded t-shirt that barely held back a substantial biker's gut. He asked where we'd ridden from and I started on my, by now familiar, recitation.

"We're going to try and ride through 33 provinces in China. Inner Mongolia is number six for us," I explained, well practiced by now not to say "*all* 33 of China's provinces" as I would when speaking English.

"You know that China has 35 provinces right?" The man replied.

I couldn't tell if he was joking and didn't know how to respond. Of course when you travel in a foreign country under any circumstance, it's best to stay apolitical. The topic of China's 34th province was a particularly sensitive one. "Hmmm, well I know about Taiwan..." I stated cautiously. "But which is the 35th?"

"Mongolia of course!" the man confidently and boisterously replied, referring to the fully autonomous country from which we were now only a day's drive away. "It's only a matter of time and everyone knows it!"

I chuckled in nervous agreement and hoped a subdued reaction would help guide the conversation onward. Inwardly though, I couldn't help thinking that Mongolians, and probably many ethnic Mongolians that lived in this actual province of China, would most likely take issue with the claim.

While we were so close to an international border I was hoping that I might be able to hop across and get my passport stamped. While Amy conveniently still had her work visa from her previous job, allowing her to stay in the country unfettered until January, I was on a tourist visa. This meant I would have to cross a border every 90 days.[18] My last entry was only a couple weeks ago, just a few days

---

[18]   This is meant as an inconvenience to discourage people from staying too long or illegally taking jobs from locals. Simply crossing a border, even to Hong Kong, for a day was enough to

before we left from Beijing, so it wasn't urgent. However, I thought that it would still be worth trying to restart the clock early rather than risk my visa running out in the middle of Tibet or somewhere similarly remote.

Unfortunately Russia was not particularly amenable to unannounced or unaccompanied visitors. While trying to negotiate with an unresponsive Chinese guard at the port of entry we met a couple of fellow motorcycle enthusiasts. Much more ragged than the high-powered Harley riders from the parking lot, the two men stood close to the entrance gate and took note of my predicament. Standing by their 250cc motorcycle they looked on as I futilely spoke *at* the unresponsive soldier. While they also couldn't speak English, the pair were helpful in that they could translate my Chinese into Chinese that the guard could (or would) understand. The result was ultimately the same though. The guard told us that there was no entry allowed, and especially not on a motorcycle.

The pair, like us, had been on the road traveling for a couple of weeks now. The first was older, looked to be in his 40s, wore glasses and was soft-spoken with a thick southern accent which made him difficult to understand.[19] The younger one, who introduced himself as Laolao (pronounced like the "Lao" in "Laos") was much more convivial. His loose, earth-toned clothing and longish hair bundled up in a head wrap gave him the look of a bohemian hipster. He communicated with a tremendous amount of energy and his persistent smile and positivity helped to take the edge off of the border rejection.

---

reset the 90 days but if you overstayed there was a heavy fine and you could be deported, and not allowed back for at least five years.

[19]   The southern accent in Mandarin tends put more emphasis on words with 's' and in fact pronounces characters spoken as *shi* or *shee* in the north (*shi* and *xi* in *pinyin*) as *si* and *see* which can make it particularly difficult for non-native speakers like myself and Amy to understand.

While we did end up having to part ways with Laolao and his travel companion we made sure to exchange contact information. They had been traveling separately from the South and ran into each other as they entered *Dongbei*. They both had plans to eventually turn west, aiming for Europe, and so decided to continue on together. The 250cc bike was the older man's, whose name we never got. Laolao was traveling on a motorized scooter and had been doing so all the way from Shanghai. They were in the process of trying to get visas to enter Russia and were still waiting for approval. If they got rejected, the backup plan was to try to cross somewhere else in Mongolia or Kazakhstan.

Like the Motorfans bikers back in Dandong, this pair of travelers were breaking the mold of the prototypical Chinese tourist, something Amy and I were encountering more and more as we got away from the big cities. Leaving behind the giant chartered busses and flag-waving tour guides of their contemporaries, there seemed to be a nascent generation of Chinese infected by wanderlust. This curiosity wasn't limited by either age or background either, as we met all types on the road. Meanwhile, there was no precedent for this in modern China, no familiar, local context to model these types of experiences off of. Their endeavors were taken up in an environment and culture that at times was hostile towards it.[20] It was fascinating to witness first hand and be privy to this unique snapshot of time. Amy and I would encounter many different manifestations of this development throughout our trip and in several cases formed lasting friendships with some of these remarkable people.

---

[20]   If you're familiar with the theory of "Tiger Moms" in China you'll have an idea of what I mean. So many Chinese that we met along our journey would lament to us how this kind of trip was not possible for a Chinese person. "The pressure on Chinese is too big" they would proclaim. "I'm envious of the freedom that you Westerners have. We could never do something like this." In these exchanges, I could just imagine their traditional mothers scolding them for not being married or having a house yet. Even Amy's mother gave us a decent amount of grief before finally giving her (still reluctant) blessing for the trip.

We ended up staying in touch with Laolao over the course of the next four months, exchanging trip highlights and photos periodically via WeChat (a Chinese smartphone messaging app similar to WhatsApp). Though of course we didn't know it at the time, this wouldn't be our last run-in with Laolao as our paths would cross two more times before our trip was over.

***

Manzhouli would be the northernmost point of The Great Ride of China. Next, the plan was to travel back south along the border with Mongolia proper. With no expressways or major cities for hundreds of miles, it was even more remote than the road we had come up on. Our trail would then eventually cut west towards the center of the province, passing within less than a day's ride of Beijing. From there we would descend from the plains and head back into the busy, industrial heart of the country.

The next morning as we prepared to leave Manzhouli, the rain we thought we had left behind when we entered the province made a reappearance. Unfortunately, mirroring our exit from Harbin, it didn't look like we could wait this one out. The whole sky was a blanket of faded grey, indicating an intention to stick around rather than a brief but torrential downpour. Like the last time, the weather was a portent of more trouble ahead.

Before heading back out into the hinterlands we wanted to make sure we left with a full tank of gas. To our dismay however the area was experiencing power shortages and was rationing electricity. This led to a frustrating 30 minutes in the rain jumping from gas station to gas station on the edges of town trying to find one with a working pump. The ordeal unfortunately did not put me in the best of moods for what was coming next.

We pulled up to a red light at a four-way intersection near the edge of town. Just beyond the crosswalks was the on-ramp for the road southwest towards Mongolia. Rather than hang back towards the end of the line of cars at the stoplight, I pulled into the bike lane and made my way to the front of the queue, coming to rest with my front tire just inside the crosswalk. Immediately after I stopped, I noticed a police officer bee-lining towards us from the street corner to our right. The cop stomped into the road, his eyes flaring wide, and pointed straight at us. Continuing to track us with his finger, he walked around the front of the bike to our left side, reached over, turned off the ignition, and took the keys with him.

The officer, trying his best to be as intimidating as possible, began to indicate with his hands that he wanted me to pull the bike over to the side of the road towards the corner where he had been stationed. To my knowledge, we hadn't done anything wrong. I was wet and frustrated from our search for gas and this unwarranted bullying annoyed me. So, in an attempt to reciprocate the inconvenience, I decided to make an exaggerated show of how heavy the bike was.

"Look," I told the cop sternly, pretending to ineffectually push the bike with as much force as I could muster, "It's too heavy with all of our luggage and you took my key. If you want me to bring the bike over there, you have to either give me back my keys or help me push."

The man appeared caught off guard by this and his face softened as he considered my offer. A moment later however, his eyebrows re-furrowed, he thrust the keys back at me and instructed me to pull over.

Parking the bike on the sidewalk next to his car, I demanded he tell me what we had done wrong. In rural China of all places, the act we were being reprimanded for and threatened with a ticket over was pulling into the crosswalk. After two weeks on the road, dealing with motorists going through red lights, opposite lanes with oncoming traffic being used for passing, and an overall life-threatening disregard for other vehicles, I was infuriated that we were being penalized for doing something that was ultimately done in the name of safety.

I tried to explain that stopping at intersections in the main car lane while on a motorcycle, particularly in the rain, runs the very real risk of being rear-ended (something that had actually happened to a friend of mine when a tailgating motorist failed to notice the brake light on the back of the bike). The officer's argument was that everyone else was stopping before the crosswalk and there had yet to be an accident. Only minutes after making this point, Amy (who had been quietly filming our exchange from the sidelines), walked up to me and pointed out that at least two cars had run a red light while we were having this conversation. I managed to actually catch one and quickly pointed it out to the officer, who seemed annoyed at having been caught in his lie. Our being pulled over must have been some act of profiling. Maybe he was looking for a bribe and two foreigners on an expensive bike seemed like an easy target.

The man's chest, which at the time of the confiscation of my keys had been fully puffed out, was starting to deflate now. His enthusiasm for giving me a ticket seemed to be waning but there was clearly some pressure to not let me off the hook. So, having reached an impasse, the cop decided it was time to bump the issue up a level.

We walked away from the car, leaving Amy to watch over the bike, and crossed the street. At the opposite corner was another car and as we approached several other policeman began to converge on the spot from their posts around the intersection. An older cop soon got out of the car and made his way over too. By his frown and the confidence with which he strode in our direction, he seemed to be the man in charge.

We met at the corner and the officer that had stopped us presented the cliff notes version of what had happened. The older man was not at all happy and didn't seem interested in my addenda. As I began to explain why I had pulled in front, he raised his voice and stopped me mid-sentence.

"The rules here in China are that you are not allowed to stop in the pedestrian crossing," he proclaimed, eyes wide and chest out. He seemed to be speaking with the unassailable authority of Moses after witnessing the Israelites worshipping a false idol before smashing the 10 commandments.

"Yes, but other drivers are even going completely through the red light," I replied.

"I don't care about everyone else. That is the rule and YOU have to follow the rule!"

"Everyone in China tells us that safety is number one." This was true, a common parting comment between drivers, particularly towards us on a motorcycle is, "*Anquan di yi*" which translates to "Safety is number one!"

"Are you saying that safety shouldn't be number one?" I asked trying to sound pleading and reasonable. "You're going to punish me for trying to stay safe?"

This really got the guy fired up. His eyes bulged out at this last comment and his face went red. "I don't care what your explanation is! This is not about punishment. This is not about what is the most reasonable. Your logic doesn't matter. This is about what the rules are! Do you understand what the rules are?"

I now saw my opening for getting out of the situation. At this point, the whole show had become about "saving face". I was starting to get the sense that I had become more trouble than they had bargained for. This was now about damage control and how to get rid of me without looking like they'd somehow lost. All I had to do was show some humility by admitting I was wrong, let them come out as the apparent authority figures, and then they could feel like they got something out of it.

"Yes," I replied, softening my voice and starting to lower my eyes. "I understand the rules."

"We have to know that you know the rules here." He said, the vein in his forehead beginning to recede but still quite red in the face. "If you admit that what you did was wrong and you tell us you won't cross the zebra lines again, then you can go."

There it was. It was like a parent's scolding of a child. Assert your power and force the offending party to admit their wrongdoing in order to assume their proper place in the pecking order. It was as good as I could have hoped for, and I tried my best to not let my relief show. They wanted to save face and I didn't want a ticket. So I bowed my head a little bit, admitted to my mistake, apologized, and promised I would follow the rules. I walked back across the street, barely holding back my glee, and told Amy that they were going to let us go. We put our helmets back on and pulled back onto the street. I parked my front wheel right behind the line and waited for the light to change green. As we waited, Amy and I watched on as a scooter cruised past in the bike lane to my right, straight through the intersection.

It continued to rain throughout most of the day as we made our way through the empty plains of eastern Hulunbeier. The area was so deserted that the weather added to a sense of serenity. The extra white noise from the droplets against my helmet and the monotonous anxiety of worrying about slick tarmac had a hypnotizing effect, lulling me into a deep focus. By late afternoon the storm had begun to pass and the sun started to come out for the last few hours of the day. I asked Amy if she'd like to look for a place to camp out for the night.

We stopped at a couple yurt camps that were set up off the highway to see if we could have dinner and set up our tent for the night. We found one that seemed pretty well built up. They were apparently set up for the tourist season and had several out-of-province cars parked in the entrance. The people that ran the camp were all ethnic Mongolians, dark skinned, high cheek-boned, stouter than the Han and with practiced standard Mandarin.[21] They told us that they didn't normally take overnight guests but with only two of us they didn't mind if we set up our tent in the open area in front of the line of yurts.

We had a wonderful meal for dinner; lots of fresh Mongolian dishes that our hosts were serving, which meant a lot of lamb and fried dough, and ample portions piled several inches above the table. The yurt we were seated in was ragged and sparsely furnished. There were no pretensions of being a place out of time – a museum piece to show how their people might have lived in the time of Genghis Khan (as we assumed the tourist yurts must have been). We guessed it might have been the staff's lodgings. It was basic, unassuming, and a bit messy. Lined around the circumference of the yurt were four beds, a TV, and a giant cooler that they kept coming in to grab stuff from, presumably ingredients for the meals they were preparing. In the center was the small table used to feed us.

They had a big group of Chinese tourists who were taking up the other dining yurts. From the sounds of it, they were running the staff ragged. One of the girls kept coming into our tent to catch a break. Sitting on one of the beds, hunched over in exhaustion, she took the opportunity to vent about the other guests to us.

"It's so tough having Chinese guests. You foreigners are much nicer," the server explained to us.

---

[21]   The Mandarin that the local ethnic Mongolians spoke was very easy to understand. Like us, they had predominantly learned how to speak *"pu tong hua"* (which translates to "common talk" but means Mandarin and is the most common Chinese dialect) in school and so they spoke with a very standardized accent. We would often find this was the case around China. Chinese ethnic minorities who had had to learn Mandarin as a second language in school spoke much more clearly than in the areas where people had their own regional dialects and accents. Without all the extra intonations and localized slang, it was much easier to carry on full conversations with people like the Mongolians, Tibetans, and Uyghurs than southern Cantonese speakers for example.

"Are they all drunk?" I asked.

"Yes," she said with an exasperated sigh. "Drunk, loud, messy. Han Chinese have very low *su zhi*."

In China, to say someone has low *su zhi* is a serious insult, and the woman was directing it at a group of people, the Han, that made up nearly 92% of the population of China. The word *"su zhi"* literally means "quality," so the best way to describe in English what it means to say someone has "low quality" is to say they are uncultured. In Chinese though, which also has a separate way to say "uncultured", commenting on someone's quality is to get more fundamentally at that person's character and who they are at their core. One might lack culture as a result of a poor upbringing or education, and thus may, under the right circumstances, acquire it later on. *Su zhi* on the other hand is not something that can be learned. It thus suggests a fundamental problem rather than simply happenstance.

That comment stuck with me throughout our trip. The dynamic between the Han Chinese and the other 55 ethnicities that made up the remaining 8% of the population was somewhat fraught. Living in China for three years, we had no shortage of negative encounters with loud, boisterous, and messy Chinese who had a complete disregard for other people and their surroundings. From this perspective it was easy to be sympathetic with our hosts. It wasn't hard to imagine what the Han guests in the neighboring yurt, on holiday and intoxicated from an afternoon of heavy drinking, were likely putting this local girl through as she waited on their tables. Of course, to hang this scarlet letter around the necks of an entire population is perhaps an unfair generalization. For every rude Chinese person there are a dozen polite, well-mannered, and generous ones. Meanwhile, in conversations with Han Chinese, it was not unusual for them to lay similarly disparaging comments on the people from other ethnic backgrounds, typically regarding their lack of class or culture. It's not something you typically associate with China, but given its ethnic and regional diversity, racial tensions are a tangible reality. It is also a reality with historical precedents.

As recently as the early 1900s, the Han were ruled by what many Chinese viewed as a foreign people. The Qing dynasty, which ruled China for over 250 years from 1644 to 1911, were ethnic Manchus. Originally from the North, they had their own language, culture, and history. After the fall of the Qing, the May Fourth Movement of 1919, which laid the groundwork for the eventual founding of the Communist Party, was a moment of intense Chinese nationalism. Born in part as an anti-foreign movement after centuries of rule by the Manchus, intellectuals, students, and political leaders came together to protest the post-WWI Treaty of Versailles, which saw many parts of China partitioned among foreign entities, including the Japanese.

Viewed from this lens, it's not hard to see where nationalism that fuels comments like the biker in Manzhouli calling Mongolia the 35th province of China come from. Chinese have a mixed relationship with their past particularly with how it relates to race. Museums claim the Mongol emperor Genghis Khan, one of the greatest conquerors in history, as a Chinese emperor, while the Manchus came to be seen as foreign invaders (as were the Mongols when they first took over). Furthermore, it was under Qing rule that China underwent its "100 years of humiliation" by Western and Japanese colonial powers. One can thus understand the sense of nationalist and, for some, racial pride that Chinese feel with a Han government that has brought the country back to a place of global prominence. With pride though can sometimes come a certain amount of bravado, something that might not sit well with the ethnic Mongolians serving you your dinner.

That night a massive rain storm made its way across our camp, hitting with its full force just as Amy and I were finishing dinner. Our yurt itself barely bordered on waterproof and we did our best to keep the water away from the beds and the electrical outlets powering the

TV and cooler. Watching from the small window in the four-foot-high doorway of the yurt we looked on as the picnic tables set up outside got picked up and thrown across the plot of land. Our tent meanwhile was blowing flat to the ground with each gust of wind. It seemed to be holding together for a time until eventually a stake popped loose and it collapsed completely. So much for camping out.

Amy and I ran out in the pouring rain to grab our stuff from the tent and laid it all out in the yurt, which our hosts had graciously offered to let us sleep the night in. As we set up I peered out one last time and watched as the storm claimed its final prize. In between flashes of lightning that lit up the pitch black of the plains, I noticed with dismay that our bike had also fallen over in the deluge. The ground beneath the kickstand had gotten so soft as it turned to mud that it could no longer support the weight of our bike. When the rain had stopped and I went to check on everything, I found the bike parallel to the ground, the stand sunk deep into the mud, but otherwise unharmed. The next morning the sun was back out, a cloudless sky that allowed us to dry out what had gotten wet the night before, and we helped the staff to clean up and recover from the storm.

The next few days through the plains, with the road skirting the Mongolian border, passed without much more incident. The monotony of the landscape carried with it a majestic beauty and its scale, disappearing into eternity like an ocean over the horizon, was mesmerizing. With no obstacles to obscure its path, the wind at times was formidable and we spent some hours leaning into its force simply in order to keep going straight. Any unexpected break in the gusts and we would have found ourselves in a ditch. The uncertainty made Amy uneasy and she maintained a tight grip around my waist as we battled our way across the plains.

Despite (or maybe as a result of) how remote the area was the roads stayed blissfully paved the whole time going back south. The only exception was a single diversion around a stretch of road that was under construction towards the center of the province. While we were thankful for the detour, the quality of the road was still more or less what we had come to expect of local National Highway management. The dirt track wound, unsigned, through fields, farmland, and villages. It was not built to handle the strain of thru-traffic that it was receiving, particularly after all the seasonal rains. In some stretches the road split off into two or three separate tracks where cars and trucks had improvised their way around unnavigable patches of pulverized mud. The landscape had been so drastically altered that twice we had to push the bike across river fords where only a week earlier a bridge wouldn't have even been considered.

The first flooded area was the most treacherous of the crossings. Lines of cars, trucks, and vans were waiting their turn on both banks which descended in slick ramps towards the water. While we unpacked some of our heavier gear and electronics in preparation to push the bike across, Amy and I watched others attempt the crossing. These passed with varying levels of success. We witnessed a sedan, one of the many urban-dwelling tourists ill-equipped for the all-terrain driving, have its engine flooded before it could make it to the other side, stalling in the middle of the river. Others opted to pay locals who had come equipped with a tractor to help them tow their vehicle across. There were plenty of other vans and cars that seemed far past their prime but still somehow barely managed to make it coughing up the opposite bank. We enlisted the help of local farmers eager to cash in on the chaos, paying two men ¥50 to push our bike across, while Amy and I walked with our bags over our heads to the other side.

Our final night in Inner Mongolia we decided we'd try once more to camp out, one last chance to enjoy the peace and quiet of the Steppe before heading back into central China. In the late afternoon we stopped through a small, one-road town to pick up some supplies for the night – noodles, vegetables, a couple beers for dinner, and some cookies and sausages for the next morning – before trying to find some open space to set up. The town where we bought our supplies, Hua De, looked relatively new and seemed to have been built for a nearby factory and power generation plant. With no thru-traffic, wide, empty roads, and sparse building clusters it felt like a ghost town. Strangest of all though was that for the second time in Inner Mongolia, as a result of electricity rationing Amy and I couldn't find any gas stations in operation. This was particularly striking in Hua De because we had just spent several hours driving through fully animated wind farms. I asked an attendant at one of the powerless stations about this and he explained that while the windmills were operational, the power being generated all had to go to Beijing. [22]

About an hour later, I pulled off down a promising looking side road. This small, dirt and gravel track eventually led us into some hilly grazing lands that seemed promising. We soon settled on a flat spot in a tree grove that sat at the bottom of a grassy knoll.

Amy and I set up camp that evening happy to enjoy a peaceful night out in the countryside and away from the maelstrom of the small cities and large towns of rural China. There were almost no people, no traffic, and everything felt much cleaner compared to the grime of city streets. Our only interaction was when a local family made their way over from a village of reddish clay huts and courtyards that could be seen just through the trees.

The family, a girl of about six or eight, her teenage brother, and their mother and grandmother, had come over to buy some vegetables

---

[22]   Given that we were only a couple of hundred miles away from the capital again at this point, the proximity made this conceivable and there is no doubt that a city of over 20 million people would be power hungry. In fact in 2008, as much as 70% of Beijing's electricity was being generated in the neighboring province of Inner Mongolia which itself had an annual wind generation capacity of 150 million kW. Despite this however, you would have thought that the bureaucrats in charge of the electricity would at least have been able to spare a couple windmills for the area where the power was actually being generated.

from a truck that had pulled up on the dirt road nearby. The kids were the first to take an interest in us and soon after the whole family was gathered round. While they were all ethnic Mongolians, the adults, and the grandmother specifically, spoke nearly incomprehensible Mandarin. The precocious young girl, who had plenty of questions of her own, was our primary conduit for communications. They seemed to be most interested in how (and why) we intended to sleep outside. How could we eat? Wouldn't it be cold? Where would we put our things? The mother even offered us a bed in their home several times. Knowing that this would likely displace some of them from a bed for a night, but that they would be too gracious to admit it, we politely declined assuring them that we would be ok. I was looking forward to a proper night in the tent anyhow.

Amy was the first to spot the ominous mountain of dark grey spawning just over the hill in the fading light of dusk. As the light grew dimmer, the wave-like cloud seemed only to grow, but I reassured Amy that with the tree cover we wouldn't have the same problem with the wind as we had in the yurt camp. So we packed up for the night and tucked into our sleeping bags. The rhythmic tapping of the rain was hypnotic, a metronomic pitter patter against the tent that increased steadily but seemed to keep within reason. I pushed the thoughts of past storms from my mind and slowly drifted off to sleep.

Nearly unconscious, I turned to change positions and found myself briefly tugged back into awareness. As I shifted on my inflated sleeping pad, almost as if dreaming it, I had the feeling that my feet were bobbing up and down beneath me, like they were pushing against the surface of a water bed. Partially awake again now, I reached over to grab my water bottle and was jerked back into full consciousness when I felt my fingers nearly fully submerged in water. I grabbed my flashlight and pointed it at where I had put my hand. To my surprise I found that there was a full current going right through our tent from up by my head and exiting again via the mesh by our

84

feet. It seemed that a stream had formed right where we had set up. As the rain picked up, the depth of the water had very quickly surpassed the height of the waterproof, bathtub base of the tent and now the current had fully overcome the two-inch high lip that had been keeping us dry.

Amy had been nervous about the rain the whole time and never actually managed to fall asleep at all. Now we both had our adrenaline pumping and were snapped into action. First we surveyed the gear in the tent, trying to put everything we could onto our mats and out of the water. Luckily, we kept most of our things in waterproof zip-locks anyway which helped to avoid any serious damage.

Next we had to hope that the whole valley wasn't flooded and find a way to move our tent to higher, drier ground. To my surprise, due to a mix of bad luck and poor judgement, it seemed we had managed to pick one of only two areas in the tree grove that had suffered from flooding. We hadn't even been at the lowest point but our camping spot (as well as the nearby footpath) had completely filled with water that was emptying off of the hill. Only 10 or 20 feet away was a flat spot that had managed to stay almost entirely dry under the tree cover. So, Amy and I proceeded to remove the tent stakes from the ground, drain the rainwater that was sitting in the bottom of the tent, and move it over to the new location.

It was a shame to have both attempts at camping on the Steppe marred by the cruel machinations of seasonal weather. Amy's confidence in particular was shaken. She had never done any proper camping at all before this trip, and would be suspicious of the weather for much of the rest of our time on the road. I'd camped out plenty of times in the rain while hiking back in the U.S., but a river flowing through my tent was a wholly new experience.

For better or worse we were now going to be putting both the challenges and beauty of this oasis of nature behind us. The plains soon began giving way to the manufacturing hubs of the lower province until we finally entered Shanxi and Shaanxi provinces. The roads dissolved into poorer conditions, accommodations and rest stops became grimier, and everything was increasingly tinged with the soot of industrialization.

Coal and factories were a big part of the economies in this area and that meant more trucks and pollution to contend with. There were, however, also things for us to look forward to. Amy and I were approaching the eastern terminus of the Silk Road, the millennia-old trade route that used to facilitate the exchange of goods with Europe via Central Asia. This meant that it was also one of the most historically significant regions in the country. After leaving the ancestral homes of the Mongols and the Manchus, we would now be entering the heart of Han civilization, with an ancient imperial tomb, a city that had been the center of Asian commerce, and the historical capital of some of the most powerful empires in history.

- Photos from Beijing to Inner Mongolia -

Scan the QR code or visit the link below to see pictures from Part 2 of
The Great Ride of China

http://book.thegreatrideofchina.com/galleries/part-1

Part II - Inner Mongolia to Kashgar

文化灿烂，历史悠久
"Dazzling culture, Age old history"
- *Old Chinese Saying*

~

峰回路转
北宋欧阳修 －《醉翁亭記》
"At each new peak, the road takes a new turn"
- *Ou Yangxiu (1007 - 1072 A.D.) from his poem "Old Toper's Pavilion"*

Chapter 5 – Smog, Silt, and City Walls

The landmass of Shanxi (山西) and Shaanxi (陕西) provinces is mostly occupied by the silty, erosion-prone Ordos Basin and the Loess Plateau (which makes up the area of the Ordos south of the Great Wall). This plateau was formed over centuries by windstorms of a yellow-colored silt called loess, from which the region takes its name. These provinces are bordered to the north by the Gobi Desert, which runs through southern Inner Mongolia and Gansu, and are divided by the Yellow River which forms their shared border. The mixture of silt and flood plains once made for extremely fertile ground, a primary reason for the area's centuries of prominence in the political and commercial development of China. Centuries of over-farming, deforestation, and over-population however have taken their toll. As you move west across the plateau, the dry, yellowish clay of the loess becomes increasingly exposed, leaving a barren and poor countryside.

At one time, Shanxi and Shaanxi provinces served as the gateway to Chinese civilization at the end of the Silk Road and were the political and cultural centers of the Qin, Han, Tang, and numerous other dynasties over the millennia. Today, both provinces are heavily industrialized. Their economies are focused around the manufacture of chemicals, heavy industrial equipment, and aircraft and auto parts. This is thanks in part to a plentiful supply of natural resources. Shanxi is the source of 25% of China's coal (which, in 2011, accounted for nearly 70% of all of China's energy consumption) with Shaanxi ranked close behind. Shanxi is also the top producer of eight different minerals, while the total reserves of Shaanxi are estimated to account for nearly one third of all minerals available in the country, estimated to be worth more than $7 trillion USD.

As China's economy has boomed so has its appetite for energy, particularly coal. As a result, these two coal-dependent provinces have been devastated by pollution and environmental degradation. While the central government has taken proactive steps in recent years to alleviate the problem, Shanxi ranked as the most polluted province in the country and was home to the three most polluted cities in China between 2003 and 2005. The situation has improved recently, and by 2013 only one city, Xi'an, remained in the top ten (it ranked ninth).

Scars still remain however, and the change was perceptible as Amy and I moved from the grass plains of the Mongolian Steppe and back into the central provinces. The roads that approached the border of our seventh province, Shanxi, became increasingly deteriorated. The trucks, which had only made mercifully rare appearances over the past week, now seemed to be reproducing at an exponential rate. More industrial activity had begat more industrial waste, fuel, and equipment which in turn begat the need for more freight to transport it all to and from the larger cities and coastal ports. I marveled at how much some of these trucks managed to fit into a single container. Cargo ranging from potatoes to pulverized cement was strapped in with complex networks of rope and webbing, precariously balanced over the lip like the foam on a glass of beer.[23]

Geological realities of desertification. Erosion-prone silt. An economy disproportionately reliant on dirty coal and heavy industry.

---

[23]   These trucks are responding naturally to economic incentives created by distorting rules. In an effort to protect consumers, recent caps on what freight companies can charge have squeezed companies and drivers whose only compensatory route is to try and fit as much in their containers as possible. As a result, many are overweight. Blocked from entering the expressways where inspections are more stringent, these deleteriously heavy trucks are thus relegated to the smaller national roads which are not built (nor maintained) to carry the load. While there is still a chance of running into a police checkpoint or weigh station, drivers factor the cost of any potential fines against the risk of getting caught. The conclusion is that it is more economical to overload their carriages. Over time this has resulted in the pockmarked network of secondary roadways throughout the country with which Amy and I had been growing so familiar.

Hordes of trucks. Thousands of swarming passenger vehicles. It was a dismal reception back to the "real" China as we returned from the periphery.

The first place we stayed overnight in was the third largest city in Shanxi. Datong, with a population of over 3.3 million, looked like most of the other faceless cities we had been through in other industrialized parts of the country. Amy and I both had trouble adjusting to the frenetic pace of the city and the self-absorbed attitude of its inhabitants. The chaos of the traffic felt claustrophobic compared to the openness of the plains. Luckily though, there was also something to look forward to here.

Now nicknamed "China's Capital of Coal", Datong has a history dating back over 1.5 millennia to when it was the capital city of the Northern Wei Dynasty from 398–494 AD. Nearly 500 years later in 1048 AD it was again made a capital by the Jin Dynasty, and then later became a major strategic center for the Ming between 1368 and 1644. This is the history Amy and I had come to the area to witness and the large stone city wall (or *cheng qiang*) that greeted us as we approached the city center served as our reminder. Stretching by the side of the road within a sea of cranes and half-built apartment blocks, the wall encircles an area of 1.27 square miles, stands 39 feet high and is 60 feet wide at the base. There are 62 watchtowers dispersed along the tops of the ramparts. These types of fortifications historically owed to the economic and strategic importance of a city and, in the particular case of Datong, its proximity to the northern plains.[24]

---

[24]   Unfortunately, as I would later find out, almost all of the Datong wall is new. Of the original Ming-era wall that was left after its construction in the 14th century, much was destroyed either during the Cultural Revolution in the process of hunting down the "Four Olds" (old thinking, old culture, old customs and old habits) or later in the 1990s to make room for new construction projects. A new initiative in 2009 by a controversial but charismatic mayor, Geng Yanbo, aimed to rejuvenate the city's past and rebuild some of its relics. Sadly not much care has been taken to adhere to original building techniques or style. Red bricks have been substituted for the rammed earth that was originally used for the core of the wall and

The city wall represented what Amy and I had been really excited to be in Shanxi and Shaanxi provinces for, despite the environment. There was nothing enjoyable about riding on the roads in Shanxi, but historically it was one of the most important areas in all of China. While the province has become relatively impoverished as the center of commerce moved away from the Silk Road and towards the coast, many of the cities still retain their historical legacy. Ancient buildings and UNESCO heritage sites litter the region and, once you get over the dreary grey of pollution, they can offer great opportunities for sightseeing. Nearby, for example, was the city of Jinci, famous for its architecture, art, and temples of the Song Dynasty. Pingyao meanwhile had been a major commercial center and home to many prominent merchant families for hundreds of years. Xi'an, in neighboring Shaanxi province, stands tallest of all as the former capital to more than a dozen dynasties spanning over two millennia. Even around Datong itself there are many famous cultural relics including the 2-million-square-foot Prince's Palace, the *Yungang* or "Cloud Ridge Cave" with over 50,000 Buddha and Bodhisattva grottoes carved into a cliff, and the 1,500-year-old Hanging Temple built into the side of a mountain 246 feet off the ground.

Unfortunately, Amy and I would not have time to visit every tourist site in the province. We settled on Pingyao to satisfy our culture itch and so that Amy could take in the local architectural styles. Modern Pingyao is a relatively small city. Although today it has only around half a million people, it was once home to some of the most famous and powerful merchants on the continent, earning the reputation as the Venice of China. With a history that spans over two and a half millennia, Pingyao first became an important commercial

watchtowers have been altered to improve on their aesthetics. This is part of an overall trend in modern China. As incomes and local budgets have increased there has been a return to an interest in the past. Unfortunately in many cases this is accompanied by a lazy disregard for a deeper respect of it.

center during the Song Dynasty in the 10th century AD with merchants known as *Jinshang* (which means simply "Merchants of Shanxi"). Similar to the House Medici of Venice, the influence of these merchant families grew during the Ming Dynasty until by the mid-to-late Qing (around the 19th century), Pingyao housed more than half of the entire country's financial institutions. The *Jinshang* were most famous for the development of a system of banking called *piao hao*. *Piao hao*, which translates to "ticket number", once served much the same purpose as modern banking services today. They were used to manage remittances, register deposits, issue loans, and track credits. One of the largest of the *piao hao* institutions, *Ri Sheng Chang*, controlled much of the silver trade and, in 1823, was the first in the country to issue checks.

It took a couple days of relatively tough riding through Shanxi to get to the outskirts of Pingyao. We got caught in several areas of very dense truck traffic on the national roads running south through the province. The two-lane roads became clogged with trucks traveling in packs, often of ten or more. Our progress was eased of course by the fact that we were on a motorcycle and I started to make a game of finding breaks in the oncoming traffic to pass the slow-moving behemoths.

Most traffic jams were usually the result of congestion – vehicles trapped in line along narrow, winding roads with no opportunity to pass. It was not long though before we were reminded of how fickle the situation on Chinese roads can be. After one stretch of ten minutes moving in and out from another bumper-to-bumper line of dust-covered trucks, we seemed to have reached the front of the line. Coming around the bend, ready to accelerate past the last of the traffic, I was abruptly brought to a near stop. At the foot of a wooded hill on the narrow two-lane turn, we found two trucks that had run into each other head on. Both cabs were completely wrecked and the force of the collision had propelled the front of the oncoming truck into a ditch on the opposite side. Its trailer meanwhile had swung around and obstructed almost the entirety of both lanes. There were no police to manage the chaos. Cars from both directions attempted to push through every chance they could, but I managed to find a gap and squeeze ahead.

Thoughts of our vulnerability swam through my head as we put the wreckage site behind us. I thought back to all the close calls of cars and trucks sweeping wide around turns and into our lane. By now it all had just blended together into an amalgamation of normal life on the road. I did everything I could to stay safe, following best practices like honking around blind turns and flashing my lights at intersections. I would have to accept though that some factors were just out of my control. The sobering sight of the demolished trucks was my reminder. If we had been nearby at the time of impact, it was unlikely that any level of skill or preparedness would have spared us. *An quan di yi.* Safety first.

One of the nice things about Pingyao, like Datong, is that there are a lot of places to see outside of the city proper. This allowed Amy and I to use downtown as a base of operations while we diversified away from just the Old City. Sitting in the suburbs of Pingyao, the Qiao Family Compound is a huge late Qing-era mansion of a once powerful Jinshang family. Superficially, preservation of the site has been well done. There was a notable effort to preserve stylistic integrity. The architecture is what you would expect of late imperial Chinese design. Triangular roofs end in ornate upturned eaves, open-air stone walkways connect a maze of one to two-story buildings, and detailed stone carvings of mythical animals litter the walls and doorways. The Qiao's old possessions are also well preserved, arranged into museum-like exhibits. Ostentatious yet still tasteful wooden furniture and European colonial-style appliances provide a glimpse into the life and habits of a turn-of-the-century Chinese merchant family.

Unfortunately, after featuring in several movies in recent decades, the site has become overrun by tourists. The most well-known of these was "Raise the Red Lanterns", a film made in 1991 and set in the 1920s during China's "Warlord Era" after the fall of the Qing. The added attention has brought hordes of domestic tourists swarming to the site. This in turn has led to a large commercial build up. After we arrived, it took a quarter of an hour for Amy and I to get from our parked bike to the compound entrance. We were forced to walk past dozens of souvenir stalls and hordes of visitors lackadaisically observing the displays. Once inside we were immediately engaged in a perpetual battle against the unrelenting current of flag-led tour groups that had inundated the premises. Remarkably, this was in the middle of the week.

There is what can only be described as a herd mentality when it comes to tourism in China. Most travelers tend to congregate around the places where the vast majority of other tourists visit. There is little appetite to diversify or explore. The Chinese also have a propensity for organized tours. When compared to Americans, twice as many Chinese tourists prefer to travel in groups of five or more. In a country that had nearly three billion domestic tourists in 2013,[25] that can make for some severely overcrowded tourist sights. Conversely, this also means that – if you can find them – less popular attractions tend to be nearly abandoned.

The two of us were fortunate enough to discover, almost by accident, a couple of such sights during our exploration of Pingyao. Counter-intuitively these felt more authentic than the more popular and better restored sites. This is likely because of, rather than despite, the neglect of local officials. The first site we visited felt somehow more genuine in its neglect. It was a temple complex on the way to the

---

[25]   The number is more than the actual population because it counts total number of trips taken by domestic tourists.

Qiao home. We never found the name of the compound itself. It didn't have the gaudy finish that many Chinese restorations seem to adopt. The paint was chipped on many of the furnishings and weeds grew on some buildings. The only person we met on-site was the old sleepy-eyed guard who sold us our $1.50 entrance tickets.

The second was a more popular destination. The Shuanglin ("Twin Trees") Temple sits to the southwest of the city and, because it is more well-known, had been more diligently restored and maintained. This made it a nice home to the more than 2,000 Ming and Qing-era painted sculptures exhibited there. The road from the city to Shuanglin however was under construction. While we managed to pay a local cabbie to take us through winding back alleys to get there, it seemed that most tourists didn't want to bother making the trip.

The main attraction in Pingyao is the Old City, or *gu cheng*, which was designated a UNESCO heritage site in 1997. The surrounding city wall, built in the year 1370 AD, runs four miles around the Old Town at an average height of 40 feet. It has four structured towers at the corners, six fortified gates, 72 watchtowers, and 3,000 battlements. It is said to be one of the best-preserved city walls in the country. Left almost entirely in its original state, the wall has only been rebuilt once after a southern section fell in 2004. The top is also open to those who want to walk up and get a view of the old streets from above.

The modern part of the city has grown naturally around the ancient fortified borders of the Old Town. Here we were able to find a hotel and place to park for the night. The streets were busy with the familiar urban entropy and thick yellowish haze in the air. Amy and I spent the evening walking around the Old Town within the wall. The narrow roadways retained their original Ming and Qing-era grid layout. Walking among the traditional one-story buildings and bustling marketplaces felt like being on the set of an old Kung Fu movie. We found a small courtyard restaurant against this backdrop to stop for dinner. The small dining room, with opened floor-to-ceiling windows and a courtyard hostel in the rear, looked out to the main street. Over a dinner of sauteed egg and tomatoes, tofu, and rice, Amy and I watched the energy of city life rush past with the consistency of frothing rapids, much as it must have over a thousand years before.

The only things disturbing the authenticity of our surroundings were conspicuous scraps of modernity that had snuck through. Hardest to ignore were the blue, six-person golf-carts that bussed tour groups between sights. Honking obnoxiously, they cartoonishly barreled along the old cobbled streets as the sun set behind the wall.

***

In the year 2000, China had over four million cars on the road. By the end of the decade, that number had grown by over 20 times, to 80 million.[26] China has since surpassed the United States as the world's biggest market for new cars, with an average of 50,000 bought each day by 2012. That's the equivalent of putting the population of Boston into a new car every two weeks. Over the course of a single decade, a generation of new drivers twice the size of California first put foot to pedal, and, as of early 2015, there are more people registered to drive in China than there are alive in the United States.

All this comes at a cost. In the West, new drivers are usually taught the rules of the road by their parents. These mentors were in turn taught by those more experienced than them still decades earlier. Driving is a practice, lessons learned and mistakes made all of which are passed on to the next generation. It is the result of over a century of cumulative experience grown in parallel with the evolution in power and versatility of roads and cars.

---

[26]   By 2015, the total number of drivers in China surpassed the number of the entire U.S. population. In late 2014, there were 300 million licensed motor-vehicle operators in the country. There are 319 million Americans, 212 million of which can legally drive.

In China, we are only now starting to see the effects of a generation that went from riding bicycles to driving cars in a matter of years. These are communities who learned road etiquette on a device with barely a two-foot width and a top speed of 15mph and are now passing on their learned habits to those driving in a vehicle that can go 0 to 60 in ten seconds and hit with an impact of 50 tons. The result has been an experiment conducted on a massive scale and with very real consequences. In 2010, there were over 450,000 car accidents in China. The World Health Organization estimates that as many as 92% of these were caused by poor or inadequate driving skills, calculating as many as 750 traffic-related fatalities per day.

Our last rest day had been nearly two weeks and several rainstorms ago. Since Harbin, all our sightseeing was organized around our riding schedule. We had to either wake up early or arrive at a place early if we wanted to see anything. Amy and I were both starting to feel the road-weariness settling in. It was about four hundred miles to get from Pingyao to Xi'an, which was our next major landmark. There, at the capital of Shaanxi province once known as Chang'an or the city of "Everlasting Peace", we planned to finally give ourselves a couple days off.

The distance would end up taking us two days to cover, which was in line with the general pace we were trying to keep. Daytime temperatures however had been rising ever since Manzhouli, matching with our decreasing latitude. The dryness of the loess was also becoming overwhelming, relentless as it covered everything with its yellowish silt. The dust from endless construction zones added to the general miasma.

On our first day out of Pingyao we ran into what would be the longest traffic jam of our whole trip. It was interminable, chaotic, and inane even by Chinese standards. With the four-lane road we had been traveling on reduced to two, it took over an hour and a half to cover 20 miles even on a motorcycle. Many of the vehicles we passed had likely been there all day. An unending conga line of trucks ran into the distance. Twice we inched towards obstructions, first a coal factory spur road and then a high-speed rail construction site, hoping the pressure would ease up after passing. Both times we were disappointed as the line of trucks persisted into the distance.

On the expressways, construction is more or less done according to international norms, with clearly marked detours and allowances made for thru-traffic. In contrast, on the national highways and provincial roads, everything seems improvised. Sometimes, as it was on our way into Shaanxi, the construction can go on for dozens of miles. Often there is either no diversion or it's not marked.[27] This leaves drivers on their own to blaze a path through the wreckage of a former road.

At this point, a Darwinian mentality takes hold. It becomes survival of the fittest, an "every man, woman, and child for themselves" approach towards road etiquette. No thought is paid to the efficient flow of traffic. If a car stuck behind a line of trucks catches a break in the oncoming traffic, he'll go for it. See a sidewalk that looks wide enough for your wheelbase? Pedestrians better watch out. Cement block barrier has a gap wide enough for your vehicle? Better hope there isn't a bridge out farther down that road. There is a manic struggle of giant trucks, farming tractors, and passenger cars all endeavoring to get to "the front of the line". Like bacteria in a petri dish, movement is slow and fluid, following the path of least

---

[27] Sometimes a gap in the barriers separating the road work from the traffic left room for us to squeeze through. Remarkably, these stretches of smooth, untravelled pavement could go on for several miles, remaining blocked off from the throng that sat just yards away, puffing out a cloud of spent fuel in its desperation to move. In one such construction zone, Amy and I found ourselves gliding along glittering, freshly laid asphalt. This led us unwittingly under the shadow of a steamroller creaking into action. The behemoth lurched forward in our direction, and between that and Amy's frantic slaps on my back, I had enough motivation to maneuver a three-point turn and join back in line with the unmoving trucks on the other side.

resistance. At no point is any thought given to the fact that if each person were to just wait in line, they could all get through quicker.

The change back to a normal traffic flow was sudden. There was no dramatic accident, no police checkpoint, not even an end to the construction. It just went from traffic jam to clear, two-lane road with the right lanes still blocked off. We had been avoiding the stoppages from this side and I barely even noticed the change as we passed.

When I realized that the road was clear again, I stopped and craned my neck to see if there was any sign of what the cause of it all was. I peered back at the knot of cars and trucks but couldn't see anything out of the ordinary. Curious, I turned the bike around to get a closer look. It still didn't look like there was anything serious enough to have shut down an entire roadway. From the direction we had originally come from was a line of trucks. On their left were a couple of overeager cars trying to pass in the neighboring lane. And, in the same lane, was a trickle of oncoming traffic unknowingly about to enter the gauntlet.

Near the almost stationary swirl of vehicles, a man leaned against the cement barrier. Shirt rolled up over his large, symmetrical belly, he stood passively observing the slow-motion drama, no more extraordinary than as if watching his afternoon soaps.

I pulled the bike up beside him and, through my helmet, asked, "Any reason for all of this traffic?"

He looked away from the road and blinked expressionlessly in my direction.

"It goes on for miles. An accident or something maybe?" I persisted.

With the same blank look, he stared back and just gave a short shrug as if to say, "I don't know. Why does it matter?" Then, he turned back and continued to watch the cars as the plodding struggle to untangle continued.

***

The next day Amy and I made it into Xi'an. Exhausted and frustrated from all the construction, dust, and traffic, we decided to sneak onto the expressway so we could make good time into the city. The site of the Terracotta Army was on the outskirts of Xi'an and on our route in. Amy and I figured that if we got in early enough we could tour the famous Qin Emperor burial site before actually finding a place to stay for the night.

The Xi'an Terracotta Army parking lot was like a giant holiday park. Huge buses were squeezed in side by side by the dozen like packs of AA batteries, to say nothing of the small army of cars. Before you even got to the actual ticket booth there was an onslaught of people and businesses trying to get a piece of all the tourists. McDonald's and KFC were both represented and had huge lines out the door. Chinese chains like "Mr. Lee's" and "Real Kung Fu" were also there to get in on the action. Any other available space was taken up by tourist shops. Everything from high-end porcelain and jewelry down to kitsch replica Terracotta soldiers was on sale. Maps, books, tour guides and plastic Chinese weapons were all on display. Here, at this two-thousand-year-old imperial burial site, was full-blown, unadulterated capitalism at work.

Before going to see the statues, we dropped our stuff off in a locker and went to look for a place to eat. We kept to the periphery of most of the activity, opting to avoid the chains and curious to see if we could find something more authentically local.

Scanning the buildings as we walked by, my eye caught a large, almost floor-to-ceiling, red and yellow sign on the side of a restaurant. Taking up most of the space on the sign was the most complicated Chinese character I had ever seen. With a general interest in the Chinese alphabet, I found myself coaxed towards the restaurant. Two men sat at a picnic table out front next to the sign, each with a bowl of noodles in front of them. One was a little shy and didn't say much, but the other was excited to talk to a foreigner who could speak Chinese and was interested in the character.

The character, which is pronounced "biang" or "byang", is completely unique even in Chinese. There are no other characters which share the same pronunciation and it didn't even turn up any results in my Chinese-English dictionary. With a total of 58 strokes (i.e. the number of pen strokes where one stroke refers to each time the pen/brush is lifted) it is one of the most complex characters in the Chinese alphabet.

The Chinese system of writing is built around radicals, which is essentially an alphabet of components that make up the character. Much in the way we use letters to put together words, most Chinese characters can be broken down into their component radicals. These in turn can give an indication as to the character's sound and meaning. Most typical characters are made up of only two or three radicals. The character "biang" however is made up of 11 different radicals, which themselves are composed of several strokes each. Some of these radicals include: "heart", "walk", "grow", "knife", and "moon". Even for Chinese, *biang* is famous for its complexity and so mnemonics exist to help remember its construction. For these, the radicals are used to construct a story. The sign hanging on the restaurant included one of these and it went like this:

A point rises up to heaven
and the yellow river has two bends.
The character "eight" opens its mouth,
and the character "speak" walks in.
A twist to the left, a twist to the right.
You grow, I grow,
and in the middle we add a horse king.
A heart is the base and a moon stands on the side.

A knife hangs on the right,
and we ride a carriage to tour the streets of Xianyang.

It all sounded rather poetic and I assumed it must have some grand, cultural significance, particularly given that we were in an area as old and historic as Xi'an. So, I asked the shirtless man eating his noodles in front of the sign about the character and what it meant. As it turns out, the meaning had nothing at all to do with moons or knives or hearts or heaven. It wasn't associated with a legend, nor did it refer to some old dynasty or forgotten religious text. Rather, *biang* was the name of a local dish. Specifically, it referred to a bowl of noodles which had been cut and prepared in a particular fashion. "*Biang Biang* Noodles" were a local, Shaanxi specialty, and fortuitously were served at this particular establishment. So of course Amy and I would have to have a try.

Ultimately and unsurprisingly, there was little unique to the dish. Served in a bowl, it consisted of normal wheat noodles, meat broth, and some vegetables. The main differentiator with other Chinese noodle dishes was the cut, which was wide, very long, and of inconsistent thickness.[28] Overall it was a nice meal, a fun story, and our shirtless tutor at the front of the restaurant got a real kick out of the two foreigners taking part in one of the local specialties of his home province. With our bellies now full, it was off to see the main attraction.

---

[28] There are over a dozen different types of noodle that can be found across China. These vary by ingredient (wheat, rice, egg, or even mung bean starch), cut (chopped, peeled, pulled, kneaded), and preparation (mixed, stir-fried, cold, boiled, braised). Different areas of the country have their own specialized noodle type. For example, the north predominantly eats wheat noodles whereas rice is used in the south (historically this is because of the types of crops available). Preparation style can also vary by region. Shanxi province is known for their *Dao Xiao Mian*, or "Knife Peeled Noodles", Shaanxi has their *Biang Biang* Noodles, and nearby Lanzhou in Gansu province has *La Mian* or "Pulled Noodles".

The figures that comprise the Terracotta Army date back to around the Third Century BC. There have been a total of 8,000 soldiers, 130 chariots with 520 horses, and 150 cavalry horses excavated so far with many more believed to still be buried.[29] The statues were built as part of emperor Qin Shi Huang's tomb. Known as the "First Emperor of China", Qin is credited with uniting the country in 221 BC after the 250-year-long "Warring States Period". Establishing his capital city in Chang'an (present day Xi'an), he was also largely responsible for reforming and consolidating the writing system. The Terracotta Army was built to protect and guide Qin, nicknamed the "Dragon Emperor", into the afterlife, interred in his mausoleum along with over 40 thousand real bronze weapons. A defining and quite remarkable feature of the statues is that they weren't built using a set mold. As if to represent real soldiers, each statue was individually carved and had their own unique facial features, hair style, and even dress.

While Amy and I had learned at this point to be skeptical of any official tourist sights and their tendency toward price-gouging and over-commercialization, the Terracotta Army exhibit felt well done. The ticket price was reasonable, about $20, and the crowds were controlled. After entering the park, several walking paths meandered through well-maintained gardens towards the excavation sites, referred to as "pits". Each pit was numbered and cordoned off into separate buildings. All this compartmentalization helped to thin traffic once reaching the observation decks. This meant actually being able to get some good views of the pits and the Terracotta soldiers inside.

The buildings that enclosed the pits were also tastefully done. White and modern, they felt appropriate for a museum and reminded me of some of the newer areas of the Natural History Museum in New

---

[29]   In fact, some have been left buried on purpose. Due to concerns that available techniques would be unable to adequately preserve the paint, these have remained un-excavated until the technology is improved.

105

York City. My only complaint was that it felt as if they had been built to maximize heat retention. The glass along the walls and on the ceiling acted like a greenhouse. Even in our cooler summer clothes, Amy and I both felt smothered by the heat and were sweating buckets.

There is speculation that the figurines on display are not the actual statues recovered from excavation but are in fact replicas. Nonetheless, the site itself is quite impressive even if it is just a representation of what was originally buried in that space over two millennia ago. And other than the overtly branded Samsung televisions placed throughout the buildings and the occasional gift shop selling information books and photos of your face on a statue, the space was notably devoid of the gaudiness that had marked the entrance.

After a couple hours touring the complex it was time for Amy and I to head back to the lockers, put our gear back on, and finish the day. The Terracotta Army sits on the outskirts of the city leaving us with about 50 miles to go to downtown Xi'an. The areas around major cities always made for nervous driving. Frequent stoplights, heavier traffic, and higher density populations make for a stress-filled environment. Amy and I were on even higher alert now since motorcycles weren't technically allowed within the city limits. Locals on their small 150cc Suzuki and Lifan motorcycles however appeared to move unperturbed among the traffic, so we plunged in toward the pillars of faceless high-rises erected before us.

Focused as I was on the pressures of the moment, the significance of the city stayed camouflaged from my mind against the backdrop of modernity. Lost in the swirl of traffic, the trance was broken by a sudden edifice that cut through the busy four-lane city street in front of us. The ancient wall of Xi'an, former city of "Everlasting Peace" and capital to some of the greatest dynasties in the world, rose up before us, an impenetrable fortification against all oncomers. The grey anachronism of stone and cement stood neck-crinklingly high above and exuded a sense of unassailable thickness. Proudly standing before us, the wall seemed eager to tell its story, to recite legends from centuries of passing armies, political envoys, and Silk Road traders. But progress doesn't stop for history. The road dove forward and the kinetic energy of the traffic continued on in haste. With the pressure of oncoming cars behind us, we advanced without pause towards a roundabout at the base of the nearest guard tower before riding the current into the bustle of 8.5 million people.

Chapter 6 – Sheep Guts and a Funeral

Xi'an marked nearly our first full month on the road. It was the longest time I'd ever traveled in China. For Amy it was the longest she'd traveled by motorcycle, period. It felt like a psychological turning point for both of us, as we grew more accustomed to our new way of life. For the past 24 days, we had hardly spent more than a couple hours in any single place. Only once did we sleep in the same bed two nights in a row. Sedentary life, its habits, customs, and predictability, were drifting into memory, replaced by the mutability of the road.

We took two days off in Xi'an. During this time, Amy and I delegated between ourselves everything we needed to catch up on. By now the process was becoming automatic. I handled emails and Chinese forum posts for CFMoto while Amy was responsible for our photos and videos. Amy also took charge of giving our gear and clothes a desperately needed scrub down in the hotel bathroom. Not trusted with such a delicate matter as laundry, I took the bike to the local CFMoto shop.

With 4,000 miles down, our motorcycle was due for a much needed maintenance check. Besides new brake pads (grit from innumerable construction sites having ground down the old ones) and an oil change, we would also finally be getting a new display panel with a working gas gauge. The shop wasn't far from where we were staying but was still difficult to find. After reconciling the address Fang Shujian had given me and the directions from the GPS, I found an unassuming line of storefronts in a quiet neighborhood of tree-lined streets. The outward-facing windows were plastered with bike brands and motorsport decals, and a phalanx of scooters stood guard out front. I couldn't find any CFMoto signs, so I asked one of the men standing outside for directions. Shirt rolled up to his chest exposing a prominent gut, he pointed me through what I had previously thought was one of several driveways for inventory drop-offs.

The road in was narrow, the width of a single car. Expecting to enter the backroom of a motorcycle shop, I was surprised when it opened into a large indoor space, the back of which disappeared into the hum of disorganized activity that droned in the background. Two stories above, an arched patchwork ceiling of semi-transparent PVC enveloped the space in yellow-tinged sunlight. I inched down this strange corridor on my bike, walled in by dozens of motorcycle and scooter shops. Each was the size of a small convenience store, often draped with large, red, slogan-clad banners. Samples sat on display in front and promotions for obscure motorcycle brands hung on the glass doorways. With each driveway out on the street opening into its own identical column, it struck me to think that there were several more rows of this, adding up to as much as a hundred stores in total.

This procession went deep into the belly of a city block. At the end I found another maze of shops. Here, the roads merged and narrowed and several additional levels of stores became visible overhead, stairwells and grated walkways weaving between them.

I finally found the CFMoto shop manager, waving to me from a catwalk above. As I waited for him to come down, I wondered at the economics of such an operation. None of the shop owners seemed to have any sort of competitive advantage over their neighbors. There was zero brand loyalty and with nothing left to compete on, that could only mean a natural race to the bottom on pricing. It was a modern bazaar in more than just appearances, with the steel and plastic goods shifting around the hive of stalls like livestock; a blur of undifferentiated commerce competing futilely for the attention of passersby.

The rest of the two days in Xi'an, Amy and I spent running about the areas near our hotel, exchanging our time between running errands and sightseeing. Within walking distance from us were the old city wall (similar in construction to the Pingyao wall) and the ornate Drum and Bell towers. The towers were large, two to three-story constructions of a type that can be found in cities throughout China. While they were originally used for timekeeping (the bell was rung at dawn and the drum struck at dusk), their parallel purpose was to warn of invading armies.

The Xi'an towers were built in 1384 by the Ming Emperor Zhu Yuanzhang. Today they are connected by a large, open causeway, which, together with the towers, marks the central axis of the city – a hub connecting the four primary roads within the wall: north, south, east, and west.[30] While the scale of the open space at the center of this former capital conjured images of an imperial parade ground, today it is occupied by four lanes of uninterrupted traffic, running in a current between the roundabouts that wrap around the base of each of the ancient relics.

Being on the move every day, change becomes the constant. Spend too long in one place, and you can quickly start to feel restless. When we'd arrived in Xi'an after several days of brutal heat and punishing roads, Amy and I had both felt pretty worn down and taking an extra day or two off had seemed prudent. By the second day, however, I was already starting to feel re-energized and hungry for something different.

---

[30] As it turns out, the Bell Tower in Xi'an is no longer in it's original location. As the city grew in the centuries following it's construction, so did it's geographical center. As a result, in 1582 AD, the Bell Tower was moved from the place where it stood through six dynasties by 3,280 feet or around 1km to the east and the new center of Xi'an. Amazingly, with the exception of its base, all the pieces of the tower are from the original construction built in 1384.

I got the impression that Amy didn't quite have the same urge to get back on the road as I did. Our goal in Xi'an had been to rest, but unfortunately our time seemed to have been perpetually occupied by laundry, repairs, shopping for supplies, mailing old gear back to Beijing, paying the deposit for our Tibet guide (who we would be meeting in less than a month's time, halfway across the country), and all our digital commitments.

For me, being on the motorcycle was meditative. On the road, the challenges we met with were straightforward, each decision black and white. This clarity made it more of a mental respite for me, and with my body recovered, I was ready to be on the move again. Amy as a passenger though had less control over our choices on the road and valued rest differently. Our time in Xi'an had been by no means restful and I don't think Amy quite felt like she'd gotten the same return on investment. This would be a struggle throughout our trip; trying to strike a balance between the need to keep in motion and our desire to make the most of our time. Xi'an was early days though. Time marched on, a Guinness World Record prodded, and Western China was beckoning.

The bike looked great when I picked it up from the "motorcycle bazaar". They'd given it a good wash and its temperament was much improved after an oil change and new front brakes. Both sets had been ground down to almost nothing in the days since we'd left Inner Mongolia, but unfortunately the shop here only had front pads on hand. We had spares with us but wanted to keep those available as we moved into more remote areas. Luckily, our next province, Ningxia, had a CFMoto shop in its capital city only a couple days away. This was farther north than we had originally planned to go but the detour wouldn't add too much extra time. I gave Fang Shujian a call and organized for the parts we needed to be sent ahead.

111

Leaving a city is always a grueling ordeal. It took us over an hour to get past the stoplights and congestion and cross the city limits. After an hour, city streets finally transitioned to a National Highway, the G312, and we hit a more even pace. By midday, we had put some pavement between us and Xi'an. At the border with eastern Gansu we turned off onto a smaller, more provincial road. Here the thru-traffic peeled away and gnarled pavement transformed, as if painted, into shiny tarmac.

We moved deeper into the rural countryside. The loess plateau exposed itself and a grid of lush ridgelines rose up above us. The road we were on began to systematically switchback its way up and down the mesas. Each nadir contained a small hamlet, a couple buildings tucked between the landscape's narrow folds. The rises opened out onto expansive plateaus of farmland, dappled with bunker-like cement huts and convenience stores. Occasionally, we spotted more traditional structures. Amy pointed out the roof of one of these, noting the presence of ceramic pigeons perched on their tiled eaves. We never found out what significance these held.

The twisties that took us across this countryside were a motorcyclist's dream. Sweeping 180-degree turns, well-paved roads, all amongst a tranquil and unique landscape. My anxieties were swept away along with any regrets either of us had had about leaving the city's comforts behind.

For our lodging that night, Amy and I decided to take advantage of the favorable weather and exceptional vistas. Climbing up a plateau, we scouted out for a flat space amongst the switchbacks. While not quite out in the bush, our sanctuary for the night, a grassy outcrop tucked in the elbow of a twist in the road, provided an adequate outpost. With the occasional hum of passing traffic, we set up our tent as the sun began to drop behind the hills. The sky looked clear and the setting sun covered the lightly vegetated ridgelines and valley below in an orange glow. It felt like we might finally get a dry night's sleep outdoors.

***

One distinguishing feature of the Ordos Basin of Central China is the honeycomb of arched doorways that are stamped into the yellow faces of its terrain. The silty loess is remarkably malleable, which makes it amenable to carving out while still able to retain its structural integrity. The first *yaodong* or "cave dwellings" were built into the hillsides here thousands of years ago. Remarkably, they still remain in wide use today. Over 30 million people use them as their primary residences across Shanxi, Shaanxi, Gansu, and parts of Inner Mongolia and Ningxia provinces.

These structures range in quality. Some caves are crudely dug into the cliff-sides, with rough edges, cramped space, and primitive doors. Others are more luxurious. These can have courtyards, steel entrance gates, and proper doors and windows built into high, ten-foot-tall archways. Cave dwellings have also recently found a place within Chinese political lore. President Xi Jinping is famous for having spent seven years in one during the Cultural Revolution when his father fell out of favor with the Communist Party in 1962.[31] While it may seem primitive to be living in a cave in the 21st century, *yaodong* are very practical even in a modern context. Economical to build and maintain, these homes are also incredibly energy-efficient. Despite brutal heat in the summer and freezing temperatures in the winter,

---

[31] This narrative has been carefully cultivated by Xi and the Chinese government. Between 1938 and 1948 the Communist Party headquarters were in Yan'an, Shaanxi and many party members located there took residence in cave dwellings, including Mao Zedong. Xi Jinping's experience plays into this nostalgia and national pride. It is also used as a propaganda tool in order to dispel the "princeling" label ascribed to second generation party members such as Xi who grew up part of the elite. The experience is said to have played a large part in the development of Xi's political outlook, making him a more sympathetic figure capable of understanding the plight of rural Chinese people.

the natural insulating properties of loess circumvent the need for air conditioning or heating.[32]

As the terrain became more barren and the valleys wider, Amy and I started to see more and more of these carve-outs in the hillsides that lined the road. Amy had read about the *yaodong* long before leaving on our trip. Eager to get a closer look, she tapped my shoulder and asked if we could stop. We found one moderately large complex by the side of the road. A gateway enclosed a courtyard and several large, yellow archways could be seen on the other side. A young woman stood by the entrance. Her face, bronzed from a life in the country, was pretty. Rosy-cheeked, she grinned a shy smile as Amy dismounted from the bike and approached.

The woman seemed to embody the welcoming and trusting nature of rural life. Disarmed by the helmeted, camera-wielding foreigner, she still did not appear suspicious. Amy walked up to the gate, asked if she could take photos, and was immediately welcomed inside. I sat observing from across the road with the bike, but followed behind as the pair disappeared behind the gate.

Our hostess confidently confirmed the practicality of the homes, and took us inside one room to prove how cool it was. She never said much but did display obvious pride when showing us her family's satellite dish. There were other modern appliances too, and she took us to the rugged, gas-powered generator that kept everything running. The home itself was made of several tunnel-like rooms arranged in a semicircle around a central courtyard. The carving out of each was so smooth and symmetrical that they felt like the inside of a cement air raid shelter. Each room was only accessible from the single entrance and was segregated according to purpose. There were

---

[32]   Unfortunately the dwellings still remain vulnerable to earthquakes. In 1556 the Shaanxi Earthquake (also known as the Jiajing Earthquake) devastated the region destroying many of the *yaodong* in the 520-mile-wide affected area that covered ten provinces. It is believed that around 830,000 people were killed as a result and most cave dwellings were destroyed.

bedrooms, a kitchen, and even a storehouse for the inventory from their seasonal harvests. The space was a three-sided sunken courtyard, cut into the hill like a Roman amphitheater. The interior was tranquil, separated from the world beyond its walls. Even the acoustics had been deliberately engineered, as I noticed the muffled sounds of nearby traffic barely crossed its barriers.

Ningxia was our 10th province (we only passed briefly into Gansu but would be returning a couple more times later on). Our road continued northward and the hilly, rigid terrain of the loess soon gave way to the windswept grass plains of the Mongolian Steppe. Tucked away between Eastern Gansu, Northern Shaanxi, and Inner Mongolia, the 25,500-square-mile (66,400 square km) province is one of the smallest in the country. Much of the northern half of Ningxia is dominated by the endless flatness of Inner Mongolia, with whom it shares all of its northern border. This geography has made it a targeted area of development for domestic wind and solar power generation. Natural resources and agriculture however still remain the primary drivers of its economy.

Yinchuan, or "Silver River", is the province's capital and where we planned to get our rear brake pads replaced. As the long, prehistoric valleys passed away behind us, I found myself, once again due to poor signage, accidentally and illegally on a highway. Suddenly we were able to maintain speeds of 75mph and hit as high as 90, with the familiar stressors of the *guo dao* suspiciously gone.

It wasn't long before we were pulled over. With nothing but endless wind-bent grass on either side and almost no traffic, the marked police SUV flashed its lights and signaled for us to stop. A thin man with a well-cared-for uniform got out of the driver's seat. He looked young, in his 30s or early 40s, and spoke remarkably good English. The dumb foreigner act hadn't gotten much traction since Harbin, and now this cop could actually explain, in plain English, how motorcycles weren't allowed on highways in China. With no better plan however, I chose to stick to script and plead ignorance.

"In Beijing, where we came from, motorcycles can go on the highways," I reasoned.

"Yes," the officer patiently tried to explain, "but in Ningxia... not allowed." The point was emphasized by a gentle finger wag.

"Oooooh," Amy and I both exclaimed in unison.

"So... why aren't motorcycles allowed here?" I appended, however futilely.

"*Tai weixian...* Too dangerous," he replied. The explanation was delivered dutifully but genially.

Throughout the entire exchange the policeman maintained an almost deferential attitude towards us. In particular, he was very self-conscious about his English and asked several times for our forgiveness. Amy and I both took some pity on the man who was clearly just trying to do his job. His demeanor was calm and considerate, not confrontational as we'd experienced in the past. Even if his logic was flawed, he seemed to genuinely want to look out for our best interests. Amy in particular felt sympathetic, especially as she knew where my questions were leading. As I went into my spiel about how the National Highway was objectively more dangerous, she patted me a couple times, signaling me to lay off.

Not too long into the conversation, we were joined by the man's partner. Rotund and rosy-cheeked, the kid (he couldn't have been older than 20) came out from the passenger's side of the car and made his way over to our bike. Smooth and sly, he approached grinning like a child ready to sneak an extra dessert. He slid up behind his partner and, rather than take notes or take part in the exchange at all, whipped out his smartphone and immediately started to snap photos. His total lack of seriousness (I got the impression that he must have been more of a trainee than a partner) added to the farcical nature of the experience.

Our little paparazzo was very enthusiastic as he moved in a semicircle around us, diligently working the different angles. His partner meanwhile was doing his best to ignore the trainee. Our demure dressing-down continued, but every once in a while he would follow the young policeman out of the corner of his eye. Tracking the bouncing behind his back, his gaze looking suspiciously like an eye roll.

The charade eventually came to an end when the older cop told us he would be our escort to the next exit ramp. It was an offer made in kindness rather than rebuke. The battle was futile anyway, so I nodded in compliance. Amy and I snapped our helmets back into place and the cop turned towards his car, trainee scurrying behind.

The next toll was only about ten miles away and when we arrived we were asked to pull over once more. This time there was a new dilemma occupying our chaperone's mind: how to find Yinchuan without the expressway. Amy took out her phone and tried to show him that we had a GPS. Visible concern on his face, the cop offered to take us there himself. Pointing towards the large building neighboring the toll plaza, he explained that we could wait in their headquarters until he was off work at six. As we spoke, I noticed the younger policeman sneak out from the car and rush down the path, disappearing into the building.

Amy and I were not at all interested in waiting another three hours before finishing the day and tried to convince him this was unnecessary. Our policeman friend relented but then nervously started to labor through directions in English. At this point, the kid popped back out from the building. Cheeks even rosier than before and grinning victoriously, he waddled back towards us, now armed with a large DSLR camera.

He snapped a couple photos to assess the scene. Apparently dissatisfied with his subjects, he paused and lowered the camera as his eyes opened wide, before suddenly hurrying back over to the car. Sticking his torso through the open passenger door, he popped back out with his prize clasped proudly in his other hand: a policeman's cap. His boss was still busy chattering about how to safely get to Yinchuan when the younger policeman made his way back over, lifted the hat, and plopped it onto his superior's head. Carefully adjusting it into place, he took a measured step backwards and reevaluated the scene. Still dissatisfied with our positioning, he prodded lightly on the back of his partner, who at this point seemed resigned to the young man's musings. After motioning the policeman towards us, he gestured for Amy and I to move closer together. We were, it appeared, finally ready. With a grin, the boy lifted his camera. His boss turned, sighed, and gave a defeated smile as the three of us posed for the photo.

***

Yinchuan was Amy's and my first formal encounter with Chinese Islam. Making our way down the wide, dusty approach, there were several pale mosques peering out to us from the surrounding road construction. It was also the second time on our trip where signs weren't written exclusively in Chinese. *Xiao'erjing* is a writing system that traces its roots back to the Perso-Arabic script, first brought over during migrations to China in the 7th century AD from Central Asia. Islam was first introduced to the region when Muhammad's uncle is said to have come as an ambassador to the Tang dynasty. Increasing trade along the Silk Road promoted further cultural exchange as Islam established a foothold in Western China that has lasted over a millennia. The Hui (the third largest ethnic group in China), Uyghurs and Kazakh Chinese ethnic minorities are the three largest Muslim populations in the country and Ningxia is officially a Hui Semi-Autonomous Region (in contrast to a standard provincial level region). Historically these groups come from the areas that are now the provinces of Xinjiang, Gansu, Qinghai, and Ningxia. Modern migrations have since seen these populations spread throughout the country.

Witnessing the sudden sprouting of mosques along the side of the road gave the feeling that we had been transported to another country. There were several times like these on our journey when Amy and I had a hard time believing we were even in China any more. Entering places like Kashgar, Tibet, or Western Sichuan later in the coming months left me with a similar sense of awe and reverence towards the scale of history. We were only two days drive outside of Xi'an, the historical capital of China, and already the city walls had been stripped away, the language that an emperor conquered a hemisphere in order to unify had been replaced, and the familiar "Chinese-ness" that we knew from Beijing had evolved into something entirely different.

The city of "Silver River", former capital of the Western Xia Empire of the Tangut people from 1038 to 1227 AD, was a surprisingly rewarding tourist find. It was even more so considering we hadn't even planned on coming. It turned out that it would still be another two days before the brake pads eventually arrived, and while the delay was unfortunate, it did give us the chance to visit some of the surrounding attractions.

Yinchuan didn't appear to be a well-known tourist destination and as a result we had most sights almost entirely to ourselves. "Mouth of the Rolling Clock" or *Gun Zhong Kou* was a nature reserve about 20 miles to the northwest of the city. Surrounded on all sides by flat grass plains, the park was an oasis of large rolling hills. Walking trails snaked at random amongst their faces and provided spectacular views of the wooded canyons below.

Amy and I hiked the paths aimlessly and followed whichever signs peaked our interest as we enjoyed the near complete seclusion. We passed solitary Buddhist pagodas and climbed up to shrines dedicated to various gods and Bodhisattvas. One trail led us down a mountain and then right through the middle of a temple where we found a whiskered old man seated in the courtyard. He sat in the shade of a nearby tree with wisps of white flowing from his face and an oxygen tank propped to his side. He invited the two of us for a seat in between puffs from the face mask. He had the air of a retired Kung Fu master now suffering the consequences of a lifetime of pipe smoking. I would have loved to stay and converse with him, but unfortunately his Mandarin was so garbled that neither Amy nor I could understand a word he said. We nodded respectfully at the prompts after each brief grunt of words, but soon bid farewell and continued down the mountain.

No more than a mile from the temple we stumbled on a mosque occupied by a community of Hui Muslims. The building was emptying out as Amy and I arrived and we heard some agitated yells from one of the scarfed women in the crowd. She appeared to be berating a nearby man while several of her friends attempted to console her. We entered the mosque after they had left and found three cheerful Hui men, unperturbed (if not amused) by the commotion outside. All of different heights and builds, they wore traditional white caps and their faces were dark and leathery. Sitting side by side on a bench at the periphery of the courtyard, they smiled placidly and invited us in with a wave. One of the men, the oldest of the three, stood up and offered us some flatbread as we entered. They didn't speak Mandarin so all of our communication took the form of nods and smiles. After taking some photos and looking around, we dropped ten yuan into the mosque's donation box and made to leave. The three men, still shoulder to shoulder on the bench, beamed as we waved goodbye.

Back in the city we visited a couple other old relics. The Haibao Pagoda is one of the oldest buildings in the province, a Buddhist place of worship built back during the Bei Dynasty in the 5th century AD. Today the nine level, 177-foot-tall brick structure is set in the middle of a well-maintained public park, a comforting respite in the middle of a provincial capital city.

In contrast, the Nanguan Mosque, the largest in the area and center for prayer for many local Muslims, was in a sorry state of disrepair. The general aesthetics were what you would expect of a Muslim place of worship. It had large domed roofs topped with crescent moons, ornate inscriptions from the Koran written on the walls and passageways, and everything was decorated in deep greens and bright gold. No park surrounded the mosque though, which instead just sat along a crowded city street. Entrance tickets were $2.50, bought from a sleepy Han guard behind a window. Entering through the gate, Amy and I were immediately greeted by the somber sight of a rusting, unused fountain. The cement of the walls was stained black from rain, old air conditioner units blighted the interior of the courtyards, and a couple of scrap piles could be seen peeking out from hidden corners. I even noticed some graffiti advertisements recently scrawled on exposed wall.[33]

Our most lasting memory in Yinchuan however was not from a cultural experience but from a culinary one. With all the different regional dishes that exist in China, one goal Amy and I had set for ourselves was to try local specialties. In Xi'an we had *biang biang* noodles and *rou jia mou*, a shredded meat sandwich served in a flaky flatbread. In Shanxi we tried *zheng rou*, a grey, pork and potato sliced pancake that we were told can only be found in the prefecture-level

---

[33]   The Nanguan Mosque that currently sits in the middle of Yinchuan was built only a few decades previously, in the 1980s. The original was built during the Ming Dynasty. It was expanded in the 1950s to over three thousand square meters but was unfortunately torn down during the decade of unrest that followed.

city of Xinzhou where we had tried the dish. In Inner Mongolia we tried not just Mongolian milk tea and fried dough in a yurt on the plains but also experimented with poor imitation Russian sausage in Manzhouli. So with the extra days off in Ningxia, we thought it would be worth asking around for their most iconic local dish.

Neither Amy nor I was familiar with the province to begin with and didn't have the first idea of what to try. So, one afternoon before heading out to tour the city, we went to the lobby of our small Chinese budget hotel and asked the young man at the front desk what he recommended.

"You want to try something local?" he asked coyly, with a smile that signaled he thought we were getting in over our heads.

"Yes," I replied with confidence. "We're traveling all around China and we want to try the local dishes of all the places we visit. We'd like to try something from Ningxia that is *didao*, something authentic."

"Ok..." the young concierge said reluctantly, "but I'm not sure you'll be used to the flavor. *Bu xi guan*. Not accustomed."

This was something that Chinese often said to us. Used to foreign tourists who haven't acquired a taste for local cuisine, they expect us to stick to safe, familiar dishes like Kung Pao Chicken or noodles. We are usually greeted with surprise and admiration when we prove to have more adventurous palates. One of the more common questions I've received is *"Ni neng chi la ma?"* or "Can you eat spicy food?" So when this hotel employee showed suspicion at our willingness to try a new Chinese dish, I brushed it aside as someone else unused to foreigners.[34]

---

[34] Another reason for this assumption could also be the general tendency of Chinese to be unwilling to go outside of their comfort zone with regards to food. When eating with Chinese friends at a foreign-style restaurant, we usually still order family-style where all dishes are put in the middle of the table and everyone picks at them individually. Italian food tends be particularly popular for Chinese tourists because of the simple flavors and the familiarity of noodles. In addition, being used to stir-fried meats cooked at high temperatures, anything less than well-done is out of the question.

"It's okay," I tried to reassure him. "We've lived in China for three years now. We're used to Chinese food!" And with that we were able to goad the recommendation out of him: *yang za sui*.

The man pointed us towards a shabby hole in the wall just down the road from our hotel. Later on, during lunchtime, we made our way to the narrow shop. Its name was simply *Yang Za Sui*, with the characters printed in large block writing on a sign above the door. The restaurant was small and very local. It was a narrow space, white walls flecked with grease and peeling paint, and there was only enough room for a couple tables. A TV hung on the wall in the back corner and a large pot sat stewing next to the entrance. Beside the door was a stool for the person serving the customers, and segmented off from the main dining area was a small side room where the food was prepared.

A middle-aged Hui woman walked over to our table with a menu, head wrapped tightly in a scarf that framed her face in a perfectly symmetrical circle. Her smile was wide but bashful and she placed the single sheet of paper between Amy and I with a short bow and a *ni hao* before scurrying back to her stool. The menu in front of us was extremely basic. All that was printed on it were the options for how to have our *yang za sui*: with or without bread, small or large bowl, and a couple of cold dishes offered as sides.

This was clearly an important moment for our host. Being a foreigner, I'm sometimes self-conscious of how easy it is to get used to being treated like a celebrity in China. You develop almost an expectation of entitlement. This woman was not used to seeing Westerners and was proud that she would have the opportunity to serve us the local specialty, and she watched us expectantly throughout our stay. It was endearing, which unfortunately made what happened next somewhat uncomfortable.

What positive anticipation Amy and I had had leading up to our meal was swept away as the reddish-brown gruel we ordered was plopped in front of us. The smell that drifted up from the bowls was sharp and pungent. Amy and I both apprehensively stirred around what seemed to be chopped noodles before looking back up at each other. The deer-in-the-headlights look Amy was giving me reflected the thoughts being conjured in my own head. With odors of rotting flesh floating up towards my nose, I thought to myself, "What have we gotten ourselves into?"

I tried a couple bites of what was in the bowl and, as if there could be any doubt, the taste was as foul as the smell. Amy decided she needed to get a drink before subjecting herself to a helping and got up to buy a bottle of iced tea from around the corner.

I hadn't thought of it before, but with Amy gone I had a closer look at the characters in the name of the dish: *"yang"* sheep, *"za"* complex, and *"sui"* pieces. *Complex... sheep.. pieces.* I took out my phone for confirmation and looked up the characters. *Zasui*: "Chopped cooked entrails of sheep or oxen; offal; mixed entrails; trivial matters."

"Oh..." full realization now passing through my mind. "Those... aren't noodles."

When Amy came back, I decided to wait to tell her what we were eating and stubbornly began making my way through the whole bowl. The side of bread we'd ordered helped to stomach the variably sized chunks of meat (the soup, it turned out, contained nothing but complex sheep pieces). I ate while trying not to breath through my nose. This made the experience bearable but the texture was impossible to ignore. Amy, not quite as bull-headed as I, decided after a few mouthfuls that the consequences of continuing outweighed the benefits. She'd tried the local dish and decided it was enough. Even with the sweet drink, she felt projectile vomit remained a real possibility and would ultimately be more damaging to our host's pride than a half-eaten bowl of sheep entrails.

Amy watched with a hint of disgust on her face as I fished around for the last of the meat. I gulped and looked down at the slightly bloody broth, now only wisps of oil left gliding over its brown surface. Hesitating a moment, I considered the soup but decided that leaving it behind would not constitute a breach of my "take what you eat and eat what you take" gastronomical principles.

Getting up from our table, the two of us thanked the still smiling woman and walked out. We made our way back to the hotel and resolutely concluded: *bu xi guan le*. Not accustomed.

***

In the past seven days we had barely managed to cover more than five hundred miles. More time had been spent standing still than in motion. The lack of progress was making me frustrated with circumstances that were out of my (or anyone else's) control. I was also eager to get started on the next leg of our trip. After Ningxia we would be heading due west and into some of the most remote regions of China. Over the next two months our route would pass through two deserts and two major mountain ranges. We would enter the third lowest inland place on earth and the hottest in China, and soon after would rise up to Mount Everest Base Camp in the Himalayas.

It wasn't just me now either. Amy too seemed bored with the lack of progress and was eager to hit the road again. So when the new brake pads were finally installed late in the afternoon of our third full day in Yinchuan, we pushed aside the thought of hanging around any longer, packed up, and headed out.

The provincial road that went south along the eastern border of the province was well paved. With only light traffic, progress away from the city was quick. Trees lined the roadway and sheltered us from winds coming off the plains. Small concrete villages of the Ningxia countryside passed through our vision like ephemeral highway billboards.

I scanned the one-road hamlets half consciously as we passed through these corridors of village life. During one of these drive-bys, I found the monotony of one-story buildings suddenly interrupted. A flash of color and sound hummed into range and a crowd of people came into view. Before there was any time to process what we'd seen, it had already fallen behind again at 50mph. Amy and I passed over so much on a daily basis that my first instinct was to just keeping going. My impatience to leave Yinchuan and the first glimmer of a setting sun were goading me onward. But then, as if by a subtle tap on my helmet from my subconscious, I was reminded why we were on this trip in the first place, and I pulled over onto the gravelly shoulder.

We got off the bike and turned to witness a crowd of people about 30 to 50 yards behind. Almost everyone was dressed in white, some in white smocks while others wore white caps. Most wore both. In front of us a line of about six people, all also in white, crouched at the edge of the sidewalk, each nursing their own smoldering nest of burning paper on the road in front of them.

Amy stayed by the bike, too polite to want to impose on the event, but I inched closer to the house where most of the action was. On either side of the driveway were piles of about two dozen large, open umbrellas. Their canopies were striking. They were made of bright, neon-colored tissue paper. Purples and greens and pinks and blues all faced out from the tops of these sculptures in ornate patterns. By the door of the house, under a tent, a band played a hypnotic song dominated by a wind instrument. The sound was whiny and distinctly Middle Eastern, bringing to mind images of a snake charmer in an old Arabian marketplace.

I noticed a black and white picture of a man hanging above the doorway of the house, but it wasn't of any of the Communist Party leaders I was used to spotting in restaurants and living rooms elsewhere in the country. Turning my head to the right, under the white tent I saw a crude, wooden casket just off to the side. We had walked into a funeral.

Not wanting to interrupt any longer, I started to slink my way back to the bike. On my way, I noticed too that the tissue paper umbrellas all had the same Chinese character printed at their peak: "奠" or *dian*, which I later learned was the character for "a libation to the dead".

I walked past what was left of the smoldering paper and saw that all but one of the mourners had left. The remaining woman had her head flat on the floor in front of her and hadn't moved in some time. Her paper was nearly burnt out like the rest, and I watched solemnly as piece by piece it broke away in the wind. She trembled then and a sob broke out from beneath her crouched head. I was back at Amy's side when we saw a man come over to console the woman, who I assumed must be the widow. The man reached out and with a hand on her shoulder gently tried to cajole her to join the crowd that was now retreating towards the house. The touch of another person seemed only to worsen the woman's pain. At contact, she let out a wail that arched her back and gravitated her off the pavement. Another man soon joined and together they lifted the mourning woman to her feet, dragging her, still sobbing, towards the building. Amy and I already felt awkward at our intrusion into such an intimate gathering, but no more so than at this point. This was a funeral, not a tourist event, and it was time we extricated ourselves.

We walked back to the bike but were intercepted by a group of four men meekly scurrying over as we put our helmets back on. I was surprised by their convivial greeting given the somber setting, as they casually launched into the ritual questions, asking what nationality we were and what mileage our bike got. Apparently not perturbed at all by our presence, the group, led by a jovial middle-aged man, invited us to join them for dinner. We were both apprehensive about intruding and worried that they were just being polite. The man, who was balding on top, wore a plaid button-down t-shirt tucked into his grey dress pants just above his belly button. He arched his back, stuck out his stomach, and, with hands on hips insisted with a grin that we join.

I parked the bike by the front of the house and then followed our hosts through a small gate around the left side. At the rear of the building a large tent had been erected that formed the roof for a makeshift dining hall. The dark grey canopy was tied at one end to the back wall of the house and sloped down making a kind of lean-to underneath which 50 people were huddled, crouched on small stools around a dozen tables. We were led through towards a table at the front and I was surprised by how few stares we were getting. No one seemed annoyed by our presence. Very aware of our obvious lack of connection to the bereaved, Amy and I felt that we were outsiders in more than just the usual way. Yet, somehow, as we were led to our seats, we appeared to be as welcome as I'd ever felt anywhere in China.

On the other side of the dining area was an open shack, a permanent brick structure with large wooden beams stretched across its ceiling. This had been converted into an industrial sized kitchen for the event. Old steel drums were repurposed into stoves. Giant wooden vats and metal cooking pots were strewn across every surface. Bags of flour and empty bottles of vinegar and alcohol littered the space. It was a beautiful chaos that represented a full day (at least) of preparation leading to the final serving of this funeral feast.

A delicious lamb and potato stew was served and generous portions were doled out into our bowls. The meal seemed graciously devoid of any entrails, although so close on the heels of our last meal of mutton, the smell gave both Amy and I pause. An assortment of freshly baked breads accompanied the dish for dipping. Amy hesitated to try until I'd given her a nod. The five people we shared our table with, including the man who invited us, watched in anticipation. They seemed more interested in whether or not we would enjoy their food than in their own bowls laid in front of them. With each bite,

Amy and I hummed our approval and looked up with a smile at the expectant stares. "*Hao chi ma?*" they asked several times during the meal. "Is it good?" "*Hao chi!*" we'd nod back. "Delicious!"

It can be easy to get caught up in the petty annoyances of travel through China. The inefficient regulations, the dangerously bad drivers ironically telling us that "safety is number one", the lemming-like policemen enforcing nonsensical rules, or the easily avoidable traffic jams that go on for miles and miles. You can rush through it in an attempt to put it behind you, but the effect just leaves a vague but persistent memory. The feeling is like that of taking a snapshot, which leaves behind a superficial impression stripped of its humanity and depth.

We may have ended up driving for an hour after dark because of the stop at the funeral, but the impact it left was powerful and enduring, the event beautiful and candid. The hospitality we received was genuine and the food fresh and filling. It even resulted in an enduring relationship as the balding man, whose name I soon learned was Qian Balun, maintained correspondence with me until long after our trip was over. The moment of indecision before I ultimately stopped to witness the funeral, and the result of the choice we made, was an important lesson for me and would affect how I would make decisions for the duration of our trip.

Chapter 7 – The Western Wall and Silk Road Oasis

I love watching the landscape change from the saddle of a motorcycle. We witnessed an amazing transformation as we went from the flat green of eastern Ningxia to the dry yellow of the Tengger Desert in Gansu. The area was significantly more arid than the loess plateaus where Amy and I had camped in the east of the province after Xi'an. We spent hours going along straight, flat highway. Sand-colored mesas followed us like the long, monotonous walls of a maze. Occasionally they shifted with the road to the right or left, but always they towered above. Cave dwellings and groupings of rustic farmhouses were some of the only signs of recent habitation that we saw. We also drove by the ruins of villages long passed from use, skeletons of clay and brick frames standing like a lattice work that radiated out from the sides of the road.

Amy grew curious about the materials and original use of the structures, so we stopped for a break to take a closer look. I waited by the side of the road with the motorcycle as she went to take photos. Leaning against the bike and trying to avoid too much movement under the heat of the sun, I lazily took in the barren valley spread out beneath the nearby cliffs. All I saw among the tufts of sparse desert vegetation was a farming village out in the distance. As I stood there daydreaming, I caught the movement of someone approaching from behind out of the corner of my eye. The woman (or man, it wasn't clear) had the hair of a caveman, puffed out in a matted mess like she'd stuck her finger in an electrical socket, and walked with a crick in her right leg. She slowed as she approached, and then stopped before giving me and the motorcycle a slow head-to-toe scan. With dreads emanating out like a halo, she stuck her tongue into the side of her cheek and cracked a skeevy, approving smile at me from the side of her mouth. I had no idea where she had come from. Miles away from any town, she turned forward again and continued her lopsided strut down the dust-covered road, headed purposefully towards nowhere in particular, leaving me feeling half violated and half like I'd just come out of a scene from a Japanese horror film.

***

Being in a desert is like being in an ocean. The scale is overwhelming. You can get lost in it and the sense of vulnerability to the elements, encroaching from all sides on your tiny strip of humanity's world, is humbling. Driving through it is meditative.

We continued west through Gansu and the terrain flattened out considerably over the following days. The wind was heavy and came in strong gusts from across the Tengger. In the distance to our left we could see the beginnings of the Altun mountain range rising up. Mostly though it was all open and dry. Amy and I passed through several wind farms; tall three-pronged windmills dotted at random across the horizon. The forests of fiberglass disappeared off in the distance, spinning lazily as they caught the gusts from across the desert plains and off the neighboring mountain tops.

As we passed through this area of Gansu, low dirt walls continued to appear along the side of the road. They looked similar to the ruined walls of the abandoned rammed earth villages from earlier and so I mostly ignored them. With unending yellow earth spread on all sides, the wandering line of the mound wove into the subconscious of my peripheral vision. All of a sudden, the wall, which had been running to our right, doubled in height and snaked towards the highway. Once there, it rose and transformed into an arched bridge that passed over our heads, crossing to the opposite shoulder where it met the ground at a collection of buildings. A small, yellow-hued rest stop.

This strange crossing in the middle of the highway made it seem unlikely that what we had been following were just the ruins of old villages, so I took note of some of the surrounding road signs. Absorbing the name of the rest stop I suddenly realized that, in fact, for the past several hours we hadn't been driving past ruined villages at all, but along the foundations of the old western portion of the Ming Great Wall.

Back in 2010, during a circumnavigation of the U.S., I spent a couple days riding through the Sonoran and Chihuahuan Deserts in the American Southwest, and I found parallels with our time in Gansu. The monotony of imposing vistas, where the only respite is a gas station among the empty vastness. The physical challenges of the heat and wind. To stumble upon the shadow of such an ancient legacy in a remote corner of Western China though was wholly unique. Amy and I had just spent the better part of a day driving along the length of one of the most consequential construction projects of all time. Lulled into complacency by the repetitiveness of a desert highway, we barely even noticed it and it was chastening to be so casually presented with evidence of a millennia-old civilization, particularly in such a hostile and remote environment.

The idea of "The Great Wall" as we understand it today is a modern construct of the Western imagination. The network of man-made barriers scattered along the northern frontiers have been known in Chinese by at least a dozen names over the centuries including *bian qiang* ("border wall"), *wai bao* ("outer fortress"), and even *tu long* ("earth dragon"). The modern Chinese name, *chang cheng* which means "long wall", first appeared in the Chinese historian Sima Qian's *Record of the Grand Historian* in around 109 BC. In his account, the phrase was a passing reference to the disparate walls built by the Warring State kingdoms and the more unified wall of the Qin that followed. It was, however, never truly viewed as a single entity or officially known by the catch-all name of *chang cheng* until the Qing Dynasty over a millennia and a half later.

When Qin Shihuang unified China in 221 BC he built three thousand miles of defensive barriers during his reign. This is considered the modern Wall's primary forebear and the first real effort to connect the many existing structures. It's actual military benefits are suspect though. It is primarily believed to have been one of the Dragon Emperor's more infamous forced labor projects that he used to keep the disparate peoples he'd conquered distracted and subjugated (the other famous one of course being the Terracotta Army with which he would eventually be buried). The Qin walls were made out of rammed earth and fieldstone. Over the centuries, these were eroded away by time and the elements. The succeeding Chinese dynasties continued building defensive barriers and fortifications throughout the north. These stretch from Yumen Pass in Western Gansu all the way to the North Korean border in Dandong. Old sections of wall are still being discovered today. Most recently, defensive fortifications have been found as far north as Mongolia proper near the Russian border, believed to have been built by the Liao, Jin, and Yuan dynasties between the 10th and 13th centuries.

Much of what we consider as The Great Wall of China today however was built during the three-century long rule of the Ming from 1368 to 1644. As part of a broader border control strategy meant to keep out invading nomadic tribes from the North, the Ming built many of their fortifications out of more permanent stone and brick (though rammed earth was still used in the West as Amy and I witnessed there in Gansu). These included as many as 25,000 watchtowers along with 5,500 miles of wall.[35] Because of the more durable material, the Ming Wall has lasted to present day. Its most

---

[35]   This includes nearly 4,000 miles of wall, 223 miles of trenches, and over 1,000 miles "of natural defensive barriers such as hills and rivers."

famous and best restored sections north of Beijing, which include Badaling, Mutianyu, and Simatai, are broad, grey, brick fortifications that snake across the craggy peaks of the Yanshan range. These Ming constructions are what have most captured the imaginations of visiting foreigners for hundreds of years and what we typically associate with "The Great Wall of China". Despite this scale however and contrary to popular belief, the Wall is not, nor ever has been, visible from space.

We were now approaching what is generally recognized as the westernmost point of The Great Wall, Jiayuguan. Jiayuguan was a mountain pass on the far edge of the Ming Dynasty's territory, with military strategic significance due to the two nearby mountains that could funnel invading armies into exposed formations. To take advantage of the defensive benefits, The Great Wall was extended out to this valley (which was also an important waypoint on the Silk Road) with a large military fort built to defend the pass. The fort today lies just outside of a city, also called Jiayuguan, where Amy and I planned to spend the night.

The section of wall and the military fortifications were both in very good condition, and Amy and I were impressed by the historical authenticity of the preservation. The contrast in materials and construction techniques used to build this section compared to the brick and stone of the Eastern Wall was distinct and highlighted the difference in terrain and available resources. The yellow of the Western Wall thrust up as if conjured from the surrounding sand. We entered the official tourist area and watched as the tamped earth rose high, over 30 feet, and wound out into the desert plain, ending in a sand-colored fortress with guard towers capped by the traditional Chinese gabled roofs.

The fortress had a permanent photography exhibit on site that Amy and I had heard about prior to our trip. The exhibition was curated by the organization "Friends of The Great Wall", a group founded by British national William Lindesay. In 2012, Amy and I had gone to a talk by Lindesay hosted by one of the foreign embassies in Beijing. The talk predated the idea for our own China adventure and turned out to be one of the formative experiences leading to its inspiration.

In 1987, Lindesay spent 78 days hiking and running over 1,500 miles of The Great Wall, traveling from Jiayuguan where we now stood to Shanhaiguan on the east coast, where the wall enters the Bohai Sea. An adventure that included one deportation and seven imprisonments, the trip ended up changing Lindesay's life, as he would later publish four books on the Great Wall and found an organization dedicated to its preservation and research. Lindesey brought together his passion for long distance running and a fleeting interest in The Great Wall into a two-and-a-half-month-long experience that would set off a three-decade-long mission to preserve, research, and catalogue The Great Wall of China.

The exhibit, called "The Great Wall Revisited", was started in 2004 and took four years to complete. For it, Lindesay and his organization collected photographs of different sections of the wall dating as far back as a hundred years when a European missionary, William Gallo, became the first Westerner to travel the length of The Great Wall. The most intriguing part of the project though was that Lindesay went to great efforts to recreate the exact shot of each of the historical photographs he found. The point of this was to highlight the various states of both decay and preservation of the wall throughout the past hundred years. It was quite striking to see not just the physical state of the wall, but also the progression of time.

The Great Wall in its millennia of transcontinental mutability has been a canvas on which China's own history is printed. The ebb and flow of its branches reflect the changing tides of imperial borders and the battles of shifting cultures. The materials and the breadth of its construction are manifestations of a civilization's technological advancement. The photography exhibit is a record of these changes that reflects the tumultuous developments that China has undergone in just the past one hundred years. In the photos, you can see the evolution from colonial subjugation to a period of internal struggle when heritage took a backseat, all the way to the present state of relative prosperity and development.

There was the Badaling section in black and white from one hundred years ago, the lone European face of William Gallo standing among overgrown grey bricks in the mountains north of Beijing. Today that same spot swarms with millions of tourists each year from around China and the world.[36] I found an interesting photograph from the 1980s depicting a child sitting next to a crumbling guard tower. The recreation was barely recognizable from the original and was apparently extremely difficult to stage. The tower had almost completely decayed, now little more than a pile of bricks, making it a challenge even to locate. Meanwhile, in the two decades since the photo was originally taken, a National Highway had been built through the town. The increased traffic from the *guo dao* and resulting development hastened the degradation of the wall (our own gear was barely surviving after a month on these roads). While many photos highlighted the opportunities for restoration that China's newfound wealth had provided, the now forgotten stone pile on the shoulder of newly paved asphalt emphasized how unforgiving the country's economic development could be at times.

Our plan was just to pass through Jiayuguan – enough time in the afternoon to visit the Wall and photography exhibit before moving on the next day. Unfortunately, after packing the following morning, I started to notice a rattling from the back of the bike. I rolled it up and down the street a couple times while Amy attempted to see where the

---

[36]   Badaling is the most visited section of the wall, receiving around nine to ten million tourists each year.

sound was coming from, but we couldn't find anything. It didn't seem serious, but this was going to be our last city of any significance for at least a thousand miles and I didn't want to take any chances. A call to Fang Shujian confirmed there was a CFMoto shop in town so we decided a visit would be prudent before pushing farther on into the desert.[37]

When we arrived, the crew at the shop seemed disproportionately thrilled to meet us. They wanted to hear all about the trip and how the bike was. The owner of the shop, Boss Li, a tall man with a combover, button-down t-shirt tucked into dress pants, and a slight overbite, was particularly enthusiastic. He introduced himself with a giddy, two-handed shake and handed over his business card displaying his title of manager of "The Jiayuguan Harley Company" (a name he likely chose himself, most likely as a marketing gimmick free from the consequences of IP litigation).

We later found out that someone at the marketing department of CFMoto had long before organized for us to visit in Jiayuguan. While Boss Li had been expecting us (apparently with great anticipation) neither Amy nor I had even been notified. If it hadn't been for our caution with the bike, we never even would have made an appearance. While I was concerned about a strange sound from near the back tire (where something like two to three hundred pounds of weight was being carried), Boss Li was treating this like a press event. It was as if Amy and I were visiting dignitaries and the work we were asking for was for show. Before I could even show him the problem, he flashed a cheeky smile asked if he could take the bike for a ride around the block. It was endearing how excited he was to take part in what he saw as a CFMoto tour of China. I was concerned though that, because of

---

[37]   After Jiayuguan there was only one more CFMoto shop in all of Western China. Urumqi in northwest Xinjiang would be our last opportunity for parts and repairs before going through the Taklamakan Desert in western Xinjiang and eventually the Kunlun and Himalayan mountain ranges towards Lhasa.

the poor communication by the factory, our real concerns were going to get glossed over (*"Mei wen ti! Mei wen ti!"*)

After Boss Li's ride around the block and some photos together with his wife, we next were led through the showroom of his store (suspiciously there was nary a Harley-Davidson in sight among the columns of small 150cc Suzukis and "Rich Lord" motorcycles[38]). He attempted to assuage my worries by informing me of the skill of his mechanic. "He'll even check the spark plugs and the oil for you for free!" he assured us (neither were problems and both had already been done recently, less than two weeks ago). In a small office in the back of the shop, we were joined by some of Boss Li's friends. His wife went around serving tea and passed around slices of fresh cantaloupe. We chatted some about the local roads and recommendations for heading west. This led Boss Li into a very enthusiastic description of a recent day trip they had all done touring some of the nearby sights. Interrupting the boisterous exposition, he suddenly began to rummage through his desk drawers before emerging with a DVD.

The short film was obviously a video that the Jiayuguan motorcycle club had had commissioned to record a weekend ride. It was a semi-professional production, shot in high definition, accompanied with appropriately cheesy Chinese pop music, and included shots of them on the road. Amy and I were already familiar with these types of local production companies, mostly from having to dodge their vans on the *guo dao*. They tended to be most prolific during the holiday seasons as this is the most popular time for wedding ceremonies. Part of this process involves a long procession of up to a dozen luxury sedans advancing at a regal crawl. While passing these parades presented a serious road hazard, most dangerous was the filming van that followed. Like the buzzing of a fly around a slow

---

[38]   Haojue Motorcycles or 豪爵 in Chinese.

moving mammal, they dodged in and out of their lane without warning, often into oncoming or passing traffic.

After the video had finished playing, Amy and I nodding along, smiling as Boss Li walked us through each event. When it was over, Li reached back behind his desk and pulled out a couple copies of the recording which he insisted we take with us on our journey.

While the bike finished going through its maintenance, Li and the guys from the shop took us out to lunch. At a nearby restaurant that advertised itself as a *Dongbei*-styled beer garden (they had cheap Tsingtao draft beer and a couple photos up on the wall of German beer maidens), we talked more about our route west. They all insisted to us that we had to visit Dunhuang, an old Silk Road oasis town only half a day's ride away by the expressway, but which wasn't on the route we had planned. They also appeared very eager to have us stay one more night in town. Neither Amy nor I were particularly interested in another night in Jiayuguan, but the group was persistent. The pitch included: a stay at a nice hotel in town, a visit to a factory where one of the men was a manager, and a dinner at the factory complete with a show by a local minority dance troupe. It seemed rude to turn them down so in the end we agreed, and after the meal we picked up the bike (rattling diminished but not completely eliminated) and were escorted to our lodging for the night.

The evening turned out to be underwhelming but our hosts were gracious nonetheless. The Huili Business Hotel where we were gifted a night's stay was starting to show its age (though we were told that it had been the choice establishment for visiting politicians and businessmen to Jiayuguan for decades). Dinner was at the "Herd Source Beach Animal Husbandry Ltd. Company of Jiayuguan City". Boss Li and his friend, a short, weaselly gentleman in jeans and a plaid button-down shirt that was a manager there, proudly explained that the factory was the largest animal husbandry company in the province. "All of their beef is sent to the first tier cities like Beijing,

Shanghai, and Guangzhou," Boss Li explained. "Almost none is sold here. That's how you know they are the best. It is just like foreign quality!"

While there was no dance performance, the factory tour did include visits to several of the stables and a garden where we were told they brought all of the high-ranking government officials that came to visit. We also were shown the company's prized breeding bull. Upon our arrival at the open-air pen, one of Boss Li's friends from the shop, a chubby, red-cheeked man in his early 30s who everyone simply referred to as "Little Fatty", was goaded into jumping in the ring with the creature. Little Fatty soon lost his nerve though and judiciously exited after being stared down by the virile bovine.

Sadly, dinner, which was hosted in the company cafeteria left open after hours for our visit, featured none of their vaunted beef (I guess it was all in Beijing already), though we were served a full Chinese feast. There was fish, tofu, soup, vegetables, chicken feet, mutton, eggplant, fruit, and more, all laid out in front of us on the XL Lazy Susan[39]. No feast of course would be complete without a couple bottles of the Chinese spirit, *baijiu*. At 56% ABV, it is a potent brew and Chinese friends are always excited to meet foreigners willing to put up with its often pungent aroma. Our congregation, which now included both Herd Source Beach Ltd.'s president and vice president, were luckily relatively tame and Amy and I were limited to only a few shots. Boss Li, our designated driver, responsibly limited himself to only two. [40]

---

[39]   Particularly because of the family-style way of eating, where dishes are shared among everyone at the table, it is important in China when hosting to serve food in excess of what is needed. While the opulence is also partly a show of wealth, it can be considered bad form if your guest has an empty plate as it means they may not have gotten enough to eat.

[40]   Alcohol is neither sipped nor savored in China in the way it is in the West. Drinking is more of a group activity where you cheers with someone or the whole table before each drink, usually downing a full mouthful of whatever is being enjoyed (with wine or beer you may be downing the whole glass). The famous Chinese saying "*gan bei*" literally means "dry glass" and is often interpreted as a prompt for an empty glass. Having any *baijiu* as a foreigner, especially in a Chinese business setting, can sometimes be a dangerous proposition. Fellow diners (especially

Dunhuang is an oasis city one hundred miles into the Taklamakan Desert, a desert that covers approximately 123,550 square miles including much of Xinjiang province to the west and merges with the Tengger to its northeast[41]. Traders traveling on the Silk Road would have to cross this 600-mile-wide stretch of hazardous land before getting to the major trading centers in Ancient China. Because of the dangers of the desert, oasis settlements played a big part in supporting this important 4,000-mile-long East–West trading route. Dunhuang, known in China as "The Gateway to the West", was the first major stop for merchants headed towards Central Asia and Europe after leaving with their goods (primarily silk) from Chang'an (modern-day Xi'an).

Because of the diversity of traffic through this commercial hub and military garrison, Dunhuang was an important place of cultural exchange which most significantly aided in the transmission and spread of Buddhism through China. First established as a frontier outpost by the Han Emperor Wudi in 111 BC, Dunhuang is home to one of the most famous collections of Buddhist grottoes, art and literature in China, the *Mogao Ku* or "Mogao Caves", located 15 miles southeast of the city. The grottoes date back nearly two millennia and the contributions by artists and monks span ten dynasties.

The road from Jiayuguan went directly west across the province. The air was hotter and drier the farther west we went and the terrain became just sand and gravel, with only the two-lane expressway to break the monotony. Amy and I exited the highway at Guazhou ("Melon State") county and dove south into the Taklamakan.

---

men) will see it as a personal challenge to see how much the *lao wai* (outsider) can drink and the flow of libations can be difficult to arrest.

[41] Dunhuang is actually right on the edge of a part of the Taklamakan known as the Kumtag Desert, a stretch of desert plains that run one hundred miles through Gansu and Inner Mongolia. The Kumtag is bordered to the north by the Tianshan Mountains, to the east by Dunhuang, and covers an area of 8,800 square miles.

As we moved down the provincial road, small three-walled shelters began sprouting up in the sand off the shoulder. Passing by at 80mph, it appeared that every one of these huts was selling melons. Piles of the white spheres stood as advertisements in front of the stands. Many also had one or two walls to their rear from which hung webs of orange slivers fully naked and exposed in the sun. Hoping to catch the sunset over the sand dunes outside of Dunhuang, Amy and I had been pushing for four hours almost non-stop from Jiayuguan, not eating anything since the slim pickings at the Huili Business Hotel that morning. I figured a break at a melon stand to try the namesake of "Melon State" was well earned.

A woman came out from the shade of the shelter to greet us as we began to dismount and peel off our dust-covered layers. She was squat, with the dark skin of years in the desert sun, and wore a pink scarf around her head. I couldn't tell if it was worn for religious reasons (she may have been Hui) or just for the practicality of protecting herself from the heat. It seemed rude to ask. She welcomed us with a fantastic smile, and her ear-to-ear grin somehow managed to widen further when she saw we were foreigners.

Without our even asking, she motioned for us to sit down at a short table under her shelter and immediately started to slice melon for us. Hami melons, the kind our host was serving us and the variety that are grown in the region, are named for a nearby city in northeastern Xinjiang, and are almost identical to cantaloupes or honeydews back home. Looking at the orange, water-rich flesh of the melon being laid in front of us, I found it hard to believe they were grown in such an arid and inhospitable climate. I asked our host about where they got the water, and she nonchalantly declared that the produce was grown up in "Melon State".

Most farmers in the area support themselves on the trade of Hami. The melon has two main harvest seasons; one in June for the summer melon and one in November/December for winter melon. The summer melons were the cantaloupe-like fruit we were now being fed. The feeding was happening at a prodigious rate, hydra-like, as two new slices seemed to appear for every one we finished.

Our melon-vendor friend entertained us for the next 30 to 45 minutes. Amy and I were happy to take some respite from the sun and were kept busy talking about life in the area. Most of all though she seemed particularly eager to learn some English. This came across as a refreshingly earnest curiosity that was unlike most locals we spoke with. It felt like much more of a two-way conversation, rather than the interrogation-like bullet point exchanges we were used to. What most impressed me though was how proactive she seemed to be.

The woman explained that she very rarely got foreigners visiting. Maybe once a year a non-Chinese tourist group would stop at her stand, and usually they were Russian. Her hope was that the next time someone did stop, she would be able to welcome them in a language the guest would recognize. Simple phrases like "Welcome!", "Please have a seat", and "Is it good?". She was a good student and throughout our conversation, as we talked about other things, she would come back to the phrases she had learned to test her memory. When she repeated the words correctly, her face beamed with childlike excitement and she'd ask for a new word to learn.

At one point the conversation took an unexpectedly melancholy turn. We had been talking about where we were from when the woman's mouth thinned, her shoulders sank, and the emotion from before drained from her face. "I'm from a small town. I'm not like the two of you," she said more to herself now than to us. "*Wo mei you wen hua,*" "I'm uncultured."

This immediately reminded me of the conversation with the Mongolian waitress near Manzhouli and the Chinese conception of personal quality (*su zhi*). I thought about how much of Chinese identity and self-worth is tied to their background. The melon vendor lamented to Amy and I about how she lacked education, her tone conveying a deep sense of futility. As an American who grew up learning about autodidacts like Frederick Douglass, the former slave turned writer and statesman, and Benjamin Franklin, I found myself frustrated at the woman's abject resignation to a low sense of self-worth. Everything about her so far indicated that she was undeserving of it. She had conducted herself with far more "culture" and dignity than many people we had met on the road who had come from wealth and education. She had made us feel welcome, engaged us in interesting conversation, fed us more than we could possibly hope to finish, and conveyed a socratic curiosity that was refreshing to engage with.

As quickly as she had entered it, the woman snapped out of her malaise and jumped up from her seat at the table. Grabbing a couple ziplock bags, she walked over to one of the walls of drying melon slices and unhooked as many as she could fit in the bags. Smile fully recovered now, she came back over to the table and plopped them down in front of us. Though she had already had Amy and I go through an entire melon by this point, she also wanted us to try some of her dried Hami and would not take *"chi hao le"* "I'm full" for an answer. We indulged her and tried a couple slices. They were tasty and reminded me of the fruit strip snacks I used to eat as a kid, but we were both too stuffed from the hydrated version to eat any more.

When it was time to finally go, we tried to pay but the woman refused to accept any money (only the second time in our conversation that she had stopped smiling). Back by the side of the bike now and packing up our stuff, Amy and I noticed the woman shuffling over to us. In her hands she cradled a full, ripened Hami melon. Once she'd reached us, she insisted we take it. We tried hard to decline, not just out of a sense of propriety but also concern that we lacked the space in our bike. Her impassioned insistence eventually wore us down and we shifted around some gear to find space in one of our panniers.

Amy and I approached Dunhuang from the north and passed through town to find a place to drop off our stuff. In ten minutes we were out again heading to the ancient oasis at Crescent Lake.

It's hard to conceive the reality of a desert oasis town until you've driven out to the edge of one. Serving as a traveler's waypoint and military outpost for over a millennia before, four miles to the south of the city lies less than two acres of water and shrubbery hidden among sand dunes. A domineering mountain of sand greets you long before you even see the lake, towering over the road and swallowing it whole at the edge of the desert. It was epic, like the kind of desert you'd imagine as a child or see in the movies.

We bought our entrance tickets but avoided the multitude of extravagant adventure activities on offer (which included camel rides, hang gliding, and helicopter tours). Instead we chose to hike, along with about one hundred other tourists scattered throughout the vista. We climbed for 45 minutes until we reached the top of the great ridge-line of sand. As we rose, the crescent-moon lake of the oasis took shape below, the water metamorphosing into the form for which it was named. We moved higher and the grey of the city slowly spread out behind us, bordering the pagoda-capped tuft of green and blue at the oasis. On the other side, over the top of the climb, we were met with an endless ocean of sand that opened up before us, undulating off into the southern horizon. Away from the crowds, Amy and I found a place between two crests of sand and sat watching as the entire scene was soon draped in the orange glow of the setting desert sun.

Chapter 8 – Growing Tensions in the Xinjiang Desert

Desert travel is hard. It's taxing. It wears you down both mentally and physically. The road quality in Western China was adequate, but the high temperatures had an invasive ability to seep under our gear and into the skin. With persistent highs over 100 degrees, not even the winds on the expressway could cool us down. Instead they had the opposite effect: the more wind there was, the more energy seemed to be sucked out of us. The heat inserted itself into every aspect of our travel, from when we were driving, to when we took breaks, to finding a place to stay at night. This meant that patience became a scarce commodity, one spent on putting up with the heat and leaving little to spare on the remaining tedium of the road. All of this to say nothing of the added strain placed on the bike.

Leaving Dunhuang after a morning visiting the Mogao Cave Grottoes, we got a flat tire less than half of the way back to the periphery of the Taklamakan. With no human habitation for at least 20 miles in any direction, and lacking the tools to do a proper patch, the situation felt hopeless. Luckily, after about 20 minutes waiting by the side of the road we were able to flag down a passing pickup truck driving back towards the city. I suspect that the family of four had stopped more out of curiosity at the flailing foreigner in a strange, reinforced, and dusty jumpsuit than anything else, but they were willing to help when asked. We managed to lift the bike onto their truck and get a ride into town, where the tire was removed and the inside patched. The following day Amy and I were on our way again, north towards the highway that would take us into our next province, Xinjiang. In Urumqi, the capital of the province still several days away, we had a pair of new tires waiting for us. I had my fingers crossed that these old ones would hold out on the hot asphalt until then.

The highway west was hypnotizing. Straight and unchanging. The hot air blowing across the sands of the Taklamakan was becoming oppressive. Highway exits and rest stops were infrequent, leaving little to break the monotony. Those we did see were not much more than extended shoulders that had muscled their way into the surrounding sands, a pasture of pavement for resting truckers. Some stops had rundown shacks which offered tire repair services[42] or noodles and bottled water. "Clear Waters", "Golden River", "Large Spring", "Grape Gully", or "Heaven's Waters" were just some of the stops sprinkled along the Xinjiang highway. All were sandy and barren, standing in mock contrast to their water-themed names. Practicing how to write the Chinese characters in my head as we passed the intermittent road signs, I thought of the small towns in America's old West that had sprung up around fresh water sources during the days of early settlement. What stand today as gaggles of gas stations, fast food chains, and kitschy tourist sights had once been important watering holes for prospectors and settlers traveling west. The "Cripple Creeks" and "Jackson Holes" of America's Wild West. There was a parallel legacy here in the sands of the old Silk Road, of travelers covering long, hazardous distances in the name of potential fortune. For these destitute watering holes of the modern Chinese highway system though, the names were where the comparison seemed to end.

Amy and I took advantage of the opportunities to break when we could. The winds on the highway were brutal and trying to stay in one

---

[42]   These tire repair shops were a staple of traveling around China, and not just in the desert, where the wear endured by the rubber on the long, hot, straight roads might justify it. It started to stick out to me, especially in contrast to road travel back home. Why was it that Chinese tires appeared to need to be changed so much more frequently? Was there such an abundance of broken tires that drivers were unable to take care of it on their own, causing a vibrant market to spring up instead?

lane was exhausting. We each had these special cooling vests that had been gifted to us by a motorcycle equipment shop in Beijing. They were built to retain moisture when soaked in water, so each morning we would submerge them in a sink or drench them with water bottles to prep for the day. Normally good for an hour or two, in this dry wind they were going stiff after less than 30 minutes on the road. If a rest stop had water for sale we'd usually buy a couple extra bottles just to re-saturate them.

Mostly these breaks were lonely and quiet, just enough time for me to have some more water, empty my bladder, and catch a break from the wind (the areas were so flat and open that unless there was an actual building with a bathroom, Amy was too uncomfortable to do the same). At one rest stop, "Calm Rivers", we found ourselves joined by two truckers stopping on their government-mandated break[43]. I had parked the bike haphazardly in the middle of the pavement outcropping as the two massive Sinopec oil tank trucks turned into the plaza. Their diesel engines roared, announcing their arrival as they turned the corner off the highway. They lined up on either side of our puny CFMoto and their hydraulics hissed as they came to a stop. Surrounding us now, they offered Amy and I the first bit of shade we'd enjoyed in hours.

The drivers hopped down from their cabs together. One was a Uyghur man and the other Hui. Both were large, hardy men, dark skinned and confident, with more prominent cheekbones and wider eyes than that of the Han majority. The Uyghur was thin with an edge of ruggedness, and his face looked more Central Asian than his paunched Hui companion. From the familiarity in their mannerisms they seemed to know each other. A member of the largest ethnic group in Xinjiang province, the Uyghur barely spoke any Mandarin and so our whole conversation went through his friend, who could

---

[43] Truck drivers are mandated by law to rest 30 minutes for every two hours of driving.

148

speak some Uyghur as well as better understand the garbled Chinese of his companion.

After making our introductions, the men offered us some Hami melon which the Hui had brought out from his truck. With no way to split it, the man asked if I could help to which I offered the services of my pocket knife. After cutting the melon into four separate sections, I handed out a piece to each. The Uyghur took his and, with a grunt, held it out with his left hand, looking at it disapprovingly. Then, suddenly, he curled his right hand into a fist, lifted it, and began to pummel the melon shell. Both Amy and I looked at each other nervously. Once he had cracked the shell, the man split the Hami into three separate pieces of more amenable size, cracked a self-satisfied smile, and proceeded to enjoy his meal.

The four of us stood there in the shade of the trucks, enjoying the coolness of the juice as it dribbled down our faces. We made small talk, chatting about the weather, life on the road, and ethnic relations in Western China. Afterwards, leaning against his truck, the Hui pulled out a pack of cigarettes. He offered one to me and his friend for the customary post-meal smoke (I declined while Amy was overlooked altogether). As they lit up, I took note again of the signage on their cargo. Large Sinopec logos, China's largest state oil and gas company, were printed prominently along the sides of each tank. Underneath, in slightly smaller, but still legible writing, was a notice: "Smoking forbidden. Risk of explosion."

***

The Turpan Basin is a geological depression that covers an area of over 19,000 square miles in Northern Xinjiang province. It is the hottest area in China with average highs in summer over 102°F (39°C) and a record high of 122°F (50°C)[44]. It is also home to the lowest place

---

[44]   The lake is believed to have once covered an area of 97 square miles (or 251 square km) but by

in China and third lowest inland place on earth at 507 feet (154.5m) below sea level. We had decided that this point, Aiding Lake, would be a nice milestone for us. Everest Base Camp in southern Tibet was one of our major goals for the trip, and it made sense that before going to get a glimpse of the highest place on earth, we visit one of the lowest.

Within a day's ride from the city of Turpan, we took a break from the highways and tried to take the smaller auxiliary roads the rest of the way. The high-speed winds had been wearing me down and the flat, monotonous scenery made me extra drowsy. I pulled off at what appeared to be an area of remote countryside, but was surprised to find signs of inhabitation. We shared the two-lane highway alongside local freight traffic: run down VW sedans and "Bread Cars" or "*mian bao che*", cheap vans named for their resemblance to a loaf of bread, used as unofficial busses or to transport goods. There were also more places to stop for breaks – collections of hovels by the side of the road where we could get water and Chinese energy drinks.

It was around midday that the bike stopped working.

We had just arrived at the outskirts of a small town. More built-up than the remote villages we had been going through, it even had a few stoplights, which also made progress more stop-and-go. Several intersections into town after accelerating out of a light, the bike began to inexplicably slow. To compensate, I turned down on the throttle but found it unresponsive. With what momentum we had left, I pulled in the clutch and eased the bike over to the side of the tree-lined road. That was the last forward motion I was able to get from it. The engine could turn over after ignition, but once I let out the clutch the bike just shut down again. I couldn't even push it in neutral. It was stuck.

1980 had decreased to less than two square miles (five square km) due to little precipitation, increased farming, and a high rate of evaporation. Today it is little more than a salt-pan and silt swamp.

Machines are frustratingly literal and logical things. There is no amount of willpower or force of determination that can make them do something they don't want to do. It's something I've come to appreciate in computers when developing websites, and it is no less true with motorcycles. As much as I felt the motorcycle should be moving forward, and certainly wanted it to, there was a bug in the machinery that no amount of exasperated pushing or cursing would be able to overcome. There is a great word in Chinese for describing these types of mechanical breaks: *mao* which can mean hair, or feather, but in this case best translates as "coarse or petty" and *bing* which simply means "illness". Our bike it seemed had come down with a *maobing*, a coarse illness, and no amount of pleading or goading would cure it.

Unfortunately my mechanical abilities are pretty much limited to checking spark plugs and changing the oil. My best guess was that something in the engine (or other part vital to movement) had overheated, expanding to the point that it lost all range of motion. I was annoyed with the inexplicable setback, frustrated with something that felt unnecessary as we had had no warning of a problem. I was starting to suffer from the heat and tried in futile anger to push the bike and get out of the sun, but it remained motionless. Amy and I stripped out of our smothering gear and spent the next ten minutes trying to diagnose the problem and figure out our next steps.

Inexplicably and with no observable impetus, the impossible grip, which had felt like a magnet pulling the bike down towards the ground, suddenly released. I took the opportunity to push the bike into the shade and off the road, where we could figure out what to do next. While there was no CFMoto shop in town, we luckily found a mechanic just around the corner. It was a small hole in the wall, tucked between two noodle shops, little more than a closet filled with old parts. A tent was set up outside for shade, with a line-up of several grease-covered farmers' motorcycles underneath and a mechanic squatting on a stool tinkering on the nearest one.

The man was intimidated by our bike at first. This tended to be the default reaction of people outside of Beijing when we approached for help. Not wanting to take any responsibility for a motorcycle this size, the assumption was usually *mei banfa*, "No way." Even before we had a chance to describe the problem, the mechanic greeted me with a violent shaking of the head and hands up in aversion. The reaction was so visceral that it was as if our bike might infect those of his other clients if we approached any further. I prodded and pleaded in an attempt to break through the primal fear. I explained that we at the very least might need to borrow tools and that we had a Chinese partner at the factory that could help over the phone.

I slowly made my case, gaining the mechanic's trust as he saw that I could at least speak some Chinese. In this time, a small crowd had gathered, forming a semicircle under the tent. Hands behind their backs, necks craned, they spectated on the unusual bit of excitement unfolding. Occasionally, in the midst of my discussion regarding our mechanical problems, someone would work up the nerve to strike up a conversation: "Where are you from?" "How much does your motorcycle cost?" Frustrated with our predicament and annoyed at the mechanic's unwillingness to help, I didn't have the patience to humor them and answered with brusque, one-word answers. Despite my attitude, each response was greeted with a giggle, a rush of excitement upon interacting with a foreigner in Chinese.

The mechanic eventually relented, but the inspection bore little fruit. We called Fang Shujian and he walked the man through a checklist of potential causes. Nothing however appeared to have been able to cause our motorcycle to seize the way it had. Coolant, engine, oil, everything seemed normal. While the temperature gauge on the dashboard had been reading higher since we entered Xinjiang, Fang assured me that it was still within a safe range. We did find a dead fuse in the bike's electrical system, and hypothesized (hoped) that it was connected to the engine's ventilation fan causing it to overheat. We switched it out with a spare but Fang still wasn't convinced that that was the source of the problem. Regardless, the bike was running again and until we reached Urumqi, there wasn't much more we could do, so Amy and I warily made our way again towards Turpan.

I did my best to keep a quick and steady pace. We navigated back onto the expressway, nervous that more stop-and-go might cause the bike to overheat again. This seemed to help and we made it the final hundred miles, finally disembarking at the exit for Turpan without another incident. Now out of the wind, we barely made it ten minutes. On the edge of town, only a few miles away from the hostel where we planned to spend the night, the throttle once again stopped responding. With the sun getting ready to set, the bike had had enough and slowly froze itself in place.

A lot of things came to a head at that moment. It had been a difficult week. With suspicious clicking sounds, a flat tire, and now whatever this problem was, our bike was starting to show evidence of wear after more than a month on the road. The high winds on the expressway were draining Amy's and my energy, leaving us exhausted at the end of each day. Meanwhile, with each problem we were moving farther away from the areas where we could find any help. Every little annoyance was amplified by the heat, whether with our equipment, other drivers, or even the staring of strangers (the novelty of which had long ago worn off). It agitated our nerves and shortened our fuses. Finally, it seemed, Amy had reached the end of hers.

As soon as we stopped and Amy realized that the problem still hadn't been fixed, she began cursing at the bike. I could hear her voice rise through the closed visor of her helmet. Pissed off at the situation and feeling helpless to do anything, her only remaining recourse was to get mad. One thing that neither of us realized at the time was that this new problem was tapping into a concern that both Amy and I had, at least subconsciously, long been carrying. It was a nagging worry we'd had ever since the factory visit to Hangzhou, one we had tried our best to ignore: how long would this bike be able to last. The motorcycle was Chinese made and it was a highway bike. Chinese products weren't known for quality and meanwhile we were taking this machine across long distances and through rigors it was never meant to handle. Even the suspicion of mechanical failure felt like our biggest fears were on the verge of being realized, the trip sabotaged and the record forfeited. When you expect things to go wrong like this, even small problems start to weigh heavy on your mental state

Neither Amy nor I had any patience to spare and when Amy started getting mad, I got mad back. I had been noticing her shortened fuse particularly at the end of each day when, tired after a full eight hours on the bike, it felt like she was becoming more and more impatient with even small annoyances. I wasn't happy either with the prospect of continued breakdowns in the desert. We still had more than a week left in Xinjiang followed by as much as a month through the even more remote Tibet, all of which compounded concerns about the quality of the bike. I was stressed with trying to figure out what was wrong and felt that getting mad at something I had no control over was counterproductive. So with no idea what the problem with the bike was and still a day's ride away from the only CFMoto affiliated shop in Western China, I got mad at the only thing left that I felt I could control: Amy!

When you travel for long periods of time with another person, particularly someone you're close to, little things can start to crawl under your skin. Small irritations fester and mutate in your mind. Long hours on the road with nothing but our own thoughts meant plenty of opportunities to play out hypothetical arguments. Not the best environment for fostering a healthy relationship. Amy and I were literally in full contact with each other, front-to-back, 24/7. While we had made a great team and already accomplished so much together, it can become easy to dwell on things that normally might go unnoticed or blow over relatively quickly.

So with tensions now boiled over, surrounded by the clay homes on the dusty fringe of this remote desert town, Amy and I started to let loose on each other. I got mad about her attitude, she got mad at my tone. Blame was thrown around. Past, smaller fights were brought up. Tallies of former transgressions were counted in contemptuous retribution. There was little chance that the few people that did pass by could understand what we were saying, so we made no efforts to control either our volume or language. There was no holding back. Sometimes when the going gets tough… you just need to scream a little.

There was a sense of claustrophobia about our situation. We were stuck in the middle of nowhere, our transportation was broken, and the person we were yelling at was the only familiar face for thousands of miles. There was no storming off, no going for a walk around the block, and no grabbing a drink with friends. After going a couple rounds and no resolution in sight, we got tired and moved to sulking. I paced nearby with a camera, taking photos of passersby, while Amy sat against a wall trying to let the emotions burn off. We cooled down as much as possible and waited for the motorcycle to do the same. Blowing off some steam had helped, but Amy was still icy with me when we got back on the bike. Luckily, waiting for us in town, there would be an opportunity to further diffuse tensions.

Since Manzhouli, almost three weeks ago in the northern reaches of Inner Mongolia, we had been keeping in touch with Lao Lao, the Chinese bohemian we'd met at the Russian border. He was still traveling around by scooter and we'd stayed in touch via WeChat, the popular Chinese instant messaging app. As we followed each other's progress, we found that we were going to be in Turpan at the same time. A familiar face is one of those happy experiences that you can take for granted in "normal" life. On the road though, it can be a remarkably comforting thing. Being able to meet up with someone that we knew, even if briefly, was refreshing. We only appreciated how refreshing when Lao Lao arrived with a knock at our door, hair wrapped and wearing an ear-to-ear smile, allowing Amy and I to put the earlier fight behind us.

We all went out for a street dinner together, joined by another traveler, a woman from Hong Kong traveling solo and staying at the same hostel as Lao Lao. Over lamb kebab and some delicious cumin-seasoned, roasted Xinjiang flatbread we talked about our trips and everything that had happened since Manzhouli.

Not long after we moved back south, Lao Lao had found himself somehow "accidentally" wandering across the border and into Russia. He never managed to get approval from the consulate to enter with his scooter. However, one day, while driving around aimlessly he had somehow managed to stumble into a town which he soon discovered was Russian. The Han merchants and Mandarin characters on street signs had inexplicably transformed into white Europeans and Cyrillic writing. According to Lao Lao's account, this happened while just driving on the road, no customs or border patrol, just in one country one minute and onto another the next. He managed to even go back a couple times, using Manzhouli as his base of operations each night after day-long Russian excursions.

Obviously it wasn't worth the risk to travel across the whole country having entered illegally, so he eventually gave up on his plans to ride across Russia towards Western Europe. From the top of Inner Mongolia he traveled west across China instead, taking a much more direct route than we had before eventually making it to Turpan. He was going to try and cross one more time, attempting the border into Western Mongolia, and from there see if it would be easier to get into Russia. If that didn't work, it would be back to Shanghai for him. Illegal border crossings and cross-country driving through deserts and rain storms, all on a tiny, gas-powered scooter. It was an impressive account and the indomitable gaiety with which he recounted it made for great company.

***

Amy and I had some prior experience with sandstorms before the trip. Beijing, being in relatively close proximity to the Gobi desert in Inner Mongolia, occasionally got them in Spring when seasonal winds swept down from the North. My first apartment in China was on the 27th floor and provided impressive views of approaching storms. Giant clouds of yellow and brown sediment could be seen from a few miles off as the sands descended on the city. It made for a dramatic sight, but, while visually imposing, they ultimately were little more than an inconvenience. Visibility was about the same as if the pollution were high and eye and mouth protection were handy if going outside, but otherwise, the only lingering damage was a thin layer of sand and dust left across parked cars.

The storm we experienced at Aiding Lake was nothing like that. In contrast to Beijing, which has some surrounding vegetation and mountains and is still a couple hundred miles off from the desert, Aiding is in the middle of a flat, open depression on the edges of one. Because of the dip of the Turpan Depression and the volatile desert temperature changes, the wind coming down through the bottom of the basin reaches extreme velocities. It's like a vacuum sucking the air down from the higher plains. Since the whole area is predominantly barren desert, a huge amount of sand gets picked up along the way. This all makes for extremely inhospitable conditions.

The actual lake at the base of the depression is little more than a shallow pond in the middle of an endless wasteland. About 30 miles outside of the city, it is advertised as an official tourist spot with an entrance fee, visitors center, and a structure marking the low point. We left when it was still dark out, hoping to catch the sunrise (and also having the practical justification of wanting to avoid the hottest part of the day given our recent mechanical problems). Most of the approach was through desert and small villages. We drove through the sleepy hamlets of clay huts as sunlight began to spread early stirrings of life through the valley. Riding past, I began to notice that many of the buildings had people, some entire families, sleeping out front in the doorways and courtyards. Lined up in rows on the stone floors with nothing but simple carpets to cover them, my guess was that, in the absence of air conditioning, this was a temperature control strategy. Soon, even these buildings peeled away. We put the villages behind us and drove on into the desert towards the bottom of the Turpan Depression.

The tickets were cheap, less than $2 paid at a toll booth in the middle of empty desert on a two-laned road still ten miles from the lake. Three guards lay across the road, sleeping on the asphalt. One stood up with heavy eyelids to take our fee. We drove the rest of the way and found the visitors center comprised of two abandoned, single-story buildings. They stood in a V-shape, funneling traffic back out to the road. Sand-colored, they blended in with the yellow background. The winds were vicious and became more intense as we got closer to the lake. I had trouble walking straight and Amy could barely stand as we wandered around the paved lot. There were some markers showing the altitudes of various cities and landmarks around the world and we took some photos before deciding we'd had enough and getting back on the bike.[45]

---

[45]   There is a very entertaining photo that Amy and I took of ourselves at this spot just as the wind was really starting to pick up. With the tepid waters of Aiding behind us, I'm smiling in almost maniacal amusement at the high winds. Amy on the other hand was not amused. It may have partially been the wind blowing sand in her face, but her expression is one of obvious displeasure. We posted the photos from Xinjiang on Facebook a few days later and a friend of ours left a comment on the picture which the succinct description: "Buck looks like a crazy man who kidnapped you".

With the exception of the heavy wind, neither Amy nor I suspected that a storm was coming. Putting the lake behind us, the wind was strong but didn't feel intolerable. Conditions worsened though as the visitors center disappeared behind us. Soon we were completely engulfed by sand. With each minute that we moved farther down the road, the orange cloud whipping around us got thicker. For the first time on a motorcycle, I felt like we were in real danger from how hard the wind was buffeting us from side to side. I was barely able to keep the bike upright. The wind was brutally trying to push us off the pavement, and I was going less than 20mph. I stopped the bike and turned my head to Amy.

"What do you think we should do?" I screamed through my helmet.

"WHAT?" She yelled back. The howling from the wind and the sand scraping across our helmets was so loud now that we could barely hear each other.

"Do you want to risk it and keep going towards the ticket booth," I yelled even louder, "or should we just turn back?"

"I'm not sure," Amy said, sounding pretty nervous now. "This is pretty bad!"

"Yeah, I know. I think we're barely halfway down this road. The storm is just getting worse!"

Sand was whipping around us in a maniacal frenzy. The view on all sides was completely obscured. We had no idea how far we'd come or how far we had to go until the next shelter, and the storm seemed to be getting worse. The safest course seemed to be to turn back and take cover in the abandoned visitor's center until the storm passed.

Managing to stay upright on the way back to the lake, we found the area to be subdued in comparison to the maelstrom we'd just come back from. I tucked the bike into a corner behind one of the two abandoned buildings. I was nervous about sand gumming up the works and wanted to avoid any more unnecessary damage to the machinery. We grabbed some gear and snacks from the bike and took shelter in the front porch area of the building. Amy and I wrapped our faces in the Buff head wraps we traveled with, imitating what seemed appropriate for desert peoples.

We spent nearly two hours waiting out the storm. Swirling sand enshrouded the area in a protective bubble, a tiny safe haven in the middle of the hostile desert. I killed time wandering around the visitor center buildings. Yellow dust from past storms permeated every crevice of the creaky wooden structures. There were hallways leading through to different rooms and offices. Several of the doors had been left unlocked, which I hesitantly tested in my exploration of the compound. The wind whistled through the cracks of the building like a flute, a high-pitched, melodious hum playing in the background as the doors creaked open. With each door, expectations of hand prints on the walls or signs of past tragedies floated through my mind. The reality of course was more mundane. Most of the rooms were left bare, an odd bench or knocked-over chair the only hint of past habitation.

In the end, Amy and I curled up on the porch, tired from our dawn wake-up. Our heads still wrapped in our scarves, we did our best to nap as we waited for the passing of the storm. I woke up an hour later to the howling of the wind and found visibility had improved. I woke Amy, and we were starting to groggily pack up our stuff when two vehicles clanked down the road towards the visitors center. One, it turned out, was a security guard. Approaching in a small sedan, he pulled up next to one of the buildings and disappeared inside. Apparently, not all of the buildings were out of use. The other driver was a local farmer or worker on a motorcycle trailer, making a delivery of some kind for the security guard.

Both men informed us that the road was now safe to pass. When we told them our plan to push on to Urumqi however, they cautioned against it and advised we wait a day. They explained that a storm like this usually signaled a 12 to 24 hour period of high winds across the whole area of flatlands within our 200-mile radius. We were not eager to endure any more storms. Not knowing if we'd be as lucky to find shelter a second time, we opted to follow the men's advice and wait a day before pushing on. So with that, we dusted off the bike and our gear and cruised down the now clear desert road across the 30 miles back to the city.

In contradiction to the Aiding security guard, several people in Turpan actually told us before we left that they didn't think the crossing was possible by motorcycle at all. But, with our tires wearing thin and each moment spent idle at an intersection the potential for a frozen bike, we had no choice but to push on to Urumqi.

Even after waiting a day to make the 100-mile journey, the wind was terrifying to ride through. I couldn't believe that these were the conditions we were told were improved. Driving through the windy corridor, we found a forest of turbines erected to utilize the wild kinetic energy buffeting us around the road. The Da Ban Cheng Wind Farm is actually one of the largest wind generation plants in the world. At the time, it ranked in the top ten by capacity (around 500 megawatts per year and an installed capacity of 1,250 megawatts). It stretches for 50 miles (over 80km) in the area east of Urumqi and experiences, on average, 100 days per year of level 8 gale force winds or above (40+mph), with highs of 90mph. For comparison, Hurricane Sandy which hit the east coast of the U.S. in 2012 had gusts between 60–90mph.

While driving through this wind corridor, I frequently had to bring the speed of the bike way down in an effort to keep from getting tossed into other lanes. My biggest concern was getting thrown into the axles of a passing truck or off the highway entirely by a sudden sideways thrust. It felt strange going so slowly on wide open desert highway, but the force of the wind made sure it was far from boring. I developed a strategy for taking breaks without needing to stop. I would ride up to a large eighteen-wheeler that was maintaining a decent speed and ride on its downwind face. The sheer size of the trucks was enough to block out most of the wind. This gave Amy and I a couple minutes' respite, an opportunity to relax our perpetually tensed muscles. If I decided to go ahead of the truck again though, as soon we overtook, the wind would smack us full-on on our side, pushing us onto the shoulder until I leaned back in to compensate.

Despite this, it didn't take us long to arrive at Urumqi, the capital of Xinjiang province and its largest city by population. After crossing the Da Ban Cheng valley, we went through a mountain gorge that blocked the winds and we again managed to reach comfortable cruising speeds.

We were greeted at the city limits by a heavy police presence. Each vehicle had to pass through a checkpoint, with many, especially the delivery vans and "bread cars", getting thoroughly searched. The political instability of the Xinjiang Uyghur Autonomous Region is relatively well known. The province had been a concern of ours since starting to plan the trip, worried that, as foreigners, we might encounter difficulties traveling alone. Much of the instability was the result of local separatist movements, predominantly Uyghur led. These had both political and religious motivations (Uyghurs are the second largest Muslim population in China after the Hui). Mostly these were expressed in the form of small protests but there had been some high-profile events including the bombing of government buildings and rioting. Two foreigners traveling alone by motorcycle would no doubt attract some level of extra attention given the sensitivity of the region. Packing about half a dozen cameras certainly wouldn't help either. The cop on the other side of the checkpoint asked for my license and passport, which I nervously handed over. Amy and I had decided before crossing to detach the video camera mounted on my helmet and hide it away. The cop looked back up at me to confirm the identification. After a short pause he held out his hand, returning the documents and flagging us on with a disinterested wave.

Since our fight a couple days before, Amy and I had managed to go without another incidence of the motorcycle seizing up. The wind had no doubt played a factor in keeping the bike cool as we made our way across the valley, but now the stop-and-go city traffic and the heat of the midday sun were taking their toll. In the middle of a busy eight-lane city street, the throttle became unresponsive and, right on cue, the bike once again froze into place.

By now used to the routine, Amy and I hopped off the bike and hurriedly emptied several bottles of water over the bike's engine and wheels to try and cool it down. When it finally regained mobility, the two of us rolled the bike off to the side of the road and up onto a sidewalk under some shade near a bus stop, wanting to let it cool some more before pushing on again. It just needed to last a few more miles and we would be at the CFMoto shop.

There was no way we could keep on going with our bike like this. We still had at least another week through the hot deserts of Xinjiang and then after that we would be trekking up into the mountains of Tibet. We had around a month of potential sand and snow storms, one desert and two high-altitude mountain ranges, all in areas that would be far more remote than anything we'd seen so far. The only place after Urumqi equipped to do repairs on a CFMoto was in Lhasa, still weeks away. We would have to know with a high level of certainty that the bike would be up for the challenge. This was not something we had learned to expect from Chinese mechanics.

As we had been riding with the stress of not knowing what was wrong with our motorcycle these past couple days, I thought to myself about what I might be able to do to help fix the problem. As easy as it was to put the blame on others, I had to admit that this was our trip, our motorcycle, and our problem. The people we went to for help, even Fang Shujian, had little to nothing at stake and I shouldn't expect them to feel as invested in the state of our motorcycle as we were. As we approached the mechanic's shop in Urumqi, I decided that I was going to be as involved as I could be with our next maintenance check. I planned to ask questions, look over shoulders while they worked, and generally make sure the pressure was clearly communicated. Our biggest challenges of the trip were still ahead of us, and regardless of our concerns, this was the motorcycle that would be taking us through them. It would need to be ready for what we had coming, with serious consequences if it wasn't, and ultimately it was my responsibility to make sure that happened.

With hours left alone to think about it (along with many other non-sequiturs), I couldn't ignore the hundreds of *"bu tai"*, "patch tire", signs I'd been seeing on the road since Beijing. The hypothesis I eventually came up with was that it was a reflection of the Chinese tendency towards a reparative rather than preventative approach towards goods and services (probably best expressed in the reputation for poor quality of "Made in China" products). In the U.S., drivers (including truckers) tend to pay close attention to the care and long-term health of their vehicles. Checking tire pressure, changing the oil regularly, spending a little extra for quality parts, etc. are all a part of the culture around driving as well as our general consumer habits. There is a comfort that comes with buying for quality and knowing that what you're purchasing will last for a longer time. Chinese consumers tend to be much more focused on bargains and less on long-term reliability. They are also distrustful of claims of quality, particularly of domestic made goods.

One side effect of this is that there seems to be a wide availability of expert tinkerers. Throughout the country we found not just tire repair shops but mechanics, amateur plumbers, even welders on almost every block available to fix things that were bound to break with reliable consistency.

It is also interesting to note that in contrast to mechanics in the West who almost always charge for their service by the hour, Chinese mechanics usually charge according to the parts used. Conceptually this is important because as a customer you're not paying for their service and so it's not where you will look for value. The rip-offs are also reversed. In the U.S., mechanics are known to charge for extra services you may not need. In China, the thing to watch out for is being overcharged for faulty or used parts.

Chapter 9 – Meet the Competition

Xinjiang quickly became one of our favorite provinces for food. The style is unique in China. Moving away from the East Asian traditions, it's more closely related to those of its Turkic neighbors to the west[46]. The usual staples of noodles, rice, and dumplings are rare outside of the Han or Hui neighborhoods, as is pork. Vegetables too are scarce. Instead, dishes are dominated almost entirely by mutton. Because of Uyghur migration to the first tier cities on the east coast, we'd already had some exposure to Xinjiang food, but it was never this fresh. Lamb kebabs or "chua'r" are popular on the streets of Beijing. Particularly during the summer months, groups of foreigners and Chinese alike can be found sitting on miniature stools, piles of metal skewers and empty beer bottles littering the small tables outside of Xinjiang restaurants. One of our favorite dishes was what I have heard Chinese friends and Uyghur waiters refer to as "Chinese Pizza", *nang bao rou*. Nang is a kind of Turkic flatbread popular in Xinjiang dishes. "*Boa rou*" simply means "enveloped by meat". The cumin-seasoned flatbread sits under a small pile of stewed mutton, onion, and green pepper, soaking up the juices of its toppings.

Even the Han meals came with their own local twist. Our first meal in Urumqi was a simple bowl of noodles. After ordering our lunch off of the menu, the motherly Han waitress asked if we would like *da rou* to accompany the dish. I thought for a second about what

---

[46] As of 2014, the population of the Xinjiang Uyghur Autonomous Region was 45% Uyghur and 40% Han Chinese, with the remaining 15% composed of a mix of 13 other ethnic groups, primarily Kazakh, Mongolian, and Hui. The Uyghur people are much more closely related to those in the region's neighboring countries like Kazakhstan and Kyrgyzstan, not just in food and appearance but also language and religion. A majority of the population in the province are Sunni Muslims, the most prominent group of which are the Uyghurs, with some Shiite populations in the mountainous regions of Pamir and Tian Shan.

those characters could mean and all I could come up with was "big meat". It sounded like something worth trying and so Amy and I asked her to add it to our order. After the noodles and our two cold beers came out, the waitress followed with a metal platter, two giant pieces of meat laid on top. She put the platter down on the table and, smiling, handed us two plastic gloves. Not wanting to make a cultural faux pas, I looked around to confirm what the gloves were for. Nearby at another table a large Han gentleman sat on a stool across the sidewalk from us. Shirt familiarly half-rolled up over his stomach, he had his "big meat" in one gloved hand and chopsticks for the noodles in his other.[47] It was a style of eating I felt pretty confident I could handle.

Luckily our bike had no further incidents after arriving in Urumqi and our anxious search for the CFMoto shop eventually led us to a heavily industrialized district. The provincial capital is a young city by Chinese standards, set up by the Tang Dynasty over 1,300 years ago as a tax collection point on the Silk Road. Relatively desolate until the Qing Dynasty conquered and began expanding the area in the late 18th century, today it is primarily an industrial and commercial hub. The cultural influences have been left to older Uyghur cities such as Kashgar in the south. As a result, our motivations for being in Urumqi were entirely practical: get our bike fixed and get ready for the tough roads ahead in Southern Xinjiang and Western Tibet.

Wide, heavily trafficked roads, gas stations, and two industrial malls, there was nothing cultural about where we would find the mechanic. The malls were filled with endless stalls selling all types of mechanical equipment. In my search for motorcycle repairs I noted

---

[47]   We found out later that the big meat was actually pork. Because most of the local population in Xinjiang are observant Muslims and follow Halal dietary practices, pork is forbidden to them. Since many of the Han that live in Xinjiang are relatively recent migrants, in an attempt not to offend the local culture while still continuing to enjoy their favorite meat type, pork is often simply referred to as "da rou".

signs for companies such as "Shanghai General Electric Welding Machine Company", "Specialty Diesel Engine Generator Group", and "The Tebian Electric Cable Chain Distributors", many advertised in Russian as well as Chinese. It was an impressive conglomeration of sales outlets, and there was a feeling of perusing the rural Chinese equivalent of a modern American mall. Rather than the American display of flashy consumerism though it was the dirty, mechanical expression of China's manufacturing industrial complex.

Among all of this was the "CFMoto / Xinyuan Motorcycle Repairs and Dealership Store". I ultimately found it on the second floor of one of the malls, led there by a slim, spiky-haired Han mechanic who took me up in a freight elevator. The repairs wouldn't be started until the following day, so after explaining what we'd need done, Amy and I left to find a place to stay. With my new resolve to play a more hands-on role in the repairs and maintenance, we chose a hotel in between the industrial malls.

Despite the familiar monotone of our surroundings, we did manage to have one interesting cultural excursion while in Urumqi when looking for dinner on our first night. Turning the corner from our hotel, in an area where only an hour before there had been nothing but dust covered cars, we found the street lined instead with food stands. The impromptu bazaar ran the full length of the oversized city block. While not officially blocked from traffic, either side was so crowded with pedestrians and a wide array of perishable goodies that it made passing infeasible.

Amy and I strolled casually among the stalls, stopping to peruse local specialties that caught our eye for dinner or otherwise. We saw a few butcher shops whose caretakers lazily swatted at flies that tried to land on the slabs of meat hanging by ropes in front. A farmer with calloused hands and dusty, ill-fitting clothes gave us a wide smile of crooked, tea-stained teeth as we stopped to take a picture. Several dozen burlap sacks were laid out in front of him on a blanket in columns. Spread open at the tops, they presented an array of different colored dried fruits, nuts, and spices creating a beautiful mosaic of East and Central Asian cooking ingredients. We found another man grinding dried beans and herbs, packaging his freshly produced spices for people to buy right there on the street. Many had retro-fitted their rust-covered trucks and bread cars to not just sell but also produce their goods, like the mobile bread-oven that churned out baked goods or the chestnut roaster with coals glowing red from the back of its owner's freight truck.

We walked the full length of the market, about 15 minutes, before Amy and I settled on something for dinner. At the end of the street we found a cart selling thin pancakes, wrapped around stuffings of your choice (sweet, sour, savory, or spicy) and then deep-fried. Behind the cart as we waited, I noticed another innovative commercial contraption – a mobile chicken coop – and while our food was being prepared, Amy and I became the unwitting audience to the slaughter and butchering of a live chicken. High enough for a person to stand and with several chickens roosting inside, the coop was built around the open bed of a pickup truck, a large cage enveloping the back. In the time we were there, the woman who ran the mobile coop had received an order and gone about preparing the meat. She was already de-feathering the poultry as our pancakes were dipped in the burning oil. By the time I paid for our meal, viscous red could be seen dripping from the truck onto the street below.

We ended up taking two full days off in Urumqi while we waited for the repairs on the bike to finish. I spent a good part of those days in the cavernous upper floors of the industrial mall with the two men helping with our bike. The skinny Han man who helped me find the shop was meek. He spoke quietly, avoided eye contact, and had a lackluster smile. His partner was the complete opposite though and dominated the relationship. A tall, jovial, mustached Uyghur man, he was balding and had a jolly paunch that pressed tightly against his fading imitation polo t-shirt. His words were loud and confident, but he was engaging and fun talk to. He had a curious background too, specifically his motorcycle credentials which included experience as a competitive racer in the Xinjiang–Gansu dirt bike racing circuit.

While I had a hard time envisioning his figure navigating the jumps and twists of a race track on the small frame of a dirt bike, he did turn out to be the most competent and confident mechanic I'd worked with in China. He easily walked me through all questions I had about the bike, explaining how to repair flats and check the wear in different parts around the machine. He even taught me how to make a makeshift fuse using old copper wire from a stripped cable in case we ran out of spares. Best of all, he was able to easily diagnose the problem of our freezing motorcycle.

To find the problem, I took the bike out onto the highway and the two mechanics followed me in the shop's bread car. We navigated our way through traffic until the issue resurfaced. As the now familiar quicksand-like feeling began to reach up through the controls, I pulled over onto the shoulder of the elevated highway. Farther ahead, the bread car also stopped and the Uyghur mechanic popped out from the passenger side. He jogged down the road towards me and my initial reaction was despair – I couldn't believe the bike had broken down again so quickly. Frustrated and annoyed, I launched into an embittered explanation of the circumstances surrounding the problem. He ignored me though and went straight to the back wheel. Within 20 seconds, he popped back up and, with a pensive but confident grimace, announced that he believed he'd found the problem. He hurriedly waddled back to his truck and returned with some tools. After just a minute of work, he declared the problem resolved, which we confirmed with a light push forward that met no resistance.

Apparently what had happened was that the last time we'd had our brakes installed, back in Yinchuan, they had been put on too tightly.

When the heat of the desert and frequent braking caused the metal pieces to expand (as they should by design), the brake plate was getting so compressed in between the two pads that it locked up the wheel, stopping the bike entirely. All we had to do was loosen the brakes and the bike was mobile again. The current brakes had been chewed up as a result of the oversight though, so the pads, along with the rest of the braking system would need to be replaced. All of that trouble through days of crossing the desert, not to mention the stress it had added to my and Amy's relationship, could have been avoided if only our brakes had been put in properly. It was a fantastic relief however to know that the problem had been identified and was serviceable.

In addition to switching out the brakes, we had an oil change, checked the spark plugs and fuses, and got our first new tires in 6,000 miles. I checked up on the repairs frequently, calling in to the shop when I wasn't actually there in person. The Uyghur mechanic hypothesized that our blown fuses were a result of us charging devices with too high amperages on our bike's two cigarette lighters. He advised using these sparingly in the future, a shame considering how many fewer charging opportunities we'd have for the next couple months.

As mentioned earlier, I'm not a big fan of staying in one place for too long. Normally, I would have become antsy after two days off. Our rest in Urumqi though was time well spent. After a couple weeks in the desert, our gear was a little worse for wear, including one camera that had broken during the sandstorm in Turpan. We needed extra food for the long stretches between rest stops in the desert, not to mention the Himalayas coming up, and we needed to re-up on some repair and maintenance equipment. Urumqi more than anything else was about getting peace of mind before going forward.

I had not yet met the owner of the CFMoto shop in Urumqi, so when I went to pick up the bike, I was compelled by the Uyghur mechanic to go up to the company offices and finally meet "The Boss" before we could leave the city. As with Boss Li back in Jiayuguan, The Boss (no last name this time, just "The Boss") was eager to meet the foreigners traveling around China whose bike his mechanics had been working on. He invited me, via a message from the Uyghur, to tea in his office. Once the finishing touches on the bike were done, I followed the two mechanics up another level of the cavernous halls.

We arrived in the sparsely populated, fluorescent-lit showroom in the upper floors of the industrial complex. I was led to the back and given a seat on a couch where The Boss met us moments later. Up to that point, the Uyghur had been the clear alpha in our exchanges. He spoke with the most confidence and led the conversations with his Han colleague. Over tea with The Boss however, this position was relinquished. The jocular man smoothly transitioned from his jovial and confident mannerisms, becoming quiet and subdued as he deferred the role to his superior.

Chinese tend to be very hierarchical. It is a Confucian-esque habit that carries over even in casual, social situations. For example, whenever you're at a meal or having tea, the head of the group will traditionally sit facing the door. Drinking won't start until this head figure has initiated the first "cheers", and the same is usually true of starting a meal too. More subtly though, if you follow the flow of conversation, this person is the one who dictates its path. You very rarely have side conversations, and if someone else starts up a new line of discussion it is usually as a tangent to the main topic. What's fascinating about this however is that despite how traditional and formal it can feel, it is not necessarily gender-specific. Though the role is typically held by the most dominant male, it is not unreasonable for a woman to assume the role too, usually a family matriarch or high-ranking company manager. I've witnessed this dynamic in everything from business meetings to family gatherings and even meals with friends.

While I had been looking forward to an early start out of Urumqi, the meeting with The Boss turned out to be very useful despite the delay it caused. Including the two mechanics and another friend of The Boss, there were five of us sitting around the (very formal) tea-serving table. Everyone there rode motorcycles and was familiar with the roads in the region. From The Boss, and confirmed by his colleagues, I learned that our way towards Kashgar was not as straightforward as just taking the National Highway south. We had two choices. The first, and the one backed up by the GPS, was to ride back the way we came and through the Dabancheng wind farm, one hundred miles to Turpan. From there we could then turn off onto a well-paved provincial road southeast. Option two was to go directly south out of Urumqi where, almost immediately past the city limits, the road launched high up into a mountain range, proceeding for the next 65 miles on unpaved, landslide-prone switchbacks. This would take us through extremely remote countryside and into a sparsely populated area, eventually going over a 15,000 foot, glacier-lined mountain pass.

I felt like I was standing at the crossroads of an old-school Oregon Trail-style computer game. It was very exciting. We had two choices: backtrack through known but taxing wind corridor or attempt a difficult, unfamiliar and potentially dangerous path with spectacular scenery judging from The Boss' photos. It was an opportunity for us to choose our own adventure. After tea, I went back to the hotel to discuss the options with Amy.

I was a bit apprehensive of going on gravel roads at high altitude just as we were breaking in our new tires. We couldn't know for sure the quality of the repairs until we'd tried out the bike for a couple days. New brakes and tires in particular can be sensitive at first and should be worn in. Under these conditions, going back to Turpan first seemed like the safest option. On the other hand, I've never liked to backtrack. I always find it tiresome, almost counterproductive, to go back over ground already covered. Between this and Amy's reluctance to reexperience the brutal winds of Dabancheng, we decided to opt in to the unknown.

The ride south turned out to be just as impressive as I'd hoped. In just one afternoon we went from an altitude of less than 3,000 feet to 15,000. As promised, the pavement didn't last long after we left the outer rings of the city but the scenery was rewarding as we switchbacked up through gorges and passes. The gravel road hugged the sides of mountains on one side and we climbed with precipitous drop-offs to the other. There was very little traffic. We saw a few sedans and bread cars, but mostly it was freight trucks rumbling past, pushing us against the side of the mountain and kicking gravel up into our faces. Because sundown was only a few hours away, we also passed several shepherds, some mounted and others on foot, coming down off the mountains with their flocks.

The bike seemed to be holding up without any problems. I took my time on the loose gravel and, though the steep drops and lack of guardrails were nerve-wracking, everything seemed to be going well. The biggest challenges had to do with the factors we had no control over. Hours of bullying trucks and unpredictable livestock left Amy's and my muscles tense and exhausted. Scarier still was when we only learned of risks we'd been facing after the fact. On the final and longest stretch of switchbacks for example, we passed by several mounds of recently cleared rubble, the refuse of recent landslides, until finally catching up with the scooper truck responsible. Amy and I dismounted at the site and waited for a clearing to be made. Incredibly, rather than being paired with a dump truck or packing the loose rocks on the roadside, the earth mover was simply dumping each scoop off the side of the road, right above the switchbacks we'd just climbed.

On one flat stretch through a valley, Amy and I found ourselves trailing a couple of other bikers. Like us, they seemed to be foolishly attempting the glacier-lined pass still ahead in the last hour of daylight. Plastic-bag-wrapped luggage gripped haphazardly with bungee cords onto their dust and oil caked bikes, they appeared to be fellow road warriors out for the long haul. In the final valley before the pass, they stopped for a break and I pulled up behind to say hi. As we all removed our helmets, I was surprised to find a foreigner and Chinese traveling as a pair. Sean, a tall, lanky Brit with a thick London accent, and Slash, his more subdued Chinese riding companion (named after the Guns N' Roses guitarist), had ridden together from Chongqing.[48] Both young, also in their mid-to-late-20s and wearing ragged gear (Sean didn't even have a riding jacket but instead just an old white sweater to keep warm in the high altitude), they were in good spirits despite the tough roads. They each had their own 250cc dual-sport bike from the Chongqing-based company, Motorhead, that was sponsoring their trip. All smiles, the adrenaline of adventure in their eyes, they leaned against their bikes and enjoyed a smoke break before the final climb as we all introduced ourselves.

It was starting to get cold as we gained altitude and the sun made it's way down behind the ridgeline. Our late start from Urumqi and bad roads meant that we wouldn't make it the full 60 miles to the next town, but we had to get over the pass to have any chance of even finding a place to camp. The four of us on our three bikes made it past the glacier and down to the valley on the other side just after dark. After the final switchback we found our way by the beams of our

---

[48]   Chongqing is one of the four municipality-level provinces in the country and is located in southwest China to the east of Sichuan province. It is also known as the motorcycle capital of China, home to the majority of the country's motorcycle manufacturing capacity, and estimated at 50% of the entire world's motorcycle production. In 2013, over 8 million motorcycles were produced in the city with 133 motorcycle manufacturing companies located there. The annual CIMA motorcycle exhibition, the one CFMoto was compelling us to attend in October, is hosted in Chongqing each year.

headlights to a small roadside station, just a couple yurts, a trailer with dorms for road workers, and a small farmyard where they kept chickens and a young cow. We found one of the caretakers and asked about camping. He gestured casually, waving towards the yard and indicated we were free to set up camp there provided we could find some space in between the cow paddies.

That night, still high up in the mountains, was the coldest night we'd had out so far, the temperature dipping to freezing. Still with our warm weather sleeping bags, Amy and I cuddled close in our tent to keep warm. The remote countryside, grand scenery, even the challenges of the bad roads and freezing temperatures were all part of what I was looking forward to entering this part of the country, and I drifted off with a smile. Only a couple thousand miles away now, I couldn't wait for more in Western Tibet.

We rode with Sean and Slash for a few days after that, both of us targeting Kashgar. We experienced some pretty wild climate changes along the way. Within about a 24-hour period we went from a glacier in the mountains back to desert again. Descending from the Tianshan range, the area at its base was relatively lush. Greenery flowed along the ridges and wild sunflowers lined the road. As we began hitting the border of the Taklamakan however, the terrain flattened, everything dried out, and we were sweating in our riding gear once more.

Bositeng Lake sits on the western edge of the desert, two days from Urumqi, and is one of the largest lakes in China. When we arrived, we explored the scattered collection of rundown lakeside resorts that surrounded it thinking it would be a nice opportunity to spend the night. The four of us, Amy, Sean, Slash and I, split a villa at one of the resorts and found that the Bositeng getaways were but a shadow of what they attempted to advertise. Looking at the moldy, battered buildings, one got the sense of what the original intention might have been, but somewhere along the way the money and enthusiasm had clearly dried up. Everything was broken from years of neglect and mismanagement. The pathway from the concierge to our villa was caked in dead frogs. The inside of our rental was most disappointing, with mold advancing along the ceilings, overgrown weeds out front, and less-than-inspiring wiring hanging from the walls. The thought was there, and the deserted beach by the lake made for a beautiful sunset swim, but in the middle of this land-bound, autonomous region of China's most western reaches there was apparently no market for, and thus no motivation to maintain, this Potemkin Adirondack village.

Because our bike was less agile than the enduro-styled Motorheads, Amy and I mostly leap-frogged with Sean and Slash. We didn't quite ride together in formation, but criss-crossed as we progressed on our southerly route around the northern borders of the desert. On open highways Amy and I could hit a higher top speed. On the rougher roads though, Sean and Slash on their dual-sports could ride more comfortably, and, because they were riding solo, they also had better endurance and didn't stop as often.

One afternoon, after a day and a half traveling separately, we ran into each other again during a long spell of desert highway. It had been about 150 miles without any operational gas stations and I was getting worried about how much we had left. Managing our speed in order to conserve gas, we all stuck together and tried to find somewhere to fill up. With our indicator already blinking empty for at least a quarter of an hour, we finally found an open station off the opposite side of the road. With three bikes to fill up, it took several trips with the designated watering can before all of us were topped back up. Just as we were about to head off again though, one of the attendants ran up to us from the station, nervously shouting something at us from across the lot. As he got closer I caught the words for sandstorm and looked over my shoulder. I noticed a thickening haze over the highway and realized that he was warning us not to go back out yet. Waving his hand to urge us inside, he walked over and offered the station for shelter until the storm had passed.

Given the paranoid resistance usually encountered at gas stations, we were grateful for the gesture and moved the bikes to the front of the shop before going inside to wait out the storm. With sparsely stocked shelves and a noticeable lack of sand covering the inside of the station shop, these were much better conditions than Amy and I had had for our previous storm. The four of us all sat around a small table that had been provided for us and we reenergized ourselves with over-sweetened coffee and Oreo cookies from the shop.

We had been chatting casually, sharing stories from the road and anecdotes about life in China, when Sean all of a sudden got serious. This was out of character for him, which made it more remarkable and awkward. He kept his gaze down towards the table and avoided eye contact.

"So… Slash and I have something to tell you," he said in his thick, Cockney accent. "We're actually not just product testing for Motorhead."

When we'd first crossed paths south of Urumqi, "product testing" was the story they had told us about the purpose of their trip. It seemed a strange thing to lie about though, and an even stranger thing to be so awkward about.

"Ok…" I prodded suspiciously.

"Actually, we're trying to break the same Guinness World Record as you two."

My larynx dropped down into my stomach and I was left speechless. Amy must have had a similar reaction because neither of us had any immediate response except to stare blankly as the information sunk in.

In retrospect, the whole situation was amazing. The chances of our two trips intersecting like this seemed astronomically low. We had left from almost opposite ends of the country, traveling in different directions, starting two weeks apart and with different timelines. Of all the hundreds of thousands of miles of highway in the country, with us both going for the same record, we happened to meet on a remote and impractical stretch of road in the far west.

The odds though were not what was on my mind. All I could think about was the more than 12,000 miles we had left to cover and how we now would have the specter of competition looming over us. From the conversations we'd had, Sean and Slash appeared to have much more sympathetic and proactive support from their sponsors. With everything from media to mechanical repairs, Motorhead were the more agreeable partners. I was also intimidated by the prospect of their endurance as riders. They were two male riders mounted on separate dual-sport bikes that were much better suited than our highway bike for the rough roads of China.

Sean and Slash had heard about us before they'd even set out from Chongqing. Sean's dad worked in the motorcycle industry in China, writing and consulting as an English language expert for foreign companies. Even more remarkable, it turned out that Sean's dad and I had had previous correspondence. I'd written a couple articles the previous year about a trip Amy and I had done for a magazine he helped run in Chongqing. I'd reached out to the magazine again before we left from Beijing and let them know about our record attempt.

Sean explained to us how, with these advantages, he and Slash initially weren't even going to tell us about how they were going for the record. The plan was to happily let us go on, unaware that our attempt was at risk.

"You two seem cool though. We've liked traveling with you," Sean explained. "So we decided we wanted to let you know that we were also planning on breaking the record."

Amy and I both stayed silent, limiting our reactions to nodding where it seemed appropriate.

"We'll let you guys get the record first though before we break it," Sean said reassuringly. He continued, as if to console us, "Maybe we'll wait a few weeks before finishing." It felt like a cynical show of compassion and the assumption that the record was theirs to give in the first place came across as patronizing.

"We feel bad about the whole situation. We wanted to see if you'd be interested in visiting us at Slash's mum's. She lives in a city close to here and we're planning on stopping there for a few days."

The offer was very kind and the truth was that we had enjoyed traveling with them as well. Sean and Slash were good people and great company, and it was a relief to have others to talk to about more than the cost of our bike and its gas mileage. It also seemed a unique opportunity to stay with someone from the area. The olive branch diffused the situation and helped loosen our jaws. It was all out in the open now and worth putting behind us. We were still a couple thousand miles ahead in our newly discovered contest anyway, and Sean and Slash barking at our heels would serve as powerful motivation in the coming months! It didn't seem like anything worth slashing tires over, at least for the time being.

***

Sean grew up in Chongqing, moving with his dad from the UK when Sean was a kid. Getting involved in the industry in the early days, Sean's dad had made a name for himself as an English language expert on Chinese motorcycles. He often wrote about the industry for foreign and domestic publications, and also worked on several motorcycle-related business ventures. Through this and his own natural interest, Sean had had plenty of prior exposure to bikes, repairing and riding them around the Chongqing/Sichuan area for years. He first met Slash at an English school in Chongqing where they both taught. The idea of taking motorcycles around the country

180

first came up in conversation at work. This was just a year earlier. At the time, the pair were only casual acquaintances; Sean brought it up as just an interesting idea, and Slash had never even been on a motorcycle before.

The two of them made for a strangely compatible pairing of opposites. While Sean was loud and boisterous with wild gestures to pair with his emotive facial expressions, Slash was much more reserved. His English was some of the best I'd heard from a Chinese who'd never been abroad. He was soft-spoken, kind, and also remarkably tidy. Amy and I often caught him cleaning up after Sean (Amy and Slash were both big proponents of the indispensability of disinfectant wipes for life on the road). Where Slash was the one setting the alarms for the morning and making sure they packed up on time, Sean was more the type to ask for "ten more minutes!"

Sean and Slash were eager to make it to Aksu, where Slash's mom lived, so after the sandstorm they pushed on ahead. 24 hours later, we met up with them again among the urban sprawl of the dusty city of two and a half million. They had driven nearly five hundred miles the day before to get there and were still a bit fried from the effort. But when we met them, enthusiastically flagging us down from the side of the road, the prospect of a couple days' rest at home at least seemed to have them reenergized.

After dropping off our stuff and stretching our legs, Slash's mom and her boyfriend took the four of us out for lunch at a Chinese restaurant nearby. Over a local Xinjiang dish called *da pan ji* ("Big Plate Chicken"), we made small talk getting to know our hosts and a little more about the area. Slash's mom was a quiet Han woman with her hair tied up in a bun. She said little but beamed throughout the conversation, content just to have everyone there. After we'd eaten we said bye to the boyfriend, thanking him for the meal, and the four of us bikers went off to run some errands around town before heading back to the house for the evening.

We spent most of our time in Aksu in Slash's mom's living room. From early evening until past midnight we sat around the coffee table chewing on leftover Big Plate Chicken and going through a crate's worth of Tsingtao long-neck beers. It was a great bonding experience between two opposing teams. We exchanged our various China stories, what had brought us here and what our plans were, talked about our trips, how we'd come up with the ideas, problems we'd run into, and the routes we planned on taking.

For the four of us, that evening was just a good time spent with new friends, fellow weary travelers sharing battle stories. Slash's mom observed from her seat, occasionally getting up to refresh the bowls of fruits and nuts she'd laid out for us on the table. We spoke mostly English, since Sean's Chinese was limited and it was what we all felt most comfortable with. She seemed happy though just to be there, taking it all in whether she could follow along or not. As the conversation went on, and we dipped in and out of Chinese, Amy and I started to learn about Slash's story.

Even though he had met Sean in Chongqing, Slash, whose Chinese name is Zhang Ying Fa, was born in Dunhuang, Gansu province. A year after Slash was born, his dad moved west to Xinjiang to find factory work, leaving Slash and most of his family behind in Gansu. A year later, Slash's mom followed with their son, getting a job in the same coal power plant as her husband. The marriage didn't survive long past the move however, and, when Slash was just three years old, his parents split up. According to Slash, his family was traditional and the marriage between his mom and dad had been pre-arranged. The way he saw it, his parents never really loved each other in the first place. The distance from their families exacerbated the problems they had, and eventually the relationship disintegrated entirely.

Slash later described his dad to me as a mean and stubborn man. After his parents split up he was forced to stay with his dad and made to cut off all contact with his mom, an excommunication that persisted for the next 17 years. It wasn't until he was 20 years old and he'd moved away from home for college that they started talking again. I asked Slash why he chose to go to Chongqing for school and he told me that actually it had nothing specific to do with either the city or the university. All he wanted was to get as far away from home, and his dad, as possible. A random point on the map to escape bad memories and an oppressive household. Over the two decades that Slash lived with his dad in Xinjiang, his mother was never far away and even continued to work at the same coal plant as his father. Ironically, it took Slash moving two and a half thousand miles away to create the opportunity for he and his mother to grow close again.

We learned Slash's story in bits and pieces throughout our conversation that night. It was a sobering reality check, learning all of this after we'd already been invited into his mom's home. We had only even met Slash just a few days earlier. As we sat around talking, you could tell from his mom's face how happy she was to have her son home again. She told us how great it was to be able to meet some of his friends, and how it put her more at ease when thinking about him on this adventure around China. At one point she even started to tear up, choking on her words as she expressed her gratitude. Later, when Amy and I had pieced together the story, we realized how impactful this experience must have been for her. I've seen the look on my own mom's face after I've come back from a long time away, at school, traveling, or in China. It is a look of happiness unique to a mother whose child has returned to the nest. For Slash's mom though the emotions must have been overwhelming, amplified to an unimaginable degree. That night with the five of us sitting around her coffee table, chatting, and drinking beers, was the first time she had seen her son in over 20 years.

- Photos from Inner Mongolia to Kashgar -

Scan the QR code or visit the link below to see pictures from Part 2 of
The Great Ride of China

http://book.thegreatrideofchina.com/galleries/part-2

Visa Run to Kyrgyzstan

Visa frustrations are a fact of life in China that almost every expat will have to deal with at some point. Enforcement by the government can be sporadic, inconsistent, and unpredictable. During one stretch of time you can have hordes of foreign English teachers "working" unimpeded on long-term tourist visas. At other times, the priorities unexpectedly change, a statement is issued by the government, and all of a sudden you have to jump through hoops to get even a legitimate work visa.

The best visa you can get is undoubtedly the Z-visa for employment. This comes accompanied by a year-long residency permit allowing its holder to move in and out of the country at will for that time. Once you reach the end of the year, renewing is relatively painless. Enforcement during the application process though can be fickle. Outcomes vary depending on who's evaluating your application, the current state of employment in the country, the status of your employer, and your past work history. It also usually needs to be processed outside of the country. With the right connections, some cash, and a bit of creative paperwork though it's usually possible to push these through.

Around when I first started working in China, they began enforcing a 50-year-old rule originally meant protect local labor from competition. In the ensuing decades, this hadn't been much of a problem (immigrant labor being less of an issue when your borders are shut to most visitors) and so the law had been applied sparingly and discriminately. However, as China's economy has opened and grown, the dynamic has changed. By 2010, the rules requiring extensive proof that your job could not be done by a local were enforced with more enthusiasm again. This included things like proving you had two years of work experience in the industry you were applying to work in, the physical copy (no photocopies) of at least a bachelor's degree, and a full physical exam which included an EKG and drawing blood at an inspection station an hour outside of Beijing. In addition, a company was limited to how many Z-visas they could issue according to a ratio of how many Chinese employees they already had (around ten to one). Even with all this, your visa application could still be rejected without any justification as it gets passed around between the different government departments involved (namely labor, residency, and entry/exit).

Amy luckily had most of the year left on the Z-visa from her prior employer and so had nothing to worry about for the whole time we would be on the road. I, however, wasn't as fortunate. My L (tourist) visa was valid for multiple entries and exits from the country for a total of six months, but required me to cross a border every 90 days. Miss the deadline and I could be fined ¥500 per day (about $80) up to a maximum of ¥20,000, and potentially deported.

At our current pace, my 90 days would be up somewhere around Tibet or Qinghai. It would also land right in the middle of China's busiest travel season, the October National Holiday in the first week of October. This was not ideal for two reasons. One, it left me vulnerable to unforeseen delays at a time when we would be in remote areas, unable to get to an airport or border in time. Two, it would be much more expensive to travel internationally during the holiday.

Sean was also on a tourist visa. While we were traveling together he told me about a visa run he had made from Kashgar to the neighboring country of Kyrgyzstan. Unlike Russia, Kyrgyzstan had no visa requirements of their own so there was no need for advanced preparation. And, because of its proximity to a major Chinese city, the border crossing could be made by bus or taxi. This seemed to be a pretty good option, particularly as Amy and I would be having to stay in Kashgar anyway while we waited for our Tibet guide to drive from Lhasa to meet us.

The prefecture region of Kashgar has the largest population in Xinjiang, with just under 4 million people (according to the 2010 census). The westernmost destination on our trip, it was also the last major area we could travel through before needing to have a guide and extensively prepared paperwork as we started to make our way east towards Tibet. Home to the country's largest mosque, Kashgar is the cultural capital of Chinese Islam and for much of the Turkic-based population in the surrounding areas of Central Asia as well. It was a great place to take it easy for a few days while we waited, but my top priority was to get my visa requirements out of the way.

According to Sean, the process to get across the Kyrgyzstan border went something like this:

1. Go to the international bus station in Kashgar, walk around the back, and catch a van to a town called Wuqia where there was a customs office and port of entry.
2. Find a certified taxi on the other side of customs to take me to the border. It would cost ¥600 (about $100) for the car, so I needed someone to split it with.
3. Take a long, uncomfortable ride to the actual border. The road was under construction so I should expect to take over three hours to travel 80 miles through checkpoints until the last passport check where I could finally get my exit stamp.
4. Walk from the Chinese border to the Kyrgyzstan border, about two miles, or hitch a ride if possible since the cab would not be allowed past this point.
5. Get the entry and exit stamp in Kyrgyzstan and run, or hitch a ride, back to China before the borders close for the night.
6. Go through the steps 1 to 4 in reverse to get back to Kashgar!

These instructions left me well equipped for my little international excursion. It was convoluted in part because they were in the process of moving the border[49]. This meant that there were two crossings, one in Wuqia and one next to Kyrgyzstan, leaving the 80 miles of legal limbo between the two.

Our first morning after arriving in Kashgar, I packed up and headed out, but immediately hit my first road block. When trying to find the international bus station, which was meant to be a short walk from our hostel in the Old Town, every person I asked for directions gave me conflicting answers that led me in circles. This included one policeman whose directions were the least accurate. I eventually gave up on walking and hailed a cab. When I arrived, it took me a while to find the van since it ended up being around back in what appeared to be an unofficial, unlicensed section of the bus station. Here, rather than proper commercial, long-range busses, there were plain-clothed drivers with unmarked, white vans viciously competing for customers. As soon as I walked around back, I was assaulted by two or three drivers who grabbed me by the arm and demanded to know where I wanted to go. I picked one and waited for nearly an hour as the van slowly filled with passengers. It was a diverse mix that joined me, including one traditionally dressed Muslim woman wearing a head wrap, a local Han merchant with a burlap sack full of potatoes, and one newly and one long-married couple. More joined us as our driver made sure that all free space was occupied before we set out.

Wuqia was a new and almost entirely unoccupied city, and once more I found myself lost as I tried to find the port of entry. Relying again on a cab, I was dropped off at the humongous and gaudy

---

[49]   The crossing is located at the Irkeshtam Pass and though its history goes back over 100 years when it was a horse path from the Kyrgyz city of Osh, it remained closed during much of the 20th century due to tensions with the Soviet Union. Russian troops were stationed at the pass until 1999, and by 2002 an agreement was reached that allowed passenger traffic to travel between the two countries. By 2008, there was an estimated 58,900 people and 520,000 tons of commercial goods that crossed the border.

customs building. Standing against a backdrop of empty mountain wilderness, the structure resembled the royal palace of some Central Asian monarch. Its scale was far out of proportion to its needs however, and I walked in to find myself alone beneath the cavernous halls apart from two sleepy-eyed customs officials.

Just as I got to the other side I noticed four Uyghur men shoving crates of fruits and vegetables into the trunk of a taxi cab. Only one, the driver, could speak any Mandarin. I helped them pack the rest of their produce (which I later learned they planned to sell in Kyrgyzstan) and the three passengers squeezed into the back while I joined the driver in front.

The road to get to the actual border was horrible. Twice we had to get out of the car to help push the rundown VW cab over large mounds of gravel that it couldn't clear on its own. Another time we were stopped for ten minutes while a crowd of drivers had left their cars to argue with a young, twenty-something construction worker. The orange-vested, Han youth was trying to tell us that the road ahead was closed and we couldn't pass. Nobody seemed content with the excuse and the horde of angry drivers bore down on him. He eventually relented and let us pass towards the closed section of road for a "toll" of ten yuan per car.

The longest stop by far was when we had to wait for a stretch of road to be paved. We were there for an hour, a mess of cars and trucks stopped in the ditches that paralleled the construction on either side. We looked on as the asphalt was laid, dried, and cooled with water before we were finally given the go-ahead.

After arriving at the Chinese side of the border and getting my passport stamped, I was pretty much on my own. The cab driver couldn't cross with us but he said he would wait to take me back the next day. After that, me and the three Uyghur men with their crates of vegetables went on by foot towards the Kyrgyzstan border. The whole experience felt illicit, as if a mistake had been made and we weren't actually supposed to be there. We walked downhill around the switchbacks of a gravel road and I kept expecting armed soldiers around each turn, guns aimed at us asking us for our paperwork. The landscape was epic and the area remote. Situated in a wide river valley, columns of snow-capped mountains loomed over us on either side as we scuttled on towards the border.

All of a sudden, as if to confirm my fears, I heard the sound of tires ripping on top of the gravel from around the switchback. A black VW sedan roared up from around the bend, skidding to a stop in front of us with a cloud of dust rising up behind. The other three men I was walking with seemed to know, or at least had been expecting, the driver and immediately started putting all of their stuff in the car. I felt like I was in a Spanish language movie about the US-Mexico border crossing. Here we were walking through the wilderness with nothing but what we could carry, and here was our cartel-connected coyote to take us on the final leg. I couldn't understand what anyone was saying but the driver seemed to be indicating that he'd give us a ride to the border (for a fee of about $5). He gestured frantically to me to get inside and so, in a rush, I complied.

The border itself was manned by what seemed to be a small Kyrgyz army platoon. In contrast to staff who typically managed Chinese borders, usually mixed gender, disinterested, and not in the best of shape, the half-dozen or more patrolling Kyrgyz officers were much more intimidating. Broad-shouldered and steely-eyed, the Kyrgyz appeared ethnically closer to Russians than their Chinese or Turkic neighbors. They had the intense, expressionless gaze of the military; neither bored, smiling, or angry. Just present. All of them were men, all were dressed in dark green military uniforms, and none seemed to be less than six feet tall. Even the customs building itself, a simple assembly of trailers, a couple one-story structures, and an area for truck and vehicle inspections, made for a harsh contrast with their impractical and lavish Chinese counterpart in Wuqia.

One of the men, a particularly broad-shouldered soldier, walked into one of the small offices and came up to an outward-facing window to inspect and stamp our passports. The three Uyghur men went first and after they had been approved, shuffled back into the car without so much as a wave goodbye before taking off down the road.

My turn at the window, the club-fisted soldier asked in broken, heavily accented English, "Too-night. You. Where stay?"

"China," I replied, and pointed back towards where I'd come.

He looked at me blankly for a few seconds and replied, simply, "No".

The soldier went on to explain, mostly with the aid of hand gestures, that there wasn't enough time to get back and that the border would close in half an hour. I told him I could run, but he refused to give in.

This continued for some time. I would run in place nodding enthusiastically. He would reply "No." I would point at my watch, point towards China, and then give the OK sign with a smile. He would say "No," then point towards Kyrgyzstan. Once or twice, he mentioned the closest city Osh and then pointed behind him.

Even when a nearby Mandarin-speaking Uyghur truck driver stepped in to translate (Uyghur being close enough to Kyrgyz that they could communicate in their native tongues), he was just as obstinate. Unwilling to continue the conversation, the man finally just stamped my passport and pointed me towards Kyrgyzstan.

Dejected, I swallowed the loss and trudged on across the lot. After clearing customs, which was inside an even smaller trailer, my trucker friend caught back up with me. He asked where I would stay that night and I indicated that I would try and rent a bed at the truck stop there at the border crossing. The man, a short, stout, but chipper man gestured the sign for "boozing", tipping an imaginary bottle into his mouth, and explained that the men that stayed there overnight got drunk and it could be dangerous. I had once had a bad experience camping at a highway rest stop in the U.S. that had involved a slightly overweight, middle-aged man in rural Illinois admitting to me that he spent nights there offering sexual favors to lonely truckers (when he turned to gauging my interest in his services, I refused as politely as possible, not wanting to offend). Cautioned by those events, I decided to take him up on the offer of a ride to Osh, nearly a hundred miles away.

Just a few minutes down the road we stopped at a weigh station. The two of us climbed out of the cab and a small group of soldiers walked over. They were led by a stern-faced man in a blue uniform, shorter than me, with the higher cheek bones and narrower eyes of people from the Central Asian steppe, and of course broad shoulders. The man, who I just referred to as "the captain" as he seemed to be in charge, pulled the trucker to the side, presumably to discuss the weight of his cargo. The exchange went on for a few minutes during which time I caught some money changing hands and a couple friendly pats on the shoulder. Afterwards, the pair came over to me. Apparently my translator friend, in addition to managing his own business with the captain, had helped negotiate for me to stay overnight with the soldiers. None of them could speak English or Mandarin, but for the sum of 1,000 Kyrgyz som, the equivalent of about 100 yuan or 20 dollars, I was welcome to stay in their barracks. Not wanting to have to take a two-hour cab ride back to the border in the morning, I agreed.

The area we were in was spectacularly beautiful. The barracks (which was really more of a mobile home with a couple rooms and a narrow kitchen) sat on a small plateau that overlooked a sweeping river gorge. We were surrounded on all sides by the ridged peaks of the Tian Shan mountains that run through the border of China and Kyrgyzstan (the same range that Amy and I had crossed south of Urumqi). Unfortunately, between the stress of traveling and the high altitude, my head was now throbbing and I had a hard time enjoying it.

Between my migraine, the unusual circumstances of my stay, and the complete inability to communicate with my hosts, the night became both strange and memorable. While the soldiers finished their shift for the night, I was left to stay in a narrow room not more than ten feet in length, with nothing but a creaky spring bed and a small CRT television. I spent the next two hours watching Russian music videos and old English language B-horror movies from the 1990s, poorly dubbed in Russian. I tried to stay hydrated but my head only kept getting worse as I sunk deeper into the mattress.

Later, when the sun had gone down and everyone was done working, five of the soldiers found their way into the room. They came under the pretense of watching TV, but were almost certainly there out of curiosity of me. Perched on the edge of the bed, the only piece of furniture in the room, I was quickly sandwiched between three of the broad and sturdy Kyrgyz soldiers. Two of them, the captain and a younger, quieter but taller soldier wearing the standard green uniform, took a particular interest in the two phones I'd brought with me. They went through almost every app on both phones. The younger man found himself particularly engrossed by a game I had on one, a colorful, cartoony game called Plants vs. Zombies. I tried to explain the game to him but he never quite got the hang of using the plants to stop the slow advance of attacking zombies.

The pair seemed most interested in the photos and videos. Recording my trip was the main reason I'd brought the gadgets along to the border and since these were military, I was nervous about getting in trouble for anything I'd photographed or filmed. In particular, I was thinking of the exchange of money between the captain and the trucker from earlier. I had managed to turn on the recorder while holding the phone discreetly in my hand and I was terrified of what they might think if they saw it. Their attention spans were mercifully short though. They quickly scrolled through the hundreds of videos and photos, including, I noted with a sigh of relief, the one of the bribe. The junior soldier seemed to be the most curious about the technology and decided to try out the camera for himself. After going through all of my albums he held the phone up and pointed the lens towards his face. Once I'd shown him how to take a picture, he then went about taking several "selfies". He made small adjustments to the position of his hat and expressionless face until he was finally satisfied with the result and handed me back the phone. As he did, I noticed the corner of his mouth lift, and he cracked into a barely perceptible smile of self-satisfaction.

Once the phones had been sufficiently perused, the captain turned to a new form of amusement. Sitting to my left on the bed, he turned to face me and handed me back my phone. He then gestured with approval that he thought my shoulders were broad. This had apparently convinced the man that I would be worth fighting. With a giant smile on his face, he pointed at me and then himself and then indicated with outstretched arms that we should wrestle. Surprised, I choked out a laugh. I wasn't sure how to gauge his seriousness and didn't want to offend him. I started gesturing to him that I didn't think this would be the best idea. The captain was persistent though. To make his case, with an excited grin he pulled out his own phone, an old, Nokia feature phone, and showed me an extremely grainy and pixelated video. In it, there were two people engaged in sort of Judo-like wrestling. I assumed this was a martial art native to the region. He looked up proudly and gestured that the one in blue (who was winning handily) was him. I tried my best to look impressed and approving but continued to try and laugh off his proposition as a joke. When it was clear I wasn't interested, he gave up on wrestling but quickly shifted his efforts on to boxing. He lifted two fists, raised his eyebrows in excited anticipation and smiled widely again.

Using the only two English words he seemed to know, I tried to explain why this wouldn't be a good idea. "Tourist," I explained, pointing at myself. Next, pointing at him, I said "Police". Then I gestured a few punches and shook my head no and waved my hands vigorously. "A tourist fighting with a police. Not a good idea!"

It seemed like a decent and diplomatic argument to me. The captain was dejected at my refusals however and turned back to the TV. Intent on trying to get me to do something, he turned back with a particularly devilish smile on his face now. A cheesy Russian pop song had just started playing on the television and he pointing at me again. Putting his arms back up, he started bouncing from side to side. "Dance!" he proclaimed.

With some effort I managed to get out of all attempts to get me to perform for the small collection of Kyrgazstani soldiers. It was weird, but ultimately harmless. Compared to a balding man from Illinois explaining to me how truckers get lonely away from their wives and girlfriends and sometimes just need a blow job, it could have been worse. The soldiers all seemed to get a kick out of it at least.

My room for the night was an empty square in the corner of the trailer. I slept on the floor and was given a blanket to serve as both mattress and comforter. I shared the space with one other soldier, the youngest and most junior of the lot. The next morning I was up bright and early. My headache finally gone, I walked out to relieve myself and found I was overlooking a beautiful network of swirling water that weaved its way across the wide valley below. The sun was only just coming up over the far side of the valley and the whole area was covered in its orange glow. A shiver climbed up my spine and a warmth crawled through my body. I stood and watched as the light draped itself slowly down the opposite ridgeline and burned off the last of the mist that still hung over the river.

Breakfast was a simple meal of bread, butter, and tea and afterwards the captain, still in his blue uniform and matching cap, offered me a ride back to the border in their small Russian-made car. Once there, I was greeted by the same club-fisted soldier that wouldn't let me cross back into China the day before. Smiling, as if to ask "Can I go back now?" I handed over my passport. He looked at me for a second and, without cracking a smile, stamped my passport and waved me through.

I hitched a ride with a truck back to the Chinese border and found my cabbie from the day before ready to take me (and a couple other travelers, a 70-year-old Japanese backpacker and thirty-something-year-old professional hiker from Italy) back to Wuqia. The ride back was much smoother than the day before, with more paved roads, no bribes, and not even once needing to get out of the car to push. We sat waiting for two hours at the Chinese customs building while the staff were on lunch before I was finally able to get my new entry stamp. Then, finally legal again, we drove to back Kashgar, back to Amy, and back to The Great Ride of China!

Photos with Road Angels and restaurant proprietors in Lioaning Province on just our third day on the road

A fellow adventurer from the Motorfans forum gaurding his group's bikes at the Friendship Bridge, near the border with North Korea

Setting up camp on the Mongolian Steppe with the rain clouds just starting to roll in

Photo-op at Aiding Lake, 3rd lowest inland place on earth, just as a sandstorm sets to strand us in the middle of the Turpan Depression

Our first meeting with the competition, Sean and Slash, on the G216 south of Urumqi

Heavy snows greet us as we enter the Kunlun Mountains at the border between Xinjiang and Tibet

A photo just as we hit the 15,000km mark, approximately the halfway point and our last day in Tibet

Waiting for a dirt road in Western Sichuan to be cleared

A crowd of onlookers gathers as a local mechanic takes a look at our broken rack outside of Nanning

Group photo with the No. 1 Motorcycle Club in Zoucheng, Shandong

Part III- Kashgar to Chongqing

"天地有大美而不言"
庄子 － 《知北游》
"The world is large, its beauty is indescribable."
- Zhuangzi (369—298 B.C.E.) from "Knowledge Wanders North"

Chapter 10 – From Deserts to Snow Storms

Being in Southern Xinjiang was like being in another world. Kashgar in particular definitely didn't feel like we were in China anymore. Everything from the people to the food to the architecture felt different from what we had experienced over the past two months. One of the most obvious differences was the people. 90% of the population in Kashgar is Uyghur. Many people who we met could speak neither English nor Chinese. Younger generations, usually in their 30s or younger, who had been made to learn Mandarin in school were often needed to help translate for the older generations who ran the shops and restaurants. With a population that was predominantly observant Muslim, most women we saw were nearly fully covered, some in hijabs and others in full burkas that left nothing but the eyes visible. From this, one could get a sense of why Xinjiang had a strong, if still minority, separatist movement. The area was a world apart from the China that claimed ownership of the land and the government that was seen as forcing a foreign culture, politics, and language on its people.

Kashgar as a city had a fantastic "old world" feel to it. The hostel Amy and I were staying at was in the heart of the Old Town, right down the road from a busy street market, and in an area that has stood as the center of the city for over two millennia.[50] We spent a lot of our time wandering the streets here, stocking up on fruits and nuts

---

[50]   The entire district is a registered UNESCO heritage site. As stated by UNESCO: "The historical importance of Kashgar has primarily been linked to its significance as a trading centre. It was a major hub along the great Silk Road as the northern and southern Silk Routes crossed here and caravans departed for Central Asia, India, Pakistan and ancient Persia (current Iran). Kashgar's livestock market named Ivan Bazaar still has the reputation to be one of the largest and most colorful markets in the region."

from the markets and trying out the different restaurants and food stalls: huge mutton kebabs cut and skewered right in front of us, delicious meat-filled pastries, and of course "Chinese pizza", *nang bao rao*.

Right on the edge of Old Town, just a few minutes' walk away, was the Id Kah Mosque. The largest mosque in China, it was built back in 1442 AD and is a major site of worship for Chinese and Turkic Muslims. During the festival at the end of Ramadan there can be as many as 20 to 30,000 worshippers who come to visit the mosque celebrating the conclusion of the month long holiday.

We spent nearly a week in Kashgar exploring the city, getting our gear patched up for the next leg of the journey, and visiting the different sights. In addition to the Id Kah Mosque and spending time in Old Town we also took a walk through the over 2,000-year-old Grand Bazaar. Here you could find everything from office stationary to brightly colored Persian rugs.[51]

A lot of the reason we spent so much time there though (six and a half days including the two where I went to Kyrgyzstan) was because we had to wait for our Tibet guide. Ciren, the guide, and Pasang, his driver, were both native Tibetans and were driving from Lhasa to meet us before we continued our journey east. With dark, Southeast Asian-like features and expressions of seemingly perpetual contentment, they showed up a couple days after I had gotten back from my visa run, pulling up to the Old Town Youth Hostel in a white Mercedes SUV. I noticed with some trepidation that the lower half of their car was still thickly caked with mud and dust from the roads of Western Tibet they had passed through to get here.

---

[51]   The Kashgar Grand Bazaar is receives up to 100,000 visitors daily. It has been around for over two thousand years and features 21 specialized markets, with more than 4,000 fixed vending booths selling over 10,000 different types of products in addition to a food street lined with restaurants.

Unfortunately, as foreigners, we were required by Chinese law to be accompanied at all times through Tibet by a certified guide. We also needed to have a separate visa just for entering the province, and to register our itinerary with local police departments at several checkpoints throughout our journey. For all of this, we had to find a registered Tibet travel agency to take care of all the paperwork and pay for a guide and a driver to take him along with us.

Our two new travel companions were both very good-natured. Calm and soft-spoken, they both had the demeanors of a culturally Buddhist society. The two dismounted from their SUV in front of our hostel, wide, white smiles contrasting with their dark complexions. Ciren greeted Amy and I immediately after we walked out by placing two white silk scarves, known as *khatas*, around our necks. The ceremony made me think of the way I've seen tourists in Hawaii greeted by hula girls placing flower garlands around their necks after disembarking from a plane.[52] Unfortunately, the gathering wasn't all happy news. Afterwards, we were informed that the pair, upon leaving from Lhasa a week prior, had forgotten to bring all of the extra gear and cold weather clothing that we had sent to their offices before leaving from Beijing. We were anticipating temperatures consistently below freezing in Tibet, but our current equipment was only adequate for warm weather climates. With over 1,500 miles until Lhasa, a stretch that included crossing the Kunlun and Himalayan mountains, we had no choice but to wait for our gear to be shipped before moving on.

Yecheng, a small Xinjiang city one hundred miles to the south east of Kashgar, was the last place on the road towards Tibet we could go to without a guide. Amy and I decided we would spend the last few

---

[52]   The *khata* is a ceremonial scarf common in traditional Mongolian and Tibetan cultures, though for Mongolians it is usually blue instead of white. They can be presented during any festive occasion: weddings, funerals, arrivals, graduations, etc. The scarf is a symbol of good luck while the color, white, is a symbol of purity.

days there, maybe riding around the area to get some extra miles in towards the record, while Ciren and Pasang waited in Kashgar for our package.

Yecheng was a relatively nondescript and unremarkable city. It appeared new and lacked the culture and tradition of its neighbor to the west. Indeed, much of its development had happened over the course of the past five years during the time the G219 highway that connected southern Xinjiang with Lhasa (and the one we would be taking east) had been completed. Amy and I also discovered on our arrival that Yecheng was under severe police lockdown. We noticed streets around the main business district being patrolled by armored trucks and cars. Some streets had roadblocks while police tents had been erected at major intersections, manned by armed cops in helmets and body armor. Some of the markets even had checkpoints and metal detectors to inspect pedestrian traffic at entrances. We found only one hotel in town that would accept foreign guests and after we checked in we discovered that the Internet wasn't working in any of the rooms. We asked about it at the front desk, and the woman casually informed us that after some recent "trouble" in the city (i.e. anti-government protests), the Internet had been shut down for the whole area.[53]

We spent four more days in Yecheng waiting for Ciren and Pasang, including one day where we did a short 150-mile ride exploring the nearby countryside. We spent four hours the morning after they arrived at the local police department with Ciren registering our upcoming itinerary into Tibet. It had been ten days with barely any progress at all. Sean and Slash had passed through Kashgar during our

---

[53]   This is a strategy that has been used by the government in the past as a way to prevent the escalation of unrest, particularly in Xinjiang. On July 5th, 2009, deadly riots broke out in Urumqi and later spread to other areas of the province. It took over six months for international phone calls, text messaging, and access to both domestic and international websites to be fully restored.

time waiting there, but after a couple days had moved on. I was increasingly anxious, thinking of our competition making their way back east across Xinjiang (Sean and Slash's route skipped Tibet, skirting the southern rim of the Taklamakan instead), brooding over the miles they were covering while we were helplessly stuck on the precipice of our twelfth province, just over a third of our goal. With nearly 7,000 miles behind us, it was now the middle of September. We were two months into the trip and had only the same amount of time left again before winter would start to descend on the Northeast.

Even more than the restiveness and competitive pressure though, another emotion was urging me on. In Yecheng, we were right on the edge of what promised to be one of the most exciting and challenging sections of our trip. It was an experience I had been anticipating for months and I was eager to dive in.

The next 20 to 30 days was something I had been looking forward to since we first came up with the idea for The Great Ride of China. With each day out of Beijing that brought us closer to Kashgar and the gateway to Tibet, it loomed larger in my mind. For the next three weeks, we would be driving along "The Rooftop of the World", never dropping below an altitude of 10,000 feet and reaching as high as 17,000 at Mount Everest Base Camp. The areas we would be traveling through included some of the most remote in all of China, with stretches of as much as three hundred miles without even a gas station. The climate would change drastically as well. It was nearly the middle of September, and we were about to enter an alpine region at the start of a long and harsh winter season.

After the build up, anticipation, and restless waiting, and almost two weeks after first arriving in Kashgar, we were finally ready to go. We had our visas, guide, and paperwork. We had registered our itinerary at the local Public Safety Bureau (PSB) in Yecheng. We had all of our gear, the bike was packed and in the best condition it had been in in weeks, and the rest of our gear stored in the SUV. Finally, it was time to set off on our journey again; onwards through the Kunlun Mountains and on to the Tibetan Plateau at the foot of the Himalayas.

***

Our first day out of Yecheng was by far the most difficult we had had the entire trip up to that point. We left the city at nine in the morning. From that time until just before sunset 8 hours later, our only opportunities to stop were for quick snacks, layer breaks, and police checkpoints. In that period, we climbed from the low altitude and dry climate at the southern rim of the Taklamakan Desert up into the sky-scraping peaks of the Kunlun Mountains. Upon breaching the borders of the mountain range, we crossed three progressively higher passes, diving deeper into the barren landscape. By the second climb, a light snow had started to fall, powdering the grey rock that enveloped us. The third and final climb was the hardest of the day, a gravel trail that brought us 17,000 feet above sea level, nearly as high as Mount Everest Base Camp, and into the heart of a swirling snowstorm that cut visibility to just 20 feet.

The nearly three hundred miles we covered was the most we'd done in a single day since starting out. It was also over some of the most difficult terrain we'd encountered yet. Besides the freezing temperatures and harsh winds now whipping snow into our faces, the steep ascents and descents over the passes meant long stretches of switchbacks over unevenly paved asphalt, warped by extreme temperatures and overweight trucks. Some of the road, such as the stretch over the final pass, had yet to even be paved. Through most of the morning and into the afternoon, our speed was limited to just 30mph.

We hadn't even entered the province yet and it was clear that our journey through Tibet would be one of extremes.

The altitude sickness didn't hit until that evening, but when it hit, it hit hard. Our first night was spent at a small trucker's outpost in the Kunluns. It was the only gas and shelter available for hundreds of miles in any direction. When we arrived at the outpost, which was still at an altitude of 15,000 feet, I had to go directly to bed. I could barely speak and felt too nauseous to attempt dinner. I crawled into my sleeping bag in the corner of a small, dark room at the back of our mangy accommodations and tried my best to get some sleep.

The second day out of Yecheng the weather was even worse. We spent nearly the entire day this time in dense snow flurries. Visibility became so poor that the only way I knew where we were supposed to go was by following the taillights of Ciren and Paseng's SUV, its white frame itself camouflaged by the snow and fog that had enveloped us. Despite three layers of gloves, my hands were getting so cold that I had to take frequent breaks where my only respite was to stick my ungloved hands down my pants in an effort to, however fleetingly, regain feeling in my fingers.

Sitting behind me throughout, Amy was having a particularly difficult time with the freezing temperatures. She had a lower tolerance to the cold already and did not have the benefit of driving to keep her mind occupied. This left her with little else to focus on apart from the stinging pain of the wind that invaded every opening in our protective gear. All she could do was curl up behind me as much as possible, using my frame to block the cold and stick her hands between my back and backpack to stay warm. All the while she fought the temptation to give up the motorcycle for the refuge of the SUV.

These two days inflicted a wild swing of emotions on the both of us. We had gone from the exhilaration of launching towards Tibet to a reality that was brutalizing us physically and that even deprived us of the views that would have redeemed it. Even sleep provided little respite. Amy and I mostly spent our nights experimenting with ways to dull the altitude-induced pounding in our heads, like chugging boiled water or trying to sleep upright. All of this and we were only two days in. Could we sustain driving at these altitudes and in this region for weeks on end? Would we be forced to face conditions like these, or worse, until we hit warmer climates in Southwest China in over a month's time? What about when we hit the east coast again in late November and early December? The two of us started to reach so low that we began second guessing the whole trip, wondering if we had left Beijing too late to be successful at all.

While the cold was a relative constant throughout our time in Tibet and parts of Qinghai later on, the landscapes we were treated to throughout the region made it much more bearable. We spent days driving through wide-open steppes and river valleys, long corridors that lay in between columns of mountains. Most striking about the area were the colors. Each natural feature added its own distinct tone to the pallet of the countryside. Greens, blues, browns, and yellows streaked as if painted on a canvas across my visor. They overwhelmed me with a sense of almost transcendental warmth that helped to distract me from the burning cold.

Once we entered Tibet's more inhabited regions, it was as if we had been transported once again. As in Xinjiang, everything from the language to the food, culture and even mannerisms was drastically different from anything we'd experienced so far. It was only the younger, recently educated Tibetans who we were able to communicate with as they too had learned to speak Mandarin in school. Ciren explained to us how guides who could speak Chinese made more money in Tibet than ones that could speak English, since, for the former, supply was far below demand. At one guesthouse that we stayed at, we met a young Tibetan girl that was helping to run her family's business. Her Mandarin was particularly clear and easy to understand, very standard and without any of the disrupting influences of a local dialect. We asked her how she could speak so well (much clearer than Ciren's Mandarin) and she explained to us that she had studied at school hoping to get into a university, possibly in another province. Unfortunately though her score on the *gao kao*, the Chinese college entrance examination, wasn't high enough, forcing her to stay back in this tiny village running the rustic guesthouse with her family.

We mostly stayed in small villages like this on our way along Tibet's southern border. The hamlets were little more than two rows of single-story buildings on either side of the National Highway, often built alongside a police checkpoint where passing motorists were required to register. Many also had a small monastery that sat atop a nearby hill, looking down over the houses and adorned with stupas and hundreds of prayer flags strung up sentry-like to nearby flagpoles. The guesthouses themselves were similarly very humble in construction and style. Neither traditional nor modern or industrial, the collection of buildings that made up these modest accommodations were made up of a single row of individual rooms, almost like an American motel, with one communal area for food and tea. The sleeping quarters comprised of a grouping of single beds, with simple bedding laid out on top, arranged in a semicircle around a heating stove. These heaters – fueled by the most plentiful combustible resource in the area, dried yak dung[54] – came in handy for the chilly Tibetan September nights.

---

[54] Almost everything in Tibetan life seemed to revolve around yaks. Most meals included yak meat, yak butter tea was believed to help with body temperature regulation and the altitude (Amy and I were not fans of the savory hot beverage however and only tried it once), their skulls were used for religious inscriptions, and their wool was used for clothing. Later, in Lhasa, we spotted "butter lamps", standing metal bowls with a wick in the center and filled with yak butter to fuel it, near holy sights such as the funeral stupas of past Lamas. The lamps never went out as they were constantly being replenished by worshippers who had traveled with large containers of the stuff, which they scooped out as an offering to contribute to the pile. As mentioned, even yak excrement was put to good use. Being far more plentiful in the area than any other flammable resource, almost every heating stove we saw was powered by it.

It took us nearly a week traveling along first the China–Pakistan and then the China–India borders[55] before making it to the secondary road that led into Mount Everest National Park. In contrast to our reception at the Kunlun Mountains, we entered the foot of the Himalayas with clear skies and beautiful, uninterrupted views up to the glacier capped peaks. The night before finally entering the park, we stayed at a small town just 15 minutes from the ticketed entrance that led up to Base Camp.

It was going to be less than 50 miles to get from from Old Tigri where we spent the night to the overnight lodgings near the camp. Such a short distance, even on switchbacked roads, would not normally have taken us any longer than one or two hours. Counter to our expectations though, these 50 miles turned out to be significantly more grueling than we had expected, taking nearly seven hours to ride from the tollgate at the entrance of the park to the overnight tents near the foot of Mount Everest.

For all of its strengths as a road motorcycle, the CF650TR is far from suited to off-road riding. The suspension is limited, the riding position is not meant for the kind of freedom of motion needed, and the thin, shallow tread in the tires can't grip onto gravel or sand. Two riders mounted on top made it even more difficult. For much of the

---

Some guest houses we stayed in even kept a crate fully stocked in the room with us so we could keep the stove burning ourselves.

[55] We encountered long caravans of military vehicles throughout this time. These were made up of as many as 50 trucks (the vehicles were numbered so we could always tell how many more we had to pass before getting to the front of the line, which could take as long as half an hour). The actual line delineating the border between China and India has been disputed ever since China's annexation of Tibet in the mid-20th century. In June of 1962, tensions led to several months of armed conflict, known as the Sino-Indian War. Though today there is an officially recognized border, disputes still occasionally arise which can lead to military build-ups on either side of the line. We later found out that there was one such standoff during the time we were traveling through Tibet, with both sides engaged in military exercises at their borders, which is why we saw so many military vehicles and encampments along the way.

distance we were relegated to speeds of 10–15mph. We crossed wide barren rock fields with stones sometimes as big as my head, each bump threatening to throw Amy and I to the ground. The road itself was often just a track worn down by SUVs. This led to multiple, unofficial pathways from which traffic could choose at their discretion. When I wasn't trying to keep the bike upright going over rocks and through gravel, I'd have to watch for obnoxious tourists ripping around the narrow switchbacks. So cocky in their all-wheel drive, all-terrain vehicles, these drivers paid little to no attention to any of the obstacles in their path, including the other motorists with whom they shared the road.

We arrived at "Tent City" (as Ciren referred to it in his thick, joyful Tibetan accent) a couple of hours before dark. The canvas shelters were arranged in a semicircle around the main parking lot. From this lot you could catch a shuttle bus to go the final two and a half miles up to Base Camp.

Exhausted and sore from the unexpectedly physical day of driving, I liked the idea that we had had to earn our view of Everest. Tent City, swarming with mostly out-of-shape tourists teeming from out of their busses and SUVs, may not quite be as dramatic a destination as the snowy peak of the highest place on earth, but it was the highest altitude we would reach on our adventure and we'd had to work to get there. It was a milestone made even more meaningful considering that we had come from the lowest point, stuck in a sandstorm no less, only a few weeks before.

On the evening of our arrival the view of Everest was obscured by cloud cover. Only the encampment area and beginnings of an ascent were visible. This was apparently the case for most of the year. Nonetheless, we got our photos at the Base Camp sign showing our elevation against a backdrop of the large, unmoving puff of white where we were told Everest stood. Base Camp itself, where the journey for us tourists ends, is a wide and flat valley at the base of

Mount Everest where the adventure for potential climbers is really just starting, the first of five camps that eventually lead to the summit. The clearing, at over 17,000 feet above sea level (three and a quarter miles up!), receives up to two hundred prospective climbers per year. With the main climbing season between April and May though, the area was a barren rock field during our visit.

It wasn't until a couple hours after arriving, on the shuttle bus back down to camp, I was struck by the sense of culture shock I recognized I was feeling. Two of the tourists on the bus held portable oxygen tanks for the altitude. They all, I thought with a twinge of patronizing superiority, seemed pampered. It occurred to me then that it had been almost two weeks since leaving Kashgar, over a month in the remoteness of Western China, and nearly two months since Beijing. Even the cities we'd been to felt distant and apart from the world we'd come from. At Everest we were surrounded with crowds again, boisterous tourists from mostly the East of China and even some Westerners. I noted how comfortable Amy and I had grown with the unfamiliar and how simultaneously uncomfortable it was to be surrounded by familiar signs of civilization again.

Even though we had been a week at high altitudes, I was still feeling its effects at night. Between the tough ride and the fact that we were sleeping at 17,000 feet above sea level, sleep was unwilling to come. Tent City was at almost full capacity, but Ciren had helped arrange a spot for us to sleep in the back of a tent near its makeshift cooking area. I curled up in my bag on the sleeping platform, separated from the kitchen by a floor-to-ceiling curtain, and tried to ignore the discomfort.

About an hour after we'd laid down to sleep, music started playing outside. It was poppy and loud, with an electronic bass that seemed to carry throughout the valley. In my head I imagined the obnoxious tourists that had been running us off the road, blaring music out of the car speakers from their SUV. As the party started picking up, I began hearing an occasional "Whooop!!!" of excitement yelled out in rhythm by one of the revelers. Finally, at around midnight, distracted and still struggling to fall asleep, I decided to take a walk outside to see what was going on.

The moon was completely full and with the clear skies you could see everything around the camp without the aid of a light. The moonlight reflected off the two ridges that rose up on either side of us, glowing in such a way that it distorted the scale of the snowy peaks. They felt almost like movie-set backdrops, fake as if you could go up and tip them over. Much more approachable than their imposing reality.

The glow of the moon, almost directly above now, also lit up the parking lot and I could get a clear view of where the music was coming from. In the center of the lot, not far from our tent, a circle of people were dancing around what looked like a small electric speaker. Now that I was outside and could hear better, I could tell that the music, though it had the predictable and catchy beat of a pop song, was not at all familiar and the words had the harmonic and rolling timbre of Tibetan. The dancers, some of which carried glow-sticks in their hands or wrapped around their wrists and ankles, were all moving around the circle in unison. No one followed any particular choreographed dance but there was still a connectedness to their movements. I looked on as they moved around the source of the music, sometimes hopping on one foot, sometimes shaking a widespread hand in the air, and sometimes bending over at the waist as they bounced up and down. Every now and then the song would approach a climax and one of the dancers would let out their high-pitched "Whooop!" rising in harmony with the energy of the music. Almost immediately after, one or two others would follow with a "Whooop! Whooop!" of their own in reply.

I went in to get Amy from the tent, thinking she might want to catch a glimpse of the festivities. Watching, you could just imagine how instead of the speaker in the center there could have been a fire pit. Where now there were pop songs, there could have been Tibetan flutes and drums. It was like a modern tribal celebration. Not long after I'd come back out with Amy, we watched the two young Tibetan women who staffed our tent pass us and join the circle. That's when it occurred to me who this small group of locals were. Here in the middle of the gravel parking lot at the foot of Mount Everest, the staff of Tent City had, by midnight, all finished tending to their guests and were finally able to unwind. What I found really remarkable about the scene though was how happy they all seemed. Most of the dancers had been up since at least dawn that morning. They had then spent the following 17 hours dealing with loud, entitled, and demanding tourists. Just a couple hours earlier, Amy and I had watched a Chinese cyclist who was sharing the sleeping platform with us treat our hosts like dirt, making a big fuss about their not making enough room for him. The Tibetan girl who was trying to help was remarkably patient despite the fact that our being there was already displacing members of her own family for whom this was normally their bed.

In the face of all this, after an unimaginably long day of working on their feet, with more reason than most to feel sorry for themselves or spend time complaining about their guests, here they all were, a perfect display of contentment and energy. It was a modern Tibetan dance party, illuminated as if with a spotlight by the full moon at the base of one of the holiest places on earth.

**

"Mr. Buck! Mr. Buck!" Ciren was calling through a whisper as he came in from the front of the tent. After the dance party had petered out by around 2:30am, Amy and I had both finally managed to doze off and get some sleep. Ciren's excitement was disorienting through my morning grogginess and it felt early. The curtain that separated us from the small electric stoves and food inventory was pulled aside and Ciren's dark face peered through, the white of his teeth illuminated against the dark of the tent. His head directly over us now, I started to sit up in my sleeping bag and he spoke again in another forced whisper, "Mr. Buck! Mr. Buck! Come see! Come see! It's out!" With Amy now also slowly stirring out of her sleep, it took me a few more seconds before my still semi-conscious mind could process what he was saying. The words finally started to make sense and comprehension settled in. The clouds had cleared from the valley, the fog was burning off, and Everest was coming out to say hi.

The sun hadn't even come up yet but people were slowly starting to rustle about, coming out of the tents as the news spread. According to Ciren, some people end up waiting around Base Camp for several days hoping to be able to catch a glimpse of the peak from behind the clouds. This made us particularly lucky since we would not have had the time to wait if the clouds hadn't cleared by that morning. One way or another, view or no view, we had to push on and Ciren wanted to make sure that we got our opportunity before we did.

Taking in the full height of Mount Everest was incredibly gratifying. Even though no extra distance had been covered since our arrival the day before, it felt like an important punctuation to our journey. We setup our camera by the still shimmering moonlight and managed to take some long-exposure shots of the mountain, the snow-covered behemoth glowing against the light with the moon gradually giving way to the sun. As I watched the mountain come into view, I reflected with Amy on what we had done to get to that point. I thought of how far we had gone, all of the things we'd seen, and all of the people we'd met. I was proud of everything we'd accomplished, and a sense of peaceful contentment swept over me, cutting through the brisk early morning cold.

There is nothing quite like the world's tallest mountain to give you a sense of proportion and scale. Having now reached the highest point of our journey highlighted not just how much we'd done but also how much there was still left to do. We were only two months into a trip that promised to take at least twice that amount of time. In terms of distance, we were still a week or two away from halfway. There was a long way left for us to go and we knew that, as we put Everest behind us, it would hardly be all downhill from there.

Chapter 11 – Barren and Holy Lands

It took another two days to get from Everest to Tibet's capital, Lhasa. The road eastward out of Base Camp was another 60 miles of unpaved gravel mountain track. Not quite as rough as the one that had taken us there the day before, progress was still excruciatingly slow – a full day of riding and sore backsides. At midday we got our last view of Everest, receding behind clouds, and by evening the road had finally turned back to smooth, well-paved asphalt on a final stretch to the small village of Lazi (pronounced "la tse"). Expecting no more bad roads on our way to Lhasa, we decided to push on for the final three hundred miles the following day, the prospect of rest and hot showers propelling us forward.

Life on the road in Tibet was highly regulated. Nearly all of our daily activities were tightly controlled. There were of course the multiple times where we had to register our itinerary with local PSB offices, informing the authorities of every place we planned to visit and lodge for the preceding days and nights. Every gas fill-up also had to be recorded, a process that involved registering with my driver's license and passport at each station.

This treatment wasn't just reserved for foreigners either. In fact, the initiative was most likely aimed specifically at local Tibetans. When we'd left from Yecheng in Xinjiang province towards the provincial border with Tibet, we'd had to pack out an extra tank of gas since our bike didn't have the capacity to cover the three hundred miles to the next station. As a Tibetan, especially one in the tourist industry, Ciren was very sensitive to attracting too much unwanted attention and was anxious about our combustible cargo. At the first checkpoint before the border, he insisted that we fill up as much as possible from the container before crossing to avoid arousing suspicion.

Gas prices were high in the province so it's possible that the controls were in place to discourage a black market in fuel sales. More likely though it was meant to preempt illicit acts of political protest by local Tibetans. Explosives could have been a concern, but the largest challenge the local government faced (and the one that received the most sympathizers from abroad) were self-immolations. The first known politically motivated self-immolation in modern Tibet is believed to have been in 2009. Between 2011 and 2013 a wave of these protests swept through China (mainly Tibet and neighboring Sichuan) with 124 Tibetans setting themselves on fire, almost all fatally.[56]

The process at gas stations was tedious, not least because they were so unused to foreigners having to fill up a vehicle. It usually went something like this: After waiting in line behind other motorists, mostly Tibetan farmers, I would approach a makeshift registration area of the gas station. This usually consisted of a table in an area that doubled as cashier's desk and staff sleeping quarters. A Han policeman would be stationed at the desk inspecting documents. I was usually met with quixotic looks by the officer and somewhat disinterested curiosity by the local motorists waiting behind. A particularly confused bewilderment would descend on the policeman when reaching the identification number field on the registration form.

"Where's your *shen fen zheng*?" I was asked once. A *shen fen zheng* is the identification card that all Chinese are assigned by the central government. These are used to keep track of the population and are needed for everything from buying a cellphone number to staying in hotels and applying for university (similar to a social security number in the United States). As a foreigner, I of course didn't have one and

---

[56]   The self-immolations have continued past 2013. As of September 2015, there have been 143 self-immolations by Tibetans in China in protest of the exile of the Dalai Lama and Chinese control of the region. All but the first have occurred since 2011.

would always offer my passport instead. With over a billion people to keep track of, the Chinese ID numbers are quite a bit longer than your typical foreign passport number and this can cause some confusion.

Ciren, who usually felt obligated to accompany me, responded by hurriedly pointing at my passport number. "This is his *shen fen zheng.*"

"I'm a foreigner," I said, adding my support. "So I don't have a *shen fen zheng.* Just my passport."

With a long line of other motorists still waiting their turn, the officer shrugged and filled in the form using the passport, his reluctance still detectable at leaving half of the required spaces unfilled.

Probably the most frustrating element of the environment of control however was the "speed controls." The speed limits imposed in Tibet, particularly in the south, were draconian. On long stretches of well-paved road, flat for as much as a hundred miles across the plateau, the speed limits could still be as low as 30mph. Indeed, it felt that as the road became more open, the limits only became more restrictive. Normally, with such impractical traffic rules most drivers in China would just ignore them, some not even slowing for police or speed cameras. In Tibet though, in order to enforce the rules, checkpoints had been set up all along the highway. At each stop, in addition to normal paperwork checks, every driver had to register his/ her vehicle and the time you had arrived at the current checkpoint. You were then given a slip of paper, tying your vehicle to this time, to present at the next stop. If you covered the intervening stretch of road faster than the speed limit allowed as proven by the time-stamped form, you were fined around ¥2,000 (or over $300).

As we got closer to the more populated and traveled areas near Lhasa, these checkpoints became increasingly frequent, often as little as 50 miles to be covered in an hour and a half. I was unwilling to go that slow on such beautiful roads, which meant that every 30 to 45 minutes of going 80mph, Amy and I would stop by the side of the road for an additional 45 minutes, waiting for Ciren and Paseng before crossing. Being locals and Tibetans they were more likely to be penalized and so were more cautious about following the rules. This meant that our last day into Lhasa, a distance which we normally could have covered in six to eight hours of leisurely driving, ended up taking us closer to twelve. The final two were spent in the dark, including the crossing of a switchbacked 14,000-foot mountain pass and heavily trafficked roads on the outskirts of the city.

***

More culture shock awaited us in Lhasa. This was the first city with international tourists that we had been to since Xi'an nearly two months previously. As a result, Amy and I found it to be a more developed and cosmopolitan place than we had grown used to. The restaurant choices were diverse, people spoke English, and the overall quality of service was improved. It all also just generally felt cleaner. Even better was that Amy's mother knew some people in the local hotel industry. When we had a date set for our arrival, a friend was able to arrange a room for us at a five-star luxury hotel. Amy and I in our dust covered gear, layers of long underwear, me with a sizable beard at this point, a hodgepodge of oblong shaped luggage, and just a general state of disheveledness about us, felt extremely out of place walking into the softly lit, elegant reception area at 10:30 at night. We had our reservation though and the staff were appropriately courteous as they checked us in. A bellboy even came over to help arrange our bags and helmets onto a luggage cart. A far cry from the single beds, simple rooms, and yak paddy fired heaters we had grown used to over the past week and a half, the room felt like paradise. Best of all, Lhasa was the first time we'd had a hot shower since first entering the province a week prior. There are few pleasures in the world as rewarding as good water pressure and a reliable boiler.

For most people, Lhasa is their first stop in Tibet, arriving there either by train from the north or by air. This means that it is their first opportunity to acclimate to the altitude. Spending the past week at significantly higher locations, our bodies had finally gotten used to the difference in oxygen level (in fact, Lhasa was around six and a half thousand feet lower than where we had spent the past few nights). We watched on, however, as new arrivals to the province struggled with the beginning stages of their acclimation. In our hotel we witnessed heavy set Americans and Europeans sitting down to catch their breath in the lobby after carrying their luggage. Other, equally rotund, Chinese tourists could be seen stocking up on portable oxygen bottles that were available at virtually every convenience store. One European tourist that had just arrived at the hotel seemed ready to call it quits after only her first day. The middle-aged woman confessed to Amy and I from her seat on the plush lobby sofa that she wasn't sure feeling this sick was how she wanted to spend her holiday. After a week of headache-induced sleep deprivation, Amy and I were sympathetic, though there was a feeling of "otherness", a tangible distance that we felt being surrounded by all of this opulence.

While it was tempting to stay in our cozy hotel room, doing nothing but sleep and eat for two days, Amy and I, as usual, had things we needed to do. In the weeks since our maintenance in Urumqi we had experienced sandstorms, snowstorms, suspension-destroying roads, high altitudes, and drastic temperature changes. After the rock fields surrounding Everest, we had also lost the use of one of our side panniers which had cracked from the vicious bumps. Fang Shujian luckily was able to put us in touch with a small CFMoto shop in town. This gave us an opportunity to brace the pannier, change the oil, and confirm everything was still in working order. With the first reliable internet since Kashgar, there were also emails to catch up on and blog posts to publish to let friends and family know we were still alive.

Being in Lhasa, one of the holiest places on earth for Tibetan Buddhists, we also wanted to do some sightseeing. As we were in the unique circumstance of having our own personal tour guide in Ciren, we were lucky enough to not have to do any of the logistics ourselves. He helped to organize an itinerary of places to see in town in the short time we had while also providing very knowledgeable explanations of the different sights we visited, including specifics about the architecture which interested Amy in particular.

Johkang Temple was our first stop. One of the holiest sites in Tibet, Johkang is a major pilgrimage destination for Tibetan Buddhists around the world. Many of these pilgrims make the journey entirely by foot, practicing a remarkable ritual of prostration. This was something we witnessed first hand as we made our way across Tibet, but we had been unable to put the travelers into context until reaching the destinations ourselves.

Progressing towards their goal from all directions, these peregrinating Buddhists are usually equipped with wooden blocks attached to their hands and knees and an apron on their front. They make their solitary progression by clapping the blocks on their hands together from a standing position then kneeling down on both knees before sliding all the way out until they lie flat on the ground. After full prostration, they slide back, take a step forward, and begin the entire ritual over again. It was a fascinating and humbling display of devotion.

One such pilgrim, dusty, ragged, and stoic, was just arriving at the temple as we made our approach to the tourist entrance[57], in his final minutes of kowtowing that had already lasted who knows how many

---

[57]   There were separate entrances for tourists and pilgrims. The two types of visitors having different priorities, this was meant as a way to facilitate the religious rituals involved for the pilgrims while making sure not to hold back tourist traffic.

weeks. The front of the temple itself was lined with rows of devotees continuing a stationary version of the same ritual. Some among the crowd of worshipers had clearly been there for an extended period of time, evidenced by sleeping blankets and hot water thermoses at their sides. There was an admirable calm with which they went about their rite, a composed humility in the act of giving themselves up to their spirituality.[58]

The other major sight we visited was the Potala Palace. Probably Lhasa's most iconic structure (though not as holy for Tibetan Buddhists as Johkang), the white and brick red stone building sits on top of a hill that overlooks the whole city. Traditionally it was the seat of Tibet's religious and political leader, the Dalai Lama. Today though it serves only partially as a place of worship and primarily as a tourist attraction. Prior to Tibet's incorporation into China in 1951, the palace's over one thousand rooms (which cover an area of nearly 1.5 million square feet) would have been filled with monks engaged in the affairs of the state and spirit. Today though the number of monks that live there is only between 30 and 50, and these have only been allowed to stay after going through an official application process through which the Chinese government selects the residents.

One thing I found particularly interesting as we toured around these religious sights was the co-existence of the new and the old. While visiting Johkang temple, Amy, Ciren, and I walked past one of its most religiously significant rooms. Housed in an almost closet-like alcove stood a golden Buddha statue. This was said to have been blessed by the Buddha himself and is one of the holiest artifacts in

---

[58]   In 2013, Lhasa alone saw an estimated 8 million tourists, 12 million total visiting Tibet that year. Johkang is the most popular site for pilgrims, with winter being the peak season for these travelers. During this time it's estimated that the temple received as many as 20 thousand pilgrims a day from Tibet and other surrounding provinces. One of the other most famous and well-trodden pilgrimages in Tibet is to Mount Kailesh (which we had passed on the G219 on our way to Everest), which also includes a 32-mile circumambulation around the high-altitude mountain.

Tibetan Buddhism.[59] A logjam had formed in front, with the pilgrims stopping to chant and pray after having made their way along the roped-off pathways of the labyrinthine building. Many of the devotees were parked at the entranceway to the statue, reading from prayer books or mumbling the chants to themselves from memory. The three of us slowly squeezed our way through, trying to make way for more appreciative and deserving parties. I noticed one young Tibetan man though who had stopped at the room but was looking at the screen of a smartphone. I thought it an odd, if not a little rude, anachronism. As I passed though, I noted the rapid movements of his lips, a subtle rocking back and forth of his body, and looked over to see Tibetan script scrolling automatically on his screen. Tibetan prayer book? There's an app for that.

We later encountered another robed Tibetan engaged in something similar when visiting the Potala Palace. As we approached one of the primary libraries for religious study, I noticed a monk seated on a solitary stool in the corner of a crooked hallway also on a smartphone. The robed Tibetan was hunched over, his shaved head deep into his activity has he busily tapped away at the touchscreen with his thumbs. As we passed, I looked down to see what he was doing and was surprised to find that rather than studying scripture, reading a prayer, or even checking email, he was, in fact, busy sending emojis to a friend on WeChat, China's most popular online messaging app.

***

At Lhasa, our route was to abruptly change direction towards our next province, Qinghai. Originally we had planned to continue east from

---

[59] The statue, called Jowo Rinpoche, is said to have been blessed by the Buddha himself and transported to China when Buddhism was first introduced to the country from India. It was later given by an emperor of the Tang Dynasty as a wedding gift when his daughter was married to the king of Tibet.

Lhasa and go directly towards Southwest China. Before we left from Beijing however, we discovered that eastern Tibet had recently been closed to foreign tourists and likely would remain that way for the rest of the year.[60] We had heard that the Sichuan–Tibet Highway was one of the most beautiful in the country for both its scenery and local culture, so Amy and I were disappointed to have to miss it.

The alternative was to take the Qinghai–Tibet Highway north. This would take us one thousand miles across the Tibetan Plateau, through the deserts of the Qaidam Basin, towards Qinghai Lake (the seventh largest saltwater lake in the world and largest lake in China), and then passing back into eastern Gansu before turning south into Sichuan. It would add two thousand miles to our original plan, reaching Chengdu, the capital of Sichuan, two weeks later than we would have via the Sichuan–Tibet Highway. It was disappointing to miss this famous mountain route (every Chinese biker we met insisted it was something we had to experience). We were however lucky to have the flexibility to adjust and I looked forward to what the new route might bring. Whichever direction we went in, there was sure be opportunities for adventure and discovery.

The Tibetan Plateau is the highest plateau in the world. With an average elevation of over 14,000 feet, it covers an area five times larger than that of France, including most of Tibet, Qinghai and parts of India. As we began to move north of Lhasa, the plateau became significantly flatter than when we were traveling at the foot of the Himalayas. We crossed fewer passes and the climbs and descents were more gradual. The barren flatlands made for high, frigid winds. The icy gusts tossed our motorcycle all over the road, but luckily the skies

---

[60]   This is a regular and unpredictable occurrence whenever there is any political unrest in the area (as there has been since 2011). The government tries to decrease the chance of international exposure by keeping non-Chinese out of the region. It is the most densely populated area of the province and the anti-Chinese sentiment is much more potent. If authorities feel the situation is too unstable, they simply restrict travel and revoke, or cease to issue, travel permits.

stayed clear. What snow we did encounter was restrained, limited to light flurries. Because the Qinghai–Tibet Highway is the main artery for trucks delivering goods to Lhasa and borders the primary train line, it was more developed than our route for the first week through the province had been. Now, rather than lodging in small Tibetan guest houses, Amy and I again found ourselves (with the help of Ciren) looking for the rundown, overpriced hotel in town that could register foreign guests. The dusty towns, reckless country drivers, and dingy convenience stores were more familiarly "Chinese", reminiscent of places we'd been to in eastern Gansu and southern Inner Mongolia.

When we crossed into a new province, there was little to indicate that we had left Tibet. The catalyst of my realization was a surprisingly streamlined experience filling up on gas. As the attendant approached us, there wasn't the familiar apathetic wave towards the nearby cement building to register nor even a frantic reaction to my pulling up to the pump on a motorcycle. I didn't even have to use the giant watering can. Surprised by the change in routine, I tentatively asked the attendant with a large smile if we were in Qinghai. Confused by the glee on my face, he replied blankly, "Yes, this is Qinghai." "So... I don't have to register to fill up gas?" A sign of understanding came over him as he lifted the corner of his lips in a smile. "Nope. How much do you want?" Hello province number 13!

With Tibet behind us now, it was soon time to say goodbye to our faithful travel companions Ciren and Paseng. With no more legal need for a guide, the pair would turn back to Lhasa once we reached Golmud, our first major town in the province. Marking our final day together were some of the most drastic changes in climate since we had left Yecheng. Within ten hours, we went from icy winds and snow flurries in a wild animal reserve, over a pass in the Tanggula Mountains bordered by a glacier, and then finally into dusty desert flatlands, bringing our Tibetan Plateau experience full circle.

That evening in Golmud, Amy and I took our two Tibetan friends out to a noodle dinner at a small restaurant next to our hotel. The conversation covered topics like our trip, where we planned to go next, and their experiences leading other tours. Amy wanted to know about how they spent their time when not guiding trips and asked about their plans for when they returned to Lhasa. Ciren was looking forward to the off-season, which was about to start now that the snows were coming, and was thinking about opening a noodle shop when he got back. He also enjoyed the opportunity to spend time with his wife and daughter. Paseng was more the strong, silent type. Though his Chinese was better than Ciren's (we got the impression that his Chinese might be better than Ciren's English too), he seemed to enjoy listening more than contributing and on our final night he mostly just sat with his beer and noodles chuckling and nodding at our conversation.

The following morning Amy and I were on our own again for the first time in nearly a month. It felt strangely unfamiliar, both liberating and disorienting. Throughout Tibet, we had left the logistics of our day-to-day itinerary entirely in Ciren's hands. This was done primarily out of necessity. He knew the roads, conditions, lodgings, and government regulations. Each morning he had dictated to us where to go, what to see, and even where to take photo breaks. Leading a tour group of our kind however – just two people, on one motorcycle, traveling independently of the guide's vehicle – had been new to Ciren. In fact, before coming to pick us up in Kashgar, he and Paseng had never even been to Xinjiang before. This led to sometimes frustrating quirks in the way he guided us, particularly whenever we asked about distances since it had never been something his guests had ever concerned themselves with before.

Once we moved past distances though, Ciren had become a fount of knowledge. Ask him the place we would end up in after the next couple hundred miles and he knew the people, the stops beforehand,

and what we had to look forward to the next day. Now on our own again, we had a flexibility that we hadn't been able to enjoy for weeks. We took the opportunity to sleep in and take care of some chores. It also meant again assuming many of the responsibilities we had been offloading onto Ciren; planning out our route for the day, scouting out lunch breaks, and deciding where to aim for that evening. We also had to re-learn how to pack our bike, no longer having the luxury of leaving anything that wasn't essential in the SUV and even having since added some new cold weather gear.

After Golmud, we continued north towards Qinghai Lake, spending over a day crossing the Badain Jaran Desert that covers the area to its south. It was still a shock passing through desert again after having just spent over two weeks in alpine tundra. For over a hundred miles through the sandy landscape, we paralleled what appeared to be the construction of a new expressway. The only other thing breaking the monotony of pale yellow extending into the horizon was a steady rhythm of highway signs erected high above our heads. I found myself trying to learn the (often ironic or heavy-handed) slogans printed across these signs, a sort of game to keep my mind alert on the otherwise boring highway.

"Production is the first step; focus on quality for the advancement of the country."

"The road connects all of us; love the road, protect the road, rely on everyone."

"Jointly establish traffic culture; share the harmony of safety."

One I found particularly odd. An optimistic and clearly artificial image of idyllic grassy hills and full, green trees was presented high above the sand and dry, desert flora below, along with a petition for citizens to "Increase tree and grass coverage; manage natural erosion."[61]

---

[61]   The area around Qinghai Lake has actually been experiencing intense desertification in recent

225

Despite being in a depression of the Tibetan Plateau, Qinghai Lake is still at a high altitude. Bordered by the Bayan Har mountains to the south and the Qilian Mountains to the north, it's over 10,000 feet above sea level. Together the area forms the source of the Yellow River, which stretches over 3,300 miles from Qinghai to the Yellow Sea by the Korean Peninsula. Amy and I decided it would be nice to take an extra day to make the more than two-hundred-mile drive around the lake. On the approach, after having made it around the Bayan Har range, road signs reminded travelers with almost compensatory repetition of the tourism bureau's slogan for the lake, "The Most Beautiful Lake in China".

Qinghai has a heavy Tibetan influence (21% of the population being ethnic Tibetans) and this was especially perceptible around the lake. Yaks and prayer flags were omnipresent. A couple yurt camps could also be seen dispersed among the flags on the busier south side. On our second day, Amy and I stopped for lunch at one such small encampment by the side of the road, enjoying locally made yak's milk yogurt and a fried potato dish. Qinghai Lake is another traditional destination for Tibetan Buddhist pilgrimages, and we passed several pilgrims in the process of the ritual prostrations as they circumambulated the holy site.

By the second afternoon Amy and I were starting to encounter signs of not just the return to areas of higher population but also the beginning of tourist season. The busiest travel season of the year in the country was only a few days away, the weeklong National Day

---

years, with a desert area increasing by 25% in just the five years between 1999 and 2004. Executing large, ambitious public works projects is of course what the Chinese government does best though. Most well-known of these are the high-speed rail network, the longest in the world at 9,900 miles as of 2014 as well as the Three Gorges Dam, the largest hydroelectric dam in the world by installed capacity. Less well known though are the years of reforestation the government has undertaken in Inner Mongolia and parts of the Gobi. These have done a great deal to reduce the severity of the sandstorms that hit Beijing and other parts of Northeast China every spring and are helping dampen the effects desertification in the country.

celebration marking the founding of the People's Republic of China. It started off as a trickle in the morning but soon the road became inundated with drivers, cyclists, and huge tour company busses from around the country. By the final collection of yurts that was nearest the entrance from the expressway, I was back on high alert for all the hazards I knew Chinese roads were likely to throw at us.

After two months in the remote areas of Western China, a region that covers nearly half the country's surface area but contains less than 5% of its population, we were returning east. The holiday meant we would be doing this at a time when virtually half of its 1.5 billion people were about to go on vacation. We snuck onto the expressway for the final one hundred miles to the provincial capital of Xining, a smallish city with over two million people. We left the Qinghai Lake Basin at a precipitous decline losing 3,000 feet of elevation in just over an hour. The dry terrain of the Tibetan Plateau abruptly began to give way to a lush, almost subtropical climate that sprouted before our eyes off the side of the road. We were entering the beginnings of the Yellow River Valley, headed towards Sichuan province only a couple days away, but, with knuckles white from dozens of cars ripping past on the crowded road, no efforts made to use breaks or lower gears on the decline, I was barely able enjoy it.

Chapter 12 – "People Mountain, People Sea"

Without the structure of a normal work week, time on the road started to blur. There were no more Mondays, or hump-days, or weekends. Instead, there was just yesterday, today, and tomorrow. Even the months started to bleed into each other. For Amy and I, our biggest concerns on a day-to-day basis were when it got light, when it got dark, and what the weather was going to be that day. Little else mattered beyond that. Breaking from the rituals and rigors of life in "the real world" and prioritizing our baser needs was cathartic, and is what makes long distance travel so liberating. The world, however, goes on turning, even if you are turning at a different rhythm. Our disconnect from the calendar meant Amy and I were caught off guard by the approach of a major holiday.

There are several official times during the Chinese calendar that offer workers time off. The biggest is Chinese New Year, which falls between late January and mid-to-late February (depending on how the Lunar and Gregorian calendars line-up) and lasts a full week. Other major Chinese holidays include Mid-Autumn Festival marking the harvest in the fall, Dragon Boat Festival at the summer solstice, and Tomb Sweeping Festival to honor ancestors in the spring. All of these are traditional Chinese holidays and so most of the customs associated with them involve family. Holidaying is thus typically limited to trips home to visit family.[62]

---

[62]   For the shorter holidays, if people live far from home they often won't take the time to travel back. The Chinese New Year, or Spring Festival, is the longest holiday and the most important time of year for people to be home with their families. The closest Western equivalent is Thanksgiving in the U.S., but the Chinese holiday is on a monumentally larger scale. With a diaspora of rural Chinese having moved to cities and factory towns all over the country, there are hundreds of millions of people that travel back home for the New Year, with billions of

The National Holiday in the first week of October celebrates the founding of the People's Republic of China in 1949. As it's a modern creation, it doesn't have the same cultural underpinnings as the rest of the Chinese holidays. With a full week off work and no customs that they feel obliged to observe, China's newly minted middle class consumers take the opportunity to travel and spend money. According to the China National Tourism Administration and the National Bureau of Statistics, there were 420 million tourists traveling during the holiday week in 2013. Revenues in the tourism, retail, and food services industries for the week were over ¥1 trillion (USD $160 billion). This is how the holiday earned its nickname, "Golden Week," and we were about to enter a heavily touristed region just as it was getting underway.

Sichuan province has an incredible amount of cultural and geographical diversity, and a lot that we wanted to do and see. Because of its proximity to Tibet and India, the province has been heavily influenced by Buddhism, particularly in the west. There are areas that have large majority Tibetan populations[63], and the region is home to some of the largest and most famous Buddha carvings in the world, including the Ten-Thousand-Buddha Caves on the Yellow River and the largest stone Buddha in the world in Leshan to the south.

Sichuan is also one of the most biodiverse provinces in the country. There are grass plains in the north, the edge of the Himalayas and the Tibetan Plateau in the west, and the lush, subtropical Sichuan Basin with its dozens of rivers and tributaries (including the Yangtze) towards the center and into the south. One of the most popular natural attractions to visit in China is Jiuzhaigou ("Valley of Nine Villages") National Park and Nature Reserve in the north of the

---

passenger journeys recorded each year during the 40 day period surrounding the holiday (three billion in 2013). This has made it the largest annual human migration in the world.

63   The Ganzi Autonomous Prefecture in Western Sichuan is 78% Tibetan. Han is the second largest ethnic group at 18%.

province. A popular destination for Chinese tourists looking to have a more "natural" travel experience, the park gets millions of visitors every year coming to enjoy the many waterfalls, crystal blue lakes, traditional Tibetan villages, and, in the right season, the colors of the changing leaves.

Our first stop during Golden Week was the Ten-Thousand-Buddha Caves, Bingling Si, in south east Gansu near the Sichuan border ("Bingling" is a transliteration from the Tibetan for "Ten Thousand Buddhas"). The temple is a collection of Buddha grottoes carved into natural caves on the Yellow River. Nearly impossible to reach by road, the grottoes are accessible via speed boat, a 50-minute journey upriver from the Liujiaxia Dam. With lines forming at the ticket office first thing in the morning, the process was a useful bottleneck for crowd control. We shared our chartered boat with six other tourists, a guide, and a driver. Our guide unfortunately served little more purpose than a chaperone. The young woman, donning a pony tail and life vest, appeared entirely disinterested in engaging with the group. As a result, when we made our first stop at a small dock on the banks of the river, Amy and I were completely ignorant of the fact that we had not yet arrived at the temple.

Ascending a steep climb up from the river, the rest of the group began to slowly peel off and after 20 minutes had all abandoned us for the docks. Not realizing that this had only been a temporary stop, Amy and I attributed the attrition to low fitness levels. It wasn't until more than a half-hour of hiking with still no sign of any Buddha carvings that we began to suspect our mistake. At a small gazebo at the top of the climb, the two of us traded theories about what went wrong and tried to get our bearings using a not-to-scale tourist map. Guessing at where we were, I found what looked like a trail that should take us back down to the river and towards the Bingling temple.

While we had completely ditched our guide, and possibly our ride back upriver, what Amy and I ended up getting was a phenomenal hike. We had inadvertently found ourselves completely secluded in a national park, a rarity in China, trekking on a path that offered stunning views of Yellow River canyon lands. Stopping at some of the overlooks, Amy and I took in 360-degree views, a protruding network of stone ridgelines draped in green. Sticking straight up into the sky like columns of soldiers, they marched in formation towards the swirling waters of the Yellow River below.

After a little more than an hour of hiking, we reached a peripheral temple two miles from the main site and were able to hitch a ride on an oversized golf-cart that was shuttling tourists between the two. When we finally arrived at Bingling, despite being among other people again, we were both pleasantly surprised by the park. The staggered nature in which people arrived and the narrow wooden pathways that hung from the red sandstone cliffs that housed the carvings alleviated the smothering of the crowds. The main attraction at Bingling Temple is a one-hundred-foot high, seated Maitreya Buddha[64]. It sits toward the back of the peninsula that contains the 183 caves of Bingling, carved directly into the exposed yellow stone of the cliff. Overlooking the bridged crossing of a Yellow River tributary, the 1,200-year-old figure remained an impressive sight despite the scaffolding and plastic that covered its limbs for restoration work during our visit.[65]

---

[64] The Maitreya Buddha is also known as the Future Buddha, a bodhisattva that has not yet appeared on earth but will reincarnate and reach enlightenment at a time when most people have forgotten the teachings of the Buddha. The Future Buddha will succeed the present Buddha, also known as Sakyamuni Buddha (of which depictions can also be found at the Bingling Temple). The large, seated Maitreya Buddha at Bingling, built during the Tang Dynasty, is also heavily influenced by the Indian artistic renditions typical of the earlier Chinese Buddhist carvings.

[65] The Temple area is a collection of Buddha statues and sculptures built and added to by a succession of Chinese dynasties. The first were begun in the year 420 AD at the end of the Western Qin Kingdom with subsequent additions made through the Wei, Sui, Tang, Song,

After Bingling, we rode south, leaving the mountains and deciduous forests of the Yellow River basin and entering the plains of northern Sichuan. One moment we were in a leafy and autumnal park, and the next we were through a tunnel and out into wide open plains dotted with yurts and prayer flags. There though, Amy and I found ourselves also bumping up against the first waves of migratory tourists.

The two-lane provincial roads seemed ill-equipped to handle the volume of traffic that had arrived. Even without any major attractions or outlooks, we got caught behind long lines of passenger cars snaking across the rolling plains. The road had no shoulder and no accommodations were made for people to stop for rests or photos without obstructing traffic. This, however, didn't stop the visiting urban dwellers. Long blockages formed throughout the valley where cars had stopped without warning for a break, one wheel in the grass and the rest blocking traffic. Once, after having managed to get to the front of one such logjam, I slowed to rubberneck, curious what the cause of our most recent ten minute delay had been. I found a Chinese family grazing on the grass, casually stretching their legs. Irritated, I noted that there seemed to be no urgency to their movements or acknowledgement of how their actions were impacting traffic. We finally made it to the stopped car and watched a man with a wide-brimmed fisherman's cap on his head, probably the father, walking over to the others and gesturing for them to gather together for a photo. Holding a DSLR camera mounted with a massive telescopic lens, he motioned them closer with his free hand. Peace sign poses of his subjects in place, the man lifted the camera and pointed at his family, which, I noted with a hint of schadenfreude, was framed perfectly by the setting sun behind them such that each

---

Yuan, Ming, and Qing. Over time much of the work has been lost due to earthquakes, looters, and exposure to the elements. Two hundred lower caves were also flooded when the nearby dam was built. There are 694 stone statues and 82 clay sculptures remaining today.

person was sure to be silhouetted into obscurity.

While the invasion was disruptive for our experience, Sichuan's ever-industrious local entrepreneurs were fully prepared to cash in on the Golden Week action. Posters on the side of the road advertised horse riding, colorful signs offered traditional Tibetan meals, and large collections of yurts were set up in the grass for overnight stays. Wild haired, rugged Tibetan men in cowboy hats stood at the road waving down cars as they passed. We encountered one or two of these street callers every couple of miles, all competing for the attention of passing motorists.

We had just over a day riding through the chilly, windswept grass plains. Riding south as we began to put them behind us, I caught a sign in passing that pointed down a small spur road into some trees. I was surprised to read that that the nondescript road apparently led towards Jiuzhaigou National Park. We hadn't even realized we were anywhere close to the park nor had we done any planning for a visit, so when I saw the sign I pulled off onto the shoulder of the road. It took me totally by surprise and given that an unknown detour could take us off schedule, I wanted to check with Amy. Jiuzhaigou was one of the original pins on the map of our planned route, and so through muffled affirmations in our helmet we decided to go for it, pulled off the National Highway, and left the swarms of tourists behind.

The hills turned into mountains and the plains sprouted forests. The climate was reminiscent of the temperate woodlands in the Eastern U.S. Switchbacks propelled us over imposing mountain passes. Mostly covered in trees in the midst of their seasonal transformation, they were warmer than the ridgelines we had grown accustomed to back in Tibet.

It turned out that this northern approach was almost completely out of use with visitors to the park. With Chengdu and a new airport specially built to service it in the south, our way was trafficked by far more pigs, dogs, sheep, and cows than cars or busses. The road itself had been ravaged by landslides and, because it was seldom used, repairs and cleanup hadn't been a priority, despite the local farming communities that inhabited the area. After a couple of hours, tourist signs for various scenic areas began to appear. These grew more frequent as we got closer to the park, and road conditions correspondingly improved along with the uptick in traffic. When I started to spot distance signs for Jiuzhaigou itself, I thought it was time to start looking for lodging.

Before we'd even arrived at any major town or settlement, Amy and I started spotting people standing by the side of the road. Too many of them to be hitchhikers, and some standing as little as a few dozen yards apart, I noticed many holding up pieces of cardboard with two characters written in black marker – "*zhu su*", lodging. Figuring a place to stay for the night would get harder to come by the closer we got to the entrance, I pulled over beside a young girl in her 20s and inquired about what was available.

It turned out that all of these people by the side of the road were neither hitchhikers nor hoteliers. Just local villagers. During the high season, many of them consolidated space in their homes, cleaned up a bedroom, and offered the now vacant room to passing tourists. I found it remarkable how these local villagers in the remote mountains of northern Sichuan had taken it upon themselves to create such a dynamic, if informal, marketplace. Though it's unlikely that many of them were aware of it, these were very similar to the circumstances under which another idea for an exchange of spare rooms had sprung up back in the U.S. This marketplace of course was Airbnb. The founders, friends from studying industrial design together in college, found themselves short on cash when they were roommates in San Francisco in 2007. They happened on an opportunity to help pay for rent when an industrial design conference was in town and local hotels were reaching capacity. Dusting off a couple air mattresses (the original name of the company was actually Airbed & Breakfast), they advertised their apartment online and found three takers for $80 each. From these humble beginnings, not too unlike the resourceful locals of Jiuzhaigou, a multi-billion dollar business was born. An area that today is saturated with large, Western hotel chains (particularly for the last few miles before the entrance), Jiuzhaigou during the National Holiday seemed to be facing similar circumstances and ripe with opportunity.[66]

The girl who we stopped to talk to was a college student in Chengdu, back home for the holiday to help her parents take guests for the week. After we had decided to accept the offer, the girl walked down a side street off the main road and we followed behind on the bike. It was a steep, narrow strip of asphalt, just wide enough for a single car. Weaving through a village, we climbed up a small hill until we arrived at a quaint courtyard home tucked away among some fruit trees and grapevines. The room we were staying in appeared to be the girl's (it had an abundance of pink and a couple posters of boyish Asian pop celebrities on the walls). It was cleaner than any "International Business Hotel" that we could have hoped for and the family was incredibly friendly. We had dinner with them on the couches in their dimly lit living room two doors down the courtyard. The girl's dad, a quiet man with a soft, genial smile, offered us each a tall glass of the special local *baijiu*. With temperatures dropping to near freezing and a long, stressful day of riding, Amy and I took him up on the offer. Thankfully, this particular Sichuan strain of the clear Chinese spirit was sweeter and more bearable than some of its other

---

[66]   Despite the remoteness of the area, Jiuzhaigou is filled with many large capacity accommodations. And it's not just local brands either. Luxury Western chains have also established themselves at the park including Sheraton, Howard Johnson, Intercontinental, and Holiday Inn. In 2015, there were over 150 hotels in Jiuzhaigou county, not including the many other inns and specialty accommodations in the area. Assuming an average capacity of 1,000 per hotel (at around 400 rooms each) this gives the area's hotels a capacity of around 60,000 people. The Intercontinental is the largest in the area, advertising over 1,020 rooms alone.

more jet fuel, urea-y inclined counterparts from around the country, bringing a comforting warmth in the frosty autumnal mountains.

Not long after we had arrived in the village, we were warned by a tourist staying at another home nearby that we should head to the park that night to pick up our tickets for the following day. He also recommended that we leave for the park before dawn, no later than 5:30 to try and beat the crowds. Even these warnings didn't prepare Amy or I for the crowds we would be facing over the next 24 hours.

While the ticket office was only 15 miles away from the village, it still took over an hour to arrive. If we hadn't been able to squeeze through stopped traffic on the bike, it would have taken twice that. The approach road, a narrow, winding, two-lane strip of asphalt at the foothills of the park, was not built to handle the volume of visitors that had arrived. Despite the abundance of high-capacity hotels that began sprouting up, it never widened, aggravating the bottleneck. We found a space where we could park the bike and walked the final bit to the ticket office. By the time we had secured our entrances passes, the sun had set and we were riding back in the dark. I noted, with some gratitude for the nimbleness of our mount, that there were still cars on the opposite side of the road which we had passed on our way up, barely moved from where they'd been nearly a half-hour before. The next morning, still on the advice on our neighbor, we left before dawn. Sadly we found the situation not much improved and it took over 30 minutes before we got close enough to park our bike.

There is a saying in Chinese, "*ren shan ren hai*" – "people mountain, people sea". This phrase has never been more perfectly embodied for me than it was getting in line to enter the park. Before we had even reached the entrance plaza, there was a mile of shops and souvenir stands. Local snacks, panda hats, commemorative postcards, it was all available before you even made it to the ticket booth. There was no purpose of direction or self-determination in how anyone walked among those thousands of people. Rather, we all had no choice but to move downstream with the tide of the crowds. To stray was perilous. The stalls of street hawkers lined the pathways like dikes where the waves of crowds sometimes broke. The slightest eye contact with a vendor and you could be sucked into a foaming eddy of multi-colored yuan notes.

At the park entrance, Amy and I slipped into the throbbing rabble of tourists, loosely structured into columns funneled towards the gates. After a long wait, we had finally made it to the front when, to our surprise, we were rebuffed by the guard. Apparently we had been in line for the busses. Our tickets however were walking only. After asking what that meant, we were quickly shooed off towards the far left of the massive entrance. There, we found a single, squat booth, separated from the rest and obscured from view by the shade of overhanging trees. Without a single person in line, it felt like we had made a mistake. We would later find out that of all the people visiting the park that day, estimated at between 30 to 50 thousand, Amy and I were two of only four people not taking the bus.[67]

There are around 40 miles of roads that run through the three main valleys of the park. These roads are reserved solely for the use of the shuttle busses which take visitors between the park's many scenic outlooks. Private vehicles of any kind are not allowed. There is only one entrance to the Jiuzhaigou area, the place where you board the busses, and it is only open between the hours of 7am and 7pm. Overnight camping is absolutely forbidden. Coming from a hiking background and having a lot of experience with the national and state parks back in the U.S., including the Adirondacks, Yosemite, the Smokey Mountains, and the Shenandoahs, I found the rigid structure bordering on the absurd (though I can't say entirely unexpected). The scenery in Jiuzhaigou was picturesque, deserving of its reputation.

---

[67]   The visitor estimate was given to us by people at the park at the time of our visit. In 2013, the year of The Great Ride of China, 2.93 million people visited Jiuzhaigou. Of that number, the park had 208,416 visitorse during the week of the October National Holiday alone.

Vivid, crystalline blues from the lakes, trees in the midst of changing colors, and the surrounding mountains made for calendar-worthy backdrops. My impression of the way it had all been organized though was that the whole experience had been transformed into a carnival attraction. Huge crowds of people were shuttled from one platform to the next, moving between lakes, waterfalls, and artificial Tibetan villages. A bus would empty at a rest stop, the crowds would disembark, pictures would be snapped, a couple plaques read, and then people would slowly drift back in line waiting for another bus to take them to the next photo opportunity.

As a result of this assembly line approach to viewing nature, Amy and I managed to have the boardwalk pathways almost entirely to ourselves. Tucked away in the woods, these trails paralleled the shuttle roads but remained relatively secluded. Somehow amongst a crowd of people numbering in the tens of thousands concentrated in a relatively small area, Amy and I had once again (and again entirely by accident) found a cloistered pocket of peace within China's zoo-like displays of nature.

We managed to hike over 12 miles that day out of a possible 80. Looking up at the surrounding peaks that bordered the valley, I lamented the potential Jiuzhaigou had as a hiking park. I thought of it being made in the same mold as the Adirondacks, Yosemite, or the Grand Canyon. Amy reasoned that maybe it had been structured in this way for crowd control. Limiting people only to a set number of places, and having full control over their movements, it seemed like an appropriate argument. My feeling though was that steep, rugged trails up the ridgelines would be sufficiently self-selecting. With a naturally high barrier to entry, the total amount of people willing to make the arduous climbs would limit themselves. Why hike for a couple hours to get a view from above what you could just as easily drive to from below for a quick snapshot at a scenic overlook? Or at least that's how it seemed to work in equally heavy-trafficked parks back home.

***

At this point, according to our original itinerary, the next stops would be Chengdu followed by Chongqing municipality for the CIMA event. After Jiuzhaigou though we were now only one and two days ride away from each respectively. Despite our greatly extended itinerary, it looked like Amy and I were ahead of schedule with regards to our upcoming obligation to CFMoto. Even with a day off to visit the pandas and see the sights around Chengdu, the motorcycle expo in Chongqing was still ten days away, which put us in a somewhat difficult position. Over a week was way more downtime than either of us wanted to take. We also couldn't stray too far away while getting more miles and seeing sights either. What if something went wrong and we ended up too far away from Chongqing to make it in time?

After making our way a couple hours from Jiuzhaigou, Amy and I sat down at a small roadside Xinjiang restaurant for lunch. I took out my phone, opened up Baidu Maps, and the two of us started to go over our options.

Currently we were in the northern regions of Sichuan province. To our east was the tip of southeastern Gansu and Xi'an in Shaanxi province. To our south were the developed areas of Central Sichuan, including the capital, Chengdu. Finally, to our southwest was the Sichuan–Tibet Highway, the well known scenic road to Lhasa that we had not been allowed to traverse within Tibet. This region of western Sichuan appeared from the map to be incredibly remote. Village names were lightly scattered along the small provincial roads and two National Highways that ran parallel through the area. This route would take us west on the G317, the northern of the two roads, as far as we could go towards the Tibetan border without being accompanied by a guide. The last serviceable southward road in Sichuan was a small, remote provincial highway that would lead us to the main Sichuan–Tibet Highway, the G318, which we could follow all the way back to Chengdu.

The challenge was appealing and the allure of this westerly road was seductive. Amy and I were wary, however, of straying too far from developed cities and roads. The accompanying risk of delays could cause us to miss the CIMA opening day, something we were required to participate in by our benefactors at CFMoto. We attempted futilely to extract more information on the area from locals and passing tourists, but neither could shed any reliable light on what to expect.

Unable to commit at lunch, Amy and I headed back on the road until a couple hours later when we reached our literal fork in the road, and were forced to make a decision: go south directly to Chengdu (the direction all the tourist busses seemed to be heading) or west into the mountains and back towards Tibet. In the end, the draw of the Sichuan– Tibet highway and our aversion to the idea of waiting in Chongqing for a week won us over and we opted, once again, for the unknown.

The first day and a half on our new route was relaxed. We made our way southwest across well-paved roads, winding through rolling grasslands. The hills were littered with herds of grazing yaks. Valleys covered in forests of brightly colored prayer flag teepees made the Tibetan influence even more tangible.

The relative remoteness of the area could be felt in the level of attention we were drawing at gas stations. Once, as I came back from the pump, fuel sloshing around in the watering can, I found Amy surrounded by wordless, dark skinned men in a circle around her and the bike. Having left their own motorcycles off to the side, the spectators were clothed in brightly colored traditional Tibetan robes, long sleeves hanging down almost to the ground (an enhancement that looked useful for keeping their hands warm when riding through the frigid wind). Reminiscent of a Tusken raider from the *Star Wars* desert planet of Tatooine, more than one had scarves wrapped around their mouths and heads leaving nothing showing but calm, dispassionate eyes. I noticed some also had long knives in decorative sheaths hanging from their waists as they silently watched me tip the gas into our tank, hands tucked into the folds of their robes.

We continued farther west. The villages became less frequent. The mountains started rising above us and gorges were sliced hundreds of feet below. Nearly every road we went down seemed to be paralleling a river, passing through increasingly lush canyons. With the green of the mountains rising up to one side and fast moving rivers down the other, the pavement became more degraded with each passing mile. We started experiencing long stretches of the tarmac that had turned almost wavy, warped from overweight traffic and harsh weather conditions. Potholes too were increasing in both frequency and severity.

We passed through towns that crept their way away from the road and up into the surrounding hills. Some appeared to be attempting, futilely, to draw on the tourist traffic from the east. We passed by stands selling prayer flags from boxes along the dusty roads and signs urging us to go visit local monasteries advertised as "AAAAA rated" tourist destinations. Nearly all the vehicles and people we passed however were either local Tibetans or road workers.

Early one evening we drove down the main street of one of these towns. Looking for a place to stay, we found mostly decrepit lodgings set up for migrant laborers. I pulled into a driveway next to one building that advertised vacancies and started to unload some of our gear. Busying myself with the layer of straps holding our bags into place, I suddenly picked up on the drifting sound of distinctly American voices. Distracted from my work, I decided to peek around the corner where I found a home appliance shop attached to the side of our guesthouse. The store was wide, with its entire shopfront taking up most of the block, and entirely open to show off the washing machines prominently on display in the center. These seemed to make up the majority of their stock, but supplementing these, along the wall that bordered our hotel, was a wall of televisions. There were nearly a dozen of them of varying sizes, and almost all of them were playing Ridley Scott's *Black Hawk Down*.

Not having had entertainment like this since our hotel in Lhasa (and even that stuff wasn't that great), I was hooked immediately. The shopkeep, noticing my hypnotic trance, walked over with a small, bright blue plastic stool. He put it down next to the washing machines facing the TV wall and voicelessly gestured for me to sit down with a smile that seemed to say "enjoy!" I spent the next two hours on that little stool, still fully dressed in all of my dusty riding gear, taking only one break to help carry the bags from the bike up to our room and grab a beer from a street vendor down the road. Amy eventually joined, at which point she too was provided with a plastic stool of her own.

The trip through Western Sichuan ended up being the most challenging section of our whole journey in China. Because of a mixture of its remoteness and a wet climate that causes frequent landslides down the steep canyon cliffs, the road conditions became rugged to the point of feeling impassible. We spent days with almost no pavement. Some days we were on the road for over eight hours without being able to cover any more than 60 to 80 miles. Once, we reached a stretch of road blocked off by a construction worker. He sat on a stool beside a sign with the contradictory notice that the road was closed but we could enter at our own risk.

These closed-off sections typically signaled a 20-minute wait while a giant scoop truck up ahead cleared away a landslide or dug into a hill to expand the nascent, dusty highway. At one section we were made to wait as one of these trucks was actually filling in what seemed to be a piece of road that had just recently collapsed and fallen down into the river that roared below. Here, the site foreman waved Amy and I through before the cars, as we were on a motorcycle and the new road was deemed still unable to hold the weight of the larger vehicles.

Everything we had with us got covered in dust during these few days. Passing cars and trucks kicked up clouds of sand which you could see from half a mile away as they approached, eventually serving us with face fulls of dirt once they caught us. Navigation was difficult too given that none of the roads seemed to have been completed yet. We more than once reached forks in the road. Choosing what seemed to be the wider, better maintained path, we would quickly find it to become ever narrower as it climbed up a mountain before disappearing towards a scattering of small homes on the escarpment, leaving us little choice but to turn back.

Getting directions was difficult too. When we were lucky enough to get GPS reception, it was rare that intersections were even included on the maps. Asking locals for directions was usually met with either blank stares or empty promises of a destination only 20 minutes away. When we finally made it to the turn south from the G317 towards the G318, a young Tibetan woman at a restaurant, wearing a purple, wide-brimmed hat and a kind mien, told us with a reassuring smile that the ride to the G318 should only take a couple hours and was paved after only 50 miles of construction. This seemed like reliable information as she said she was from a town we would pass along the way. Unfortunately, nearly the whole thing was unpaved and ended up taking us nearly two full days to cover.

The G318 itself was only marginally better. Given that it was the official Sichuan–Tibet Highway, it had more traffic than the G317, however like its parallel counterpart to the north, it was also in the midst of being repaired (or built). We crossed several traffic stops where they were laying down new asphalt. Long lines of cars would wait on ridgelines overlooking the edges of the Tibetan Plateau while steamrollers made their slow progress overtop wet pavement. We were still always allowed to pass before the waiting cars, who weren't to be trusted on still steaming asphalt. With all of our luggage and two riders, the soft road could be felt bending underneath the wheels as we cautiously advanced. Later, I'd usually find bits of tarmac picked up from these passings still stuck in the grooves of the tires.

One of the most challenging things about the G318 was the long caravans of military trucks traveling in and out of Tibet. We had encountered a similar situation in our crossing of Tibet where it had been tedious, but far easier, to pass the lines of as many of 50 trucks on the wide highways of the plateaus back in southern Tibet. In the mountains of Sichuan however there was no way to avoid them. In the sections of road that were still unpaved, deep parallel grooves had been left in the still exposed earth. The way these dried after heavy rains left very little flat dirt to drive on. At times we had nothing but the tire tracks to drive along, uncertainly surfing along a tightrope of dirt ditches. These precarious pathways were so deep in some places that the gutter walls rose a foot on either side, halfway up our wheels, leaving no flexibility to react to the capricious veerings of wayward traffic.

Despite all of these challenges, the weeklong excursion into Western Sichuan turned out to be one of my favorite parts of our trip. The scenery was stunning. Despite the lack of pavement and mouthfuls of dust, the deep greens and roaring rivers of the gorges when we first diverged from our itinerary put a huge smile on my face. As we moved west on our approach to the eastern foot of the Himalayas, the hills shot up into mountains and the valleys widened out. Small snow flurries greeted us as we passed over high-altitude passes but the views of endless rows of mountains were reward enough to make up for it. Amy's memory and lower back were not quite as forgiving of Western Sichuan. With little control over how we confronted uneven surfaces and the back of my helmet depriving her of the views, there was less for her to enjoy.

Something we were both able to appreciate however was the opportunity to enjoy an unfiltered version of one of China's most scenic regions. In contrast to Jiuzhaigou, which delivered a highly structured, strictly controlled environment perpetually swarming with tourists, the areas of Western Sichuan were devoid of any of the cheap attempts at commercialization that we were used to. We drove through small Tibetan villages composed of traditional homes, authentically built in styles we hadn't seen anywhere else in the country. Mostly wooden constructions, the cube-like buildings rose several stories high, mounted with triangular roofs and brightly colored trimmings.

It also felt like we were getting an opportunity to experience "Tibet Lite". The cultural influences of the Tibetan ethnic majority in the region could be seen everywhere from the prayer flags that lined the roads to the impressive monasteries garnished with golden roofs, built into the sides of mountains that overlooked raging rivers below. At some restaurants in small villages, Amy and I would find ourselves seated next to a group of monks from a nearby temple. At others, we met elderly nuns smiling through wrinkled faces, hands outstretched for alms from the patrons. Considering that our entire experience in Tibet had been tightly controlled, with the need to be accompanied everywhere, facing constant roadblocks and speed controls, and requiring us to register at every gas station and major town, this relatively restriction-free exposure to Tibetan culture felt more genuine in every way. Amy and I both felt extremely fortunate for the experience, especially considering that as the National Highways neared completion, the area was likely to be completely transformed in the proceeding years.

Our last night before Chengdu, the roads finally seemed to hold out and the last of the major construction faded behind us. With the sun starting to set, we found ourselves in a beautiful valley walled on both sides by tall mountains. A river cut through the center and the colors of the fading light metamorphosed it into a crystalline, bright orange. Dotted across the valley on either side of the river were the Tibetan cube-homes. I started to see some people holding signs with the now familiar characters for lodging on them. Considering it would be getting dark soon and we were nowhere near the next town, Amy and I decided to pull over and enquire with a group of locals with their "*zhu su*" advertisement.

The group was a family made up of an elderly couple, a youngish-looking woman with hair wrapped and a surgical face mask for the dust, and two young children. The woman and two kids ran over to where we had stopped and we asked them about staying the night. They offered us ¥50 per person including breakfast, ¥80 (about $13 total) if we wanted dinner too. Watching the sun set behind the mountains, Amy and I agreed that in addition to it being a good deal it would be an amazing location to spend a night. After we accepted, the elderly couple walked away down the road without so much as a goodbye, having apparently served their purpose of helping their neighbors attract guests. We were shown down a sloped driveway by the woman and two children, towards a beautiful wooden house on the banks of the river.

After getting the bike settled for the night and unloading all of our bags, we were shown around the house. Next to the main building was a small, one-story structure for keeping animals, mainly yaks. The house itself was three stories high. A narrow and steep stairway led up to the second floor. This was the primary living area which included bedrooms, a living room, and the kitchen and dining area. Our room looked like it was meant as a dorm-style living room with single beds arranged in the same way as the guesthouses we had stayed at in Tibet, forming a semicircle around a stove that sat in the middle.

We were told that eight people called this home, but apparently the men were all away working. It sounded like they were truck drivers and so weren't home very often. There was one other woman who was home, but who had been out with the family's yaks when we had pulled over. The interior of the house had a wonderfully cozy and rustic feel to it. It felt like being in a log cabin, with unfinished wood flooring, large wooden supports running up vertically from floor to ceiling, and small wood (and yak paddy?) powered stoves in each room used for heating and, in the kitchen, cooking.

Our hosts were extremely kind and welcoming. They could all speak Mandarin, including the children, so we were able to communicate with them. The two women were dressed casually, wearing sweatshirts, long, floor-length skirts made from what looked like denim, and comfortable, flat walking shoes. The one that had been holding up the lodging sign kept her hair in a bandana-like hair wrap, but eventually took off the face mask when she got indoors. Both wore long hanging earrings. They had the subtle beauty and kind facial features of Tibetans and remained soft-spoken, though opened up more as the night went on. At first Amy and I thought the two women were sisters, appearing to be almost the same age. We were surprised to find out later though that the one who wore the hair wrap was actually the others' mother-in-law and grandmother to the two young children.

The kids themselves were also enthusiastic hosts. The younger, a small boy of about six, had a wily way about him, a Tibetan Dennis the Menace that knew how cute he was and liked to see how much he could get away with because of it. His older sister, aged ten, had a childish air of faux maturity about her. Eager to prove herself, she confidently went about the various chores she was assigned to help with around the house. These included helping her mother put away the family's yaks for the night (locking the barn house door whose latch was just barely within her reach) and taking care of the cleaning in the kitchen.

With electricity only switched on by the local government during the night, anywhere between 9 and 10pm, the six of us had dinner together by candlelight at a small wooden table against a wall in the kitchen. Dinner was very simple but still nourishing (and very fresh) – peanuts, rice, preserved eggs, cabbage stew, and some extremely spicy roasted peppers. When the power eventually turned on, we plugged in all of our cameras for the night and Amy and I promptly collapsed into our warm winter weather sleeping bags, exhausted from rough roads and pushy trucks, hoping for better conditions for the final day into Chengdu.

The next morning we were treated to a breakfast of freshly made yogurt as well as some cheese, both of which were made from yak's milk. The texture and look of the cheese reminded me almost of string-cheese that I used to have as a kid, but the flavor was sour. They prepared it all right in front of us, separating out the fats from the milk using a tool composed of a large metal bowl that syphoned out the components through two spouts in the bottom. The cheese was then kneaded and stretched by hand (assisted by the young girl) before being served to us on the table with some Tibetan sweet tea.

We tried to get an early start to cover the two hundred miles to Chengdu, a distance we hadn't been able to cover in one day for nearly a week through western Sichuan. With the mists still burning off from the valley we waved goodbye to our hosts and drove off eastward toward the capital. That day took us over one final mountain pass, snow-covered ridges on either side, and down to the mountain tourist town of Kangding, a city built entirely on the near-vertical slope of a mountain. The road continued winding its way down, eventually passing through wide, industrialized river canyons with swirling, brown waters that raged over 1,000 feet below the road, before leading into the subtropical forests of central Sichuan. Traffic steadily increased until we finally started to enter busy municipal counties and National Highways. It had been a week now since we were last within driving distance of Chengdu, and after several hundred miles through unknown territory we had finally rejoined with our original itinerary. Better yet, "Golden Week" was now officially over.

Chapter 13 – The 12th Annual CIMA Motorcycle Exhibition

The onslaught of Golden Week tourism the week before Chengdu was a shock. Traversing remote countryside over the past week had been challenging, but it was the kind of challenge we had expected. It was all baked into the cake of a trip like this. What we had coming up, however, was not, and as a result it overwhelmed and exhausted us both.

The day after we arrived in Chengdu, we found out from Chen Guanping, the Director of China Marketing from CFMoto, that Amy and I would be giving two presentations during the opening day of the CIMA Exhibition, just four days away. This meant that in addition to preparing what we had to say (all of which would be in Chinese), CFMoto would also need an outline for a powerpoint presentation as well as photos and video to play on the screen before and during the talk.

It was only a one-day drive to get to Chongqing and we still had a few days before the opening ceremonies. So with what spare time we had in Chengdu, Amy and I made time to stop by the world famous "Chengdu Research Base of Giant Panda Breeding" to view the their rescued Giant Pandas[68]. With 80% of the world's Panda population in Sichuan province, the base is an extremely important center for research and conservation efforts. Disregarding the giant TV screen playing Kung Fu Panda as you entered it was a tasteful and well-organized animal sanctuary.

---

[68]   Though they are the main attraction, Pandas aren't the only animals on the base. The space acts as a general research facility and sanctuary for over 20 species of rare and endangered animals from Southwest China, including red pandas, black-necked cranes, and white storks.

Amy and I arrived early in the morning, just in time for feeding when the Pandas are at their most active (i.e. slovenly munching on bamboo) and concluded with a walk through the Panda nursery. With all of the vegetation, including a couple bamboo forests and lily ponds, exploring the exhibits over the 92-acre space felt like a walk through a park more than visiting either a zoo or research facility.

Aside from Pandas and Buddha grottoes, Sichuan is also renowned for its food. The most distinctive characteristic of Sichuanese cuisine comes from its generous use of a local peppercorn that induces a powerful numbing sensation upon contact with saliva. The most well-known dish in the region by far is "hot pot" (Sichuanese and Chongqing hot pot dishes can be found all over the country as well as in Chinatowns around the world). Hot pot meals are organized around a simmering stew heated at your table in a large, metal cauldron. Diners cook their own food in the broth which is usually heavily seasoned with Sichuanese peppercorns, beans, garlic, ginger, and sometimes meat stock. When you're having hot pot at a proper restaurant, your table (hot pot is best experienced in a large group) orders a wide range of different raw ingredients brought over on a cart. These dishes include thin slices of mutton or beef, different mushrooms, leafy vegetables, fish, noodles and much more, all of which you can cook at your own leisure. Finally, you get to mix your own sesame-based dipping sauce. With extra seasonings like salt, chives, and even oyster sauce, the sauce makes for a great complement to the freshly cooked food fished from the pot.

Nothing is better than being able to enjoy local food with someone who is actually from the area. You can both avoid any ordering faux pas as well as have the flexibility to be a little more adventurous. The company that helped organize our Tibet tour was based out of Chengdu and our account manager, Jessie, who had helped directly with the logistics when we were in Tibet, was in town as we were passing through. Jessie had given us a lot of support over the past half a year. She even helped us get a 15% discount off the cost of our tour because of our work with Free Lunch for Children. When she heard we were in town, she invited us out for a hot pot dinner, an exciting opportunity to not just meet face to face but also to have a local food guide.

Jessie and a coworker that came along for dinner grew very excited when I told them we wanted to try local dishes as we passed through each province. Chinese frequently ask us before we sit down to a meal, "*zhong guo cai xi guan le ma*?" "Are you used to Chinese food?" Amy and I still get this question after years of living in the country. Apparently many Chinese expect a foreigner of having only a basic familiarity with dumplings, plain rice, and Kung Pao Chicken. Even after reluctant acceptance of adventurous palates by our hosts, moderately dexterous use of chopsticks can still be met with wide-eyed amazement. "*Waaaa* You can use chopsticks too!"

"Are you sure you want to try ANYTHING?" Jessie asked, suspicious that we didn't know what we were getting into.

"Yep. If it's authentically local, then we'd like to try it!" I answered. My confidence however was contrasted with a low groan of protest from Amy, no doubt related to conjured memories of sheep entrail soup.

Jessie and her friend looked at each other with coy smiles. "Ok, well there are a couple of things. It's a bit strange though. Not everyone likes it. But they are definitely local."

"Ok then. Sounds great! Let's go for it." Not wanting to go into this completely blind, I prodded with some apprehension, "What are the dishes exactly?"

"Um…" she said with a hesitant chuckle. "Duck blood… duck intestines… aaaand… pig brain." Jessie's smile was noticeably more nervous as she waited for my response. Amy groaned louder.

"Alright, bring it on!" I said with exaggerated bravado. At the very least it would make for an interesting story. I tried to reassure Amy that this was unlikely to be as bad as our previous experiments with animal innards.

In the end, the reality landed somewhere between our two expectations. We had both actually had duck blood before, which comes served in sliced, gelatinized rectangles. The other two "specialties" however were most definitely new. Because the flavors and aromas of the hot pot broth are so strong, dishes that are cooked in it usually end up being overwhelmed by its flavor. So in the end the most uncomfortable thing about them was the texture. (This was particularly true of the brain. The way in which it quickly liquified in your mouth reminded me a bit of Jello. I even almost began reflexively to squish it around my mouth from cheek to cheek as I would have as a kid). Between the peppers and the sesame dipping sauce, the brain, intestines, and blood were all more than palatable, certainly when compared to our experiment with Ningxia's "complex sheep pieces".

***

A light drizzle had started up as we packed the bike for the two hundred mile ride to Chongqing. Eager to make good time, Amy and I decided to jump on the main expressway after leaving our hotel. Rather than face the likely prospect of village drivers and construction pits on the smaller roads, this felt especially prudent in the rain.

After a couple of hours, we were making pretty good time and decided to break at a roadside rest stop for lunch and respite from the precipitation. As we parked in front of the main service building, a couple of older Chinese men, dressed in what looked like security uniforms and orange safety vests, started making their way over to us. Peeling off her helmet and gloves, Amy became concerned about getting kicked off the highway. We were used to being approached at these types of rest areas though. Usually it was just people curious about us and the bike. In the past, answering with short one-word answers and nods or pretending not to speak Chinese at all was enough to be left alone, even by inquisitive cops. There seemed to be little point once we were already on to try and kick us off. These men however were scowling as they walked over and, when they arrived, were neither thrilled nor dissuaded by the "dumb foreigner" routine.

"*Mo tuo che bu yun xu shang gao su!*" "Motorcycles aren't allowed on the highway!" one of them said to us, wagging a finger at our motorcycle in indignant disapproval.

Acting like I couldn't understand I smiled and pointed down the road, "Chongqing, Chongqing."

Then, acting as if we had satisfactorily answered their question, I began to walk toward the building entrance. I mumbled to Amy that she should play along and we left the two men standing next to our motorcycle, growling at our backs.

Their reflective orange jackets indicated they were either volunteers or low level security guards at the service station. They didn't seem to have any actual authority. I figured that it would be too much trouble for them to kick us off and we'd be left to eat our lunch in peace.

Their resentment however ran more than skin deep, and it wasn't long after we were seated with our trays of half-day-old cafeteria-style Chinese food, Amy and my rain gear dripping puddles on the floor next to us, that the two volunteers had returned. This time though we were outnumbered and outgunned. The disgruntled duo had come equipped with patronizing smirks and two official police officers.

"Can... you... speak... Chineeeese?" the lead cop asked us with a nervous smile and tortured English.

"No, I'm sorry we can't." I replied innocently. "Why? What's the problem?"

The officer turned to his partner with an anxious, wide-eyed grin. It was the kind that we had come to expect from people trying to find the nicest and easiest way to communicate that we were breaking a rule. He struggled for several minutes, stumbling over the familiar arguments. I continued to play dumb by either just curiously asking "Why?" or pretending I couldn't understand what he was saying. Meanwhile, as this conversation progressed, a small crowd had formed behind the two policemen, an audience of other motorists and rest stop employees, spectators to the curious drama unfolding in front of them.

Eventually, the lead cop, who I assume had given up on receiving any language support from his partner, pulled out an old Nokia feature phone from his pocket and called someone. I listened as he explained the situation to the person on the other line, asking for help translating. After giving the full rundown, he handed the phone over to me so that I could start speaking with his friend.[69]

The cops were being extremely persistent and it looked like they had the support of the crowd. In addition to the two guards from earlier, there were a couple of other staff members that seemed to be especially eager to see us brought to justice. One female janitor in particular, leaning on her mop as she watched, kept smirking at every answer we gave and watching with perverse glee as the police (who themselves were actually quite friendly about the whole thing) kept pushing. It was starting to seem increasingly unlikely that we were going to get out of this and be allowed to stay on the expressway.

---

[69]   Calling up a bilingual friend and handing the phone over to someone you need help communicating with is a common practice in China. Tourists in major cities often can confidently hand over a cellphone to a cab driver to have him or her speak to someone from their hotel or travel agency. The cabbie will immediately comprehend the request, letting loose a flurry of dialogue with the person on the phone (often intoning a strange familiarity as if catching up with an old friend or arguing with a relative) until the exchange has been concluded. This ends with a wordless handing back of the phone and either a vigorous shake of the head, or a grunt of "okay".

I am stubborn by nature however (possibly in part thanks to my New York City upbringing). I genuinely believed that, especially in the rain, the highway was a safer place to be than the smaller provincial and national highways. There were no construction pits with miles of dug up pavement and dirt, no dogs running out from marketplaces, no electric scooters suddenly swerving into the street against traffic, and no honking commuter busses or freight trucks pushing us off onto the shoulder. After three years of riding motorcycles in China, covering tens of thousands of miles on both kinds of roads, I had been in three traffic accidents. Fortunately none were serious but all were on smaller roads and all were with smaller electric scooters or low displacement engine motorcycles that couldn't even reach speeds suitable for the highway in the first place. Generally in China, government slogans might as well be gospel and according to the government it was too dangerous for a motorcycle to be on a high-speed roadway, even if that motorcycle is built for high speeds.

Amy, I knew, never really thought these principled stands of mine were worth it. She was generally of the opinion that it would be better to just let it go. And I would… eventually. So, while it was ultimately hopeless to resist, I was determined to make this as difficult for them as possible. I explained to the man on the phone, who introduced himself as a coworker of the policeman and whose English was only marginally better than his colleague's, that we had gotten on the highway because the smaller roads were too dangerous in the rain. This was so contrary to what he knew to be true that the man questioned if he'd heard me properly and didn't know how to respond. After some silence, I handed the phone back to the cop who had my message translated.

In disbelief, he repeated what I had told his friend, "*Ta shuo gao su lu GENG anquan ma??*" "He says that the expressway is MORE safe??" There was a collective gasp from the audience behind him. The more malicious of the crowd laughed out loud. Some exclaimed in disbelief,

"*GENG anquan??*" "MORE safe??" heads shaking with patronizing grins as if to say, "These foreigners really don't know anything!"

The passing back and forth of the cellphone went on for a few more minutes. The cops tried their best to explain to us how the highway *wasn't* safe. The speeds were too fast and the rule was motorcycles were not allowed. There was no reason to the argument but there was no way it would ever move in my favor. We still had more than a hundred miles left to Chongqing and the cops would not be cowed. Finally, ready to submit, I took the phone back.

"So just to be clear, you're saying you want us to get off of the SAFER road, the highway, and onto the more dangerous road, the national road?" I asked defiantly.

"Yes yes!" the man said in exasperated celebration, relieved that I seemed to finally understand what he was asking.

"And we have to get off of this road because it's too dangerous here?"

"Yes. That is why," he replied. "The cars on highway too quick. Very dangerous."

I thrust the phone back towards the officer and finally nodded in obstinate acquiescence.

We were allowed to finish our lunches, which by now had gone from lukewarm to cold, while the crowd dispersed and the two policemen waited for us at another table. After we had finished, Amy and I put all of our rain layers back on and followed them down the highway to the next exit.

At the risk of sounding overly smug, I wish the cops could have kept coming with us once we were off the highway. Luckily we did not get into an accident, but the road conditions were terrible. There was one stretch of nearly 20 miles of pure construction. Long tracts of dirt had been transformed by the rain into slick mud. There were potholes so wide they nearly reached the full width of the road. Amy and I slid our way through one village that was mud from beginning to end, made to swerve off onto the sidewalk several times as oncoming cars forced their way down the road that had been narrowed by temporary blue, tin barriers walling off construction on the opposite side.

The rain never let up, and between the run-in with the cops, the horrible roads, and a second attempt at the highway thwarted, it wasn't until after dark, all of our gear soaked through and everything from our bike to our helmets splattered with mud, that we finally pulled into our hotel on the outskirts of the city.

***

Chongqing is one of the four provincial-level municipalities in China and the only one inland. The other three are Beijing, Tianjin, and Shanghai. This meant that Chongqing marked province number 15 out of 33 for our trip!

Though the main urban center has an estimated population of between eight and ten million residents, the municipality region of Chongqing itself covers an area of 31,800 square miles (or 82,400 square km) with a population of almost 30 million people. To put that into perspective, that is an area larger than that of Belgium and Switzerland combined, with almost twice the combined populations. Chongqing held particular significance for our trip as it is the motorcycle manufacturing capital of China. The municipality accounts for 60–70% of national motorcycle production with 133 associated companies located within the municipal boundaries. It is also the only major city in the entire country that officially allows motorcycles within its main urban center.[70]

---

[70] Despite the relative openness to motorcycles, the city still bans them from highways even the primary ring roads that encircle the city. Contrary to other cities we had been to around China, where it seemed like once you were in, no one paid you much attention, in Chongqing, the police were much more attentive and strict about kicking us off of these roads. My impression was this was probably due to the fact that motorcycles *were* permitted to enter, so traffic cops were more diligent about enforcing the other rules.

CIMA is an annual event jointly hosted by the city of Chongqing and the China International Motorcycle Trade Exhibition (CIMAMotor). It is a trade show for both Chinese and international companies to showcase their products and brands. The exhibition first started in 2002 and it is the largest motorcycle show of its kind in Asia. With 80% of China's motorcycle production capacity represented by the companies in attendance, it is also the largest exhibition for the commuter motorcycle industry in the world.

For our sponsor CFMoto, CIMA was the most important marketing event of the year and included by far their largest promotional initiatives. So, obviously, it was important to them that we were able to make it to Chongqing for at least the opening day and participate in some of the events they had planned.

It was the evening of October 15th when we arrived, in time for one day of preparation for the opening. CFMoto was putting everyone up in a nice hotel not too far away from the exhibition center, and there were some familiar faces already there to greet us when we arrived in the parking lot. After three months of new people and new surroundings almost every day, it was surreal and jarring to see people that we knew. Most of the staff from our factory trip back in May, including those we had been communicating with while on the road, were there. Fang Shujian, the head technician; Hu Hai, the professional stunt driver; Chen Guanping, the Marketing Director; all these and at least a dozen other staff were waiting for us out front.

Fang Shujian and Hu Hai, both relatively short Chinese men in their 30s, were most enthusiastic about seeing us again. Hu Hai, before I had even turned the bike off, immediately started to help us unload our luggage, though he quickly got lost in the tangle of straps. Fang Shujian had a huge smile on his face and shook my hand vigorously as I got off the bike. I had gotten to know Fang especially well over the previous few months as he had been closer than anyone else to the various challenges we had been facing. The gas leak in

Harbin, our flat tire in Gansu, and the stalling in the desert. He was always the first person I called, and was usually on the receiving end of my frustration. The evening we arrived at the hotel though he seemed so genuinely happy to see Amy and I, and me in particular (since I was usually the one who spoke to him). It made me feel a little guilty about all of the times I had yelled at him over the phone. He was our main contact and my fuse had grown noticeably short with regards to the problems that surfaced. With Fang's childlike excitement though, wide-eyed and eager to hear about the trip, it all seemed to be water under the bridge.

Chen Guanping was another we had been communicating with regularly. Slightly built, taller than Fang and Hu Hai but not quite as tall as I, he had a squirrelly way about him. He never seemed comfortable sustaining eye contact and shifted around a lot when talking. He also had the habit, unfortunately common in China, of giving distressingly limp handshakes. Every time he greeted us it elicited memories in my mind of the worm-like children's toys filled with gel which would squirm out of your hand when you squeezed it.

Chen and I had always seemed to have a tenuous relationship. It wasn't just the eye contact or weak handshake either. Throughout our project he never seemed fully supportive of what we were doing. He would frequently ask additional responsibilities of us (and me in particular) like writing more frequent Chinese blog posts from the road or uploading more high-definition photos and video, even as we went through areas where there wasn't any Internet or where the riding was particularly challenging. One conversation we had had in Yecheng especially had stuck with me.

He and one of his staff had called me up and asked us to upload and post more photos[71]. Yecheng of course was the town at the

---

[71] In general, Amy and I tried to give them access to our media as often as possible, posting photos on Chinese social media from our phones and uploading to cloud storage when we had the opportunities. Chen's objection tended to be that we should post each of these on all of the

gateway to Tibet that had just had its Internet cut off and was under tight lockdown after recent protests.

"You know, we have limited wireless data we can use, and uploading photos will take up a lot," I tried to explain as diplomatically as my temperament would allow. "We don't even always have cell reception."

"No no. You don't understand. Hotels in China will have Internet. You just have to ask them," he tried to rationalize as if to educate me on the local customs.

"Well we don't always stay in hotels. Sometimes we're camping. We're about to enter Tibet too which will be even more difficult. What do we do then?"

"No problem, no problem. Just next time you're in a city, you can get Internet and post more."

"Chen, I don't think you understand the types of areas we are going through. We are in a city right now, but the Internet everywhere is turned off because of recent protests in Xinjiang."

"Oh... Protests?" he asked.

"Yes, protests. Things are not always *wen ding*, they're not always 'stable' where we go."

"Oh..." he said hesitantly, "Ok..." He appeared to be processing this new information, unsure with how to deal with a problem like social unrest and surprised we were faced with conditions like that at all. "*Mei wen ti, mei wen ti.*" "No problem," he mumbled. "*Zhu yi an quan.*" "Stay safe." And that was that.

In general, working with both a Chinese charity and Chinese sponsor, there seemed to be a large disconnect between their expectations of our trip and the reality of actually riding 20,000 miles around China. The marketing team at CFMoto seemed to have this

---

platforms individually, adding to the already two to four hours of non-motorcycle work Amy and I were doing on a daily basis.

vision of Amy and I on a leisurely road trip from big city to big city. Some, like Chen Guanping, almost appeared to resent us for it; privileged foreigners staying in comfortable hotels and riding on well-paved asphalt at their company's expense. The idea that we were spending up to ten hours a day going through construction sites, sand storms, rain, snow, and a host of other exhausting conditions never factored into their calculations.

Amy and I walked into the Chongqing hotel with Chen so we could get checked into our room. Standing at the front desk, now under the bright lights in the lobby, he scanned us slowly from head to foot. He noted holes ripped in the rain gear, mud covering everything, and the disheveled and exhausted looks on our faces after a long day of riding. I imagine our smell wasn't all that inspiring either.

"Oh," he mumbled, almost to himself, eyes averted. "You guys look really tired." It was said in a way as if he was doing us a favor, as if letting us know how bad we looked. He also seemed surprised to see us so ragged in the months since the press conference when we last met face to face.

"Yeah," I replied. "It was a pretty tough day. Raining all the way from Chengdu."

"Your rain suits look really dirty," he said, still surprised as he commented on our CFMoto-branded gear. "We should get you new ones."

This was the first (and only) time he voluntarily offered us support the entire duration of our partnership. I was too tired to respond anymore, and simply nodded my thanks. Amy and I both shared a brief look though, noting our small victory.

Neither of us lingered on the exchange too long however. As Chen finished checking us in, both our thoughts quickly turned to the forthcoming warm shower and soft bed.

We spent the next three days in Chongqing. The whole thing went by in a blur of activity and none of it was under our control. For the people at CFMoto this was already the busiest time of the year, their most heavily invested event, and one that they had worked towards all year. With everything to organize including their huge booth in the main exhibition hall, motorcycle displays, prize giveaways, contests, and press events, there was plenty to do. CIMA was a huge corporate event with people from all over the industry and across the globe setting up for the week. Everyone from small parts manufacturers to domestic Chinese brands like Zongshen and Jincheng to global household names like BMW and Harley-Davidson was represented, a flurry of banners, displays, and scurrying laborers.

Our trip and the Guinness World Record attempt wasn't even close to the most important thing for CFMoto at CIMA either. That year, after several years of negotiations and bureaucratic red tape, the company had finally signed a formal joint venture agreement with one of the top brands in adventure and racing motorcycles, Austrian company KTM.[72] The partnership was going to be announced at a special unveiling on opening day and would mark KTM's official entrance into the Chinese market. It was also a major international validation for CFMoto.

All of the busyness and stress was a huge change of pace for us. With no time to adjust, we went from worrying about bad weather and poor road conditions to corporate dinners and tight deadlines for powerpoint presentations. There was barely even any time for the culture shock to set in.

---

[72] KTM is the bike that Charlie Boorman and Ewan McGregor had originally wanted to take on their round the world trip which became the TV show "Long Way Round". The pair was rebuffed by the company in the end, by representatives claiming that they didn't believe the trip would be successful. They ended up going with two BMW 1200GS's and KTM has probably been kicking themselves ever since.

With two presentations to give, both in Chinese, Amy and I were only able to get a few hours of sleep the night before opening ceremonies. After breakfast at the hotel, the whole CFMoto team packed into a bus to go to the exhibition center about 20 minutes away. A member of the marketing staff, Yang, sat down with Amy and I on the ride over to explain the itinerary for the day. The complex was the size of several aircraft hangars and CIMA was only occupying two out of at least a dozen on site. Both halls were packed with thousands of visitors, press, hobbyists, trade specialists, and international buyers. CIMA was everything you'd expect from an automotive industry show. Scantily clad models, bright lights, new bikes high up on pedestals, and massive screens with promotional videos and generic, high-adrenaline rock music playing on loop. The CFMoto/KTM booth was set up one position away from the entrance. The first spot was occupied by Honda. Covering an area almost three times the size of ours, it could barely be called a booth anymore. Honda had a big announcement they were making at CIMA as well, a new 300cc commuter bike, a small displacement machine specially being released for the Chinese and other developing countries' markets.

Our first presentation was just after the KTM announcement. This took away a lot of the momentum for Amy and I but it was helpful to ease into the experience. We had tried to get the A/V team to time our photos with our script, but they rushed through much faster than we could explain them to the audience of a couple dozen until being shuffled off stage again. Amy and I posed for a few photos with some people from the audience next to the display motorcycles and in just 15 minutes the first event was over.

The second talk was later that evening. It was part of a special event hosted separately from CIMA, one jointly organized by CFMoto and Moto8 (known as *Moto Ba*, a transliteration of "Motor Bar"), the largest online motorcycle forum in China.[73] The event was hosted a little farther out of the main city area at a hotel with conference space able to hold the 400–500 people in attendance.

Guests had ridden from all around the country to be in Chongqing for this special week of motorcycles. The hotel parking lot had an interesting array of bikes covering the full motorcycle spectrum. There were large, expensive BMW tourers, old 750cc Chinese sidecars[74], and smaller Chinese-brand commuter bikes. Before the event, there was a dinner where Amy and I were introduced to CFMoto dealership owners (the "Boss Chen"s and "President Li"s) from around the country. Later we were all filed into a large room with a stage for a show that would last for the next couple hours. There were presentations by different motorcycle hostel owners from around the country, dances by (more) scantily clad women, and even a cross-dressing standup comedian. Amy and I took our turn on stage before one of the dance routines and after a prize giveaway. Our tortured Chinese speech came out a little more comfortably the second time around despite the larger audience. The crowd of Chinese bikers were incredibly receptive to what Amy and I were doing, showing their support with cheers at the applause lines and laughs at our improvised jokes.

The last day in Chongqing was almost as busy as the first two. Without any time during the previous days to wash any of our clothes or catch up on posts for our website and social media, there was a lot we wanted to get done before hitting the road again. In addition to our normal "town day" tasks, I also had to drive across the city to the

---

73   Moto8 has over 1.1 million registered members, with the second largest, Motofans, totaling just under 700,000.

74   The CJ750 is a very popular sidecar motorcycle in China. A copy of the Soviet-era Russian Ural M72, which itself is a copy of a German BMW from the 1930s, the bike has a classic WWII-era look to it. The aesthetics are likely the primary reason for its appeal however given that the build quality is more or less what you would expect from a 1980s Chinese-built copy-of-a-copy.

local CFMoto shop where Fang Shujian had generously (and enthusiastically) volunteered some time to give the bike a full look over. He set us up with a sorely needed new chain, changed the oil and spark plugs, and made some adjustments to the brakes.

While we were in town, Amy and I had also found out that a local radio station was interested in interviewing us. A totally new experience for both of us, it was pretty cool getting invited into the tightly packed recording room and speaking for an hour to the two hosts about our trip. The show was more freeform than our presentations the day before, but the hosts were incredibly patient with our Chinese and very good at keeping the conversation going. They also asked some of the best questions we had received from Chinese media. We covered topics that included the roads, the bike, the charity, and even what some of our thoughts were on China's environmental protection.

***

Stressful and fast paced, while these were technically rest days, Chongqing had drained us. Amy and I were more tired than when we had arrived, after two hundred miles of rain and mud, five days earlier. We had been completely knocked off of the routine we had grown comfortable with since Beijing, which left us disoriented and overwhelmed. From the relatively simple day-to-day goal of going from point A to point B, we had been thrown into the swirl and excitement of one of the world's largest trade shows. We gave presentations in front of hundreds of people in another language. We did meet and greets with company presidents and did a one-hour-long radio interview.

Being ripped out from the simple realities of our trip and dropped so abruptly into the fast paced machinations of the real world made it feel like the trip was almost done. Adding to this, Chongqing had been a major milestone. Just like Harbin in Heilongjiang, Xi'an in Shaanxi, Kashgar in Xinjiang, and Everest and Lhasa in Tibet, it had been one of the major pins on our map since the planning stages. Hitting that goal while at the same time being displaced from our normal routine had been a major shock.

The reality though was that the trip was still far from over. There was still a lot left to do and see on The Great Ride of China. Ahead of us were more than half of the provinces and over 8,000 miles of road left to cover. We had the mountains of southern Sichuan and Yunnan provinces, the sunny tropics of Hainan Island, the rainy areas of the central provinces, and what was sure to be a chilly drive up the east coast at the beginning of winter.

All of these thoughts went through my head as we were finally back on the bike again. Putting all of the excitement of CIMA behind us, we snuck onto the highway and headed back west towards Sichuan. I couldn't help but think how at home I felt being back on the motorcycle. We were heading out towards the unknown. The likelihood of getting stopped by police, bullied around by traffic, and obstructed by road work were all very real possibilities, but a feeling of comfort and relaxation swept through me. It was a feeling that emerged from a place of deep familiarity. All of a sudden I noticed my muscles, from my hands on the grips, to my upright shoulders, to my feet pressing on the foot pegs, all slacken for the first time in days. A smile spread across my face as I gave Amy's knee a comforting squeeze at my side and pulled down on the accelerator. On to the next adventure.

- *Photos from Kashgar to Chongqing* -

Scan the QR code or visit the link below to see pictures from Part 3 of The Great Ride of China

http://book.thegreatrideofchina.com/galleries/part-3

Part IV- Chongqing to the Pearl River Delta

"锲而不舍，金石可镂"
《荀子劝学》
"Through perseverance, even metal and stone can be carved away."
- *From the collected writings of Xunkuang (c. 310 – c. 235 BC)*

~

行百里者半九十
《战国策》
"90 miles is half way in a 100-mile journey."
- *From "Strategy of the Warring States" (380–284 BC)*

Chapter 14 – Giant Buddhas and the Final Days of Sichuan

Asphalt passed underneath our feet at 80mph. There was little trouble skirting tollbooth barriers. Passing cop cars were ignoring us again. After so much time spent off the bike, first in Chengdu and then in Chongqing, the monotony of the highway was grating to me. Deciding that we hadn't come all this way just to ride on an expressway indistinguishable from those back in Beijing, Amy and I took our first opportunity once back in Sichuan to pull off onto a provincial road and meander through the countryside.

We were putting the cities behind us again, and the S305 was well paved with little construction. Our motorcycle dipped and weaved on the long sweeping turns as we waltzed our way through the subtropical hills of the landscape. The road was elevated above surrounding farmlands. Palm trees, thatch-roofed huts, and rice paddies lined the alleyways below. It was a portrait of the "real China", like the one you see in movies rather than the evening news. A place stuck in time as our sliver of modernity blazed a trail through its belly.

With evening approaching, we began to hit up against waves of commuters and were soon drawn in by the eddy of early rush hour traffic. I became entranced by the pure kinetic energy of the scene, a swirl of vehicles notably composed almost entirely of motorcycles. The entropic buzz added to the sense of otherness. Amy and I were surrounded by hundreds of bikers mounted on small capacity two-wheelers. Many wore fake construction caps as a substitute for helmets. They zipped around us in a cloud of industry, sometimes carrying two or three additional passengers, most likely coworkers, on a Chinese-style carpool.

***

Buddhism has left a large footprint on Sichuan, something Amy and I had been cognizant of for weeks. There are over 1,700 years of Buddhist history in the area, with 1,828 operating monasteries run and occupied by over 57,000 monks and nuns. One of the most famous relics in the region is the Leshan Buddha. Built in the early 8th century during the Tang Dynasty, it is the largest stone Buddha in the world and in 1996 was officially named a UNESCO World Heritage Site.

Before we arrived at Leshan however, Amy and I would find ourselves making an unplanned pilgrimage to a site overshadowed by its more celebrated neighbor. Ranked as the second highest stone-carved Buddha and tallest stone depiction of the Sakyamuni Buddha in the world, the over 900-year-old Rongxian Buddha is nonetheless a much lesser known and less frequented site than Leshan. When I first saw signs for a "Giant Buddha of Rongxian County" it was just after we disembarked from the expressway. I thought we were being directed to Leshan just by a different name and so I followed out of curiosity. Had it not been for our decision to get off the expressway and wander the provincial roadways, it's likely we would have missed the signs and the Buddha altogether.

In contrast to Leshan, which we would find the next day packed with hundreds of tourists, there was almost nobody at the temple when we arrived in Rongxian. The park is tucked away on the outskirts of a small village. To arrive, visitors must drive down a narrow road that parallels a small stream. The softly smiling face of the Sakyamuni Buddha can be seen from a quarter mile out on the approach road, peering out over the top of several stories of layered roofs with upturned eaves.

It felt like Amy and I may have been the only tourists in the park. Most of the other visitors were staff or locals who could enter the attraction at a heavily discounted rate.

We parked the bike and chained up our helmets in the parking lot before going to buy our tickets. This was an unplanned stop and we still had some distance to cover before nightfall, so we left the rest of our gear on, hoping to make this a quick visit.

The temple complex was constructed according to traditional feng shui conventions. The gate opened into an open courtyard, framed on either side by single-story buildings. Taking up sentry in the rear was a hill into which the Buddha was carved. Amy and I walked across the courtyard and climbed several flights of stone steps on our way to the pagoda. As we entered the cover of the mountain's vegetation, a gaggle of three girls and two boys ran around the corner of a paved pathway, intercepting us as we walked towards a map of the park. As soon as they became aware of us, two foreigners lumbering around in cumbersome riding armor, two of them immediately blurted out reflexive gasps.

"*Whaaaaa*! Chinese people." I echoed their exclamation back as they slowed their run.

Curiosity piqued having now confirmed we could speak some Chinese, the group began to congregate. "Where are you from?" One of the more rambunctious of the two boys in the group exclaimed.

Around eight years old, they were all dressed in a mishmash of clothing. Their wardrobe looked as if it could have been sourced from a thrift store, Crocs for shoes, deliberately patched denim, and more than one instance of Chenglish labeling.

"American and British." I panted back, still slightly out of breath from the climb.

"Which do you think is which?" Amy asked, trying to quiz the inquisitive eight year olds on our nationalities.

"American. British." the other boy said, pointing at each of us in turn. As soon as I declared the guess correct, the first boy chimed in repeating the answer, vying for attention in an attempt to receive some praise for himself.

I reaffirmed my acknowledgement and walked closer to the posted map of the park. One of the girls now took it upon herself to play tour guide.

"Let me show you where to go!" she said, pushing her way to the front of the group. "Here, here, here, and aaaall over here." She finished with a flourish of her finger that encircled half of the map.

"You had to pay sixty *kuai* to get in didn't you?" one of the boys asked. Before either of us had time to respond, he proclaimed with a puff of his chest, "We only had to pay ten! It's because we're from Rongxian. We come here to play all the time."

The kids waved goodbye as we made to continue down the path, but shadowed us on our approach to the pagoda just short of temple entrance. Amy and I then proceeded to climb up the narrow, almost vertical, wooden staircase on our own. By the time we reached the top level, even with the smiling face of the over 180-foot Sakyamuni Buddha, Amy and I were both feeling the effects of over three months of little to no aerobic exercise, panting heavily as we looked out on the foggy view of the semi-urbanized Rongxian county.

On our way out of the park the kids caught up with us again. Their buzzing excitement was a clear contrast to Amy's and my panting. Their curiosity was admirable, as the children went to great lengths to learn as much as they could about every detail of our exotic-looking gear. In addition to asking after the helmets, the camera mounted on top, or the straw that lead to the water pouch in my pack, they also wandered into the more familiar territory of the economics of our bike:

"What brand is it?"

"How fast does it go?"

273

"What mileage does it get?"

…and (of course) "How much does it cost?"

Neither Amy nor I had any idea what context an eight year old would have for making a judgement on gas mileage. I certainly couldn't see how they'd know what the current market prices were for large (or even small) displacement motorcycles. Through the months and miles following that exchange however, I would think back to those kids after almost every conversation, questions repeated almost word for word, and how remarkably consistent these seemed to be across nearly every generation of Chinese we met.

We arrived in Leshan a bit before dark. It was too late to visit our second giant Buddha that day so we looked for a hotel nearby to spend the night. The town itself was a nondescript, archetypal, small Chinese city. With over half a million people, there was little to set the place apart, filled with not much more than the swarms of people and traffic that Amy and I had grown used to. The town's most defining characteristic were the two wide brown rivers, the Dadu and Min, which ran through its borders.

We wandered the streets after dark, looking for somewhere to eat, and ended up at a safe-looking "*Jia Chang Cai*" or "Homestyle Food" place with a menu of familiar offerings. The food was good, no surprises, and well priced, with most dishes costing less than $4. Towards the end of the meal we were approached by a man in his 40s who Amy and I took to be one of the owners. He walked up to the table and lazily mumbled something to us under his breath.

"What was that?" we both asked in Chinese.

The man's eyes went wide and he seemed to panic at the thought of interacting with foreigners.[75] Shifting around, his anxiety increased as

---

[75]   As we made our way through the various regions of China, one of the more difficult challenges we faced with locals was the difference in dialects. Particularly as we started moving south, the Mandarin that was spoken in some areas varied so greatly that it was like speaking another language. For example, words that would be pronounced with a 'sh' sound in the northeast are

he averted his gaze to the floor. He began mumbling again and nervously shook his head from side to side, *"ting bu dong ting bu dong"* "Don't understand, don't understand."

"No, no. We can speak Chinese. We just didn't hear you clearly," I replied.

"Ooooohh!" He exclaimed, an excited smile spreading across his face. *"Waaaaa.* Your Chinese is so good!"

We hadn't really said anything that couldn't have been picked up in any standard guidebook, but I accepted the compliment with the denial that Chinese modesty demanded. "No, no. It's not that good."

"Where are you from? What nationality are you?"

"I'm British and he's American," Amy responded. "My mother is from Beijing though, so I'm mixed blood."

"Ooooohh! Mixed blood!" the man said, his excitement growing more tangible. "Wow, I didn't know. You don't look Chinese."

"Yeah I know," Amy replied with a chuckle. "Most people say that. I grew up mostly in Europe."

The man paused for a moment then, as if trying to remember something that he had wanted to say. Then, suddenly, he perked up, standing up straighter and smiling in a moment of apparent inspiration. "Can you drink *baijiu*?"

Always excited for an opportunity to drink with a local, my ears perked up a little at this. I looked over at Amy who, less enthused than I, nevertheless smiled knowingly (and graciously?), a look of implicit permission to accept.

"Yes," I replied, smiling back, "we drink it sometimes."

---

often pronounced with an 's' sound down south. If you consider that Chinese writing is character rather than phonetic based, it's easy to see how the sounds of this millennia-old language could transform so drastically across geographies, without a unifying phonetics system. This made annunciation even more important for communication. Often Amy's and my requests for clarification however could be frustratingly brushed off, interpreted as incomprehension and inability to communicate in Chinese at all.

275

At that, the man's face really lit up. He pivoted towards the back of the restaurant and shot off in a shuffle. Within a minute, he was back. In one hand the man held a large, one-gallon, glass jug about one third full of clear liquid sloshing around the bottom. In the other hand, he held three small, six oz. glasses. He placed the container down with a plunk, turned behind him to grab a chair and sat down with us before pouring out three, nearly full glasses of the spirit, one for each of us.

"Welcome to my restaurant!" the man exclaimed lifting his glass, boisterously gesturing a "Cheers!" Amy and I lifted our glasses with his, touched in the middle and took in a mouthful each. The man watched us expectantly as the *baijiu* made its way down our gullets with the familiar burn. He seemed pleased with our reaction to his drink. Nothing, not the ability to speak the language nor having acquired a taste for Chinese food, is more impressive to a Chinese man than being able to stomach their sorghum spirit.

"You know, this *baijiu* is very special," he explained, proudly thrusting out his chest and placing a hand on the jug. "I made it myself. It's eleven years old!"

"Oh really?? It's really nice!" we replied together, Amy more out of her British disposition towards politeness than any genuine enjoyment of the brew. For my part, it wasn't quite like what I imagine sipping on an 11-year-old scotch would have been like, but it also definitely wasn't the worst *baijiu* I'd ever had.

"Thank you, thank you." He nodded, bowing his head in an attempt to suppress his pride. He quickly recovered, looked up, and continued on.

"Yes, I'm taking it out because it's a special occasion. I'm happy to welcome my new foreign friends!" he said, lifting his glass for a new round of cheers.

After another generous gulp, he went on. "You know I didn't even bring it out for my daughter's graduation party! There were more than fourteen people there. I didn't want them all to finish my special *baijiu*."

This was obviously meant to be taken as a compliment but Amy and I were both a bit shocked at this. We felt bad that he was wasting his "good stuff" on us, simply for the fact that we were foreigners able to communicate with him. It seemed especially wasteful as surely there were people who could appreciate the nuances and subtleties of a well-aged *baijiu* more than we.

The man threw his head back and laughed out loud before lifting his glass up in the air and inviting us to another drink, teeth bared in a full smile. It only took three cheers' total for the man to finish his glass, to which I felt obliged to catch up (Amy felt no such obligation). This was a special drink for our host, but for Chinese, alcohol is not something meant to be sipped or savored. Even with expensive bottles of *baijiu* costing hundreds of dollars that you might enjoy at a banquet, the ritual is the same. You lift your glass, cheers at least one person at the table and take as big a swig as you can stomach. The more important the occasion for your drinking, a business dinner, a government banquet, a wedding, the more you ingest with every clink of glass.

We went through three glasses each of the drink as we sat and talked. Most of the talking was done by the man (in all the excitement we never exchanged names). He spent a lot of time telling us about his own personal story, which was told with great enthusiasm and pride. Our host, as it turned out, was Han Chinese but originally from eastern Tibet. He had grown up poor, living mostly in the streets. The first job he had ever held was hauling loads of garbage to dumps. He boasted about how he had been able to lift himself out from that situation thanks to hard work ("eating bitterness" or *chi ku* in Chinese). Through his perseverance he had raised himself to a point where he was married, owned his own restaurant, and even had a daughter who was going to college in the big city of Chengdu.

With each new exclamation, he laughed heartily, lifted his glass, and celebrated with another swig of *baijiu*. As our host became increasingly inebriated, the conversation got more contemplative. Soon we moved from personal history to economics. He explained to us how the opportunities he'd had to be able to start his business never would have been possible with the old system, before Deng Xiaoping and the era of "Reform and Opening Up". Politics soon were also covered and the man's Chinese became more difficult to follow. He elucidated on how, despite the improvements, the central government was still very corrupt and usually was not to be trusted. At one point, the conversation even turned towards religion and the freedom (or lack thereof) to practice it in China.

As the topics became more complex, the language approached a level above both of our heads. I was able to follow somewhat, but mostly I could only pick up the basic subjects being covered, getting lost in the specifics. Amy and I would still nod at what seemed to be the appropriate times, occasionally supplemented with words of affirmation congruent to the topic, and this seemed to suitably content him. Every now and then I was able to add in a few thoughts of my own, but ultimately it was a one way conversation. We were however both happy to oblige his opportunity to vent. Amy and I found it an enlightening experience and for the man, the unique chance to speak with foreigners was likely cathartic.

I'm not sure how much more *baijiu* we would have been invited to drink if the discourse had not been abruptly brought to an end by a yell from the back of the restaurant. "HEY! Husband!" a woman's voice screamed from around the corner of the second, larger dining area.

"Yes yes yes," our host replied back, trying to brush off the admonitions of his spouse.

"That's my wife," our friend jovially explained, turning back to us with a smile. "She runs the restaurant with me."

Soon his wife's face peeked back from around the corner, clearly losing patience with her husband. We had actually seen the woman walking around the restaurant throughout the conversation but she had finally lost patience in being left to do all the cleaning up while he indulged himself talking to guests and drinking.

"Husband!" His wife yelled again. "What are you doing??"

"I'm just talking with our guests," he offered matter-of-factly. "They're foreigners and their Chinese is really good!"

"Come on!" his wife exclaimed, clearly not impressed with his excuse. "Have you taken out the garbage yet? Head to the back and grab the garbage!"

Obediently, the man rose from his seat. He asked if we wanted to keep drinking, offering to leave the glass receptacle behind. We graciously declined and he, cheeks significantly pinker than when he first joined, grabbed the *baijiu* and backed away from the table apologetically. "Ok, I've got to go now. Good night!" he proclaimed with a smile.

"Good night!" we said back. "Thanks for the *baijiu*. It was really good!"

He headed to the back of the restaurant, as we paid our bill with one of the other waiters and grabbed our stuff to head out the front door. Just as Amy and I turned to head down the street, we heard the man coming back out from the kitchen and we turned to wave goodbye. He reciprocated with an energetic wave and beamed at us, the picture of a man proud of having taken control of his own destiny. Three decades later now, the bags of garbage he hauled behind him, he owned himself.

***

The Leshan Buddha is carved into a red sandstone cliff, seated overlooking the point at which three turbulent rivers, the Min, Dadu and Qingyi, all converge. The statue stands 233 feet tall. It's a scale that's hard to appreciate if you're not visiting in person. It's ears alone are 23 feet, with fingers that measure over 26 feet long and shoulders over 90 feet wide.

In the early 8th century AD, a local monk by the name of Haitong was moved to help protect local fishermen and tradesmen who depended on the nearby rivers for their livelihood. The currents, particularly in the spot where the waters converged, were treacherous and caused a large number of boating accidents and deaths each year. Haitong devoted the remainder of his life to the construction of the giant Maitreya Buddha to stand watch over the waters and protect those who relied on it. The project took 90 years to complete, eventually finished by Haitong's disciples after his death. Interestingly, the construction project did indeed result in calmer, safer waters. Because of the sheer amount of debris being dumped in the river from the carving out of such a large sculpture, the currents were altered, calmed, and ultimately made more navigable.

Amy and I woke up early for our visit to the site, hoping to get back on the road by lunch time. After a quick breakfast of soy bean milk and hard boiled eggs, we took a cab across town. With a mix of fog and smog still rolling its way up from the rivers, we began our traverse of the park.

The pathways through subtropical greenery and stone dragon-head carvings gradually led us up to a point on the cliffs high above the rivers. Through overhanging trees, Amy and I suddenly found ourselves under the gaze of the Leshan Buddha. The pathway we had been climbing up led us to the statue's right side and only its face was immediately visible above the cliff wall. The Buddha's pupils, visible from the corner of its eye, were painted black and could be felt scanning just over the heads of the hundreds of visitors lining up for the cliffside viewing walkway. The eyes looked forward and the corner of the Buddha's mouth could be seen lifting into a barely perceptible smile. As soon as you were in its presence, you could tell it was aware of you.

The statue sat in a notch, carved into the cliff to make space for the seated Buddha. The narrow steps were chiseled into the stone wall itself. They zigzagged from the head down to its feet, segmenting the viewing experience into digestible chunks: eyebrows three times my height, hands the size of a tractor-trailer, and an instep large enough to seat one hundred people. The aesthetics of the statue inspire a sense of belonging, as if it was always meant to be there rather than an artificial scar forced by human hands upon the banks of the river. Moss grows on the Buddha's shoulders and knees, vines and trees drape its back, and aside from the light coloring of black on the hair and eyes, the shading of its robes and skin come almost entirely from the deep reds and browns of the stone from which it is carved[76].

We could have spent the whole day exploring the Leshan scenic area. Aside from the main attraction there were smaller carvings and statues, walking paths, temples, and even a mock, old-style fishing village and market whose main street was lined with plastic buckets half-filled with water, with shrimp, lobsters, and crabs climbing over one another inside the various containers.

***

The lush green vegetation persisted as we continued on after Leshan. The road dove deep into a region of remote river gorges. Mountains rose high above us, cloaked in deep greens. The road, meanwhile, stayed low and twisted in and out with the movements of the river as we proceeded downstream. Getting farther away from the industrialized center of the province again, we experienced hardly any

---

[76] The Leshan Buddha had been originally brightly colored as well as protected from the elements by a temple housing similar to the Rongxian Buddha's construction. The colors and temple both had since been degraded and looted by time.

traffic. Mostly we saw trucks transporting road-building materials or construction equipment. These barreled past us down dusty, partially paved roads, at times navigating around the feet of giant pylons holding up portions of a still incomplete highway. The only buildings we passed by through the canyons were old factories and abandoned aqueducts. Once we saw a still functioning smelt, the glow of molten metal reflecting off canyon walls from beside the river.

Sometimes, with nothing but roaring white water below and impassable mountains above, the road penetrated straight through the obstructions themselves rather than attempting to navigate around. In one afternoon we drove through at least a dozen tunnels. Most had not yet even been completed. At times, the only thing that illuminated our path was our single headlight pointed at the yet unpaved gravel tracks.

The longest tunnel we encountered was over two miles long. As we drove farther into the silence that lead us into the unknown depths, visions of the abandoned mines of Moria from the JRR Tolkien's *Lord of the Rings* floated through my mind (Amy and I are both huge Lord of the Rings geeks). I imagined the narrow, uneven walls of our tunnel suddenly opening up before us into a grand hall, our light nothing but a small sanctuary pushing against the encroaching darkness. While we didn't encounter any underground palaces of legend, Amy and I were given momentary pause when we encountered an unmarked, unlit intersection deep in the mountain. The mystery of this undeclared road, cragged mouth threatening to swallow our forward progress, further tempted the imagination as the road dove still deeper into the Sichuan mountains.

Soon, the subtropical river canyons gave way to a new kind of scenery and the ravines opened up into valleys. The road in turn began taking us around large, placid, man-made lakes. The vegetation changed too. Soon the deep greens melted into the oranges, yellows, and reds of a deciduous forest at the beginning of autumn. It became noticeably more humid too as the moisture began seeping through our riding gear, adding a deep chill to the wind.

The local culture transformed in turn with the atmospheric and geological changes. The road signs were no longer just in Mandarin now, but shared the space with a new kind of writing belonging to the local Yi minority. This was a vertically oriented script that shared no resemblances to any writing system either of us had ever seen before. Circles mixed with sharp lines connected together conjured images of crop circles. The road soon took us through traditional Yi villages. These homes here were all uniformly constructed and dotted across the valleys: single-story, rectangular buildings, white washed outer walls, and brown-tiled, triangular roofs. Almost all of these homes had two of their four walls painted with a large brown pictograph, a long-horned ox printed up near the roof. The bottoms of the buildings were lined with a repeating pattern that looked like a red wave with a yellow background, bordered on the top and bottom by blue. It appeared that Amy and I were passing through the Yi lands just after the harvest season, as each home we passed was also adorned by massive bushels of corn, strung up in human-sized oblongs on the walls of the homes.[77]

As we continued moving southwest the mountain weather got wetter and colder. At first there wasn't much rain, but it was foggy and the moisture in the air made the wind increasingly biting. The road wound into the mountains and the fog at the higher altitudes became

---

[77]   The Yi People are the second largest ethnic group in Sichuan after the Han Chinese. They make up around 2.6% of the population. There are about 7.7 million Yi people in China, living in Sichuan, Yunnan, Guizhou, and Guangxi, with over half of the population in Yunnan. Communities can also be found in Vietnam and Thailand. The language is Sino-Tibetan in origin and a subset of the Tibetan-Myanmese Language Group.

The cultures actually vary widely between different groups which are classified either as Ni, Lolo, or "Other". Even their script developed differently by region, with apparently around 40 different ways just to write the word for "stomach".

an impenetrable sludge. Each turn and every forward yard appeared without warning like a snapshot that quickly faded again into the mist. What traffic we did encounter seemed to make no additional considerations for the weather as they drove with the conventional amount of abandon. Amy gripped tightly to my waste. I kept to a speed of 10–20mph and turned on the hazard lights. I honked furiously around each turn, always anticipating the worst, and Amy's hold would harden.

Our last day in Sichuan we headed deeper into the Hengduan Mountain Range at the border between northern Yunnan and southwestern Sichuan. In an effort to shave off nearly one hundred miles to our next destination, the tourist city of Lijiang in Yunnan province, Amy and I decided to leave the two-lane provincial highway we had been on for an unmarked county road. The area was inhabited by little more than squat, one-room, wood huts, unclear if they were meant for shepherd or sheep. The pavement soon crumbled to dirt and we were already halfway down the road when we were hit by a heavy rain. With just as much mud behind us now as there could be in front, we were left no choice but to push on at a crawl through the deep sludge that climbed into the mountains.

Chapter 15 – Old Towns, Chinese Bohemians, and Our Broken Rack

We slipped and slid our way out of Sichuan province. Some mud pits were so thick that Amy would get off to lighten the load as I duck-walked the bike through. There was no sign welcoming us, but the change was convincing as we crossed over into a new province. The mud road led down into a small ravine, suddenly paved again. The rain stopped and we were in Yunnan. Amy and I spent that night in a dark, rural village in the hills, untouched by tourism or development, and warmed ourselves over a dinner of *ma la tang*, a popular street food where diners pick out raw ingredients set on skewers to be cooked in a pot of boiling water, at a hole in the wall down an alley. The following day the clouds and fog cleared and we were able to enjoy spectacular views of the mountains of northern Yunnan.

Near the road to Shangri-La, the landscape was similar to southern Sichuan but somehow more elegant. Maybe it was the better condition of the road, but the mountains, which were taller now, somehow felt more welcoming. The road hugged tight to the hillside, with deep valleys running between the peaks. It was as perfect a road as a motorcyclist could hope for, wiping away the mud and stress we'd accumulated in the days left behind.

The first time I ever came to China was on a three week holiday back in 2006. I was with two friends and most of our time was spent hiking in the mountains of Yunnan. Those experiences in this unique province played a big part in my falling in love with China, leading me to study the language and move back after I'd graduated from college. Accounting for only around 4% of China's landmass, Yunnan is home to half of the country's bird and mammal population as well as 25 of the 56 total ethnic groups in China. The climates cover everything from snow and glacier-capped mountains near the border with Tibet to tropical and subtropical rainforests in the south where it borders with Vietnam, Laos, and Burma.

The idea for The Great Ride of China had initially been born from a plan for a cross-country trip from Beijing to Yunnan. This made Yunnan an important milestone for Amy and I. Our arrival came with a sense of accomplishment as we finally realized the first challenge that we had originally set for ourselves. Amy in particular had a personal and academic interest in the province. Because of it's diversity of cultures, the vernacular architecture in the region is wide-ranging and with deep historical roots. Our two main stops in the province were picked by Amy: Lijiang, a UNESCO heritage site and former capital of the Naxi people, and Dali, an area that included several small villages around a lake and capital of the agrarian and mercantile Bai people. Despite their close proximity (just one hundred miles apart), the landscape, history, and architecture of the areas vary greatly.

Something that had been occupying my mind since putting CIMA and Chongqing behind us was the timeline of the rest of our trip. The additional distance we would need to cover because of the new world record meant we were already going to be on the road nearly a month longer than we'd planned. While they had run into some difficulties, Sean and Slash were still making their own progress towards the same goal. Meanwhile, we were nearing the end of October, with winter nipping at our heels and over 6,000 miles left to go. I was getting anxious about our time constraints, something Amy was finding increasingly aggravating each time I hurried us on past a waypoint. There were so many places that we would have liked to spend more time, and no stops more so than those in Yunnan.

The other thing restricting our schedule were more events planned further on, this time focusing on the charity. Over the previous few weeks we had been in the process of finally organizing some fundraising opportunities with Free Lunch for Children. The charity was an aspect of our trip that, up to that point, had been far less fruitful than we had hoped. Because charities are a relatively new phenomenon in China, Free Lunch for Children (themselves less than three years old at the time of our trip, despite being one of the biggest domestic non-profits) seemed to be unfamiliar with how to effectively capitalize on our partnership. This had led to several missed opportunities to organize fundraising events. Entering into the second half of our trip now, and getting into more densely populated areas of the country again, Amy and I decided to be more proactive. The first such stop was a luxury hotel whose owner we knew through Amy's mom. It didn't take much to endear their management to what we were trying to accomplish and they ended up taking it mostly upon themselves to plan an event. Amy and I were now just over a week and several provinces away from the hotel, at the southern tip of the island province of Hainan.

***

Lijiang has stood as the cultural and political center for the Naxi people of Southwest China since the 7th century AD and was an important stop on the Ancient Tea Horse Road, an old trading route that stretched from Iran through India, Tibet, and Burma. The Naxi are believed to have originally come from the northwest of present day China, descended from the Qiang people that formerly inhabited areas of the Tibetan Plateau. The whole metropolitan area of Lijiang has a population of over one million people, but only about 150,000 of those are actually in the old town district, Gu Cheng Qu. The areas outside were familiar – road construction, buildings plastered with billboard advertisements, and inescapable traffic congestion. The noticeable exception however is the surrounding mountain landscape, clear, smog-less blue skies, and a *relative* dearth of tall, faceless skyscrapers.

The Lijiang Old Town is 435 square miles of one to two-story buildings. It is a web of narrow cobbled streets, and a temple park on a hill that overlooks the network of triangular tiled roofs. At night, the paths, storefronts and waterways that pass through the city are lit up by lanterns. Unfortunately, despite (or more likely, as a result of) this quaint and traditional atmosphere, Lijiang has become overrun with tourists to a point that it has lost much of its charm. Everything seemed to be a bit too overdone, leaving it crawling with inauthenticity. The roads were lined with kitschy souvenir shops and overpriced jewelry stores selling "cultural" trinkets to the loud travelers who were all too happy to part with their yuan. At every restaurant Amy and I walked past, passersby were aggressively urged to dine by someone dressed in the brightly colored traditional clothing of the Naxi.

If you focus really really hard, walking along those stone cobbled alleyways, you can almost imagine what the actual, traditional Lijiang might have been like. Take away the crowds of people with oversized cameras around their necks, the cheap, mass-produced trinkets that can be found in almost any tourist district in the country, and the excessive flower decorations at each street corner, and you get a sense of the former charm and character of the place. Empty it all out and you could see the streets being used as a film set for an old Kung Fu movie. Unfortunately this feeling is ephemeral at best, and even Amy felt little regret at moving on again after a half-day and evening of sightseeing.

The next stop while in Yunnan was another area of cultural significance, the nearby prefecture of Dali, home to the Bai people. The region of Dali is in a valley surrounded by mountains on all sides with Erhai Lake at its center. The history of the region and Dali Old Town, which sits on the southwest corner of the lake, spans back over a millennium. It was a leisurely half-day ride from Lijiang along a less mountainous but still scenic road. The Bai, similar to many of the other 56 ethnicities in China, have their own traditions and language distinct from the majority Han. Most however can speak Mandarin fluently. 80% of the Bai population in the country live around the Dali Bai Autonomous Prefecture, with the rest spread out around Yunnan and parts of nearby Guizhou and Hunan provinces.

20 miles north of Dali city is a small town called Xizhou (which translates to "Happy Prefecture"). In Xizhou is a small boutique hotel called the Linden Centre run by an American couple. Amy had first heard of the Linden Centre through research into Chinese building restoration and cultural preservation for her website, *Project: China Building Restoration*.[78] The hotel was originally an old Bai merchant's mansion in the outskirts of the village, discovered and restored by Brian and Jeanee Linden. Through their work on the mansion, in cooperation with the local government, the couple had become well known for the authenticity of their restoration work. In the year it took to renovate the property, they took immense care to use materials, colors, and building techniques all true to the original. The construction was done by local build teams and local artisans were used for any new or extra furnishings needed. Amy had managed to get in touch with the Lindens for her website, interviewing them on their work in Xizhou. Dali had been one of the first pins on the map when we were planning our trip and Amy had managed to organize a visit ahead of time.

---

[78]   Project: China Building Restoration (www.chinabuildingrestoration.com) was started by Amy in 2013. One of the first and only English language websites dedicated to reporting on news and sharing of information related to the building restoration industry in China, the site was one of the big contributing factors for Amy's interest in joining me on The Great Ride of China. She saw it as a good opportunity to get more first-hand exposure to the different types of architecture and building styles around the country. She had especially been looking forward to visiting the old cities around China's South and Southwest such as Dali and Lijiang.

We were lucky enough to catch both Brian and Jeanee (as well as their two sons) during our visit, as they often travel around China and the U.S. on business. We got private tours around the Centre and their nearly complete *Yang Zhuoran* sister restoration project, also in Xizhou. One of the staff from the hotel guided Amy and I through Xizhou itself as we walked between the sites. The locals of the town, just a small settlement in the flatlands of Erhai Lake, were a mix of primarily Bai and Hui Chinese. We watched as they went about their daily routines, carrying fresh produce to the markets, squatting on small stools playing cards outside of their shops, and working on various construction projects among the small, whitewashed buildings of the town.

We learned from our guide that in the middle of the 19th century this now-sleepy hamlet had been part of a major rebellion by the local Muslim Hui farmers against the ruling Qing. The rebellion lasted for over 16 years from 1856 to 1872 and ultimately ended as a very bloody massacre for the outmatched Hui rebels. Estimates for the number of dead are in the hundreds of thousands, with the Qing troops leaving only a small population of Hui survivors, between 40 and 50 thousand, behind. Present day Xizhou had no signs left of this bloody conflict and the Hui, Han, and Bai all seemed to be co-existing peacefully with observant Muslims and non-religious Chinese, traditional Bai buildings and mosques, all side by side in this quiet village by the lake.

We had a very enjoyable tour of the two properties, which we found living up to their reputations of exemplary restoration work. Exposed wood pillars supported the upper floors, open air courtyards lay just within the entrances in traditional fashion, Buddhist artifacts and artwork decorated the walls, and warm, friendly staff all made for a very pleasant atmosphere. Watching the guests calmly move about in the various activities offered at the hotel, it wasn't hard to imagine that the Linden Centre would have made for fantastic holiday getaway.

We moved on from Xizhou towards Dali where we ended up spending the night. Amy and I found a small courtyard Bed & Breakfast just on the edge of the old town. While Dali still had its fair share of tourists milling about, it was nowhere near as busy or crowded as Lijiang. The streets were wider, mostly paved rather than cobbled, and the style of the buildings felt newer than those on the streets of Lijiang. There was a general sense of having more space. Despite the impression of being less "ancient", Dali still retained more of its authenticity. This was owing in large part to the attitude and demeanor of the inhabitants, who were more focused on normal day-to-day activities than on catering to tourists. Everyone was much more natural and at ease. Women walked around with giant baskets on their heads, farmers could be seen setting up impromptu vegetable markets on the streets, and local artisans stood in storefronts selling their wares. Amy and I had a much easier time believing their handmade goods were actually made by hand (maybe even by *their* hands).

The city also had a very bohemian feel to it. I couldn't help but think of Dali as a Chinese version of Burlington, Vermont or Boulder, Colorado. Small cafes and bars were everywhere, each with their own eclectic decorations and individual style. It was the type of place that artists from around the country might come to spend their days ruminating over a cup of coffee and letting their imaginations wander. As Amy and I walked along the old streets I even noticed one or two dreadlocked Chinese twenty-somethings hanging out in the afternoon sun much as you would on the streets of Burlington, playing guitar and humming out songs in Chinese. Probably not entirely a coincidence either, but Yunnan, and particularly this area of the province, is well known as the marijuana-growing capital of China.

We left Dali in a much different mood than the day before after Lijiang. The beautiful weather, fresh air, laid-back atmosphere, and overall beautiful backdrop of the small city and surrounding villages left us wishing we had more time to spend in the Erhai region of the Bai people. Before leaving, Amy and I stopped at a popular haunt for foreigners, a bar and cafe called "The Bad Monkey" that we'd heard about from friends that had taught English in the area in previous years. There, we enjoyed a Western-style breakfast in their outdoor cafe and watched the locals going about their morning routines. We sat enjoying bacon, fried eggs, and the first cup of real coffee we'd had in months as the town of Dali prepared for the day ahead.[79]

***

Moving east across Yunnan, the scenery was becoming less dramatic than when we first entered from Sichuan. We had three more days in the province after Dali and managed to spend one night away from the crowds and busy traffic of Chinese cities. Just west of Kunming, the provincial capital and largest city in Yunnan, Amy and I decided to wander off of the National Highway and towards the Purple Brook Mountain Scenic Area in the Chuxiong Autonomous Region. There was a ticketed entrance to the park, but by the time we had arrived, a little after 6pm, no one was manning the gate. There were no barriers set and the only person there, a woman closing down her convenience shop when we arrived, simply shrugged in confusion when I asked about going in and camping.

---

[79]   Yunnan is one of the only places in China where you can find easy access to proper cups of coffee. The province's humid, semi-tropical climate makes it agreeable to coffee plants. Up to that point, most coffee we'd had over the past couple months, even in the self-proclaimed "International Business Hotels", was made with instant coffee mix rather than brewed with beans. The cafes in Lijiang and Dali all offered real, fresh-brewed coffee, a very welcome opportunity for Amy and I to over-caffeinate ourselves.

292

One important axiom Amy and I established for travel (and life) in China is that it's usually better to ask for forgiveness than to ask for permission. With this in mind, we conferred in the parking lot and decided to risk getting kicked out of the scenic area, far from any hotels, and drove around the unattended gate into the park. We set up our tent inside a tree grove, just up the road from a small man-made lake. Never even seeing another person, Amy and I spent a relaxing night enjoying a dinner of instant noodles with chopped tomatoes by our small campfire, accompanied by a nightcap of Yanjing long-neck beers we'd picked up at the convenience store.

For all of Yunnan's strengths as a tourist destination, you wouldn't be missing much if you passed over its capital city, Kunming. The traffic of a Chinese urban area of over three million people was not something either of us was particularly eager to subject ourselves to either. Even though our route towards the next province, Guizhou, would take us by the city, we did our best to stay in the outskirts. Unfortunately, this is also what all the long-haul freight traffic does. Since most trucks are not allowed to enter the city center, the really large, and usually overweight, trucks keep to the outer rings and secondary highways.

The truck congestion was unlike any we'd had since Shanxi, months earlier. It was bumper-to-bumper, slow moving behemoths for miles. They kicked up dust in our faces, ripping through the gravel of the torn up roadway. I tried my best to weave ahead of these trucks but found it a futile exercise trying to get to the front of a line that didn't seem to end. The sound of rattling axles rang out from the underbellies of the poorly maintained trucks, deafening as they made their way into ever-expanding potholes and over speed-bump-like mounds of gravel and dirt.

Our bike was not faring much better in these conditions. There were too many road hazards for me to avoid, and the endless queue of trucks provided even fewer options for a level advance. With all our luggage and two passengers, the suspension of the bike was bottoming out regularly from all the weight. Each time the springs reached their full compression I could feel the impact reverberate up my back. Amy was already subjected to a much more narrow and less cushioned seat than I, and after each hard knock of metal-on-metal, I could hear her groan through the noise of the traffic.

Towards the end of this quagmire I was caught unawares by a pothole whose depth I greatly underestimated. I decelerated as much as I could but we hit it straight on. The bike came down on the other side with a loud "Crack!" Amy yelled out, tapping me on the shoulder to signal something wasn't right, but I brushed it off, telling her it was just our suspension again. A little farther on, after finally making it to a paved and less trafficked section of road, we stopped at a gas station to grab a quick lunch of "convenience noodles". I walked around the bike, unpacking things we would need for our meal, when I caught a glimpse of our taillight and noticed a crack in the glass. It turned out Amy had been right to worry.

Looking around the bike some more, I found the aluminum supports that anchor the rear luggage rack to the motorcycle had cracked, and appeared to be on the verge of snapping off entirely. This left all the weight of our rear, 12-gallon, hard plastic case and the waterproof bag strapped on top, to fall backwards onto the taillight.

At a loss for what to do, I attempted a temporary solution. We had some spare compression straps which I added to our already Gordian knot-like setup. Attempting to lever the weight forward, I threaded the straps around the far back of the bags and then forward towards the seat, tightening them in the front. This transferred the weight back towards the center of the bike and off of the light. The effect seemed to be sufficient and the taillight decompressed as the pressure shifted. After lunch we chose to sneak onto the expressway, thinking it would be safer to stay on roads that were as flat as possible. Amy kept a close eye on the new straps, tightening them as necessary.

We made our way around the north of Kunming without incident, but about 30 miles east of the city, I felt Amy's now-familiar tapping on my back. She yelled through the wind that the straps were feeling loose and I pulled over onto the shoulder. The crack through the taillight had doubled in size, the straps I had attached were now slack, and the aluminum braces were almost completely snapped through.

Our panniers were fully packed. There was no space left in the backpack I wore, which already left Amy squished between me and the rear case. This case and the bag on top were now barely hanging on to the back of bike, but were the only options for carrying the things we needed. Computer, charging equipment, spare clothes, camping gear, travel documents, and journals. We needed to find a way to keep it all on the bike.

I made some small adjustments to the straps, hoping it would at least keep everything attached long enough to get us off the highway and figure out our next steps. I cautiously kept to the shoulder, not risking going over 40mph. We got off at the next exit and entered a small city on the outskirts of Kunming, keeping our eyes out for a repair shop. There was no chance of acquiring replacement parts for our particular bike here, but what we did find was someone who could help us MacGyver together a way to keep the braces attached long enough to get to a place where we could.

An observation I'd initially had back in the desert, with the frequent tire repair shops we encountered there, would now be working in our favor. The happy byproduct of the notoriously questionable quality of everything that is produced, bought, and sold in China is that many Chinese are expert tinkerers. There tends to be little interest in prevention, but when something goes wrong, they usually find a way to fix it. Even during repairs mechanics remain blasé about quality. In the past when I've tried to recommend some minor qualitative improvement to a repair or enquire as to the reliability of a new part, I am almost invariably greeted with a smile and a nonchalant *"Mei wen ti! Mei wen ti!"*, "No problem!" The philosophy, and another important China rule, boils down to "save costs and labor now, deal with potential consequences later".

Songming county, an outer suburb of Kunming where we found the bike repair shop, was grey and enveloped in smog when we arrived close to dusk. Our spirits were already depressed and the mechanic showed the familiar initial reluctance, but after a glance at the cracked frame of our bike, his confidence seemed to grow.

A small crowd of observers from nearby stores and other patrons of the repair shop gathered to watch as we attempted to reinforce the luggage braces. A few newly drilled holes, some thick metal wire twisted around in a clever way, and a new method for strapping the bags to the bike, and it looked like everything was more or less holding together. I suspiciously, and with some reluctance, tested out the braces. There was some give, but they held together. With the wires between my fingers, I looked up at the man, drill still in his hand, and asked if he thought it would hold. With an assured smile as if to pat himself on the back for a job well done, he replied, *"Mei wen ti!"*

And so it was... for a time.

***

The next province on our list, Guizhou, was a bit of an add-on in terms of our route. Our long-term trajectory over the next week was to head down to the coast, eventually getting on a ferry to take us to Hainan. Guizhou though is landlocked and inland from where we needed to go. You can actually see on the GPS track of our trip a stretch of a few hundred miles where it looks like we got sidetracked, almost as if Amy and I got lost for a couple days. We went from moving purposefully southeast through Yunnan to taking a sharp turn to the northeast and into Guizhou. The truth is, I had almost forgotten about the province until the day before we had to make our detour. I had been looking at the map, planning our route for the day and suddenly realized we were about to miss one of the 33 provinces!

The two days we spent riding through Guizhou turned out to be a pleasant surprise. We essentially circumnavigated the western half of the province, riding in from the west, going northeast towards the capital in the center, and then back down and slightly westward again in order to return to the coast. The entire time it was either raining or there was extremely dense fog. This reduced visibility to as low as 20–30 feet and was particularly precarious during the several tunnels we passed through, as the beam from our headlight reflected off the water particles and decreased visibility even further.

Most enjoyable about Guizhou was the scenery. The incredible geological formations that rose up out of the mist off the sides of the elevated highway were otherworldly. Towering stone pillars stood as high as small mountains, marching out from the fog. Some were covered in lush green moss and small trees, while still others laid bare the grey of their craggy limestone surface. It was our first encounter with the iconic limestone karst formations of southern China.[80]

Being landlocked, Guizhou is still quite a poor province, 31st poorest per capita in the country. This had an atmospheric effect however, accentuating the anachronistic, mystical authenticity of the landscape. Small villages could be seen tucked away at the feet of the mist covered hills. Amy and I observed, from the back of our 650cc machine, farmers commuting on the highway with their oxen and

---

[80]   The University of Texas at Austin describes the formation of the distinctive karst topology: "[It is] a landscape formed from the dissolution of soluble rocks including limestone, dolomite and gypsum. It is characterized by sinkholes, caves, and underground drainage systems." China is home to some of the largest carbonate rock deposits on earth and the South China Karst is one of the largest karst landscapes in the world, covering around 230,000 square miles including most of Guizhou as well as parts of Guangxi and Yunnan. In 2007 the South China Karst was designated a UNESCO World Heritage Site.

wheelbarrows.[81] All of it together; the fog, the mountains, the farm animals, the thatch-roofed homes, made it feel as if somehow we and the highway had been dropped into the backdrop of an old Chinese scroll painting.

Guizhou was a real hidden gem of the trip and it would have been nice to have had more time to explore the villages and smaller mountain roads. The province felt like a perfect travel destination for those more willing to get off the beaten path. It's not as popular a place to visit as it's neighbors Yunnan to the west and Guangxi to the east, so there were far less people. This made it much easier to get a sense of what life is and was like there rather than some artificial recreation of what the local government expected tourists to want. The incredible scenery came as a complete surprise to me. The Guizhou cuisine too has a good reputation and they also specialize in a rice-based *baijiu* that is far easier to drink than its more pungent sorghum-based cousins from other regions. These are all things Amy and I regretted not having had more time to explore.

We pointed the bike back towards the coastline just short of the capital. We moved through the center of the province and within an afternoon the landscape went through another dramatic transformation. The towering karst obelisks melted down into rolling hills and river ravines, which eventually gave way to flat farmlands. The fog and rain too began to burn off. Within a couple hours Amy and I had shed almost all of our extra layers. One by one we peeled off our gloves, rain gear, jacket liners, and long underwear, until I was even getting warm in our normal padded riding gear. Then, with banana plantations starting to spring up along the side of the road

---

[81]   Guizhou and Yunnan were actually some of the only places in the country where we were allowed on the highway. Once in Guizhou we passed through a tollbooth and were pulled aside to a police inspection station. The cop looked surprised to see two foreigners, and smiled goofily when he saw our faces. Amy and I were nervous about a confrontation for our being on the highway. After looking through our identification though he simply waved us on without so much as a warning.

(the large, almost human-sized leaves recognizable to me only from photographs and TV) I started to catch a familiar scent in the wind blowing through my helmet. It was distinctively fresh and slightly salty. We were finally almost there, the southern coast of China and the South China Sea.

The road was opening up and flattening out, and my adrenaline was pumping. With memories of not just rain but also snow still fresh in my mind, I was propelled forward towards the tropical climate and our first glimpse of the sea. The pavement, however, was wavy, asphalt distorted from poor build quality and overweight trucks. This caused our frame to undulate in parallel on top of our suspension, a movement exaggerated by the speed we were moving. It was certainly better than most of the National Highways we had been on though and I was undeterred.

Amy was more cautious and less enthusiastic about the milestone of the coast. Sitting with her back to the precariously attached luggage on the rear of the bike, she kept giving me nervous taps on my shoulder asking me to slow down. At one gas stop, she berated me for it, pointing out that she could feel the weight of the bags shifting up and down with every wave in the road. I was having fun though and attributed the movement to the natural give in the metal. I was also a little worried about getting caught in the dark if we didn't hurry, so I brushed off her concerns, promising to take it a little slower but self-assuredly telling her we'd be fine.

The dates were set now for the event at the hotel in Hainan. Some of the local volunteers for Free Lunch for Children were planning on meeting us, and the hotel had organized local media to come too. The event was set in stone and so we found ourselves on the clock – two days to get to Sanya over five hundred miles away, including a two-hour ferry crossing. Sanya also had a CFMoto shop where we hoped a new rack would be waiting for us.

Making it to Nanning in southern Guangxi province would have made this more than doable. With the sun about to set and just about a half-hour left to get there, I was feeling optimistic we could make it with minimal night riding. Unfortunately though, our luck with the rack had finally run out.

On the back of my shoulder I started getting the rapid-fire slapping from Amy that meant I needed to pull over. I slowed down, pulled in the clutch, and rolled over onto the shoulder.

"The rack!" Amy yelled to me as soon as I could hear her through the wind. "I think it's really broken now!"

I stopped the bike, put down the kickstand, and hopped off to take a look. The wire supports we had used to keep everything together the past few days were not holding any weight any more. The taillight was now missing pieces of glass, which had splintered after getting crushed by the luggage. And our two bags were barely hanging onto the bike, ready to fall off completely at the next pothole. There wasn't going to be any brushing this off.

Chapter 16 – Fundraising in Paradise

Dusk was just starting to give way to the night sky. The road was still roaring with activity even as dark set in, and the pounding of nearby construction equipment and rumbling of passing trucks meant Amy and I had to yell to hear each other over all the noise. Thousands of dust particles, kicked up by passing traffic, hovered in the air all around us, shimmering in the glow of the streetlights. Amy and I stood there, staring helplessly at the luggage rack of our bike. The hard case and waterproof bag, a web of yellow compression straps keeping it all precariously together, was hanging over the rear wheel. It looked pathetic, like a limp tooth about to fall loose, the final sinews of gum barely holding on.

Snapping out of my self-pitying daze, I jumped over to the bags and lifted them up to take the weight off of the now broken taillight. I called Amy over and we started to unwrap all the straps and remove both pieces of luggage from the bike. Night had fully descended now. Still another 20–30 miles from the city limits of Nanning, we talked over trying to flag down a "bread car" in the dark to take us into the city.

As we stood there, both of us feeling helpless and annoyed at our misfortune, a man ambled up to us from across the street. He had noticed that we were having problems, felt compelled to rubberneck, and asked about our troubles. He nodded nonchalantly at my explanation, a look of unsurprised understanding on his face, and then casually pointed over to the intersection we'd just passed. There, he told us, we could find some repair shops that should be able to help. Of course we could.

I rode the bike over to the opposite corner while Amy waited with our luggage. There, I found a string of shops right where the man had pointed. Each stall, of which there were about a dozen wrapped around the corner, was little more than a single-room hole in the wall. Inside of each, the walls were lined with makeshift shelves filled with jumbles of whatever that particular stall was selling. One had different types of piping, from PVC to copper plumbing. Another farther down sold power tools and home-repair equipment. Others, it wasn't clear what they sold, the disorderly arrays of equipment piled around the room leaving few clues. Most of these also served as home to the families that ran them, evidenced by the mattresses peeking out from around the back walls. Because it was just around dinner time I caught meals being prepared towards the backs of one or two, steaming pots tended to over solitary hotplates.

There wasn't much differentiating them. It all looked like the partitioned remains from a salvaged junkyard. You could, however, tell which did motorcycle repairs by the line of scooters parked out front. On this particular corner, there were two such stalls. At the first, the *Lao ban* (or the "Boss") stubbornly refused to help. The man was standing out front when I approached and his eyes opened wide in apprehension at seeing a foreigner with an unfamiliar motorcycle. Regaining some composure, his eyes snapped shut and he shook his head, waving his hand vigorously. "No no no no," he said when I asked if he could help. This reaction didn't come as much of a surprise, all part of the routine of asking for help as a foreigner in China, and while he stood his ground on the refusal he did refer us to another shop around the corner.

I passed by a couple power tool vendors and arrived at a storefront where I found a man and woman both fiddling over a small-bore motorcycle. They stood over the space where a seat had been removed, tinkering with the innards of the machine. To my relief, they did not immediately rebuff my plea for help despite the late hour. Instead they simply gestured for me to wait my turn, something I was more than happy to do. I set the bike down and ran over to help Amy bring the bags from across the street.

Once the couple was done with the smaller bike, they walked over and I started trying to explain the problem to them in greater detail. It wasn't long before a small crowd of people had formed. The families and customers from neighboring shops as well as passersby started gathering in a semicircle, like an audience at an amphitheater. No one was sure what to make of us as I continued on in my somewhat beleaguered and exasperated Chinese. Through monosyllabic responses, the man indicated that I needed to remove the rack so that they could take a look. When I asked for tools, he went to his shop and came back with a screwdriver and a desk lamp, plugged into an extension cord that led to the back, to light my work area.

Working my way through the dozen or so screws, I listened as the onlookers started speculating amongst themselves as to who Amy and I were and what we were doing there. I noticed, and this wasn't the first time this had happened, that they gossiped as if we couldn't hear them. Despite most of the bystanders having already witnessed both of us conversing in Chinese with the shop owners, few seemed to have internalized that we, as foreigners, could understand Chinese. Even when a person like this could hear us communicating completely in Mandarin with someone nearby they still felt the need to find a "translator". This is exactly what was transpiring as I disassembled the rack and new people joined the group.

"Oh. Foreigners!" One slightly overweight woman exclaimed as she walked by, peering over one man's shoulder to see what I was doing. "What nationality are they?"

"I'm American and she's British," I answered, not breaking from my work.

"Oh, American and British," the woman repeated, nodding with increased interest. "Where did they come from?" she asked, directing the question at the man whose shoulder she was looking over.

"Where did you come from?" the man then asked us, in more or less the same Mandarin and with the same accent.

"Uh... We came from Beijing," I replied, slightly bemused at this strange and inefficient way of communicating.

"They came from Beijing," the man said, matter-of-factly transmitting our response back to the woman.

"Ooooh. Beijing." she replied to the man.

The conversation proceeded in this way for a couple minutes as the woman caught up on all of the relevant information (the brand of the bike, how much it cost, what gas mileage it got, etc.). The man who was translating or someone else from the crowd would interject every now and then with a question of their own.

Unfortunately, after about 10–15 minutes of fiddling in the dark with all of the screws and disassembling most of the rack from the bike, we concluded with the mechanic couple that there was little we could do to fix the bike that night. In addition to the aluminum rack itself that had snapped, the two primary bolts that attached it to the frame had also broken clean through leaving two broken screws stuck in the bike. Luckily, they would be able to help with the bolts and for the rack there was someone in the neighborhood that could weld aluminum (something that apparently required a certain level of expertise above the welding of other metals). If we came back in the morning, they should be able to get it fixed.

There didn't seem much point in pushing it any longer. It was getting late and most of the shops around us were already closed. I pressed the man to make sure that there really would be someone in the morning and he wasn't just trying to get rid of us. Once I felt we'd received sufficient confirmation, Amy and I headed off down the dusty road to find a place to spend the night. We ended up in a shabby, narrow hotel, the type of place migrant workers stay at on the way to the factories in Guangzhou. The room was small, barely enough room for the bed, and smelled of stale cigarettes. I was nervous too about leaving our bike outside unattended. Being close to the coast again, theft was a bigger concern with more developed markets for stolen goods, including motorcycles. Though the hotel owner assured me of its security by showing me their security cameras, Amy and I remained nervous. But, with few prospects of getting anything better deeper in the village, we made do, securing our things as best we could for the night.

A welder turned out to be exactly what we needed. It only took a couple of hours the next day, during which time we enjoyed a street-side noodle breakfast and explored the local fish market, to have our aluminum rack good as new again and everything bolted back into place. They seemed to have done good work too as I warily tested the strength of the joints, slowly increasing pressure on the back of the bike until I was confident it would hold. I strapped our two bags back onto the bike and everything looked solid. By noon we were on the road again, heading southeast and towards the ferry crossing to Hainan island.

***

It was a complete transformation of mood in only a day. With palms and banana trees lining the roads, temperatures in the mid-80s, and bright blue skies overhead, the troubles of cold rain and a broken luggage rack had become fading memories. To catch up on lost time and avoid construction on the National Highway, we skirted around the expressway barriers and by sunset had made it the 300 miles to Xuwen and the Qiongzhou Strait where we could catch the ferry the following day.

The ferry that connects the island province of Hainan with Guangdong and the rest of mainland China is massive. I took the bike into the main vehicle container area, riding over the deep ridges of the metal grating in the belly of the boat. Amy hopped off and I weaved around passenger cars as well as about a dozen 18-wheelers that were packed in like sardines on their way to make deliveries to Hainan.[82] Because the boats are so large, they don't operate on a set schedule and can only afford to leave once they are sufficiently full. Nobody really tells you this though, so for two hours while Amy and I waited for the boat to disembark, the only answer I could get from anyone onboard about when we would be leaving was "*Ma shang*", "Soon."

It took 90 minutes after leaving port to make the ocean crossing, a pleasant journey with the freshest air in all of China blowing past as we made our way across the crystalline water and towards province number 19. It wasn't until early afternoon that we'd finally landed in the port of Haikou on the northern end of Hainan. Meanwhile, we were expected at the Horizon Resort on the completely opposite end of the island, a couple hundred miles away, by evening. Luckily, Hainan was the only province in the entire country where they didn't have any tolls on the expressways. This allowed not just motorcyclists on the highway, but even cyclists were allowed to brave the high speeds on the shoulder. We breezed down the highway at a comfortable 80mph, racing against the setting sun. The sea air and beautiful tropical scenery made for a terrific ride, as we traversed the idyllic landscape of what has become known as the "Hawaii of China".[83]

---

[82]   As of January 2003, Hainan and Guangdong also now have a train line connecting them. The Yuehai Ferry carries both freight and passenger trains across the Qiongzhou Strait. Trains are essentially disassembled and put into the boats in pieces, with tracks leading directly onto the lower levels of the boats. The Yuehai Ferry line had only two boats in operation until February 2013, when two more began service. The boats are 616 feet long by 75 feet wide and 50 feet high, with space for cars on the upper deck and passenger compartments in addition to the loading areas for the train cars.

[83]   This nickname is owing to both its tropical climate as well as its popularity as a holiday spot. Tourism makes up between 13–15% of the province's GDP, in 2013 bringing in ¥42bn ($7bn). In an effort to further encourage growth in the industry, visitors from 26 different countries can visit Hainan visa-free. In 2011, of the 30 million tourists who visited Hainan only 814,600 were foreigners. Nearly 30% of that number were Russian!

We reached Sanya, the southernmost city on the island and the outskirts of which was our destination for the night, just as the sun was starting to set. This provided a beautiful backdrop of glowing orange against the stony foothills of the Wuzhi Mountains. By dusk we had disembarked from the highway and entered the peaceful roads of the resort district, Yalong Bay. As we pulled into the driveway of our hosts, the Horizon Resort and Spa, the stress from a difficult few days on the road started to set in. Muscles tense from long days of troubleshooting and about a thousand miles straight on the bike, Amy and I were both eager for a couple days' rest.

Coming around the roundabout in front of the hotel lobby, I was completely taken aback by an unexpected sight at the main entrance – to the left of the lobby doorway a massive poster had been erected, at least 20 feet wide, with Amy's and my names printed in huge lettering along the top. The giant billboard-like display had a blown-up image of the two of us on our CFMoto, one of the photos we had taken looking towards Everest across the Himalayas, photoshopped onto an orange background. In big bold print across the banner was a message in Chinese: "Welcome Buck & Amy on their Guinness World Record Breaking Trip to the Sanya Horizon Resort Hotel". Under this were a couple more lines in smaller font introducing our trip. Amy and I were of course blown away by the gesture, not at all expecting this professional or high-profile of a reception. We were also suddenly conscious of how out of place we must have seemed in our grimy motorcycle gear and my unkempt, three-month-old beard.

With barely enough time to dismount from the bike and before we'd had a chance to take off our helmets, two staff in brightly colored Hawaiian shirts and pristine white pants greeted us each with a colorful flower garland placed around our heads. Standing in the driveway and looking into the luxurious, open-air lobby with tropical flowers draped over our sweaty necks, the uncomfortable feeling of self-awareness bubbled up further. Amy and I looked at each other and then back at our welcoming committee, wearily but graciously accepting the gesture.

Next we were greeted by the hotel's head of PR, Hai Xiao, the short but confident, bespectacled woman with whom we had been in contact the past couple weeks. Hai Xiao, who had her phone in hand throughout as she attended to various articles of business, was accompanied by an overeager young reporter, her camera man, and the General Manager of the hotel. The portly GM walked briskly over to us from across the lobby, a wide, jovial smile across his face. While Hai Xiao was dressed in formal business attire, he wore the same pink Hawaiian shirt and white pants as the rest of the staff. After making his way across the hall and over to our bike, the GM grabbed my hand and, shaking vigorously, introduced himself, maintaining the enthusiastic grin the entire time. It was a face that seemed to fit in naturally with the luxurious, holiday surroundings.

It was all a bit overwhelming, a blur of activity after a full day of travel, and difficult to take in all at once. The prospect of a few days at a luxury resort however was refreshing. From the sound of her voice as we made our introductions, Amy was in noticeably higher spirits. It was hard to believe that just the day before we had been unsure if we would even be able to make it to the Horizon. After about 30 minutes of small talk, helmets and riding jackets piled onto a luggage cart with the rest of our gear, we figured out our schedule for the following day with Hai Xiao (and rescheduled an interview with the reporter) and were finally led away from the entrance, across the lobby and to the elevators to check into our room.

Amy and I could not have asked for a better southern terminus for our trip. Our room, up on the 8th floor of the hotel, had a 180-degree view of the whole of the resort grounds as well as the ocean itself. It was by far the nicest place we had stayed in all trip. Our room even came with its own washing machine, which we would put to good use over the next couple days. Arriving in our room at this idyllic seaside resort, peeling off the rest of our grimy gear, and laying down on that bed felt like one long exhalation, a decompression as Amy and I looked forward to our first day off in the two weeks since the CIMA Motorcycle Expo in Chongqing.

***

The days we would spend in Sanya were not quite as relaxing as we would have liked. Everything we had to do with the hotel, with Free Lunch for Children, not to mention the maintenance on the bike and gear after a tough few weeks on the road, gave us barely enough time to enjoy our tropical surroundings. In terms of places to be kept busy in though, we could have done worse.

The first thing we had to do was an informal press conference the following morning that Hai Xiao had organized for us in the main grounds of the hotel. About a dozen local volunteers from Free Lunch for Children had arrived by bicycle to take part. Even though the organization did not yet have any partner schools in Hainan, they were in the process of applying to work with three in the rural countryside of the province and already had an impressive network of young, eager volunteers looking for a way to help out.

Amy and I were asked to wear our (newly scrubbed down) riding gear and helmets for photos, and I brought the bike around back for the small event. Rolling along the lawn that lay between the towers of the hotel and the pool and beach behind, I was surprised yet again when I saw that Hai Xiao and the rest of the Horizon had actually prepared a second poster for us, this one laying out a mosaic of photos from our trip so far that I had sent online a week prior.

The press conference took a couple hours. After photos and a Q&A with the local media, as Amy and I were preparing to head off to lunch, Hai Xiao asked if we would be free that evening to participate in another event. She went out of her way to assure us it would be short and that we would only need to spend 20 or 30 minutes before dinner. After everything that they had done for us so far, we of course had no objections. The plan was to meet in front of the lobby at 6pm with our bike and dressed once again in our gear.

We arrived on time to meet her and a couple staff in the lobby. Neither of us were quite feeling rested, but Amy and I were at least more refreshed after a day of fresh air and blue skies (there may have been one or two tropical drinks involved too). I hopped on the bike, turned on the engine, and started to make my way around the back of the hotel in the direction Hai Xiao pointed out. I duck-walked the bike beside her and Amy along one of the pedestrian walkways that meandered through the rear gardens of the hotel. The sun was already starting to set and our way was lit by the fading blue glow of dusk. Hai Xiao began to explain that the hotel wanted to organize an opportunity to share our trip and the charity with some of their guests. In typical, modest Chinese fashion, this turned out to greatly underplay what was planned.

Coming down the stone path, I saw ahead of us on a grassy clearing, silhouetted by the recently lit promenade lamps, what seemed to be a large crowd. As we got closer I could make out what must have been a group of around three hundred people standing there on the grass. In front of them was an amphitheater-like clearing, fully lit up, and with a stage backed by a large wall.

The rotund GM of The Horizon came out from the crowd as I approached on the bike, and greeted me with the same firm handshake and wide smile as before. He thanked us both for coming and then gestured for me to go around the back of the wall. The wall, as it turned out, was actually the larger of the two banners that had been made for us – the orange one we had first been greeted with on our arrival the previous day. Big and orange, the banner was lit up on the stage that, I now noticed as I came around to the front, was facing out onto an elaborate setup of dining tables and a buffet spread. It appeared that we were to be a part of an evening show, a twice-weekly event and beachside seafood cookout organized by The Horizon.

We had the bike set up on the stage in front of the banner, mirroring the blown-up photoshopped image behind us, while Amy and I dutifully took our spots on stage in front of the hotel band. The GM took center stage, enthusiastically introducing us to the guests who were just starting to sit down for dinner. Meanwhile, Hai Xiao walked on with a large box in both hands, which she placed at center stage. The GM looked over at us and, with his jolly grin, thanked us for what we were doing. Projecting his voice for the benefit of the audience, he proclaimed that all the employees of the hotel wanted to do their part for Free Lunch for Children and donate to the cause. With that, he turned to the box and pulled a small wad of pink, neatly folded 100 yuan notes from his pocket. He posed for a picture with his hand over the box and then placed the cash inside the slit on top. Next, he walked over to Amy and I, shook each of our hands and thanked us profusely before walking off the other side of the platform. The GM had no sooner stepped off the stage than his number two, who we'd only met briefly the night before, started walking over and put his own pad of money into the collection box.

With the band starting to play a kind of elevator-like background music, a procession began to make its way across the stage. Amy and I turned to look at each other as it dawned on us now who the crowd of people we had seen on our approach was. One by one, each member of the Horizon staff was lining up to make their own donation. Everyone from the hotel managers to the cleaning ladies, cooks, and maintenance workers had taken a break from their evening tasks and (perhaps with some pressure from above) come to donate what they could. Each person after leaving their offering walked up to Amy and I and shook each of our hands in turn. For maybe 15 minutes straight we stood there shaking hands and thanking them for their donations. The faces of some were completely lit up, evident pride and joy shining through their smiles at having the chance to support a charitable cause, even if ¥5 or ¥10 was all the support they could afford. We noticed others however that looked somewhat disgruntled at being forced to come out and participate at all. In sharp contrast to the enthusiasm of their colleagues, they offered us the familiar limp-fish handshake and barely made eye contact before quickly shuffling back off the stage.

In all, it was quite a strange and enlightening experience. On the one hand we were touched that so many people had been moved enough by our trip and our desire to partner with a Chinese non-profit that they had gone above and beyond the donation already made by the organization that owned the hotel (around ¥20,000 or $3,000). On the other hand though, the expressions of pride expressed by some and the dispassionate resentment on the faces of others made Amy and I uncomfortable, and the ostentatiousness of the display left us very self-conscious. Even though it wasn't organized by us, here we were, an American and a Briton traveling around China, coming into a Chinese holiday resort, and asking Chinese staff and Chinese guests to donate to a Chinese charity helping Chinese school children. What did we foreigners know about China and why should we want to help? It felt like there was a touch of Western patronization to it all. There was nothing malicious in it of course, but shaking hands with each member of the staff as they walked by, Amy and I both felt awkward at being made the center of attention.

To be sure, these thoughts were secondary to the primary emotions of the moment, more of an uncomfortable feeling that we were only able to identify fully after talking it over together. Overall we were both extremely moved by the remarkable generosity and wholly unnecessary gesture by the hotel, its staff, and the guests in attendance that night. It helped add an unmistakably positive tone to what ended up being one of the best stops we'd had all trip.

Several days later, when we had already left from Sanya and were making our way back north again, Hai Xiao messaged us to let us know what the final count from the donations that night had been. In all, the event had managed to raise ¥10,000 from staff donations and an additional ¥9,700 from guests, for a total of ¥19,700 (over $3,100), nearly matching the amount donated by the hotel directly. This made our three-day stop in Hainan by far the most productive time to date in terms of fundraising for Free Lunch for Children, more than doubling the total we'd raised so far.

After a maintenance stop at the Sanya CFMoto shop, we had a brand new luggage rack attached to the bike and new brake pads to replace old ones which had been ground down from weeks of rain and mud. Amy and I also felt like we were finally making an impact on one of our other goals of the trip which was to support a local charity. Hainan was undoubtedly a high note for us, so it was a shame when we discovered that we would soon be forced to rush out of the province.

Chapter 17 – A Race Against Time and Typhoon

On November 3rd, a couple days after our arrival in Sanya, a storm system began developing 265 miles southeast of Micronesia, 3,000 miles away from Hainan. Two days later the storm was classified as a typhoon and by the 6th of November it had reached the status of a Category 5-equivalent super typhoon. Super Typhoon Haiyan (which means "Sea Sparrow" in Chinese) ended up being the deadliest and costliest typhoon in the South China Sea's modern history, resulting in thousands of deaths and severe damage across Micronesia, the Philippines, Vietnam, and Southern China.[84]

Amy and I were watching the growth of the storm closely during our time in Sanya. All indications were that by the time Typhoon Haiyan hit mainland China, much of its strength would have already dissipated. Everyone at The Horizon Resort remained uneasy however. The central Chinese and provincial governments were also taking precautions. The State Flood Control and Drought Relief Headquarters eventually issued a level three emergency alert in Hainan, Guangdong, and Guangxi, all provinces we planned to be spending time in over the coming week and a half. Aside from concerns about riding conditions in heavy rains, we had an eye towards how the storm would affect the ferry schedule. Given that we were completely cut off from the mainland, there was a very good chance that if ferry services were suspended, we could end up stranded in Hainan until the storm passed.

---

[84]   The storm was most devastating in the Philippines, causing a total of 6,300 deaths and USD $2.02 billion in damages. Seven provinces of the country were placed under a state of "national calamity" allowing the government to "effectively control the prices of basic goods and commodities for the affected areas and afford government ample latitude to utilize appropriate funds for rescue, recovery, relief, and rehabilitation efforts."

As we neared the final leg of our trip, Amy and I were becoming increasingly conscious of our timeline and more sensitive to delays, an anxiety exacerbated by the impending storm. For one, it was now already the beginning of November. It may have been a comfortable 80 degrees in the bright sun of southern China, but the longer we were on the road, the colder it was going to be for our last couple of weeks back up the east coast, still a month away. Remarkably, we were also now within spitting distance of our original goal of 15,500 miles, the distance that we had been originally aiming for when we set out from Beijing. However with all of the changes in the Guinness World Record and our route, Amy and I still found ourselves with 13 provinces left to cover.

It wasn't just the baked in travails of weather and itinerary we had to deal with either. Aside from the already busy travel schedule in the coming two weeks that would have us going through seven provincial-level regions – back into Guangxi then on to Hunan, Hubei, Jiangxi, and the Pearl River Delta region that included Macau and Hong Kong – we also had two more events coming up with Free Lunch for Children. One was a program visit at the *Longping* School in the remote mountains of eastern Guangxi province. The other was a fundraising event at a luxury hotel in Shenzhen a week and a half later. Because we were being invited as guests to independently arranged events, it meant that, like the CIMA expo a month prior, the dates weren't flexible. Regardless of any potential mechanical problems, difficult road conditions, or adverse weather, we were afforded very little latitude for delay.

So with the looming Typhoon Haiyan threatening to strand us on Hainan island, and plenty to keep us busy during our stay at the Horizon, there was little opportunity to enjoy our idyllic backdrop over the three days we spent in Sanya. With still a couple days before the storm made landfall in the Philippines, we had crossed back to the north of the province, boarded the ferry, and made it safely across the

Qiongzhou Strait back into Mainland China.

Our first stop was only a couple days' ride away from the ferry crossing. Situated in the mountainous region between two small cities, Shuikou (or "Water Mouth") was a tiny village in the Zhuang Ethnic Minority Autonomous Region of eastern Guangxi province and the location of the *Longping* ("Level Dragon") Lower School. The area was so remote in fact that we would need to meet with the representatives from the charity in Wuzhou, a small city to the south of the village, so that we could follow them along the largely unmapped twisty mountain roads to the school.

Wuzhou itself ended up being a fascinating stop, one of those unanticipated gems of traveling by motorcycle that we might otherwise have missed by more convenient and traditional means of transportation. It turned out that one of the Free Lunch employees, Jia Ning, who ran the Guangxi region operations and was the one to invite us to the event at the Level Dragon School, was a native of the city (though she now lived in the larger city of Guilin to the north). When she arrived in preparation for the event, along with another colleague, Lü Lele, and three photographers contracted for the occasion, she offered to take us all on a little tour of the main street market neighborhood.

We met up with Jia Ning, Lele, and the photographers for dinner near the hotel the evening prior to the event. Jia Ning and Lele were both young, bubbly Chinese girls in their mid-20s. Their cheery dispositions seemed to be well suited for working in a non-profit that helped children, and they were both very excited that we were able to join them at the school. The photographers, two skinny, young Chinese guys and a 7-foot-tall 20-year-old Swede, none of whom had any official partnership with the charity, had come by train from Nanning (the city in southern Guangxi outside of which our rack had snapped).

After we'd finished dinner, Jia Ning put the seven of us into cabs and we went out for a night on the town. The main attraction of the city was a district known as "Stilt City" or *Qilou Cheng*, which had a distinct European colonial aesthetic reminiscent of the French Quarter in New Orleans. Its most unique feature however was the stilt-like pillars that held up the second stories of the buildings. With the ground floors recessed into the structures, this is what gave the style its name.[85] The sidewalks that lined the brightly lit storefronts proceeded underneath the upper stories of the buildings, and created a covered promenade area with the columns bordering the walkway.

As Jia Ning showed us around, she explained that the style had both a practical as well as aesthetic appeal. Wuzhou, which is situated at the confluence of three major rivers, the Xun, Gui, and Xi, as well as being more broadly in the watershed region of the Pearl River Delta, is prone to heavy flooding. As we walked down the streets of "Stilt City", Jia Ning pointed out metal railings that lined the outside of the pillar-supported second stories. During the rainy seasons, she explained, this downtown area near the rivers used to experience such heavy flooding that boats were needed to travel along the streets. These railings were used as a means for the boats to anchor to the buildings, allowing residents to enter and exit their homes through the *shui men* or "water doors" above the stilt-pillars. This was of course why the second floors were raised on stilts in the first place – they became the ground level of the buildings when the lower levels were submerged.[86]

---

[85] *Qilou Cheng* directly translates to "Riding-Building City", where the word for "riding", *qi* (pronounced like "chee"), is the verb used for anything you would mount such as a horse, bicycle, or motorcycle.

[86] This was primarily during the time before the city dykes were reinforced a couple decades prior. Jia Ning explained to us that it used to be the case when she was a kid that the entire city would shut down during this period, which used to last from May to August each year. Businesses were shuttered, kids stayed home from school, and people only ever left their homes to buy groceries.

In addition to walking along the stilt promenades she also had us try a few local snacks. The first was a sweet, jelly-like treat served at the end of a wooden skewer. The street-side stand sold these in a variety of flavors including mango, strawberry, and even chocolate. We were also introduced to a more traditional local food, a delicacy harvested directly from the lush Guangxi countryside – field snails. These came in a bowl filled to the brim with pre-boiled, bite-sized spiraled shells served like the peanuts you're given at a bar to munch on with a beer. To eat them, you pick the shells up one at a time and, with a toothpick, scoop the snail out, popping the de-shelled mollusk into your mouth and working through the chewy meat as you reach into the bowl for your next target.

We made our way back to the hotel, and as we walked along the rivers I thought about how lucky and Amy and I were to be able to visit a place with someone who is actually familiar with the area. Without Jia Ning, our visit to Wuzhou would likely have been brief and unmemorable, hectic traffic the only thing to leave any sort of lasting impression. Instead of just passing through on our way to Guangxi's more popular destinations farther north though, we got to experience the culture and sights of this small Chinese city that barely registered as a blip on the pages and websites in most China travel guides.[87]

The following day we made the two-hour journey towards the school, 60 miles north into the surrounding mountains. Amy and I

---

[87]   Wuzhou, though most westerners would never have heard of it, in fact has played an important historical and cultural role in the region. The city has shown up in historical records going back over 2,000 years to the Han Dynasty (206 BC–220 AD) and is first referred to by the name Wuzhou in the Tang Dynasty in the year 621 AD. Later, during the reign of the Ming (1368–1644), it was made the military and political center of the Guangxi and Guangdong area. This place in history is mostly due to its favorable geographic conditions at the confluence of major transportation routes, particularly the rivers. It sits at the center of both the Lingnan mountainous region of southern China and the Pearl River Delta, and 85% of all of Guangxi province's water flows through it. In 1897 Wuzhou was formally set up as a trade port and has since become one of the top ten inland ports in China.

followed behind a procession of a half-dozen cars that included our five friends from the night before, the local government official that was guiding us, a film crew from a local news station, and a group of about ten representatives from the September 3rd Society, one of China's eight political parties and the organization for whom the event was being organized in appreciation for a recent ¥50k donation.[88]

Shuikou, where Level Dragon Lower School is located, was made up of little more than a scattering of buildings carved into the forested hillside. The landscape had an otherworldly feel to it, lush vegetation covering the vertical spires of karst formations was like something out of Peter Pan's Neverland. The school itself sat at the very top of one of these hills, like the crow's nest perched atop a ship's mast overlooking the rolling ocean of green below. The driveway up to it was so steep that Amy implored me to let her off before I made my way up the 45-degree incline to the modest schoolyard above.

We spent the rest of the morning and much of the afternoon at the school for the event. There was a long stretch of about an hour or so where Lele and a couple speakers from the September 3rd delegation gave some speeches to the kids and staff while an official Free Lunch for Children plaque was given to the school by the donors.

Amy and I were blown away by the patience and discipline of the kids. They were remarkably quiet and well behaved despite many of them probably not even knowing what was going on other than that their lunchtime getting delayed.[89] Afterwards, we were all treated to

---

[88]   The *Jiusan*, or September 3rd Society ("Jiu" means nine and "San" means 3) is a member of the Chinese People's Political Consultative Conference, which serves as an advisory legislative body with representatives from twelve different parties of which the Communist Party holds the most dominant role. The name, *Jiusan*, comes from the date when the Chinese beat the Japanese at the end of World War II, September 3rd, 1945. The party is mostly ceremonial however. Holding little legislative or administrative power, the nationwide organization of nearly 150k members as of 2014, is made up primarily of intellectuals and those working in the areas of science and education.

[89]   Aside from them just being young children (between the ages of 8 and 12), almost all of the children were of the local Yao ethnic minority and for whom Mandarin was not their first

the "free lunch" that is procured by donations to the charity, with visitors and kids all enjoying the same meal. We all lined up single file along with the kids and were served generous portions of rice, a meat and potato stew, and greens out of large cauldron-like pots. We were told that this was the same quality of food the kids got every day. There was no way to verify this but it was a great meal all the same, with seemingly fresh ingredients, well prepared, and served warm. It was probably among the best lunches we had had on our whole trip.[90]

After lunch, we hung around a bit longer at the school. I played basketball with some of the kids in the yard out front, Amy and I chatted with the other guests about our trip, and we all took some photos together with the kids after getting a few to sign the extra-large commemorative "Free Lunch for Children" and "Great Ride of China" flag we'd been carrying since Xi'an. By about mid-afternoon though it was time for Amy and I to start moving on again. While the rest of our party was going to head back to Wuzhou for the night, we would have to continue inland, north towards the central provinces of Hunan and Hubei. The next closest city where we could stay for the night, Hezhou, was still a hundred miles away, which included several hours through remote country roads. So we said our farewells to everyone, thanked Jia Ning and Lele for hosting and made our way back down the steep driveway of the school and into the mountains.

---

language. In fact, we were only able to communicate with the older kids who had been studying Mandarin the longest and who helped to translate for the younger, shyer kids less familiar with the language. This meant many of the children probably couldn't even understand the speeches apparently being made for their benefit.

[90] One of the appeals to us of the Free Lunch for Children mission was that it was a simple message of donating a small amount of money to buy a kid a lunch. This simplicity also ensures a high level of transparency, helping to avoid graft by having donations go directly to the purchasing of food. Rather than just donate to local schools and governments, where the money could get "lost" in bureaucracy, the schools had to publish their accounts publicly, showing exactly where the money was going (e.g. x-hundreds of yuan going to buy x-kilos of rice, vegetables, and meat).

***

The next scheduled event, a celebrity golf tournament in Shenzhen, wasn't for another week and a half. Unfortunately though there was still a lot of ground we needed to cover, about 2,000 miles, and the rain from what was left of Typhoon Haiyan, which was just making landfall in China, would be catching up with us any day now.[91]

The region coming up was also one we had been particularly looking forward to for tourist destinations. Guilin city and Yangshuo county were only a day's ride away from the Level Dragon School. Famous for the snaking Li River set against the backdrop of tree covered karst formations, the area has been the inspiration for Chinese landscape art for centuries (a scene of the Li River in Guilin is even featured on the Chinese ¥20 note). Weaving amongst the stoic colossuses that overlooked the Li was something Amy and I had been looking forward to since we had first set out. After Guilin we would move north to Phoenix City, a 300-year-old UNESCO World Heritage site in the mountainous area of western Hunan province. The walled city is located on the Tuo river, with distinctive Ming and Qing architecture with Miao and Tujia ethnic minorities making up more than 50% of the population[92]. After that, and also in Hunan, we planned to visit the second most popular national park in China,

---

[91]   Despite the fact that the severity of the storm had significantly decreased by the time it hit Mainland China (particularly compared to the devastation it caused in the Philippines), the damage was still significant. The cost of the storm reached USD $803 million in Hainan and $45 million in Guangxi as a result of property damage and evacuations that affected over 3 million people, including seven deaths.

[92]   The city garnered national attention in April 2013 when it began instituting an entrance fee to visit the historical village. The fee of ¥148 (about $20), was levied against all visitors regardless of whether they were tourists or not. This was controversial as the town was still a functioning community with native residents who needed to be able to do business with people coming in and out of the city. Local businesses claimed that the high ticket price, which had risen to over ¥200 by the end of 2013, had also had a deleterious effect on tourism, a claim that local officials refuted.

Zhangjiajie, best known for the otherworldly landscape that inspired the floating "Hallelujah Mountains" in James Cameron's *Avatar* movie.

This schedule led to one of the more exhausting weeks of riding of the trip. The rain from Haiyan first hit us in Guilin, soaking us through the morning before we left while out touring a local park and bird sanctuary[93]. It didn't let up for several days and followed us north into Hunan. Because we were so short on time, and with a lot of distance to cover, the only way Amy and I could effectively sightsee was to wake up early in the morning before the sun was up, eat a quick breakfast before touring the nearby sights, and then head out on the road again by lunch. This we would do rain or shine, weekday or weekend.

Luckily we had gotten efficient enough with our daily routines and the maintenance of all our gear that we were still able to get 100–200 miles in per day. Making sure everything was packed first thing in the morning gave us a good head start. There was, however, only so much we could do to hedge against unplanned difficulties. After Guilin, and on our first day in Hunan, the highway rose up into the mountains and visibility decreased significantly as dense fog rolled in with the rain. Slowing down on the twisty mountain roads to compensate for the precarious conditions, we passed by a veritable procession of traffic collisions. In the span of about ten miles Amy and I saw a car in a ditch, an overturned truck, one car rear-ended by another, and even an emergency response vehicle that had itself gone into a ditch, presumably on its way to help with one of the other accidents. It was almost comical in its slapstick-like severity. Wide-eyed, I pre-empted Amy's nervous tap on my shoulder and slowed down by a few more mph as we made our way deeper into the mountains.

---

[93]   The "Hundred Birds Sanctuary" was located in *Die Cai* Hill Park and we found it occupied almost exclusively by chickens and chicks (though we did spot a couple peacocks and one or two other less common birds).

Bad traffic wasn't the only challenge getting in the way of our schedule. A couple of days after the accident-riddled hills of southern Hunan and not too long after our morning through the old town of Phoenix City and some of the worst mud we'd seen since Sichuan, we started to run into mechanical difficulties. After nearly four months and 15,000 miles of rain, snow, ice, and sand, our battery had finally reached its limits and the bike underneath us twice whimpered unprompted to a stop. The pistons refusing to fire, and with an unresponsive electric starter, it took us a couple of rain-soaked push-starts (Amy pushing from behind as I duck-walked the bike forward until we had enough speed for the engine to turn over on its own) to convince us to try and find the nearest CFMoto shop ASAP. Wuhan, the capital of Hubei province, was the closest one to us, only a couple days' ride away. Luckily this unplanned stop just after our visit to the "Avatar Mountains" didn't cause too much of a delay in our schedule. An evening of wine and spicy Hubei food with the local CFMoto boss and some of his friends, a couple of hours overseeing repairs at the shop the next morning, and by early afternoon we were on our way again with a new battery.

Wuhan was the farthest inland we would go before once again pointing our nose towards the sea. We spent almost the entirety of Hubei and Jiangxi provinces on the expressways as we rushed to get back down to the Pearl River Delta region and Shenzhen where the event would be held in only a few days' time. Though both safer and faster than riding on the smaller roads, I preferred to not ride on the expressways when I could avoid it (though I think Amy was agnostic towards, if not preferred, them due to the relative level of predictability and safety). My basic reasoning was that riding on the monotonous and perfectly paved roads felt like cheating. The purpose of our odyssean motorcycle journey through China was to have an immersive experience, exploring the environments and cultures of each province as we passed through. The high-speed roadways though, with fences and cement barriers keeping vehicles in their lanes and village traffic out, was boring and sheltered. If it weren't for the writing on the signs and the traffic police who tried to chase after us as we went around the tollbooths, we could have easily been riding on a highway back in the US.

We passed by the flatlands and farming villages of southern Hubei in about a day and a half. Watching as the nondescript homes and humble plots of cleared land flew past in a blur, I was reminded of the pastured and forested countryside of the northeastern United States (Amy made a similar observation, commenting at one rest stop that the area reminded her of the pastural British landscape).

Jiangxi got hilly again. The Da Bie Mountains rose abruptly out of the level, grassy terrain and threatened the progress of the stubborn G45. Refusing to be diverted, the highway cut straight through the topography and passed under mountains via dozens of tunnels, brushing them aside as if nothing more than a passing nuisance. A major geographical feature that would have once been a significant obstacle for both trade and military endeavors (and today seduced me with the thought of sweeping, scenic mountain roads) had nonetheless been relegated to an afterthought on the road south towards the coast.

To keep alert and fight the boredom, I developed a strategy to help pass the time – tracing out Chinese characters in the air with my head. One game I played was to try and recall the road signs we passed on the road. As we approached the large slogan-like proclamations, I would read them closely as many times as possible in an attempt to commit the characters to memory.

"Don't follow too closely. Tailgating is dangerous."

"Treasure the highway, everyone has a responsibility."

"Jointly establish cultured transportation, share harmonious safety".

After passing, I would move my head around in the air as if writing out the strokes with my forehead to test myself. If I was ever unsure of a character, I could check on my phone at the next stop or just wait until the next time we passed the words again.

Another game I played was to see if I could remember all the provinces we had been through so far on our trip. I would go through each one in order, trying to trace out the character abbreviation that was used on the license plates for each province. There were the easy ones like 京 (jīng) for Beijing, or 甘 (gān) for Gansu. The central and southern provinces though, like Chongqing, Hubei, Hunan, and Jiangxi, stubbornly used older and less obvious characters for their abbreviations. For example, the Jiangxi abbreviation was the character "Gan" written 贛. For Hubei, rather than 湖 (hú) or 北 (běi), the single character 鄂 (È) was used.[94] Hours of fun to be sure.

Watching the swaying and twitching of my helmet in front of her, Amy spent many hours behind me curious, and somewhat nervous, about what was wrong with me. Finally, at one gas stop, I explained the new form of entertainment I had developed for myself, assuring her that I was neither falling asleep nor losing control of the motor functions in my neck.

The ability to easily cover hundreds of miles per day via the expressway allowed us to make up a good amount of distance and avoid delays from some of the bad roads we would have been sure to encounter otherwise. Despite the rain, sightseeing, and battery troubles we managed overall to keep to our schedule and it looked like we were going to make it in time for the event in Shenzhen. By more or less staying ahead of the rains from Typhoon Haiyan (that had hit most heavily in the south after we had already left) and keeping to a

---

[94]   In most cases these single character abbreviations are anachronistic references, official titles for the regions from centuries past and a time when the nation was divided into warring kingdoms or run by warlords, rather than having any relation to their modern entities or even borders.

strict schedule of taking care of tasks and tourism in the morning while putting miles behind us in the afternoon, our progress remained steady.

The boring roads and dirty, nondescript commuter cities we had to pass through were regrettable sacrifices to our unfortunately rushed schedule. It was a common theme throughout the trip though, not just now that we were getting closer to the end. Amy and I had two primary goals, and frequently we found they were in conflict. One of these goals was to experience the diversity of culture, history, food, and people throughout China. At the same time we had the more material aims of covering over 20,000 miles through each province, and in a reasonable amount of time so that we could break a Guinness World Record. Oftentimes Amy and I would rush out of a place, whether the deserts of Xinjiang, the yurts of Inner Mongolia, the ancient minority towns of Yunnan, or the mythical landscapes of Guilin, thinking how much we would have liked to stay but knowing that we would have to budget our time if we wanted to realistically see it all. When talking about the trip together, Amy and I would frequently compare our time on the road to more of a taste testing of China's 33 provinces rather than a full course meal. Every place we passed through was like a brief swish around the mouth, an opportunity to get an idea of the unique features of each but not enough to get to intimately know any single one.

These were the thoughts going through my head after several days on expressways as we approached the southern coast of China for the second time in as many weeks. It also occurred to me as we got closer to the Pearl River Delta that this would probably be our last time heading south. After our visits through the Special Administrative Regions of Macau and Hong Kong, and a stop in Shenzhen for the Free Lunch for Children fundraising event, our direction of travel would be, for all intents and purposes, homeward. There were still plenty more miles to cover and ten more provinces that we planned to visit, but it felt like a turning point, both literally and figuratively. Each day on the road now was one where we were getting closer to the end. The roads would be getting more familiar, the cities more bustling and modern, and soon, the temperatures colder. Every mile we moved forward now was no longer taking us farther from the start, but rather closer to the end.

- *Photos from Chongqing to the Pearl River Delta* -

Scan the QR code or visit the link below to see pictures from Part 4 of The Great Ride of China

http://book.thegreatrideofchina.com/galleries/part-4

Part V - The Pearl River Delta to Beijing

我欲乘风归去，又恐琼楼玉宇，
高处不胜寒。
起舞弄清影，何似在人间！

转朱阁，低绮户，照无眠。
不应有恨，何事长向别时圆？
- 苏轼《水调歌头》

I'd like to ride the wind to fly home.
Yet I fear the crystal and jade mansions
are much too high and cold for me.
Dancing with my moonlit shadow,
It does not seem like the human world.

The moon rounds the red mansion,
Stoops to silk-pad doors,
Shines upon the sleepless,
Bearing no grudge,
Why does the moon tend to be full when people are apart?

- Su Shi (1037–1101 AD), "Prelude to Water Melody"

Chapter 18 – The Pearl River Delta and Celebrity Golfers

After traveling inland around the south central provinces, Amy and I turned back down to the coast and into the bustling mega-metropolis of the Pearl River Delta (PRD). The official PRD Economic Zone covers a space of 4,000 square miles. It is made up of nine cities, the largest and most well known of which are Guangzhou and Shenzhen. In 2012, the area had a gross domestic profit of over USD $757 billion, a number that does not even account for the neighboring Special Administrative Regions (SARs) of Hong Kong and Macau. Together these make up the Greater Pearl River Delta. Combined, this region has a total population of 73 million people and, as of 2012, an economic output of over USD $1 trillion, the equivalent to the 16th largest economy in the world.

I've always been fascinated by the story of Shenzhen's growth. It is a remarkable narrative that has reached near-mythical status emblematic of China's economic development in the latter decades of the 20th century. Back in the 1970s, before Deng Xiaoping initiated his "Reform and Opening Up" policy, the area that is now occupied by the sprawling metropolis of Shenzhen was a modest county by the name of Bao'an. It had a population of 300,000 and an economy sustained primarily by fishing. Hardly a hint of the manufacturing and trade powerhouse it would later become. Unlike its counterparts like Shanghai and Hong Kong, or foreign cities such as London or New York, it had no real historical precedence or deep roots in commerce.

In 1978, Deng formally announced his signature open-door trade policy on a visit to Bao'an county. This would launch one of the greatest economic growth stories in history. By 1980, the area was established as a Special Economic Zone. This designation entitled the region[95], and the businesses located there, to receive preferential tax treatment and more freedom from the economic and trade policies of Beijing. Shenzhen was the first of these cities, established as a way to experiment on a smaller scale with measures that could help modernize the national economy and spur economic growth. By 2013 there were a total of 20 cities designated as Special Economic Zones. As a result of these efforts, Shenzhen has grown from a rural scattering of farmers and fishermen, to a thriving city with a population of between 10 and 15 million, and the 4th largest economic output in the entire country. Foxconn, the Taiwanese electronics manufacturer, employs over 300,000 people in Shenzhen alone, equivalent to the entire population of Bao'an less than 40 years prior.

Amy and I had just spent two weeks going through some relatively backwater areas of central China, winding our way around misty mountain roads and sleeping overnight in budget hotels attached to bleak city train stations. Getting back to the heavily industrialized and more developed coast now, there was a noticeable difference in the levels of economic development and infrastructure investment. We spent a total of four days traveling around the PRD, including one day each for Macau and Hong Kong. The growth of the area has been so dramatic that the knot of cities seemed to have just melted into one another. In the half-day it took to drive the three hundred miles from the east end of the delta towards the border of Macau in the west, we passed north of Shenzhen, near the border with Hong Kong, underneath the city of Guangzhou, and finally into Zhuhai at the Macau border crossing. There were countless highway interchanges

---

[95]   These regions are usually a city, as with Shenzhen, but sometimes they can be districts, regions, or even whole provinces, of which Hainan is the only one.

along the way and we got lost several times. Amy was attempting to navigate us through using her phone's GPS, but the road signs often seemed to conflict with the directions she was giving.

Sometimes in China, especially around the major cities, the development has been so quick that online maps such as Google or Baidu (China's own homegrown search engine) have a hard time keeping up. It's not uncommon for a major highway to head straight into a blank spot on the map. Signs can be similarly inconsistent and unreliable. One example of this was on one of Amy's and my first multi-day motorcycle trips in China back in 2012. As we set out from the port city of Qingdao in Shandong province, both the street signs and GPS led us towards a bridge that headed north out of town. I didn't think much at first of the exiting cars we crossed paths with on the on-ramp. This was a Chinese road after all. "No rules, only suggestions" as Amy and I liked to quip. Pulling to a stop in the middle of a dozen deserted traffic lanes that funneled towards a row of unmanned toll booth, we quickly discovered the reason for the break in protocol. Just behind the signs that cheerily invited us to visit Qingdao again, the bridge we had been directed to abruptly ended, with exposed rebar and nothing but blue ocean connecting it to the land on the other side. Qingdao is no backwater either. This was all in a city with a population larger than that of Chicago.

With this kind of uncertainty, driving around the highway systems of the PRD was somewhat hectic. Without bluetooth headsets, and with the high-speed winds of the highway making it impossible to speak directly, Amy and I communicated by the more primitive means of taps, points, and head shakes. Using a mixture of what I read from signs, the directions Amy pointed in, and a little bit of instinct, we made our way towards the Macau border. A couple of times however, I didn't like the road Amy was pointing down. With no better way to communicate my intentions, I simply shook my head from side to side and drove past the exit ramp she had been indicating.

This was an undiplomatic way to brush aside Amy's navigational efforts. No discussion, just refusal to take her advice. I didn't feel however that I had much choice but to make my own decision, and, consequently, veto hers. It's not that I didn't trust Amy, but rather I didn't of course fully trust the maps. In the end, it turned out I was right not to trust them as our path stayed on course. To Amy though, particularly after the first couple of times I ignored her, it came off as insulting.

Something I never fully appreciated about the differences in our experiences is how comparatively little Amy had within her control as we traveled. As the driver I was able to take charge of everything, from our speed to the steepness of our lean and even to when to stop for breaks, Amy as a passenger had to passively accept whatever happened to us (something that can be particularly stressful on Chinese roads). Navigation was the one thing she was in charge of and could control. Having to use Chinese maps that often weren't precise, she got very good at approximating distances, prepping me for turns, and adjusting the route when necessary. Each day, we would discuss together where we were aiming for, and the rest would be up to her. Amy took these duties seriously and didn't like being responsible for going in the wrong direction (which can happen to anyone in China, even with the best GPS). So when I repeatedly overruled her on the PRD highway system, it was, needless to say, a disarming experience and one she ultimately was not happy about.

Of course I didn't see it this way at the time, so a fight ensued at lunch around the outskirts of Guangzhou. My knee-jerk reaction of macho posturing, explaining why I knew better and would make whatever decision I thought best at 80mph, didn't quite win me any boyfriend points. Eventually cooler heads prevailed and we each arrived at a more empathetic understanding of each other's positions.

Better to yell on a random Chinese street corner than stew with our own thoughts for days inside of our helmets!

***

Macau and Hong Kong were short visits for us. One reason of course was our schedule – with the charity event in Shenzhen only a couple days away, we didn't have much time to hang around. The other reason though was that we weren't allowed into either territory with our motorcycle. Both cities, rather than being provinces, are classified as Special Administrative Regions. This has to do with each municipality's former status as a colony under the Portuguese and British respectively. When the handovers for each were negotiated (Hong Kong in 1997 and Macau in 1999) certain allowances were made to each in how they would be governed. This was done to both ease the transition of the local citizens, whose sovereignty was being transferred from European colonial powers to the Chinese Communist Party, as well as provide additional ways for the Chinese to benefit from the more open markets of the two cities (a similar idea as was behind the establishment of Special Economic Zones like Shenzhen). It was under these initiatives that the slogan "One Country, Two Systems" was popularized.[96] For Amy and I though, having two systems meant that neither the plates on our motorcycle, my Chinese driver's license, nor our insurance would be valid in either territory.

---

[96]   The slogan was first introduced by Deng Xiaoping in 1984 when negotiating the handover of Hong Kong from then Prime Minister of the UK, Margaret Thatcher. The general framework for these agreements was that both colonies would be able to self-govern their territories, receiving a large level of autonomy from the socialist principles of Communist China, for a period of 50 years after reunification. This strategy has also been proposed for a reunification with Taiwan. As such, Taiwanese in both the pro and anti-mainland camps have watched the relationship between the two former colonies and the mainland government closely, wary of any breach of the 50-year grace period and how it might affect the local populations.

That didn't stop us trying futilely to convince the border patrol to let us pass from Zhuhai into Macau on our bike. When that didn't work, we decided to look for a place near the border where we could stay overnight. Because of the high density of urban areas around the Pearl River Delta, there were luckily plenty of hotels where we could park both bike and gear close to the border crossings. Once we'd stashed our gear, we made our way to the former Portuguese colony by foot.

We both really enjoyed our afternoon in Macau. The city had a fantastic mix of colonial European atmosphere with Chinese energy and commerce. Because Macau itself is relatively small, only 11.3 square miles, we were able to cover over half the length of the island in just a few hours of walking. Signs were in Portuguese as well as Chinese. The streets were narrow and, in most cases, cobbled. The traffic was orderly and quiet (pedestrians and drivers actually obeyed stoplights)! Amy and I walked by old Portuguese churches, listened to a school chorus and band practicing on top of tiled mosaic walkways, and climbed up to an old Portuguese fort that sat on a hill in a park. The buildings all had a very "Old World", Mediterranean feel to them, a unique energy made particularly poignant by the fact that the 60th annual Macau Grand Prix had only just ended earlier that day. It felt reminiscent of the way places like Monaco or Casablanca are depicted in movies.

To commemorate our visit to Macau, we ended our walk at the city's version of the Las Vegas strip, which is of course to say the area where most of its casinos are concentrated.[97] Finding the most gaudy and ostentatious casino we could, The Grand Lisboa, which also

---

[97] Probably in large part due to its proximity to 1.5 billion Chinese who have a historical proclivity for gambling (and whose government forbids it), Macau's gambling revenue in 2013 was nearly seven times as large as that of Las Vegas' (USD $45 billion to Vegas' $6.5 billion). Hong Kong, which also lacks casinos, is working on bridges to connect the two cities so people (gamblers) can travel between the two. There are a total of 33 casinos in the Macau SAR, 23 of which are on the Macau peninsula.

happens to be Macau's tallest building and shaped like a giant, glimmering lotus flower[98], Amy and I decided to put a day's worth of food and gas money on the line (¥200 or about $32) and try our hand at some roulette.

Amy was reluctant to gamble at first, and feeling out of place in our grimy "town clothes" as we walked around five star hotels didn't help. I eventually convinced her however with the theory that since our goal was to see as many of the sights in each province as possible, what better sight for Macau than the inside of a casino! It did not take much to turn Amy to my view and she soon became a more enthusiastic gambler than I. It helped of course that we caught a hot hand at the cheap table. We spent about an hour at it (with a quick break at the slot machines which we cut short after a couple losses) and managed to turn our ¥200 into nearly ¥500. When our lucky streak ended, I convinced a now fully enthused Amy to quit while we were ahead and cash out our winnings. We took our profits and bought a nice local dinner around the corner from the casino, before taking a bus back to customs and across the border to the Mainland.[99]

After spending the night in Zhuhai, we traversed the width of the PRD economic zone once more, this time heading back to Shenzhen to find a place to keep our stuff near the Hong Kong border. Hong Kong was less eventful than Macau, mostly because we'd both already been before but also because it's quite a bit bigger and so it took us most of the afternoon just to get downtown.

---

[98]   The Grand Lisboa stands at 47 stories and 856 feet tall. It is owned by Sociedade de Turismo e Diversões de Macau ("The Society of Traveling and Entertainment of Macau Limited"). It is built to resemble a giant golden lotus flower, the symbol of Macau, with an egg-shaped base symbolizing prosperity. According to a press release by the hotel, "The design also [owes] its inspiration to a feather crown worn by a dancer, which [symbolizes] the vitality of the entertainment business."

[99]   The border crossing to the mainland, with all the Chinese heading back to Zhuhai after a day of gambling, took over an hour to cross. This was in contrast to the ten minutes it took that morning going in the opposite direction.

The big reward of this visit was that a friend of ours had a house on the far south side of the city, a beautiful cliffside home overlooking Stanley Harbor. Amy and I arrived at the house just after dark, tired from a day on the bike and over four hours on public transportation. After much needed showers in the room that had been prepared for us, we were given a tour of the gorgeous eight-story home. The tour ended at a rooftop patio where we closed off the day with foreign beers and an amazing steak barbecue, which we enjoyed under the light of the full moon as it made its way up over the cliffs of the harbor.

***

I never played much golf growing up. I suppose that's because of the need for equipment and space – it was hard to get into on my own and no one in my immediate family played either. Amy's situation was much the same. So, with our combined golfing experience limited to a couple of visits I'd made as a kid to the Chelsea Piers driving range in New York and neither of us being anywhere close to celebrities, Amy and I were somewhat out of place for the celebrity charity golf tournament we had been invited to participate in on the outskirts of Shenzhen.

Like with the school visit in the mountains of Guangxi a couple weeks previously, this was an event organized independently of our motorcycle trip. We had been invited to join by the charity almost as a matter of convenience. One of Free Lunch for Children's corporate donors, the luxury hotel that was hosting the event, had organized a high-profile tournament involving Chinese celebrities. These dignitaries of the entertainment industry were put into three teams organized by where they were from, one team each for Hong Kong, Taiwan, and the Mainland. The teams would then compete for overall best score as well as other individual contests such as best shot and lowest single score. In an effort to try and fit us into the festivities, Amy and I were told that we would present the prize for longest drive. (Get it? Because of our longest motorcycle drive in a country!)

While it was nice to be invited for the event, have the opportunity to participate in the fundraising, and have a couple days' stay at a nice hotel, the event itself was regrettably unorganized. Amy and I were given essentially a day and a half off to prepare for the evening banquet when the awards ceremony would be held. One of our contacts at the charity explained that we would have our trip introduced by the hosts, a short video presented, and then we would be asked to give a five to ten minute speech in Chinese about our work with the charity. Thus, Amy and I spent the time that we weren't doing laundry and catching up on our other work preparing materials for the video and working on a speech. Both of us were relatively competent in Chinese, enough to have meetings and engage in conversation, but to give a speech in front of media and celebrities we felt was something best prepared for ahead of time.

It was clear from the start that the event would prove frustrating and ultimately unproductive. Amy and I showed up on time, at 7pm, but nothing seemed to be happening yet. Dressed in our full motorcycle gear at the request of our hosts, we walked into a nearly desolate reception area. A few Free Lunch for Children volunteers could be seen scurrying about like windup toys messing with superfluous tasks; some tables and banners were laid out and a red carpet paved a walkway to the banquet hall, but otherwise it was clear the event was a long way from starting.

We flagged down one of the dithering deputies clad in their charity branded white and red polos and asked where we should wait. Amy and I were led to a small, sparsely furnished sitting room to the side of the lobby where the spare decorations and party favors were being stored. It was over an hour until the celebrity golfers, changed from their cleats and plaids and into full black-tie attire, finally started to trickle in. They strolled along the red carpet, a feigned aloofness in their stride, as they made their way to the entrance. Pictures snapped away as the couples and groups walked down, signing a large poster board that had been placed at the end of the walkway before entering the hall. After about 15 minutes of this, one of the managers of the event suddenly rushed over to Amy and I. We had been standing off to the side with the rest of the onlookers, watching the procession of personages, and had apparently been forgotten until spotted by the volunteer. We were nervously ushered towards the top of the carpet and then motioned to walk along the same rug we'd only moments before been standing beside. Feeling severely out of place and underdressed, Amy and I walked awkwardly down in our padded cycle pants and boots, signed the board with a pen that had been shoved at us, and then apprehensively made our way into the hall.

After entering the main room, a small group of curious attendees started to crowd around us. They appeared interested in our extraneous presence and out of place dress but too nervous to make any inquiries. One middle-aged woman (short, a little overweight, and dressed in a long, white ballgown) finally began speaking to us in tortured English. Stepping forward precariously in ill-fitting heels, she practically yelled the over-annunciated words at us.

"HEEELLLOOOO! WHERE... YOU... FROM??" she inquired with an almost manic look in her eyes as she strained through the question.

"*Ni hao. Wo shi mei guo ren. Ta shi ying guo ren.*" "Hello. I'm American and she is British," I replied.

The woman's eyes went wide in amazement when she realized we could speak Chinese. She began frantically looking around at the people nearest her as if to find someone to share this revelation with.

"*Waaaa! Ni hui shuo zhong wen ma??*" "Waaaa! You can speak Chinese??"

We smiled politely and nodded. Excited and not knowing how to deal with this fascinating new discovery, the woman suddenly whipped out her phone and handed it to one of her male companions.

"TAAAKKEE A PICTURE?" the woman asked, for some reason switching back into English and motioning the action with her hands.

Amy and I agreed and the woman shuffled over. Standing in between the two of us, she whipped her arms around our torsos, posing for the photo. After seeing that we were taking pictures, several other people, both men and women, some giggling but all sheepishly, asked if they could take one too.

It was something we had grown used to traveling around China. Oftentimes at a scenic spot, the foreign tourists are as big an attraction for the Chinese tourists as the site itself, and it is not uncommon for people to come up to you and ask to take a photo. It's novel at first, but after a while it becomes a little tiresome.

For this event, I had figured that most of the people in attendance, in contrast to a person from rural China visiting Tiananmen Square for the first time or young girls in a second tier Chinese city seeing their first foreigner, had had plenty of exposure to Westerners. Looking around the room though, I quickly saw that we were in fact the only non-Chinese in attendance. Our bilingual friend asked us briefly what we were doing there at the event, but it became clear that she had no interest in our association with the charity. She quickly grew bored and changed the subject back to the prototypical topics of how good our Chinese was and how long we'd been in China.

Amy and I both felt a little absurd, standing there in the middle of a crowd of Chinese taking our photos for no other reason than the fact that we were foreigners. Our outfits were completely out of place but no one seemed concerned with why we might be dressed in dirty, reinforced motorcycle gear at a black-tie event. Rather than talk about our experiences around China or ask about our work with Free Lunch for Children, people were instead yelling at us the couple of words they knew in English as if we had a hearing impediment, and snapping photos like we were some sideshow attraction.

In fact, no one really ever got the chance to find out what we were doing there at all. Everything was so far behind schedule before the event had even gotten underway, that the agenda became compressed. Dinner didn't start until nearly 9 o'clock and was served in parallel with the first half of the speeches. The announcement for the "Longest Drive" award came rushed and out of order. There was no warning from the organizers, just someone hurrying up to Amy and I at our table and shooing us towards the stage just as the segment was starting. We made our way up and stood next to the hosts. Expecting a video, we were surprised when someone handed us a small plaque from off stage. Then, one of the hosts announced a name and we were brusquely motioned to hand the award to the man who came to receive it. The video and photos we had been asked to prepare were never put to use, and I thought of all the things that could have been done in the time we'd been preparing speeches never spoken. Adding salt to the wound, with the night dragging on late, Amy and I didn't end up getting to bed until after midnight. This made the 6am wake-up we had planned for the next morning, in order to get a good start on a day of riding, increasingly unlikely.

The experience confirmed a suspicion Amy and I had begun to develop that Free Lunch for Children didn't really have a good idea of how to use our trip. We had been on the road for four months already and had been working with their organization for over half a year. Every fundraising campaign we'd had the opportunity to take part in seemed half-baked and poorly thought out. With this cynical backdrop and the bad taste that the mess in Shenzhen had left, Amy and I had become despondent with our charitable efforts and partner.

Throughout our time working with the organization we discovered that the idea of fundraising drives or "walkathon" style events (where some sort of challenge is tied to donations) was a foreign concept to the Chinese non-profit sphere. When first bringing up the idea of The Great Ride of China with the people at the charity, one of the questions we were asked was "What does a motorcycle have to do with hungry kids in China?" We tried for months before and during our time on the road to receive some help organizing fundraising events. This included many hours in direct meetings. One idea we had proposed was to hold joint events with some of their corporate sponsors in areas we would be passing through. Another that we would have really liked to see materialize was to have multiple school visits across the country. The appeal to us of Free Lunch for Children in particular was that they had operations in 20 provinces, a scope that Amy and I felt complemented tremendously our goal of riding through all 33. To our minds it seemed like the perfect opportunity to raise both local and national awareness for the cause. Not only did none of this ever come to fruition, but after months of prodding I was not even able to get them to setup a donation platform for foreign funds.[100]

This apparent lack of motivation from the charity is what spurred Amy and I to start being more proactive, organizing opportunities like the one with the hotel in Sanya and another one later on in Shanghai. Given our travel schedule however, we were limited in what we could accomplish on our own and had become disheartened and disappointed at the partnership.

As we learned more about the organization itself and the non-profit industry in China more generally, our views morphed and we became more sympathetic. Not entirely unsurprisingly, working as a non-profit in a political climate unwelcoming to non-governmental organizations and self-organizing civil society can be very tricky. For

---

[100]   By the end of our trip, Amy and I had raised over $1,000 from foreign donors, mostly friends and family. This was enough for 2,000 lunches. Nonetheless, because Free Lunch for Children was never able to set up a platform, we had to collect these donations in a private PayPal account and could only wire the money to the charity months after our trip was over.

one, there are incredibly unrealistic expectations of how and where funds should be spent. Donors don't like to see their money used anywhere other than directly on the cause itself. So in the case of Free Lunch for Children, people would only donate if their money went directly to buying school lunches. This attitude may seem altruistic and constructive on the surface, however it makes investment in development, growth, and staff incredibly difficult to fund.

The other problem was a credibility gap with the general public. This had especially built up in recent years as a result of several high-profile corruption scandals.[101] The effect was to both dampen the number of people willing to part with their hard-earned money as well as increase the level of government scrutiny attracted by charities both foreign and domestic.

Combined with a newly burgeoning middle class and the fact that non-profits are such a recent development, all this can cause structural problems for charities operating in the country. Free Lunch for Children compensated for this in two ways, which both created further problems but also contributed to their growing into one of the largest domestic non-profits in China in just two years. The first was to operate mostly through volunteers. This helped to keep HR costs down, with the few full-time employees they did have getting paid very little. The other strategy was to rely entirely on their large donors to organize events. This meant that everything from the venue, to media, to actual programming and fundraising activities was managed by these outside organizations.[102] This led to a huge deficit

---

[101]   The company most at the center of these scandals in China has been the Red Cross, which endured two major publicity mishaps. The first was after the 2008 earthquake in Sichuan when donations apparently went missing while local officials appeared to be profiting. The other was an alleged employee of the Red Cross, Guo Meimei, who was found showing off a lifestyle on her social media presumably beyond the means of someone working in a non-profit. This included most famously posting photos of herself with luxury cars and designer fashion accessories.

[102]   Conversely they had also learned to be very effective at deploying social media to attract large

in experience when it came to what is known in foreign non-profits as "development", i.e. the operations involved in increasing donor bases and organizing events. Poorly paid management and lack of practice doing on-the-ground fundraising was not fertile ground for strong organizational skills.

A clear example of this lack of experience was when we first told Free Lunch for Children that we had received sponsorship. When we called up the manager of the Beijing office (one of the few paid employees) to inform her that we would now be able to move full steam ahead with the trip, rather than seeing the fundraising possibilities that a Guinness World Record attempt could open up, she instead replied curtly and brusquely, "*Na... wo men de qian ne?*" "And... how about our money?"

---

numbers of small donors while keeping costs low. Their simple message of "¥3 can buy a child a lunch" proved both fruitful and scaleable.

Chapter 19 – The Motorcycle Crews of Southeast China

There was an ironic contrast between the unpredictability of the challenges of the road and the near robotic consistency with which we executed our daily routines. Each day was more or less structured the same. Wake up and plan out the day's route, pack up all of our gear, find a place for lunch, gas and supplies, convince a local hotel to register foreign guests that evening, and, finally, explode all our gear again at night. No matter the deviations brought by weather, confrontations with police, interactions with locals, or deteriorating roads, these were the immutable pillars of our day-to-day lives. While Amy and I rarely spent two nights in a row in the same place, we could always take solace in our routines.

Any variabilities revolved around our map and, to a lesser extent, the weather: where we had been, where we were going, and where we still had to go. From this perspective, Shenzhen and the Greater Pearl River Delta region were pivotal milestones for us. Our visit to the SARs and the charity event had been constants on our calendar for weeks. Now our map was taking us back northward again. Under normal circumstances, this might seem trivial. But when some of the biggest decisions you make each day revolve around which direction to go in, it assumes more meaning.

The PRD was not just the literal turning point but the figurative one as well. As we started to make our way east and north, we were getting closer and closer to familiar territory. Not far off now was Hangzhou, the home of our sponsor CFMoto and the place that in some ways marked the beginning of our adventure half a year earlier. Next after that would be Shanghai, Qingdao, and Tianjin, all places

Amy and I had travelled to by motorcycle before and all on the road back to Beijing.

The end was at the edge of my thoughts as Amy and I set out from Shenzhen along the coast, but immediately at hand were still new places to explore. Located right beside Guangdong, and less than a day's ride away from Shenzhen by expressway, was Fujian province. After the stress and formality of participating in the fundraising event, plus the built-up urban sprawl of the PRD, a return to the open road brought Amy and I a sense of relief. Especially liberating was the reliable consistency and familiarity of our daily routines.

An escape was not our only reason to look forward to Fujian, province number 26 on our list. Fujian was a place we had been looking forward to for some time, drawn primarily by its rich history. For the better part of two millennia, the province persisted outside of the political dramas and dynastic machinations of the major Chinese empires ebbing and flowing around it. During this time, the region existed mostly as an ancillary kingdom, known as the *Min Yue*. The *Min Yue* oscillated between independent, tributary state and conquered province of various contemporary Chinese dynasties, including the Qin, Han, Ming, and Qing. Surrounded by mountains, the province's topography made it difficult for these empires to maintain a strong hold on the area. This afforded the *Min Yue* a unique degree of autonomy.

Throughout the centuries, the region attracted large numbers of migrants from northern and central China. Because of Fujian's geographic separation, many refugees moved south to escape the destruction of warring kingdoms and invading hordes. The resulting legacy from centuries of attracting disparate migrant populations is that Fujian became one of the most linguistically diverse provinces in the country, a fact that has persisted to this day. The province has a total of seven different Chinese dialects spoken within its borders (eight including Mandarin). Some of these can be broken down further into sub-classifications, and many of these are so diverse that they are unintelligible between groups.[103]

One of the largest populations of migrant peoples that moved to Fujian are the Hakka (also known as the *Ke Jia* or "Guest Home" people), an ethnic group related to the majority Han but who traditionally speak a different language, "Hakka Chinese". Though they migrated first to Fujian, settling in the mountainous region in the southwest, they can now be found throughout southern China. Today the majority can be found living in Guangdong. They were also some of the first Chinese migrants to Taiwan during the end of the Ming dynasty, c. 1644 AD. With their settlements in Fujian, the Hakka brought a distinctive agrarian culture and, most appealing for us (and especially Amy), architectural styles. It was some of these old settlements, which dated back as far as the 12th century, that we were most eager to visit while in the province.

One other notable aspect we were looking forward to was that Fujian was the tea capital of not just China but, arguably, the world. Way back on just the fourth day out of Beijing, Amy and I were treated to a tea ceremony by a family that had invited us into their roadside dispensary in Liaoning. As we sat drinking tea with them, we learned that the family were migrants who had moved from the area of Fujian we were now passing through. The three primary tea processing techniques for Oolong, Green, and White teas all originated from Fujian, as did the special "Kung Fu Tea Ceremony" we had been treated to by the family months earlier. Having only just finished the box of vacuum sealed Iron Bodhisattva tea gifted to us on

---

[103] In a piece for the New York Times in 2005 investigating the present difficulties for Chinese who wish to unite the country under a single language, Howard French used Fujian province to highlight the challenges. In the article he quoted one Fujianese linguist, Zhang Zhenxing, (a professor at the Chinese Academy of Social Sciences in Beijing) who told French about a local saying: "If you drive five miles in Fujian the culture changes, and if you drive ten miles, the language does."

that visit, our arrival at the special Oolong tea's home was a fortuitous opportunity to resupply.

That we were now entering more developed and populated areas of the country again meant that we would also have something else new to look forward to: local motorcycling communities. This seemed largely to be thanks to year-round favorable weather conditions and prosperous economic development, where a growing GDP meant both investment in great roads and populations able to afford expensive hobbies like recreational motorcycling. Because we had been regularly sharing updates online about our trip in both English and Chinese, members of these communities had been following along with us throughout. Now that we were finally in the neighborhood, we would have the opportunity to meet up, and even ride, with some of them.

We met the first fellow two-wheeled enthusiasts on just our first day out of Shenzhen in the small, industrial town of Yunxiao, a couple of hours east from the border with Guangdong. Mike (who was fully Chinese, but introduced himself by his English name) was a middle-aged, tall, and sturdy-looking Chinese man. He showed up just after us at the hotel he had recommended to us in town, rolling up on a gas-powered scooter which he parked next to our 650TR in the parking lot. He was both warm and welcoming, greeting us each with a large smile and firm handshake (a welcome change from the dead-fish grip we'd grown accustomed to).

After we'd put our stuff away in our room, Mike took us to a restaurant attached to the hotel. It was comfortable and relatively upscale (for rural China), arranged in a semi-open-air layout where you had to walk outside to get between the different rooms.

Before we found a place to sit, the waitress took the three of us into a room separated from the seating areas. There, we found the walls lined with glass tanks and one massive tank in the center. All of these were filled with live fish, with aquarium-level diversity on display.

Everything from sea cucumber to abalone to lobster and shrimp was available (as well as many more slimy creepy crawlies that I would not be able to name). More than just for show, the transparent cages would be serving as our menu.

Mike, playing the host, talked through our order with the waitress. He asked which fish were available and discussed with her how they should be prepared. This was a strange way of ordering but it wasn't the first time Amy and I had encountered it. In the past when we'd been escorted into the kitchen after asking for a menu, the process always felt intimidating. Without guidance, we had no idea what to ask for or how it should be prepared. Requesting recommendations yielded few results.

"What do you recommend?" One of us would ask the chef or waiter.

This was usually just met with a shrug. "Whatever you want!"

We'd try and probe further. "What's a good local dish?" The response was usually more or less the same, replying by pointing to a wall of raw ingredients and a prompt to pick.

"Ok… braised eggplant then," we'd say, picking a safe dish we were familiar with from Beijing.

Then came the vigorous shake of the head. "We can't do that here!"

The uncertainty of this process was exponentially more unnerving with seafood.

Mike went through the orders one by one as the waitress effortlessly, and without expression, fished out each with a nearby net, lifting it up for our inspection before moving on to the next. Amy and I meanwhile stood passively to the side, deferring to Mike's tastes on what to have for dinner, nodding our approval to whatever our host recommended.

After ordering, we went back outside and into the seating area, finding a place by a window that looked out at the courtyard. As we waited for the dishes to start arriving, the three of us began exchanging stories about our travels. We talked about motorcycling and about China. As the conversation progressed, I got a feeling of stately confidence from Mike. He was easy to laugh and had an air of quiet contentment, as if he had seen enough in his life to leave him perfectly at ease. As Amy and I started to learn more about his backstory, it became clear that this wasn't just a show he put on for guests. The more we learned, the more I started to think of him as the Chinese "Dos Equis Man". If he wasn't the most interesting man in the world, he was certainly one of the most interesting people the two of us had ever met in China!

Though he was ethnically Chinese and his mother tongue was Mandarin, Mike was born and raised in Vietnam. When he was in his late teens and the Vietnam War broke out, he, along with thousands of other Vietnamese, left the country to find refuge from the fighting. He managed to leave by boat, as many others were forced to do. He would, however, soon encounter a problem experienced by refugees throughout history – nobody wanted to take them in. Mike explained to us that after days at sea they eventually reached the shores of Malaysia where they asked for asylum. When their plea was rejected, the local government rerouted them to a nearby island where they were forced to find shelter on their own.

As the months went by, while Mike and the rest of the people from his boat continued to be denied refuge, the numbers arriving from Vietnam continued to increase. This just exacerbated the problem – more refugees made it harder to convince local governments to accept them, while at the same time their swelling numbers made the status quo more and more unsustainable. The population of refugees on the island grew larger and larger, until a community numbering in the thousands had developed. From the way Mike described it, we gathered that for no other reason than perhaps his sheer force of presence and relative organizational competency, he eventually became the de-facto mayor of the island. In his new role he assumed responsibilities that included resolving disputes, establishing rules, and helping set up local marketplaces.

After the war, Mike was able to get an education in engineering and eventually relocated to Houston, Texas, getting a job in the oil industry. He shared some stories of his decade and a half there, including once spending a night in jail after going over a hundred miles per hour on his motorcycle in the middle of the night on a Texas highway. After making a good living in oil, he eventually moved back to China in the early 2000s in order to be closer to family, many of whom had since relocated to the mainland around Fujian and Zhejiang. He started off owning some factories in neighboring Zhejiang but later sold them, and now ran a door and handle fixtures factory in Fujian with his brother.

Among Mike's many surprises was the incredible collection of motorcycles he had accumulated over the years. At one point in the conversation, he casually mentioned to us that in one of his warehouses he had almost 50 bikes. It was a collection that included everything from custom cafe racers to broken down Chinese farmer bikes all the way up to high-end Ducatis and BMWs.

Despite his accomplishments and wide range of experience, Mike was incredibly humble, the type of guy that's easy and enjoyable to talk to. He was like a fun uncle that everyone loves to visit and who you later find out, after years of not suspecting anything remarkable, was a famous war hero or led some harrowing expedition in his youth.

After dinner, Mike (who refused to let Amy and I pay for anything) told us that he unfortunately would not be able to join us for the next day's ride. It was a weekday and so duty would be calling him into the factory in the morning. He did however have some good recommendations for which roads to take northeastward towards our

351

next destination, the famous Fujian rammed earth buildings, or *Tulou*, of the Hakka people.

The *Tulous*, which directly translates to "earth building" in Mandarin, are a legacy of the Hakka who migrated south to Fujian province nearly a millennia earlier. The unique circular buildings, which can get up to five stories high and house as many as eight hundred people, were built between the 13th and 20th centuries. They are made primarily out of tightly packed earth and mixed with readily accessible materials such as stone, wood, and bamboo. The structural design, a donut shaped building with walls up to six feet thick, no windows except narrow slits on the top floor, and only one outward facing gate made of reinforced wood, was conceived primarily for defensive purposes at a time when bandits posed serious risks in the southern provinces. These rural fortresses were known to be able to withstand even the most punishing of canon fire and were incredibly efficient at protecting the residents inside. The buildings are completely unique in the world, an architectural wonder, and as such, the Fujian Tulou "clusters", which comprise a total of 46 buildings spread among counties throughout the area, were officially registered as a UNESCO World Heritage Site in 2008.

Each of these clusters is made up of four to five buildings, essentially forming a *Tulou* village. One could spend a couple of days driving around the nearly 100 miles of roads visiting all of the clusters in the region. Each cluster has its own unique buildings and each of these in turn has their own distinctive characteristics reflecting the clans or families who originally constructed them. Unfortunately though, as was usually the case on our trip, Amy and I were limited by our schedule. This meant that we would only have time to visit one cluster. For our single visit, we decided on the *Tian Luo Keng Tulou* or "Snail Pit Earthen Buildings" cluster, which had been recommended by Mike the night before as well as others we'd spoken with online.

The "Snail Pit" cluster consists of five rammed earth buildings – three round, one oval, and one square. This arrangement of shapes has earned it the nickname *si cai yi tang* or "four dishes and one soup". While it had become noticeably built up for tourists, with locals along the stone pathways aggressively trying to pull us aside and sell us ice cream or trinkets, the buildings themselves were well preserved and allowed for an immersive historical experience. Similar to our visit back in Yunnan to the Naxi capital of Lijiang, if you used your imagination to look past the commercialization, one could get a good idea of what life would have been like for the original Hakka residents before the UNESCO listing and newly laid asphalt brought the hordes from the nearby cities and beyond.

Amy and I visited each of the *Tulou*s in the cluster. In the first, a circular one near the periphery, we climbed up a creaky wooden staircase and walked the circumference of the upper stories of the earthen castle. The dozens of narrow rooms, arranged side by side like a circle of dominos, offered a fascinating look at the culture of a people that reached back nearly two centuries before Columbus stumbled upon the Americas. Old sets of tools and farming utensils leaned against the walls. On the upper stories, the narrow windows offered views of the village outside through the thick wall of packed earth. Amy and I had the promenade entirely to ourselves. A look over the railing revealed the bustling tourists and villagers four stories below.

Each of the buildings seemed to have its own purpose in the community. For example, one of the buildings had a freshwater well at the center. Looking at it, I imagined a time when matriarchs from the various families gathered there to collect water in the early mornings. I envisioned children playing nearby as the women chatted about the local goings-on, sharing gossip like coworkers at the water cooler in a modern-day office building.

Another had a bustling marketplace on the ground floor. The courtyard within the walls was populated by a scattering of wooden huts with thatched roofs. This was in addition to the shops and restaurants that greeted you as soon as you walked in through the gate, a frenetic buzz of commerce radiating from the inward-facing stall-like rooms around the circumference.

In contrast to Lijiang and more similar to the authenticity of Dali, Snail Pit did not feel like it was trying too hard. There were people here that seemed to be legitimately going about their everyday chores rather than just putting on a show. Alongside the tourist shops that sold portraits of Mao and mass-produced paintings of the Fujian countryside, we looked on as still others went about the daily work of living among the plantations of Southeast China. Some were outside, hanging up recently harvested tea leaves, drying them next to sliced fruit in the hot, southern sun. There were others busy with laundry in the center of the *Tulou*, scrubbing the fabric clean in the building's courtyard. We even saw one woman slaughter and de-feather a chicken right in front of us. It eventually became clear that she ran a small restaurant in one of the buildings and was preparing the meat for customers that had just walked in for lunch.

As midday set in, the area began to fill up more. The crowds and increasingly hot sun began detracting from the charm. Amy and I took this as a sign to push on rather than stick around and be pedaled what was sure to be overpriced food. With an eye on Xiamen for the night, a nearby city of four million, it seemed best to get a head start on the traffic.

For our trip out of the mountains that house the *Tulou* clusters, we were lucky enough to be joined by another local biker. Kai Di (pronounced "kai" which rhymes with "sky" and Di like "dee") had been following us on Weibo and through posts we had made on online forums. As we got closer to his home province, he reached out and offered to show us around. Kai Di was part of a group from

Xiamen called the AMOY Motorcycle Club and so he, as well as the head of the club A Tai (pronounced "ah tie"), had decided to meet us on our visit to the Snail Pit cluster and accompany us for the ride to Xiamen. The club also ran the Xiamen Motorcycle Inn and they offered to put us up for the night when we arrived.

Kai Di was in his 20s, skinny, and had an endlessly cheery disposition. He and A Tai, who was in his late 30s or early 40s, with black framed glasses and a more subdued demeanor, met us at the ticketed entrance gate to Snail Pit after we had completed our visit. Before we pushed on to the city, the pair took us to a nearby restaurant for lunch, one farther removed from the tourists. After eating, A Tai led us around the corner from the restaurant where a friend of his had a tea shop. The building was like a storehouse – a single open area with high ceilings, populated with with shelving and furniture. The stoic owner of the shop, a thin, quiet man in his 50s, treated us to the full Kung Fu tea ritual. He delicately steeped the locally sourced leaves at deliberately timed intervals. After dumping the first round, which he explained was too bitter, the man served the second from a glass beaker and out into the shallow, ceramic dishes we each had in front of us. Enjoying the rich flavor of the expertly prepared tea, Amy and I realized that this, surrounded by the terraced hillsides of tea plantations, would also be the perfect opportunity to resupply our store of Iron Bodhisattva Oolong tea.

As we sipped on our tea, A Tai explained that the southern region of Fujian we were in was also well known for its tobacco, which our host also sold. After the tea ceremony, the sun-aged shopkeep smiled widely and proceeded to prepare a couple of hand-rolled cigarettes. Though I don't smoke, I thought it could be counted as a cultural experience and decided to try a couple of puffs. While I've had the occasional cigarette here and there, this Fujianese tobacco wasn't like anything I'd ever had before. Even without any filter, the smoke felt as smooth as from a hookah and, in contrast to the smell of old ashtray and second-hand smoke that permeates most Chinese restaurants and bars, the flavor was remarkably pleasant. While Amy decided to abstain, I accepted when it was passed to me and inhaled from the tightly rolled cigarette, letting the smoke pass over my tongue. It left an almost sweet aftertaste as it rolled backwards into my lungs. My head buzzing from the nicotine, I left the tea house with a giant smile on my face knowing that we could not have asked for a better reception to the province of Fujian.

***

We had a great stay that night at the Xiamen Motorcycle Inn, which also doubled as the home for A Tai, his wife, and his ten year old son. Despite having no experience traveling abroad and being unable to speak much English, A Tai had knowingly or not created a place with the cozy familiarity of a Western hostel. There were beautiful photos hung up on the wall of past trips their members had made to places like Tibet and Yunnan. Upstairs was a communal area with satellite TV and a fridge filled with sodas and beer for guests to enjoy at their leisure. Best of all were the clean rooms, well furnished and with private bathrooms that even had sit-down toilets (a rare commodity, treasured when encountered after months on the road in China). Even the neighborhood, which Amy and I spent time exploring to find breakfast the next morning, was charming – little narrow streets crisscrossing with no particular purpose, small shops that faced out from the whitewashed one and two-story buildings, and restaurants and shops bustling with people buying their meats, vegetables, and noodles for the day.

The evening of our arrival we had dinner with A Tai, his family, and Kai Di, Chinese food ordered from somewhere nearby, and chatted about our different motorcycle trips. I found it once again refreshing to have a conversation in China that went beyond the cost, gas mileage, and brand of our motorcycle.

Our discussion that evening also made me appreciate the value of community. Despite the language and culture barriers, there was so much that was familiar and comfortable about our time at the Xiamen Motorcycle Inn. Talking about our bikes, gear, and past trips felt just like a conversation I would have had with a local biker or fellow traveller back home. We had these common passions, and in the end that seemed to be enough to bridge any gaps that otherwise existed.

After dinner, A Tai and I went over a road map of Fujian that he had hanging up on the dining room wall. We started talking over possible routes we could take through the province, and I sketched out the one we'd planned out along the coast. It felt reminiscent of when I'd seen my dad having similar exchanges at gas stations or biker hangouts on highways back in the US. Not only was the familiarity in a foreign setting refreshing, but it was also nice to just be able to get decent and reliable route suggestions at all!

"Avoid Fuzhou city if you can," A Tai advised, cautioning us against the provincial capital of over 7 million people just a day's ride away. "The National Highway between here and Fuzhou is horrible. Where are you trying to head to next?"

I told him that our next stop was Ningbo, a city on the east coast of Zhejiang near Shanghai. We had planned to mostly follow the coast until Ningbo where we would meet with yet another local motorcycle group that had reached out to us online.

"Have you thought about going up this way?" He traced out a path that deviated completely from our original plan, going northeast around Fuzhou and towards the inland border with Zhejiang.

"No actually. I'm never sure how the smaller provincial roads will be. Sometimes they're a mess – muddy and filled with potholes. Sometimes there's not even a road at all!"

A Tai reassured me that these roads were great for motorcycles, scenic and perfectly paved mountain *wan qu* (Chinese motorcycle speak for "twisties") – lots of fun to be had on two wheels. He then marked out the major towns and landmarks along the way so I would know which roads to take and where to turn. With a grin growing across my face, I grew excited at the next couple of days' ride Amy and I now had ahead. Being spared several days on dusty, truck-infested road, I was savoring the idea of a locally endorsed route.

Our ride north out of Xiamen was as promised. We were led along beautiful roads, smooth, black Tarmac that snaked through small villages, and the promised *wan qu* wove their way among the lush Fujian mountains. Nary a truck was present to hinder our progress. After a full day's worth of great riding, Amy and I decided to take advantage of the nice weather and idyllic scenery and try and find a place to camp for the night. Hoping for the same luck we had had back in Yunnan, we found a scenic area on our GPS, hoping its security would similarly lax. This time unfortunately we were greeted by an active, ticketed entrance, staffed by people not keen on the idea of letting us spend the night.

So, with the sun starting to set and not enough time to travel much further on, Amy and I started wandering around the gorge we had ended the day in, looking for some out-of-the-way space among the villages and farmlands to set up for the night.

The area was very rural. In the vicinity of the provincial park was a scattering of small courtyard homes but almost everything seemed to be abandoned. Along the small one-lane roads that reached out from the provincial highway, we passed by what looked to me like a messy cluster of wooden shacks. Amy pointed out as we passed however that the knot of buildings was actually another local architectural tradition called *Weilongwu* (pronounced "way long woo") or "Encircling Dragon Rooms". These, like the *Tulous*, were a very community-centric design unique to the area. The buildings would have originally started off with just a single building or room. As the founding family grew, these would be added to as succeeding generations made additions to accommodate their own growing families. More and more contributions would be added to the structure, until these "Dragons" ended up being as many as one hundred rooms long.

Unfortunately though, this *Weilongwu*, despite being at least a couple of dozen rooms long, was in a state of severe disrepair. It seemed to have been abandoned, the only signs of life were the one or two female members of the family that we could see busying themselves with chores around the structure. In fact, very few of the homes we drove past seemed to have any people in or around them at all. As Amy and I tried to inquire at some of the homes, even one that had a sign advertising lodging, it became clear that the valley was almost completely deserted.

While we saw barely any people, it still seemed like any bit of useable space had been occupied in some way. Whenever Amy and I found ourselves looking for a place to camp, we ran into the same problem: space was always being used for something (a reflection in my opinion of the resourcefulness of the Chinese). This made it difficult to reliably find room to set up a tent. And unlike in the West where roadside campgrounds and state parks are plentiful, public spaces were not amenable to sleeping overnight.

While Amy and I spotted plenty of farms and residences, it did not look like anyone was home to watch over them. So, after wandering around for another 20 minutes, I pulled over and asked Amy how she felt about camping in the courtyard of one of these empty properties.

Crawling around the narrow strips of asphalt in the woods off of the highway, we soon settled on a village ten minutes out from the main road. There we found a dark home with flat space in front, bordered by crops on its right, a hillside on its rear flank, and a narrow village road to its left. The structure was built in a U-shape, with an empty courtyard in the middle and a grassy space in front where we could stake in our tent. The house itself looked as if it could have been haunted. The windows were covered by dark, water-stained, wooden shutters. There was no lighting and an obscure emblem was posted on the doors. The occasional "shhhk shhhk shhhk" sound of scurrying rodents made it all the more suitable a setting for a horror movie. But, aside from the risks of the paranormal, this seemed like the safest and most convenient place for us to spend the night.

We spied a woman farming a plot of land nearby as we pulled up. She was the only other person we saw in the village and not wanting to impose we decided to ask her about camping at the house.

"Excuse me auntie," I yelled across the field, using the polite but colloquial Chinese greeting for older women. "Do you know if it's okay if we sleep here tonight?" I yelled to her across the field.

Her first reaction was to just look at me with befuddlement. Confused about the idea of our sleeping outside, the woman explained that the family who lived there had all moved to the city for the winter to work while the crops were out of season. As to the notion of our camping on their property, she simply shrugged. So, with the sun already having set behind the hills and the last bits of light left lingering in the valley, Amy and I started to unpack.

Setting up in this nearly deserted valley in the hills of central Fujian was quite a contrast to our experiences over the past week. We were within one or two days' drive of the Pearl River Delta, among the most economically vibrant places in the world. Tonight though we had just spent a half-hour driving past dozens of farmhouses and seeing only a small handful of people. I was struck by the thought of these villages just emptying out during the autumn and winter months and couldn't conjure an equivalent type of migration back home.

It was strange to me how even the act of asking about camping on someone else's land had appeared so alien to the local farmer. The annual abandonment of homes reflected a similar lax attitude towards property that felt foreign to me as an American but was common throughout China. Whether because of its recent socialist past or because of some deeper cultural norms rooted in ancient feudal, Confucian, or Buddhist traditions, property ownership in China just isn't as personal as it is for people in the West (and Americans in particular).

In my travels around the U.S., by motorcycle and foot, signs reading "Private Property" are everywhere. Occupying space, private or public, where you're not welcome can carry penalties. I learned from experience that a guy threatening to shoot you if you come on his property is not just something that happens in the movies. In China in contrast, if we asked locals if we could set up camp somewhere, mostly people would look at us perplexed and just answer "*mei wen ti*" "no problem", almost as if they were annoyed we even bothered to ask. Follow up by asking who owned the land and the response was a shrug, "*mei ren*," "no one."

In fact, in China, as with many countries outside of the U.S., Chinese do not actually own land outright. This was a state of affairs exacerbated by its recent Communist past. After the victory of the CCP over the Kuo Min Dang (KMD) in 1949, almost all of the land in the country was confiscated from the landlords. Afterwards, it was organized into communes that were governed by collectives of peasants. By the late 1950s, nearly 90% of the land had been "collectivized".

One of the major reforms implemented by Deng Xiaoping in the "Reform and Opening Up" period that started in the 1980s was to begin to relax these initiatives, moving to a more semi-privatized, market-driven system. Despite this, all land today is still officially owned by the government, with individuals able to lease their land for set periods of time. After this policy was put into place, China began to develop two separate national systems of property ownership to manage these leases. In areas classified as urban, residential leases were structured as renewable, 70-year terms which residents could buy, sell, or put up as collateral for loans.[104] Rural land however is much more restrictive in that the land is still owned and controlled by the local governments. In many cases, land sales are the local government's sole means of raising revenue, which has a distorting effect on property management. Here, the leases are renewable for 30 years rather than 70 and the families that own them are not even able to transfer them as they are still considered owned by the "collective". [105] Economists and "China watchers" have long suspected that this asymmetrical property management regime, as well as the Hukou residency system that underpins much of it, has led to the large wealth and development disparities between rural and urban Chinese populations today.

Not long after we set up camp, a second woman, another local farmer whom we hadn't seen from across the road, became drawn to our activity as well. Apparently an acquaintance of our current audience member, she called down from her work up on a nearby hill on the other side of the road, and asked her friend who we were.

"*Lao wai!*" the woman yelled back, "Foreigners!"

"Ooooo, foreigners!" the friend said in affirmation, still calling across the narrow valley. "Where are they from?"

Rather than consult Amy and I, as if we could somehow *not* be aware of this dialogue being yelled from across opposite sides of the village, our woman screamed back, "I don't know!"

The friend, deciding she would have to come closer if she wanted to glean any more information, soon made her way over from her

---

[104]   The three categories of lease are 30 years for commercial, 50 for industrial, and 70 for residential.

[105]   At the Third Plenum of the 18th CPC Central committee it was announced that the Party would begin to push through reforms to modernize this system, including an effort to clarify the holder of land rights and allow farmers to hold and mortgage their leases for loans.

farm, waddling down the hill and across the road to stand at her friend's side.

The two women, both squat, with skin dark and creased from years in the sun, stood shoulder to shoulder and calmly studied us from their perch on the road. After several minutes of observation, the newcomer had apparently managed to piece together a theory regarding our machinations for the small plot of land we had just recently settled.

"Waaaaa!" she exclaimed. "Where are they going to sleep??"

Rather than let our neighbor try and explain, I tried to preclude the third-party, Chinese-to-Chinese translations and called over in response.

"We're camping!" I said through a confident grin. "We're going to sleep in our tent."

"Oooh! They speak Chinese!" the woman replied to her friend, momentarily distracted from her prior line of questioning. Her next comment was mercifully directed at us. "Won't you be cold at night though?"

"*Mei wen ti*," Amy replied. "No problem. We have sleeping bags. They help keep us warm."

This got a chuckle out of the woman. The patronizing undertone was one Amy and I were familiar with. No malice to it, just something we've picked up in the past when someone thinks a foreigner just doesn't understand the way things are in China (as if Chinese nights are colder than what we could be used to back home), but deciding there's no use in trying to convince us either. There was a maternalistic quality to it too though, almost as if to say "Oh kids these days with their silly notions of sleeping outside!"

Still concerned that we probably didn't know what we were doing, she next moved on to our food situation. "Do you need hot water?" she asked. "Let me get you some boiled water!" She made to turn, not wanting to give us the opportunity to refuse.

"No, no! That's alright," I said, interrupting her. "We don't need it. Thank you though!"

"Waaaa! What do you mean you don't need it??" she replied. "How will you eat dinner? Do you need me to give you food too?"

"Nope," I said. "We have a stove and water so we can boil some for the *convenience noodles* we brought."

"Ai ya!" she said, shaking her head with a laugh. Her smile seemed to indicate that she had resigned herself to the fact that we didn't know what we were doing but couldn't be convinced to change our minds.

The two women stood watching for another ten minutes or so, leaning on their farming tools, quietly observing as Amy and I finished packing everything up for the night. As the light began to fade from the valley, they asked once more if we were sure we didn't need anything before slowly meandering back down the road and to their homes for the night.

***

On November 26th, a couple of days after camping in the Fujianese hills and crossing into Zhejiang, province number 27, Amy and I crossed mile 18,042 of our trip. This marked our unofficially breaking the Guinness World Record for longest motorcycle journey in a single country, passing the standing record of 18,041.5 miles, set by Steve Miller in the U.S. (who himself broke the record that had been set just as we were setting out from Beijing).

We reached this milestone while riding with a local biker, this time a foreigner named Jon Sims, a Brit who had been living and riding motorcycles in Zhejiang for nearly two decades. Jon had heard about our trip via the English-language motorcycle forum My China Moto (a place where foreigners and some Chinese discuss motorcycling in China covering topics like trip reports, how to get licensed, and reviews of local brands). Jon met up with us near where we crossed the provincial border and was taking us across Zhejiang to his home in the suburbs outside of Ningbo.

The GPS on my phone, which had been tracking our progress every day for the past four months, ticked upward closer and closer to our target. Every five minutes it announced the latest mileage in my headphones. I passed Jon, who had been leading the way through the mountains, and slowed the pace down as our long awaited goal approached. Then, when it finally hit, I pulled over to the shoulder and announced to Amy and Jon (who hadn't realized we would be breaking a record that day) what had happened.

It was surreal. Here we were back in Zhejiang again. The last time we'd been in the province was in May of that year for a visit to the CFMoto factory in nearby Hangzhou. At that time, less than two months before departure, Amy and I were still struggling to get this dream of ours off the ground, lacking even a motorcycle. Now, after 133 days on the road, having travelled through the grass plains of Inner Mongolia, the deserts of Western Xinjiang, the snow-covered mountains of Tibet, and the rains of south and central China, and having met so many fascinating people and faced countless challenges, here we were in sunny Southeast China, riding with a local foreigner and marking with a stone on the asphalt the point where our tire had finally crossed the record marker.

We had stopped to mark other major milestones along the way on our trip – the 10,000km mark[106], the estimated halfway mark around the Tibet–Qinghai border, even when our odometer read exactly 22,222.22km- but this milestone was different (for obvious reasons). Reaching the record felt a little bittersweet for me. Both Amy and I had grown used to life on the road. It was engaging, always

---

[106]   Our distance measurements on the road were all in metric as that is the standard used in China.

interesting, and in its way, comfortable. Each day brought with it something new – new people, new places, new roads, and new challenges. This would change now though as we drew nearer to the end, only a few weeks away. Coming up we had stops planned at the CFMoto factory in Hangzhou and with Amy's dad in Shanghai. Afterwards there were a few other people, sights, and cities we planned to visit as we passed through the remaining half-dozen provinces. Now, the countdown had started towards Beijing and the end of the road.

Chapter 20 – When Everything Comes Full Circle

Jon and Denis, aka "Biker Doc", were both middle-aged foreigners. They had moved to China separately years before and at some point decided it was where they wanted to settle down. Denis was a doctor by trade (thus the nickname "Biker Doc"). From New Zealand originally, he was now, like Jon, working in Ningbo while keeping active in the Chinese motorcycle scene via the My China Moto forum. He was a big supporter of CFMoto on the site and kept busy on the side helping foreigners get hold of Chinese motorcycle parts from abroad. He had also been following us online since almost the beginning of our trip.

Jon had been living in Zhejiang for 18 years. He owned a factory near Ningbo where he also lived with his Chinese wife and 8-year-old son. We arrived at his house in the suburbs just after dark the evening we cracked the record. As with so much new construction in China, the buildings of Jon's neighborhood seemed to be a textbook duplicate of something out of the West. In this case it was as if a Chinese property developer had simply shown his planners and architects an episode *Leave it to Beaver* (or some such 1950s American sitcom) and told them to make that – homes duplicated with cookie-cutter precision, each topped with a triangular roof, a driveway, a one-car (or two-motorcycle) garage, and a small front yard. It wasn't clear what percentage of the suburban homes was actually occupied, but the area appeared deserted.

After unpacking the bikes and parking them in the garage, we joined Jon and his family for a delicious seafood paella at their home. Afterwards, Jon drove Amy and I into the city for a quick tour of downtown Ningbo where went out for some drinks and a walk around the old British settlement *Lao Wai Tan* or "Foreigner Beach", also known as "The Old Bund" in reference to The Bund in Shanghai.[107]

Zhenhai, now a county of Ningbo where the Old Bund is located, had formerly been a British concession, occupied after the First Opium War as per the Treaty of Nanjing in 1842. Today, while no longer under the control of the British, the former port continues to earn its nickname of "Foreigner Beach". The markets and trading centers that formerly inhabited the two-story colonial-style stone buildings have, in recent decades, been replaced by bars and cafes. These have become, in the 21st century, congregation points for a different sort of foreigner (if only a marginally better behaved one).[108]

The next morning, heads pounding slightly after a late night out on Foreigner Beach, the three of us on our two bikes rode off from Jon's house. This time Jon had traded in the Chinese dirt bike he had picked us up on a couple days earlier for another bike of his, a CFMoto 250cc scooter. Since Denis, who we would be meeting that day on our way towards Hangzhou, also owned a CFMoto, a red version of our CF650TR, we thought it would be appropriate to all ride up to the factory in Hangzhou together, a surprise for our hosts and sponsors now less than a day's ride away.

The area we were in now, and had been since arriving in Ningbo, is known as the Yangzte River Delta region or YRD. Reminiscent of the

---

[107]   Both "Bunds" had their origins as beachheads for foreign governments and merchants in China in the late 19th and early 20th centuries, when the Europeans, Americans, and Japanese divided many coastal ports in China into "Concessions", i.e. extraterritorial land ceded by the Chinese to foreign powers, primarily for trade purposes.

[108]   As part of the Treaty of Nanjing that ended the war, the city of Ningbo, along with Shanghai, Fuzhou, Guangzhou, and Xiamen, was forced to open its borders to foreign trade. "Foreigner Beach" retains much of its Old World charm, with narrow, cobbled streets and bars occupying the colonial-style buildings. Next to the boardwalk running along the Yong River that flows through the city, there is an old church that Amy, Jon, and I visited after a few drinks on "Bar Street". The Jiangbei Cathedral was originally built by French missionaries in 1878. Sadly, less than a year after our trip, in July 2014, a fire consumed much of the wooden portions of the building, collapsing the roof and leaving only sections of the stone structure behind intact.

Pearl River Delta a couple weeks before, the YRD is made up of a tight knot of 15 large cities in the drainage area of the Yangtze, all with economies fueled by manufacturing and foreign trade. In addition to Ningbo and Hangzhou, these include several others we would be passing through in the next few days: Shanghai, Nanjing, Wuxi, and Yangzhou.

The YRD is considered to be the world's 6th largest economic zone. In 2013 its GDP was ¥12 trillion (about USD $1.8 trillion), or 20% of the entire country's economic output. The region is also responsible for nearly 40% of China's foreign trade. That level of development usually translated to an unbearable amount of commuter and truck traffic (not to mention stubbornly obstinate traffic police). It was lucky then that we had a local like Biker Doc (who also happened to be a bit of a mapping geek) to show us the way around all of the heavy traffic. Jon and I drove behind as Denis took us zipping along a maze of hidden side streets in the villages and small towns that filled in the in-between-spaces of the YRD urban sprawl.

***

It had been early June last time Amy and I had been to the southern manufacturing city of Hangzhou, less than two months before the start of our trip around China. Midday temperatures then were already reaching into the 100s as Amy and I were preparing to meet with the CFMoto executives for the first time. We were two untested foreigners proposing to spend over four months riding their motorcycle around China in order to break a world record. There we were, arriving at this world-class manufacturing facility hat in hand. I had been so nervous about making the presentation, one that would be entirely in Chinese and which could make or break our trip, that I'd barely slept on the overnight train down from Beijing.

This time around, winter was the threatening. Even though we were still in the South, temperatures were getting colder and the days shorter. Our bike, gear, and clothes were showing the wear of over 130 days on the road, I was now sporting a beard a couple of inches thick, and just one day ago Amy and I had surpassed the record that, over six months prior, we had promised the company management we would break. It was a triumphant homecoming for the road-tested 650TR, and a noticeably more relaxed visit for its passengers.

After getting buzzed in by security at the entrance to the factory grounds, our mini CFMoto motorcycle gang-of-three rolled past the lines of massive, sterilized, aircraft-hangar-like buildings. We made our way to the entrance of the office, the one non-industrial building on the grounds, and dismounted. There we were greeted by the now-familiar faces of the CFMoto team; Chen Guanping, Fang Shujian, Hu Hai, Manager Zhu, people that Amy and I had been working with regularly over the past few months and many of whom we had last seen only a couple of months earlier at the CIMA event in Chongqing. We left the three bikes at the factory for the night where they would get a full maintenance checkup (complimentary of course, including for our two riding companions). Then we were driven into the city for the night to be put up in a hotel.

Before moving on to our next stop, Shanghai just a hundred miles away, we were told that the company wanted to host an event with us for the factory employees. So, just before lunch the next day, the four of us were led into a large conference room where we found seating for around two hundred people. Almost all of the staff on site had been invited, a few hundred employees dressed in their white assembly line coveralls seated and facing the stage. There were a couple speeches from management about our trip and our work with the company and then Amy and I were invited up to speak. I said a few words thanking CFMoto for their support and Amy and I gave the presentation that we had first prepared for CIMA, with a few more slides amended this time for the past month's latest activities (a little better practiced now too after a couple months of experience speaking about our trip).

At the end, just like had been set up back on Hainan island at the Horizons Resort, a box was placed on stage and Chen Guanping, who was emceeing the event, announced that CFMoto wanted to show their support for Free Lunch for Children. The upper management stood up first and walked towards the stage. After smiling for photos, they each took out some cash from their pockets and placed the folded bills into the box, donating a few hundred yuan each. Following their employers' lead, all the other jumpsuit-clad assembly line workers got up as well, lining up to donate to the charity. In all we raised another ¥9,000 (about $1,500), a very kind and entirely unexpected gesture from a company that had up to that point seemed apathetic to the charitable aspect of our endeavor (it had been all "Guinness World Record or nothing" for them so far, so maybe they were feeling more charitable now we had passed the record). With just an hour until sunset once it was all over, we said goodbye to the CFMoto team and to Jon and Denis who would be riding back to Ningbo.

Our arrival into Shanghai later that evening was our third YRD city in as many days. Our visit happened to spontaneously be coinciding with Thanksgiving. This was a totally unplanned coincidence, not only because Shanghai had the largest population of foreigners in China, which meant one of only a handful of cities in the country where we'd be able to find a traditional Turkey Dinner to celebrate, but it was also where Amy's dad and brother lived which meant that we would be able to celebrate with family!

Amy's dad, Tim Mathieson, had made reservations in preparation at a nearby American sports bar that was serving a special Thanksgiving set meal. Joining us would also be Tim's girlfriend, Mae, and Amy's youngest brother, Tristan. Thanksgiving of course is a family-centric holiday, much like the Spring Festival for Chinese[109], so even though I was the only American and also only peripherally related, it was nice to enjoy the meal with family. The experience was made more meaningful in my mind by how diverse the company was. Amy's background is eclectic and her family includes a wide range of nationalities. With her parents both remarrying after they split when she was a toddler, Amy now has three younger brothers with no two siblings who actually share the same ethnic background – one Swiss-Indian-German stepbrother, one Swiss-Indian-British half-brother (Tristan), and one full Chinese half-brother. This is without even mentioning family on the side of her mom's sister, who also married a foreigner, bringing American, Australian, and Belgian into the family tree. Turkey, wine, a melting-pot family, and pumpkin pie. It was a great way to spend this most American of holidays as Amy and I neared the end of our Chinese adventure. Our venue being a sports bar, the Dallas Cowboys game playing downstairs was an added bonus.

Shanghai marked the last days off Amy and I would take on our trip and the impermanent reality of our adventure was starting to sink in. We were in familiar surroundings again and with familiar company for the first time in months. Taking two rest days, Amy and I spent a good portion of our time in Shanghai preparing not just the final days of the trip, but also our post-Great Ride lives. Having moved out of our apartment before setting off, we would have no place to live once we we got back to Beijing and I took the time in Shanghai as an opportunity to start apartment hunting online. We also began to think about something else that we had kept out of

---

[109]   While both holidays are the busiest times of year for travel in each respective country, the number of Americans in transit on Thanksgiving pales in comparison to the number of Chinese traveling for Chinese New Year. Lasting for approximately 40 days, it is the largest annual human migration in the world. In 2013 there were over 3 billion trips made during this time. This number includes 43 million who traveled by boat, just 1 million less than the 44 million Americans in transit total for Thanksgiving that year.

mind since first extending our itinerary back on July 19th – setting a target finish date.

What was really beginning to emphasize the mortality of our trip now was that, not only had we been to Shanghai before, but Amy and I had also come by motorcycle before. Over a year earlier, in 2012, we had taken a trip down the coast together – an eight day, 1,500-mile each way ride from Beijing to Shanghai on the used Honda Shadow I was riding at the time. Prior to The Great Ride of China, that had been the longest continuous motorcycle journey the two of us had ever done in the country.

Sitting in Amy's dad's apartment planning our route back to Beijing, I couldn't help but compare it with that last trip. Then, Shanghai was the halfway point in a week-long road trip rather than the tail end of what was now a five-month, record-breaking adventure around China. The first time, the thought of just another four days along the industrialized coast of China had been daunting. Now, even as much as the two weeks we had left felt all too fleeting.

I remained cautiously apprehensive of the remaining miles, ones that would be relatively mild compared to some of the remote and varied geographies we had crossed to get to this point. It was a minor concern though. Instead, the worry that occupied my mind most as I mapped out our route through the final five provinces was the thought that the adventure was almost done. After 130 days, even two consecutive nights in the same place made me restless and eager to get back on the road. Amy had never done any sort of traveling even close to this long before and had no idea what to expect when it all came to an end. Beijing may have been where we lived but, after getting rid of our apartment, selling half of our stuff, and quitting our jobs, the road was where we now felt most at home.

***

While a straight shot from Shanghai to Beijing can be done in only a couple days by expressway, there were still some remaining boxes we had left to tick off before we finished up. The Yangtze River Delta region is a great place for sightseeing, with a high concentration of culturally significant relics and cities in a relatively small area.[110] So rather than head due north along the coast, we first planned to spend a couple of days winding our way through a few of the sights around the area. Our route would first take us past the world's 8th largest Buddha statue in the outskirts of Wuxi. Next we would pass through Nanjing, the capital of six different Chinese dynasties including the Republic of China (before the Communists moved the capital back to Beijing). Finally we would visit an area of old Qing-era merchant gardens in the city of Yangzhou, a town whose history dates back 2,500 years and which is home to some of China's richest historical figures.

The days passed quickly, our rituals for visiting tourist sights and covering miles by now was second nature. Daylight was increasingly scarce and compressed our available riding time even further. The grey, industrial landscape in between destinations blended into our peripheral view.

After Yangzhou, a day in which we crossed the Yangtze river twice, once by bridge and then by ferry, Amy and I turned our sights south for a couple days and towards Anhui, province number 30. There, in the southern quadrant of the province, we paid a visit to the Huangshan ("Yellow Mountains") Range, a UNESCO heritage site and

---

[110]   The Yangtze River is the 3rd largest river in the world and the longest to flow through only a single country. It's waters carry the glacial melts from the Tibet–Qinghai Plateau through nine provinces over nearly 4,000 miles, until it empties out in the East China Sea off the coast by Shanghai. The Yangtze or *Chang Jiang*, which means "Long River" in Chinese, is considered along with the Yellow River to be the cradle of Chinese civilization. One third of the country's population lives within the Yangtze river basin. This of course has given it a dominant position in the economic and cultural development of the country for millennia, contributing particular significance to the coastal region, the YRD, at its terminus.

a popular inspiration for traditional Chinese paintings (any depiction of steep craggy peaks shrouded in mist is usually a Huangshan landscape). Huangshan is also one of the most popular scenic tourist spots in the country, receiving nearly three million visitors per year.

Amy and I rolled up to the park entrance just an hour before sunset (so close to the winter solstice now, we were getting less than ten hours of sunlight per day). Because it was late and in the middle of the slow season, the area felt uncharacteristically peaceful for a Chinese tourist sight. The park was devoid of the frantic activity typical of other scenic areas we had visited on our trip; places like Jiuzhaigou, the park in Sichuan we visited during the October holiday, or Zhangjiajie, home of the "Avatar Mountains" in Hunan, areas that had suffocated us with teeming tourists. The wide roads that led to the entrance were built to accommodate large volumes of cars and busses, but we found them almost completely empty. The space felt like a partially built suburban town that had yet to fill up with any residents. The granite cliffs of the mountain range sprouted up from the valley in front of us, a wall of layered shark teeth. True to their name, they shimmered yellow in the light of the setting sun, with splotches of red, brown and yellow accenting the verdant ascents. With time and ticket prices keeping us from entering the park itself, Amy and I took our commemorative photos and promptly put the fading Yellow Mountains into our rear-view mirrors, leaving the scenic valley to find a place to spend the night. That was the last tourist spot we would visit on our trip.

As we traveled north through Anhui and into Henan province, the terrain flattened out and the roads straightened. Making our way to our final three provinces, it was back to the industrial east of China. We found ourselves once more greeted by assertive trucks and entitled busses who threw their weight around, claiming ownership of every bit of asphalt they could. Potholes littered the neglected National

Highways and the all too familiar spinal compressions greeted each bottoming out of our suspension if I didn't keep a close eye out.

Worse than all of this though was that, with the official arrival of winter and temperatures dipping down into freezing territory, coal plants throughout the Northeast had begun to fire up. The (literally) government-mandated heating they provided to millions of homes meant a thick blanket of smog that we woefully found encroaching from all around and which would follow us for days. After spending months traversing and experiencing some of the most breathtaking scenery in the world, blue skies in the regions from Xinjiang to Tibet to Yunnan and tropical Hainan, being back on the east coast, the area in which Amy and I had started our China motorcycling careers, felt ruefully anti-climactic.

***

The last planned stop we had for our route back, aside from passing through the remaining provinces, wasn't a place you'd find listed in many travel guides. Google the city of Zoucheng and you're most likely to learn that it was the birthplace of Mencius, the famous Confucian philosopher, back around the year 300 BC. The heyday of Confucian scholars has long past though and today the Song Dynasty-era Mencius Temple and Mencius Forest located there have since been overwhelmed by the coal-dominated industries of Shandong province. It now comes across as little more than just another prefecture-level town of a third-tier city in an industrialized coastal province of China.

The reason we were stopping though was not to make some pilgrimage to a run down Confucian temple or ticketed city park. Rather, Amy and I were there to visit friends. Back in 2012, on the ride back from Shanghai on my own (Amy had taken the train back to Beijing to get back for work while I returned with the motorcycle), I found myself with a broken bike in this same, grey corner of the country.

The day before my first visit to Zoucheng over a year earlier, the battery on my used 2001 Honda Shadow, a 750cc cruiser-style bike, exploded just a day out of Shanghai. Battery acid leaked on the chassis and let loose a foul stench of rotting eggs. When the scooter battery I had found to replace it in the town of "Five Rivers", Anhui also lost its juice just 12 hours after I'd bought it, I thought I was sunk.

Progressing with a battery that would only move in fits and starts, I made my way to the outskirts of Zoucheng, a suburb of the prefecture-level city of Jining, where I managed to find a car mechanic. The situation was desperate when my best hope seemed to be to strap a larger car battery into my saddlebag, have it wired to my electrical system, and hope it would give me enough power to get to a larger city that would hopefully have some more experienced motorcycle mechanics and parts. It was in the driveway of this car repair shop that I met *Xiao Hei*.

Xiao Hei or "Little Black" (a nickname his friends gave him because of his tanned skin), was part of a local club, the Zoucheng Lan Bo Wan Motorcycle Club[111]. Pulling up on a dirt bike with his girlfriend riding pillion, rather than start off on the "20 questions for a foreigner" routine for which I had little patience left, he seemed genuinely interested in engaging me in conversation. When he heard about the troubles I was having, he immediately offered to take me to his club's mechanic and what started off as one of the lowest points of my China experience quickly turned into one of my most treasured memories. By that evening, I had a new rectifier to keep the smaller scooter battery charged until Beijing and about a dozen new friends

---

[111] The characters for *lan bo wan*- 蓝博万 – have no real meaning on their own, directly translating to something like "Blue Vast Ten Thousand". Their meaning rather comes from their pronunciation – *lan bo wan* is a phonetic stand-in for "Number One". Say it out loud and you'll see what I mean!

as Little Black had assembled the whole crew for a rural feast (accompanied by a not trivial amount of beer and *baijiu*) at a private restaurant owned by one of the club members located in the woods up a mountain. The next day, noticeably more sluggish but also in much higher spirits than 24 hours earlier, I was at the Lan Bo Wan clubhouse where everyone I'd met came to see me off to Beijing. An escort of five motorcycles mounted up and took me out of town and onto the expressway back home.

For our latest visit to Zoucheng though, in early December of 2013, we had the benefit of foresight and were able to give the Lan Bo Wan Club a few days notice before we arrived. After dropping off the bike and unpacking our stuff at the same 7 Days Inn I had stayed in over a year earlier, we walked down to the clubhouse to say hello and introduce Amy to the club.

This group of motorcycle enthusiasts from small-town, coastal China that had adopted me into their group were all members of the culturally significant *ba shi nian dai* or "80s Generation" of Chinese. This generation has become extremely important in the context of the country's development – they were the children born in the 1980s, at the turning point after the cultural revolution and before or during the "Reform and Opening Up" period. They had grown up in parallel with their country and their economy, as much victims as facilitators of the historic pace of development. They weren't "princelings", the sons of powerful CCP members that you hear about in the news crashing luxury cars, nor were they poor farmers or downtrodden factory workers that make for compelling newspaper features. Little Black and his friends seemed to be relatively well off for residents of small-town China (in some ways suspiciously so with giant BMW touring bikes that I couldn't hope to afford myself). They had leisure time and hobbies and clearly had some disposable income. At the same time, none of them appeared to have had any higher education, none had spent much time out of the province, and little about their outward appearance, from their clothes to their accessories to their mannerisms, seemed to indicate much money.

The reality was that the Zoucheng Lan Bo Wan Motorcycle Club represented China's middle class. They were the faces behind the statistics when you read about China's growing consumer spending or the millions of new Internet users that are added each month. They were the group that every developing country hopes to establish to maintain growth, but whose stories people rarely find interesting enough to relate to beyond the one-line opinion quotes or online Weibo posts. From Joe the Plumber in the U.S. to Little Black the coal factory worker in China, both were the center pieces of stump speeches, the cogs in the faceless crowds of hardworking individuals that keep it all going.

The end of that night was... a blur. The pain and grogginess the next morning however were clear enough. I remained nearly incapacitated for a couple hours, but Amy had luckily been more prudent in her moderation and so could help with most of the morning prep. It was late morning by the time we managed to stumble out and get everything packed on the bike. By the time we were driving off from the hotel, the smog from the past few days had thickened into haze with an AQI (Air Quality Index, a sliding scale from 0–500 that measures the number of pollutants in the air) of 400,[112] a level designated as "Hazardous" by the WHO. Visibility as we

---

[112]   2013 was the first year that the government started publishing numbers for the AQI around the country and specifically PM2.5 (particulate matter smaller than 2.5 micrometers). PM2.5 measures the pollutants most harmful to a person's health, the ones that can be absorbed through your lungs and into your bloodstream. 2013 was also the year that saw the popularization of the term "airpocalypse" among foreign news outlets and expats to describe pollution levels that reached unimaginable heights, as much as AQI 993 that year, nearly twice as high as what was thought to be the theoretical maximum of 500 (for reference, the AQI is around 300 in areas with forest fires). It is estimated that the country's smog causes between 350,000 and 500,000 premature deaths and an economic loss of between 2–10% of GDP per year.

made our way down the street had been reduced to only a couple of hundred feet.

In contrast to the previous year when I was joined by five other motorcycles on my way out of town, only one rider was brave enough to join us and suffer the cold for our Lan Bo Wan escort to the highway. The rest of the parade was composed of a sedan, a giant F-150 pickup truck, and a BMW Z-series convertible. We took our final photos in front of the club, and said our final goodbyes at the highway on-ramp before sneaking past the expressway ticket booth and riding off into the smog.

As we made our way east across the province and towards the coastline, the pollution slowly gave way to genuine fog, condensation from the colder winds coming off of the nearby East China Sea. We noticed the change from the consistency of the air itself. Moisture was starting to pierce through the four layers of clothing and gear we were wearing, leaving us chilled and numb. The weather, long days, and I think probably the emotions of getting close to the end (and no doubt some contributions from the *baijiu*) were starting to get the better of me and that night, at the major port city and former German concession of Qingdao, I could feel my body start to give out on me.

These conditions persisted for our last few days on the road. Each morning Amy and I would sleep in to give my body time to rest before getting on the road. We'd cover as much ground as we could to our next waypoint before the sun set by 4:30pm. The temperature was settling consistently in freezing territory now, even during the day, and the sharp bite of winter wind was exacerbated by the high speeds we were riding at. Amy spent her time huddled behind me for shelter, sticking her hands in between my back and backpack for extra warmth. Lacking the same protection, my extremities felt like they were in a constant battle against frostbite. Each break at a gas station or rest stop, Amy would go off to find some hot water for tea or instant coffee while I shoved my hands down my pants, the only refuge I found to regain feeling in my fingers. Our last day on the Shandong peninsula, the piece of land that sticks out into the East China Sea less than 120 miles away from North Korea to the east, we experienced our first snow flurries since the Tibetan Plateau in Qinghai nearly three months earlier.

Our last province was Tianjin, the municipality province whose border nearly touches with that of Beijing. The journey north from Shandong back into Hebei province was a drive through an industrial wasteland, a place inhabited by little else aside from a zombie-army of trucks. With no natural barriers, the wind blowing off of the nearby sea was hitting with force that Amy and I hadn't felt since hiding behind the trucks in the Da Ban Cheng Wind Farm outside of Urumqi. Hunched over and tensed as I leaned into the wind, I marveled at the vast greyness of the post-apocalyptic expanse. The pallid water from the sea merged with the equally grey road off in the horizon, and the interminable onslaught of trucks continued along this feeding channel of nearby coastal ports and some of the busiest trade hubs in the world.

Tianjin is a beautiful city that has maintained much of its European and colonial-style architecture from the days when it was broken into colonial concessions over a century ago. The city prides itself on being a major cultural hub of the Northeast as a result of these 150 years of outside influence. Its population is also particularly proud of its stuffed buns and dumplings. We were so close to Beijing now though, and the weather had become so cold, that Amy and I had little left on our mind but the end of the road.

Less than 100 miles away, we would finally close the circle. It was a journey that we had started 146 days earlier, leaving Beijing in the midst of a heatwave. We had trekked our way into the Northeast and eventually through all 33 provincial-level regions of one of the largest and oldest countries on the planet. The journey took us through grass plains, ancient cities, deserts, and mountains at the "Rooftop of the World". We argued with traffic cops and with each other, sat in on a funeral feast, and snacked on melons with a solitary Hui woman in the desert. We dealt with faulty equipment, raised thousands of dollars for disadvantaged school children, and swapped stories with a new generation of Chinese adventurers. After everything, it had come down to this final strip of a well traveled, modern highway, sneaking around the toll and onto an expressway that connected two of China's largest cities.

The traffic signs rushed past at 80mph. The cold seemed less harsh than it had the days before. With each posted distance, I counted down in my head how far we had left until Beijing city center.

100 miles...

50...

5th ring road...

4th ring..

3rd...

Traffic jam.

146 days, 21,221 miles, and 33 provinces of The Great Ride of China had led us back to Beijing. Here, Amy and I found that life had gone on much as before. Commuters on the inner ring roads went about their daily travels, moving at a crawl, and unperturbed at their almost complete lack of movement. A housing agent and our new landlord impatiently waited for us in the apartment we planned to sign for that afternoon. They asked about our clothing but thought we were joking when we told them we'd just ridden a motorcycle around China for half a year. There was an awkward chuckle and they presented us with the contract. We accepted the keys, cash exchanged hands, and we called a moving van to drive out to the suburbs where our stuff was in storage. A couple of hours later, surrounded by boxes and suitcases, far more than we could have ever packed onto a single motorcycle, Amy and I sat in our new, semi-furnished apartment,

feeling lost as we thought about how to plan for the days ahead without the help of a map.

- Photos from the Pearl River Delta to Beijing -

Scan the QR code or visit the link below to see pictures from Part 5 of The Great Ride of China

http://book.thegreatrideofchina.com/galleries/part-5

Acknowledgements

In many ways, riding a motorcycle around China was the easiest part of this whole adventure. Without all the help and support Amy and I received leading up to and during our trip there would not have been anything to write about in the first place. A huge thank you to Ying Mathieson and Li Qiang. The connections and guidance you gave us for navigating the often opaque intricacies of Chinese business culture were absolutely invaluable. Thank you as well to Ying and Tim Mathieson for letting this odd American with an even odder name take your daughter on a crazy motorcycle ride around a foreign country. Thanks to Chelsea Eakin, John Hanrahan, and Amanda Tang for being our anchors in Beijing while we were on the road and to Sean Abagnale, Kristen Faiferlick, Victoria Yuan, and Julie Qiu for helping take care of our two troublesome cats for the five months we were gone.

For first introducing me to China and the adventures to be had, I owe a huge debt of gratitude to Gregory Root, Anthony Root, and Hong Yu and an extra special thanks to Greg for being a partner in crime for so many of my schemes and adventures over the years. Speaking of schemes, Alex Bell, without that first trip to Ketchikan, Alaska in high school I don't know if any of this would have ever happened!

To all the Road Angels along way, many of whom we only met briefly, without the hospitality you showed to two foreign strangers the road would have been a lonely place. Thank you for making us feel at home in a foreign land. And to the people that helped with planning, logistics, support, and being a friendly face along the way, Oliver Blockland, Da He, Li Lei, Wang Zhenzhen, Uncle Du, Ning Jia,

Li Bin, Yang Fan, Jon Sims, Dennis aka "Biker Doc", Carla King and many more thank you for helping make this possible.

Motorcycles are dangerous. Motorcycles in China are even more dangerous and I can't imagine what it was like letting your first born go out on a trip like that so far away from home. To my mom and dad, the support you've given me throughout my life has made taking risks and trying new things not just easier but more enriching. Thank you for paving the way and setting an example for how to be a good, honest, and hard working person.

And last of all, Amy. I'm not sure if you knew what you were getting yourself into when you agreed to start going on motorcycle trips with me, but I'm glad you did. Your patience with me as I quit my job (and then another one), took you on a trip where you were only allowed to bring one spare change of clothes, and then as I spent the next three and a half years putting it all down on paper is beyond any thanks I could give. The faith you have in me is a source of inspiration and strength and I look forward to spending the rest of my life with you.

Appendix I – Chinese Words and Definitions

an quan di yi - 安全第一 - "Safety is number one"

bai jiu - 白酒 - Literally "white wine", blanket term for Chinese fortified white wine there are a range of varieties spread across the country, with ABV ranging from around 35% to 70% made with a range of different ingredients usually sorghum bean but also rice, corn, and others.

ba shi nian dai - 八十年代 - "80s Generation", used to describe the generation of Chinese born during the 1980s, and just after the cultural revolution and the beginning of China's "Reform and Opening Up". Also related, "九十年代", jiu shi nian dai or "90s generation".

Biang biang mian - Biang biang noodles - type of noodle originating from Xi'an, Sha'anxi province

bu tai - 补胎 - Tire repair or "Patch tire"

(bu) xi guan - (不) 习惯 - (not) accustomed

cheng qiang - 城墙 - City wall

chi hao le - 吃好了 -"I'm full" or "I've eaten my full". A polite way to indicate you enjoyed your meal

chi ku - 吃苦 - Literally "eat bitterness", to indicate enduring difficulties or hardships

da pan ji - 大盘鸡 - "Big Plate Chicken" a chicken stew dish served in the western provinces of China

da rou - 大肉 - "Big meat" the polite name for pork in Xinjiang or other observant Muslim areas

Dong Bei - 东北 - Northeast, used colloquially to describe the area of Northeast China that composed Manchuria

di dao - 地道 - authentic

fang bian mian - 方便面 - "Convenient noodles", instant noodles

feng shui - 风水 -"wind water" The name for the traditional Chinese custom of organizing everything according to their most "auspicious" placement or structure.

gan bei - 干杯 - "Cheers!", literally translates to "Dry glass"

gao kao - 高考 - "High exam" the Chinese college entrance exam taken by high school students across the country applying for university.

gao su / gao su lu - 高速 / 高速路 - Highspeed highway, Expressway

gu cheng - 古城 - Old/Ancient city

guan xi - 关系 - Literally, "relationship", often used to describe cultural system of relationships as a form of social currency

guo dao - 国道 - National Highway

hao chi ma? - 好吃吗? -Is it good/tasty?

huan ying - 欢迎 - Welcome

jia chang cai - 家常菜 - "Homestyle Food"

jin shang - 晋商 - "Merchants of Shanxi"

kang - 炕 - raised brick platform, hollowed out underneath to burn wood.

lao wai - 老外 - Impolite word for "foreigner"

lao ban - 老板 - The boss, boss

ma fan - 麻烦 - Trouble, annoyance

mao bing - 毛病 - Literally "disease" or "sickness" can also be used to refer to a mechanical problem, as in "Does your motorcycle have a *sickness*"

ma shang - 马上 - "In a moment", Literally to "get on a horse"

mei ban fa - 没办法 - "There's no way"

mei (you) wen hua - 没（有）文化 - Without/doesn't have culture

mei wen ti - 没问题 - "No problem"

mian bao che - 面包车 - "Bread car" the colloquial name for a van because it's shaped like a loaf of bread

ming bai ma? - 明白吗？ - "Do you understand"

mo tuo che bu yun xu shang - 摩托车不允许上 - "Motorcycles are not allowed on"

nang bao rou - 馕包肉 - "Nang bread stuffed with meat", a dish popular in the western province of Xinjiang of cumin spiced flatbread topped with a lamb and vegetable stew.

neng chi la ma? - 能吃辣吗？ - "Can you eat spicy food?"

piao hao - 票号 - Literally "ticket number", this was the banking system of deposit receipts created by the Jinshang of Pingyao.

qing zuo - 请坐 - "Please sit"

ren shan ren hai - 人山人海 - "People Mountain, People Sea", a metaphor used to describe huge crowds of people.

shen fen zheng - 身份证 - Personal Identification Card

shui men - 水门 - "water doors", found in the buildings of the southern city of Wuzhou, they are situated on the second stories to allow people to enter and leave their homes by boat when the streets are flooded.

su zhi - 素质 - Translates to quality. When used to refer to a person or group of people it speaks to their quality of person or level of cultural.

tai wei xian - 太危险 - "Too dangerous"

ta shuo gao su GENG an quan ma?? - 他说高速更安全吗？？ - "He says the highway is MORE safe??"

ting bu dong - 听不懂 - "Don't understand"

tu lou - 土楼 - the rammed "earth buildings" of the Hakka people

wan qu - 弯曲 - "twists and turns", used by Chinese motorcyclists to describe "twisties" or windy roads.

wen ding - 稳定 - Stable/stability (e.g. political, cultural stability)

yang za sui - 羊杂碎 - Sheep entrails

yao dong - 窑洞 - Cave dwellings

yi lu ping an - 一路平安 - "Safe Travels" Literally- "One road, calm and peace"

zhong guo cai xi guan le ma? - 中国菜习惯了吗? -"Are you used to Chinese food?"

zhong guo - 中国 - China. Literally- Middle Kingdom.

zhu su - 住宿 - Lodgings

zhu yi an quan - 注意安全 - "Stay safe"

Appendix II - References

Chapter 2

"Chinese Green Tea and Your Health", Ping Ming Health, accessed July 5, 2014, http://www.pingminghealth.com/article/562/chinese-green-tea-and-your-health

"N. Korea, China discuss annual trade fair", The Korea Times, accessed July 14, 2015, http://www.koreatimes.co.kr/www/news/nation/2015/03/485176083.html

"Trade between North Korea and China: Firm-level Analysis", Editorial Express, accessed July 14, 2015, https://editorialexpress.com/cgi-bin/conference/download.cgi?dbname=WCCE2015&paperid=168

Chapter 3

Bakich, Olga Mikhailovna, "Emigre Identity: The Case of Harbin", The South Atlantic Quarterly, Vol.99, No.1 (2000): 51-73.

National Bureau of Statistics of the People's Republic of China. 2010 6th National Census for Heilongjiang Province Report . February 28, 2012. Accessed May 15, 2017. http://www.stats.gov.cn/tjsj/tjgb/rkpcgb/dfrkpcgb/201202/t2012022830390.html.

"Statistics Communique on National Economy and Social Development of Harbin, 2013", Harbin Municipal Statistics Bureau, March 18, 2014.

Zhou, Wanqing. "Food Waste and Recycling in China: A Growing Trend?" Food Waste and Recycling in China: A Growing Trend? | Worldwatch Institute. February 11, 2013. Accessed May 15, 2017.

Junguo Liu et. al., "Food Losses and Waste in China and Their Implication for Water and Land", Environ. Sci. Technol. (American Chemical Society) 47 (18) (2013): pp 10137–10144, http://pubs.acs.org/doi/abs/10.1021/es401426b

Chapter 4

"China builds on border trade", China.org.cn, accessed July 23, 2014, http://china.org.cn/china/NPCCPPCC2013/2013-03/04/content281193322.htm

"Manzhouli (Inner Mongolia) City Information", HKTDC Research, http://china-trade-research.hktdc.com/business-news/vp-article/en/1/1X07375A.htm

"2013 Railway Statistics Report." National Railway Administration of the People's Republic of China. April 10, 2014. Accessed May 17, 2017. http://www.nra.gov.cn/xwzx/zlzx/hytj/201404/t201404105830.shtml.

"Tapping China's luxury-goods market", Yuval Atsmon, Vinay Dixit, and Cathy Wu, McKinsey & Company, April 2011, http://

www.mckinsey.com/insights/marketing*sales/tapping*chinas*luxury-goods*market

"Why Harley-Davidson Can't Break Through The Wall Of China", Forbes, Jan 31, 2014, http://www.forbes.com/sites/greatspeculations/2014/01/31/why-harley-davidson-cant-break-through-the-wall-of-china/

北京电力70%来自内蒙古 成奥运供电"大后方""Inner Mongolia Supplies 70% of Beijing's Electric Power, Becoming the Rear Guard for the Olympic Games", Sohu, March 8, 2008, http://news.sohu.com/20080308/n255594877.shtml

Chapter 5

Laflen, John M, "Soil Erosion and Dryland Farming", 2000, CRC Press, 736 pages

U.S. Energy Information Agency, http://www.eia.gov/countries/cab.cfm?fips=ch

"The China Business Handbook: Shanxi", Alain Charles Asia Publishing, 2014, accessed June 2014, http://chinabusinesshandbook.com/the*book/2014-edition/provinces-2/shanxi-2/*

"China's Glorious New Past", Ian Johnson, The New York Review of Books, June 1, 2011, http://www.nybooks.com/blogs/nyrblog/2011/jun/01/chinas-glorious-new-past/

"In Banking's Shadow; Pingyao." The Economist (US), October 18, 2014. Accessed May 17, 2017. http://www.economist.com/news/china/21625827-former-financial-hub-now-begs-patronage-tourists-bankings-shadow.

"China's Travel and Tourism Market Takes Off", Joseph Luk, China Business Review, January 1, 2011, http://www.chinabusinessreview.com/chinas-travel-and-tourism-market-takes-off/

"Number of domestic visitor arrivals in China from 2004 to 2014 (in millions)", Statistica, http://www.statista.com/statistics/277254/number-of-domestic-trips-in-china/

"Ancient City of Ping Yao", UNESCO, http://whc.unesco.org/en/list/812

"Pingyao City Wall", Travel China Guide, http://www.travelchinaguide.com/attraction/shanxi/pingyao/city*wall.htm*

"China Soon to Have Almost as Many Drivers as U.S. Has People", Rose Yu, Wall Street Jornal, Nov 28, 2014, http://blogs.wsj.com/chinarealtime/2014/11/28/china-soon-to-have-almost-as-many-drivers-as-u-s-has-people/

"China and cars: a love story", Tania Branigan, The Guardian, December 14, 2012, http://www.theguardian.com/world/2012/dec/14/china-worlds-biggest-new-car-market

"Forces in Car Crashes", HyperPhysics, http://hyperphysics.phy-astr.gsu.edu/hbase/carcr.html

"Global status report on road safety 2013", WHO, accessed August 16, 2015, http://www.who.int/violence*injury*prevention/road*safety*status/2013/en/

Lu Yanchou, Zhang Jingzhao, Xie Jun, "TL dating of pottery shards and baked soil from the Xian Terracotta Army Site, Shaanxi Province, China", International Journal of Radiation Applications and Instrumentation. Part D. Nuclear Tracks and Radiation Measurements 14 (1–2) (1988): pp 283–286.

Jane Portal, "The First Emperor: China's Terra Cotta Army", Cambridge, Massachusetts: Harvard University Press, 2007.

Chapter 6

"In China, millions make themselves at home in caves", Barbara Demick, Los Angeles Times, March 18, 2012, http://articles.latimes.com/2012/mar/18/world/la-fg-china-caves-20120318

International Association of Engineering Geology International Congress. Proceedings. (1990). ISBN 90-6191-664-X.

Chapter 7

Arthur Waldron, "The Problem of The Great Wall of China", Harvard Journal of Asiatic Studies (Harvard-Yenching Institute) 43 (2) (1983): pp 650. JSTOR 2719110

"China's Wall becoming less and less Great", Reuters, August 29, 2007, http://www.reuters.com/article/us-china-wall-idUSPEK27469920070829

"Great Wall of China 'even longer'", BBC, April 20, 2009, http://news.bbc.co.uk/1/hi/world/asia-pacific/8008108.stm

"World's Most-Visited Ancient Ruins", April Orcutt, Travel + Leisure, http://www.travelandleisure.com/slideshows/worlds-most-visited-ancient-ruins/

Chapter 8

"Don closing in on Texas; 91L a potential threat to the Lesser Antilles", Jeff Masters, Weather Underground, accessed July 29, 2011, https://www.wunderground.com/blog/JeffMasters/don-closing-in-on-texas-91l-a-potential-threat-to-the-lesser-antilles

"China's First Depression - Aiding Lake", Turpan City Government Website, Jan 17, 2013, http://www.tlf.gov.cn/info/409/80322.htm

Qi, Wu. "China – Dabancheng Wind Farm now has a combined generating capacity of 500 MW." REVE (Wind Energy and Electric Vehicle Magazine). October 5, 2010. Accessed May 17, 2017. https://www.evwind.es/2010/10/05/china-dabancheng-wind-farm-now-has-a-combined-generating-capacity-of-500-mw/7664.

"Xinjiang 18 Peculiarities", Tour118, http://www.tour118.com/

Chapter 9

"Xinjiang territory profile", BBC, November 17, 2016, http://www.bbc.com/news/world-asia-pacific-16860974

"2015 China Motorcycle Industry Sales Analysis", China Industry Information, December 14, 2015, http://www.chyxx.com/industry/201512/368651.html

"Chongqing Motorcycle Monthly Production Statistics, January to December 2013, ", China Industry Information, April 21, 2014, http://www.chyxx.com/data/201404/239023.html

"China's Chongqing – World's Leading Motorcycle City", Dave McMullan, Ultimate Motorcycling, July 16, 2013, https://ultimatemotorcycling.com/chinas-chongqing-worlds-leading-motorcycle-city/

Chapter 9.5

"Important Statistics on the Xinjiang Uygur Autonomous Region from the 2010 National Census", National Bureau of Statistics of the People's Republic of China, February 28, 2012, http://www.stats.gov.cn/tjsj/tjgb/rkpcgb/dfrkpcgb/201202/t2012022830407.html

"Irkeshtam Pass." Adventour. Accessed June 19, 2017. http://www.advantour.com/kyrgyzstan/irkeshtam-pass.htm

Wang, Shaoyi. "口岸下迁，迎接边贸大发展." NetEase News. July 11, 2009. Accessed June 19, 2017. http://news.163.com/

09/0711/08/5DU7IAU9000120GR.html.

Chapter 10

"Kashghar", UNESCO, https://en.unesco.org/silkroad/content/kashghar

"Id Kah Mosque", Kashgar Travel, February 11, 2014, http://ly.mlxks.com/zjks/kswhms/574.html

Middle Eastern International Trade Market, Kashgar City Government, October 24, 2012, http://www.xjks.gov.cn/Item/138.aspx

Chapter 11

"Self-immolations by Tibetans", International Campaign for Tibet, last updated December 9, 2016, http://www.savetibet.org/resources/fact-sheets/self-immolations-by-tibetans/

拉吉卓玛 . "Johkang Temple Welcomes Large Numbers of Pilgrams." Qinghai Lake Online. November 19, 2013. Accessed May 19, 2017. http://www.amdotibet.com/.

"The People's Republic of China Project: Qinghai Ecological Environmental Improvement Project", JICA, 2007.

"China boasts world's largest highspeed railway network", Xinhua, January 30, 2015, http://news.xinhuanet.com/english/photo/2015-01/30/c133959250.htm

"Three Gorges breaks world record for hydropower generation", Xinhua, January 1, 2014, http://news.xinhuanet.com/english/china/2015-01/01/c127352471.htm

Chapter 12

"Trillions of Bookings Made on National Day Golden Week: Who Won, Who Lost?", Zhao Moon, China Economic Weekly, October 14, 2013, http://www.ceweekly.cn/2013/1014/65863.shtml

"2010 6th National Census for Sichuan Province Report (No. 1)", National Bureau of Statistics of the People's Republic of China, February 28, 2012, http://www.stats.gov.cn/tjsj/tjgb/rkpcgb/dfrkpcgb/201202/t2012022830404.html

"State of the Provincial Tourism Industry in 2013." Website of the Sichuan Provincial Government, Tourism Bureau. October 09, 2013. Accessed May 21, 2017. http://www.scta.gov.cn/sclyj/lydt/szdt/abz/system/2013/10/9/000477413.html.

Chapter 14

"Survey of the Religions of Sichuan." Committee for the Communist Party of Sichuan Unified Front(中共四川省委统战部

网站）. September 22, 2013. Accessed May 21, 2017. http://
www.sctyzx.gov.cn/web/detail.asp?id=22.

"Rongxian Giant Buddha." Baidu Baike. Accessed May 21, 2017.
http://baike.baidu.com/item/荣县大佛.

"Leshan Giant Buddha", Travel China Guide, http://
www.travelchinaguide.com/attraction/sichuan/leshan/
buddha*statue.htm*

"The Yi Ethnic Group", China.org.cn, http://www.china.org.cn/
english/features/EthnicGroups/136960.htm

"Yi", ScriptSource, http://scriptsource.org/cms/scripts/page.php?
item*id=script*detail&key=Yiii

Chapter 15

Yang, Y., Tian, K., Hao, J. et al. Biodiversity and Conservation 13
(2004): pp 813. doi:10.1023/B:BIOC.0000011728.46362.3c

National Bureau of Statistics of the People's Republic of China.
2010 6th National Census for Yunnan Province Report . February
28, 2012. Accessed May 21, 2017. http://www.stats.gov.cn/tjsj/tjgb/
rkpcgb/dfrkpcgb/201202/t2012022830408.*html*

"What is a Karst?", Environmental Science Institute: University of
Texas, http://www.esi.utexas.edu/outreach/k12-resources/caves/
karst/

"South China Karst", UNESCO, http://whc.unesco.org/en/list/1248

Chapter 16

"The China Business Handbook: Hainan", Alain Charles Asia Publishing, 2014, http://chinabusinesshandbook.com/the*book/ 2014-edition/provinces-2/hainan-2/*

"Sanya big draw for tourists", Xinhua, May 1, 2012, http:// news.xinhuanet.com/english/china/2012-05/01/c*131562175.htm*

Chapter 17

"Proclamation No. 682, s. 2013", Official Gazette, November 11, 2013, http://www.gov.ph/2013/11/11/proclamation-no-682-s-2013/

"China issues higher Typhoon alert as Haiyan nears", China Daily, November 10, 2013, http://usa.chinadaily.com.cn/china/ 2013-11/10/content*17093250.htm*

"Wuzhou Travel Guide", Travel China Guide, http:// www.travelchinaguide.com/cityguides/guangxi/wuzhou/

"Wuzhou", Wikipedia, http://en.wikipedia.org/wiki/Wuzhou

Central Committee of the Jiu San Society, http://www.93.gov.cn/

403

"Typhoon Haiyan Leaves 7 Dead in South China." China Radio International. November 13, 2013. Accessed May 21, 2017. http://english.cri.cn/11354/2013/11/12/3521s797859.htm.

"Phoenix City Faces Entrance Ticket Shockwave", China Broadcasting Network, April 15, 2011, http://native.cnr.cn/pic/201304/t20130415512357272.html

"New fee put off May Day visitors, Fenghuang hotel operators claim", Laura Zhou, South China Morning Post, May 5, 2013, http://www.scmp.com/news/china/article/1230274/new-fee-put-may-day-visitors-fenghuang-hotel-operators-claim

Chapter 18

"The Greater Pearl River Delta", InvestHK, April 2014, http://www.investhk.gov.hk/zh-hk/files/2014/05/InvestHKGPRD-BookEngApr2014.pdf page 22

"Macau's gambling industry dwarfs Vegas", Charles Riley, CNN, January 6, 2014, http://money.cnn.com/2014/01/06/news/macau-casino-gambling/

"China's Red Cross fights to win back trust", Celia Hatton, BBC, April 22, 2013, http://www.bbc.com/news/world-asia-china-22244339

Chapter 19

"Uniting China to Speak Mandarin, the One Official Language: Easier Said Than Done", Howard W. French, The New York Times, July 10, 2005, http://www.nytimes.com/2005/07/10/world/asia/uniting-china-to-speak-mandarin-the-one-official-language-easier.html

"The Hakka : The Jews of Asia", Edu.ocac.gov.tw, accessed April 23, 2015, http://edu.ocac.gov.tw/lang/hakka/english/a/a.htm

Joseph Needham, "Science and Civilization of China", V.6, P.V, od Science pp 561. Cambridge University Press ISBN 0-521-65270-7

"Fujian Tulou", UNESCO, http://whc.unesco.org/en/list/1113

"Land Reform and Collectivization in China"; 2 July 1958. **Electronic record.**; Background Report; Records of the Radio Free Europe / Munich; Open Society Archives http://osaarchivum.org/files/holdings/300/8/3/text/9-9-239.shtml Retrieved on May 21st, 2015

"After The 70 Years Of Property Rights Expires, Who Does A House Actually Belong To?" The People's Paper. January 26, 2016. Accessed May 21, 2017. http://www.thepaper.cn/newsDetail*forward*1425711.

"China will increase farmers' property rights", Liu Qiang, China.org.cn, November 14, 2013, http://www.china.org.cn/china/2013-11/14/content*30599289.htm*

Chapter 20

"The Old Bund (Lao Waitan)" Bamboo Compass, http://www.bamboocompass.com/ningbo-travel-guide/the-old-bund-lao-waitan-4865.html

"Jiangbei Cathedral", Bamboo Compass, http://www.bamboocompass.com/ningbo-travel-guide/jiangbei-cathedral-4759.html

"GDP of Yangtze River Delta Economic Zone reached 12 trillion in 2013", China Industry Research Network, May 5, 2014, http://www.chinairn.com/news/20140505/101423684.shtml

"The Yangtze River Delta", Baidu Baike, http://baike.baidu.com/view/48994.htm#reference-3-48994-wrap

"Amazing statistics: China's Lunar New Year by the numbers", CNN, February 6, 2013, http://www.cnn.com/2013/01/21/travel/gallery/china-new-year-stats/index.html

"Number of Thanksgiving holiday travelers in the United States from 2005 to 2016 (in millions)", Statista, http://www.statista.com/statistics/372271/number-of-thanksgiving-holiday-travelers-us/

"China's 'airpocalypse' kills 350,000 to 500,000 each year", Malcolm Moore, The Times, January 7, 2014, http://www.telegraph.co.uk/news/worldnews/asia/china/10555816/Chinas-airpocalypse-kills-350000-to-500000-each-year.html

Haakon Vennemo et. al., "Environmental Pollution in China: Status and Trends", Rev Environ Econ Policy (Oxford Academic) 3

(2) (2009): pp 209–230, http://reep.oxfordjournals.org/content/
3/2/209

"Not all those who wander are lost"
- J.R.R. Tolkien

***

Visit us online at
www.thegreatrideofchina.com